Oracle SQL Recipes

A Problem-Solution Approach

Grant Allen, Bob Bryla, and Darl Kuhn

Apress®

Oracle SQL Recipes: A Problem-Solution Approach

ISBN-13 (pbk): 978-1-4302-2509-6

ISBN-13 (electronic): 978-1-4302-2510-2

Printed and bound in the United States of America 9 8 7 6 5 4 3 2 1

President and Publisher: Paul Manning
Lead Editor: Jonathan Gennick
Technical Reviewer: Stephane Faroult
Editorial Board: Clay Andres, Steve Anglin, Mark Beckner, Ewan Buckingham, Tony Campbell, Gary Cornell, Jonathan Gennick, Michelle Lowman, Matthew Moodie, Jeffrey Pepper, Frank Pohlmann, Ben Renow-Clarke, Dominic Shakeshaft, Matt Wade, Tom Welsh
Coordinating Editor: Debra Kelly
Copy Editor: Sharon Terdeman
Compositor: LaurelTech
Indexer: Becky Hornyak
Artist: April Milne
Cover Designer: Anna Ishchenko

Distributed to the book trade worldwide by Springer-Verlag New York, Inc., 233 Spring Street, 6th Floor, New York, NY 10013. Phone 1-800-SPRINGER, fax 201-348-4505, e-mail orders-ny@springer-sbm.com, or visit http://www.springeronline.com.

For information on translations, please e-mail info@apress.com, or visit http://www.apress.com.

Apress and friends of ED books may be purchased in bulk for academic, corporate, or promotional use. eBook versions and licenses are also available for most titles. For more information, reference our Special Bulk Sales–eBook Licensing web page at http://www.apress.com/info/bulksales.

To George, for teaching me everything he knows.

—Grant

To the gang at home, even with my long hours I was still able to make the football, volleyball, and basketball games!

—Bob

To Heidi, Brandi, and Lisa.

—Darl

Contents at a Glance

Contents

About the Authors

Grant Allen has worked in the IT field for 20 years, most recently as Chief Technology Officer for a leading Australian software vendor before taking on his current role at Google. He has worked across the industry, as well as in government and academia around the world, consulting on large-scale systems design, development, performance, technology innovation, and disruptive change. Grant is a frequent speaker at conferences and industry events on topics such as data mining, collaboration technologies, relational databases, and the business of technology. He is now a team leader at Google, using database technologies to tackle problems of Google-scale and beyond.

Bob Bryla is an Oracle 9i, 10g, and 11g Certified Professional with more than 20 years of experience in database design, database application development, database administration, and training. Bob is an Internet database analyst and Oracle DBA at Lands' End, Inc., in Dodgeville, Wisconsin. He is the author of several other Oracle DBA books for both the novice and seasoned professional.

Darl Kuhn is an Oracle DBA and developer. He has coauthored three other books: Linux Recipes for Oracle DBAs, RMAN Recipes for Oracle Database 11g, and Oracle RMAN Pocket Reference. He also teaches advanced database courses at Regis University and performs volunteer DBA work for the Rocky Mountain Oracle Users Group. He has a graduate degree from Colorado State University and currently lives near Mauricio Canyon, Colorado with his wife, Heidi, and daughters, Brandi and Lisa.

About the Technical Reviewer

■**Stéphane Faroult** first discovered relational databases and the SQL language back in 1983. He joined Oracle France in its early days (after a short spell with IBM and a bout of teaching at the University of Ottawa) and soon developed an interest in performance and tuning topics. After leaving Oracle in 1988, he briefly tried to reform and did a bit of operational research, but after one year he succumbed again to relational databases. Stéphane has been continuously performing database consultancy since then, relentlessly improving queries and trying to teach good SQL manners to developers. He is the author of The Art of SQL and of Refactoring SQL Applications.

Acknowledgements

I would like to thank the many people at Apress for helping me along this now well-traveled road, especially Jonathan Gennick for convincing me to get on board in the first place, Debra Kelly for her relentless but appreciated schedule reminders, and Stéphane Faroult for his keen technical edits. Thanks also to all of my professional colleagues, both past and present, who provided me with inspiration, guidance, courage, and many other intangibles without which this book would not have been possible. The list is long, but I would be remiss if I did not mention my co-workers, friends, and managers at Lands' End who provided expertise, advice, and many other incentives: Jesse Piascik, Brook Swenson, David Schwake, and Jennifer Sisk Merino.

Bob Bryla

Special thanks go to Jonathan Gennick as he skillfully guided and directed every aspect of this book, from inception to printing. Huge thanks go to Stéphane Faroult who provided ingenious and witty feedback along with creative SQL scripts and suggestions. Also, it has been a pleasure to work with my two coauthors, Grant Allen and Bob Bryla; they are experts with SQL and displayed a keen sense of humor throughout the project.

Thanks to my co-workers who indirectly (and directly) contributed to this book via inquisitive and insightful SQL questions: John Lilly, Dave Wood, Joey Canlas, Todd Wichers, Jeff Shoup, Casey Costley, Pascal Ledru, Eric Wendelin, Peter Schow, John Goggin, Brett Guy, Kevin O'Grady, Steve Buckmelter, Zack Tillotson, Randy Carver, Aparna Bharthulwar, Jeff Hanson, and Jim Johnson.

Also thanks to the numerous DBAs and developers from whom I've learned SQL techniques over the years: Sujit Pattanaik, Scott Schulze, Dave Jennings, Kevin Bayer, Shawn Heisdorffer, Pete Mullineaux, Doug Davis, Abid Malik, Mehran Sowdaey, Tim Gorman, Janet Bacon, Sue Wagner, Barb Sannwald, Ulises Llull, Ken Roberts, Mike Perrow, Roger Murphy, Dan Fink, Margaret Carson, Jed Summerton, Guido Handley, Tim Colbert, Nehru Kaja, John Liu, Inder Ganesan, Shari Plantz-Masters, Denise Duncan, Bill Padfield, Glenn Balanoff, Brad Blake, Mike Nims, Mark James, Sam Conn, Dan Likarish, Arup Nanda, Charles Kim, Sam Alapati, Bernard Lopuz, Ravi Narayanaswamy, Abdul Ebadi, Kevin Hoyt, Trent Sherman, Sandra Montijo, Jim Secor, Sean Best, Don Shade, Krish Hariharan, Buzzy Cheadle, Mike Eason, Ken Toney, Mark Blair, Mike Hutchinson, Karen Kappler, Joe Hernandez, Bob Suehrstedt, Ennio Murroni, Beth Loker, Tom Wheltle, Debbie Earman, Greg Roberts, Gabor Gyurovszky, Chad Heckman, Mihir Shah, Gary Smith, Michael Del Toro, Mark Lutze, Kevin Quinlivan, Dave Bourque, Kevin Powers, Roy Backstrom, James Jackson, Greg Oehmen, Tim Goode, Gaurav Mehta, and William Chua Tan.

And thanks to supportive colleagues: Dinesh Neelay, Will Thornburg, Tae Kim, Steve Roughton, Ambereen Pasha, Thom Chumley, Jeff Sherard, Dona Smith, Lori Isom, Karolyn Vowles, Deni Staheli, Brad Vowles, Kristi Jackson, Chirstian Hessler, Arvin Kuhn, Mohan Koneru, Amin Jiwani, Liz Brill O'Neill, Mike O'Neill, Doug Cushing, Joe Darby, Paul Kuhn, Mike Tanaka, Darcy O'Connor, Kye Bae, Peggy King, John King, Katharyn Sindt, and Jim Stark.

Darl Kuhn

Introduction

Welcome to Oracle SQL Recipes. You have in your hands a book of ready-made solutions to common problems encountered while writing SQL to run against an Oracle database. We've written this book for the person in a hurry who needs to solve a specific problem and then get on with the job. Each recipe addresses a specific problem and presents a solid, working solution to that problem. For those who are interested, each recipe also provides an extended discussion of the solution, and sometimes of alternative solutions.

We've tailored the recipes to take you to the heights of a gourmet chef, at least as far as SQL for Oracle is concerned. Though we've split the recipes into logical chapters covering topics like data types or report generation, you should feel free to sample and use the recipes in any order, as well as in any combination.

Who This Book Is For

This book is for everyone working with Oracle SQL, be they DBAs, developers, report writers, or even end users. No matter what level of expertise you currently possess for writing and using SQL, there are recipes within Oracle SQL Recipes that will appeal to you. This book is not designed to teach you SQL or to act as a facsimile of the Oracle SQL reference. Instead, what you'll find are elegant and sometimes tricky solutions to real problems that you'll never see presented in a language manual.

How This Book Is Structured

We've split the book into five parts, each covering one broad aspect of writing SQL for Oracle databases.

Part 1 deals with the fundamentals of SQL for Oracle and the basics of all facets of SQL.

Part 2 covers the intricacies of Oracle data types and recipes to manage and manipulate data in different forms.

Part 3 discusses working with Oracle as a development environment and introduces recipes to help the developer and DBA solve complex tasks in SQL.

Part 4 is a compendium of special topics and ranges from XML to generating dynamic reporting web pages straight from the database.

Part 5 is for database administrators and shows how SQL can be applied to many of the problems and tasks administrators face on a daily basis.

Choosing Tools

All of the recipes we've included in Oracle SQL Recipes are designed to work without the aid of special tools or applications. You should be able to pick a recipe and use it in an ad-hoc fashion through SQL*Plus, or include it in your application code calling the Oracle OCI or similar client library.

Those of us who've been avid users of SQL*Plus for some time appreciate that its "vintage" approach to formatting and aesthetics—OK, we mean 1980's throw-back output with all the beauty the Courier font can offer—sometimes takes something away from the recipes, especially those that show off neat tricks with output formatting. For years, Oracle has made SQL Developer available and we've been keen users of it. SQL Developer is part of the standard install as of Oracle Database 11g, so you may already have it without realizing! We're happy for you to use any tool you like when working with these recipes, but if you are in any doubt, start using SQL Developer now, and you'll be glad you did.

Working With Example Data for SQL Recipes

For many of the examples we'll use in Oracle SQL Recipes, we'll take advantage of the excellent sample schemata that Oracle provides as part of every installation—all the way back to Oracle Database 9i. Gone is the venerable Scott schema, so you can forget the password "tiger". Taking the place of the Scott schema are the following six schemata that show off many of Oracle Database's technical capabilities:

BI The Business Intelligence schema is new to Oracle Database 11g and is used to illustrate the growing power of BI capabilities in Oracle. The BI schema will appeal to those who are—or are thinking of—using the OBIEE products.

HR This is the most basic of the schemata and models the very common notion of employees and the departments in which they work. Close observers will note that this is what happened to the old Scott schema.

IX The Information Exchange schema illustrates the power of Oracle's Advanced Queuing and IPC technology. We explore this toward the end of the book.

OE Order Entry is another classic example schema, dealing with concepts of sales, orders, order items, customers, and the like. It will strike a chord with anyone who's dealt with the sales process, retail systems, or online commerce. Oracle has enhanced this schema to the point where it also has its own sub-schema, Online Catalog (OC), and quite a few interrelationships between them.

PM In the Product Media schema, Oracle's strengths in multimedia object manipulation are highlighted. This includes advanced features for large object manipulation, which we explore in Chapter 16.

SH Sales History is best thought of as a mini warehouse or datamart, perfect for exercising data mining, analytic, and other tools like cubes and rollups.

We should warn you now that we will be taking many liberties with the sample data, changing it as well as the objects that house it, slicing and dicing and even deleting and destroying. Fear not, as by the time you've finished the book, you'll be happily doing the same to more than just the sample schemata.

In a typical Oracle Database installation, the six sample schemata are installed if a full installation is performed through the Oracle Universal Installer. If this wasn't done for the database you propose to use, don't panic. You can add (or refresh) the sample schemata at any time by running the script `ORACLE_HOME/demo/schema/mksample` under Linux or Unix. Under Windows, the equivalent script is `%ORACLE_HOME%\demo\schema\mksample`.

We recommend you rerun the Database Configuration Assistant to have it do the dirty work for you, as it will save you from having to search around for some of the obscure options for which the manual script will prompt.

And if you really want to become an expert in sample data, you'll be gratified to know that Oracle's sample schema are now so large as to have a dedicated manual all to themselves. You can download the Oracle Database Sample Schemas 11g Release 1 guide (complete with the incorrect plural "schemas") from the Oracle documentation site at `http://www.oracle.com/docs`. The part number is B28328-03, and you'll find both an HTML and Adobe Acrobat version of the material.

Conventions

Throughout the book, we've kept a consistent style for presenting SQL and results. Where a piece of code, a SQL reserved word or fragment of SQL is presented in the text, it is presented in fixed-width Courier font, such as this (working) example:

```
select * from dual;
```

Where we discuss the syntax and options of SQL commands, we've used a conversational style so you can quickly reach an understanding of the command or technique. This means we haven't duplicated large syntax diagrams that better suit a reference manual.

Contacting the Authors

Should you have any questions or comments—or even spot a mistake you think we should know about—you can contact the authors via the book's web site, at `www.oraclesqlrecipes.com`. To contact Bob Bryla directly, e-mail him at `rjbdba@gmail.com`.

PART 1

Foundations of
Data Manipulation

■ ■ ■

CHAPTER 1

The Basics

This chapter presents lots of basic recipes to get you started—or rekindle old memories—on the core building blocks of SQL statements. We'll show you recipes for selecting, changing, and removing data from Oracle database tables, plus some common options you usually want to include when doing this kind of work.

Those of you with a firm grounding in SQL should feel free to delve into this chapter in an *à la carte* fashion. We've included one or two clever recipes at this early stage to make sure you get the most from Oracle SQL Recipes from the very first chapter. To continue the menu metaphor, feel free to consume the recipes herein in any order you like, and mix and match code fragments and techniques across the chapters to derive your own recipes.

■ **Note** We'll move through the basics quickly, and avoid such niceties as syntax diagrams and discussing every permutation of every recipe's options. Don't fret if you see commands and techniques you don't immediately understand. Try them out yourself in an Oracle test instance to get a feel for them, and remember that complementary books like *Begining Oracle SQL* (de Haan, Fink, Jørgensen, Morton) and *Beginning SQL Queries* (Churcher) help with learning SQL itself.

1-1. Retrieving Data from a Table

Problem

You want to retrieve specific row and column data from a table.

Solution

Issue a SELECT statement that includes a WHERE clause. The following is a straightforward SELECT statement querying a database table for particular column values, for those rows that match defined criteria:

```
select employee_id, first_name, last_name, hire_date, salary
from hr.employees
where department_id = 50
  and salary < 7500;
```

The SELECT statement returns 45 rows when run against an Oracle 11g database loaded with the sample HR schema. Here are the first 10 rows you will see.

```
EMPLOYEE_ID FIRST_NAME LAST_NAME   HIRE_DATE SALARY
----------- ---------- ----------- --------- ------
        198 Donald     OConnell    21-JUN-99   2600
        199 Douglas    Grant       13-JAN-00   2600
        123 Shanta     Vollman     10-OCT-97   6500
        124 Kevin      Mourgos     16-NOV-99   5800
        125 Julia      Nayer       16-JUL-97   3200
        126 Irene      Mikkilineni 28-SEP-98   2700
        127 James      Landry      14-JAN-99   2400
        128 Steven     Markle      08-MAR-00   2200
        129 Laura      Bissot      20-AUG-97   3300
        130 Mozhe      Atkinson    30-OCT-97   2800
...
```

How It Works

The SELECT statement was formatted to help you understand (or refresh your understanding of) the basic elements that constitute a working query. The first line of the query explicitly states the five columns we wish to include in the results.

```
select employee_id, first_name, last_name, hire_date, salary
```

The next line is the FROM clause, naming the table or tables to be referenced to pull out the columns we want to see:

```
from hr.employees
```

In this example, we use two-part object naming, specifying both the table name, EMPLOYEES, and the schema to which employees belongs, HR. This disambiguates the EMPLOYEES table in the HR schema from any other employees table that may be present in any other schema, and more importantly avoids the implicit selection of the table in the user's own schema or the currently set schema, which is the default where no schema is specified.

Next we list the WHERE clause, with two criteria that must be satisfied in order for rows to be included in our results.

```
where department_id = 50
  and salary < 7500
```

Rows in the EMPLOYEES table must satisfy both tests to be included in our results. Meeting one, or the other, but not both will not satisfy our query, as we've used the AND Boolean operator to combine the criteria. In non-technical terms, this means an employee must be listed in the department with an ID of 50, as well as have a salary below 7500.

Other Boolean operators are OR and NOT, and these follow normal Boolean precedence rules and can be modified using parenthesis to alter logic explicitly. We can modify our first example to illustrate these operators in combination

```
select employee_id, first_name, last_name, hire_date, salary
from hr.employees
where department_id = 50
  and (salary < 2500 or salary > 7500);
```

his query seeks the same columns as the first, this time focusing on those members of department 50 whose salary is either less than 2500, or more than 7500.

```
EMPLOYEE_ID FIRST_NAME LAST_NAME   HIRE_DATE  SALARY
120         Matthew    Weiss       18/JUL/96  8000
121         Adam       Fripp       10/APR/97  8200
122         Payam      Kaufling    01/MAY/95  7900
127         James      Landry      14/JAN/99  2400
128         Steven     Markle      08/MAR/00  2200
132         TJ         Olson       10/APR/99  2100
135         Ki         Gee         12/DEC/99  2400
136         Hazel      Philtanker  06/FEB/00  2200
```

Only 8 rows in the sample HR schema match these criteria.

1-2. Selecting All Columns from a Table

Problem

You want to retrieve all columns from a table, but you don't want to take the time to type all the column names as part of your SELECT statement.

Solution

Use the asterisk (*) placeholder, to represent all columns for a table. For example:

```
select *
from hr.employees
where department_id = 50
  and salary < 7500;
```

Our results show wrapped lines and only a partial listing to save space, but you can see the effect of the asterisk on the columns selected:

```
EMPLOYEE_ID FIRST_NAME LAST_NAME EMAIL PHONE_NUMBER HIRE_DATE JOB_ID SALARY
COMMISSION_PCT MANAGER_ID DEPARTMENT_ID
----------- ---------- --------- -------- ------------ ---------- --------- ------
-------------- ---------- -------------
        198 Donald     OConnell  DOCONNEL 650.507.9833 21-JUN-99 SH_CLERK   2600
                   124         50
        199 Douglas    Grant     DGRANT   650.507.9844 13-JAN-00 SH_CLERK   2600
                   124         50
        123 Shanta     Vollman   SVOLLMAN 650.123.4234 10-OCT-97 ST_MAN     6500
                   100         50
```

How It Works

In SQL, the * is a shortcut that stands for all of the column names in a table. When Oracle's parser sees SELECT * as part of a query, the parser replaces the * with a list of all the possible column names, except those that have been marked hidden. Writing SELECT * is a quick way to build ad-hoc queries, because you avoid having to look up and type out all the correct column names.

Before you succumb to the temptation to use the asterisk for all your queries, it's important to remember that good design usually means explicitly naming only those columns in which you are interested. This results in better performance, as Oracle otherwise must read the system catalog to determine the fields to include in the query. Specifying explicit columns also protects you from problems in the future where columns may be added to a table. If you write code expecting the implicit order from using the asterisk, you could be in for a nasty surprise when that order changes unexpectedly, such as when a table is dropped and re-created in a different way, or a new column is added to a table. For the most part, the asterisk is best reserved for interactive querying, and ad-hoc analysis.

1-3. Sorting Your Results

Problem

Users want to see data from a query sorted in a particular way. For example, they would like to see employees sorted alphabetically by surname, and then first name.

Solution

Oracle uses the standard ORDER BY clause to allow you to sort the results of your queries.

```
select employee_id, first_name, last_name, hire_date, salary
from hr.employees
where salary > 5000
order by last_name, first_name;
```

The results are as follows.

```
EMPLOYEE_ID    FIRST_NAME    LAST_NAME    HIRE_DATE    SALARY
-----------    ----------    ---------    ---------    ------
174            Ellen         Abel         11/MAY/96    11000
166            Sundar        Ande         24/MAR/00     6400
204            Hermann       Baer         07/JUN/94    10000
167            Amit          Banda        21/APR/00     6200
172            Elizabeth     Bates        24/MAR/99     7300
151            David         Bernstein    24/MAR/97     9500
169            Harrison      Bloom        23/MAR/98    10000
148            Gerald        Cambrault    15/OCT/99    11000
154            Nanette       Cambrault    09/DEC/98     7500
110            John          Chen         28/SEP/97     8200
...
```

How It Works

The ORDER BY clause in this solution instructs Oracle to sort by the LAST_NAME column, and where values for LAST_NAME match, to then sort by the FIRST_NAME column. Oracle implicitly uses ascending ordering unless instructed otherwise, so numbers sort from zero to nine, letters from A to Z, and so on. You can explicitly control sorting direction with the ASC and DESC options for ascending and descending sorting. Here is an example:

```
select employee_id, first_name, last_name, hire_date, salary
from hr.employees
where salary > 5000
order by salary desc;
```

Our explicit descending sort on salary has these results:

```
EMPLOYEE_ID FIRST_NAME LAST_NAME HIRE_DATE SALARY
----------- ---------- --------- --------- ------
        100 Steven     King      17-JUN-87 24000
        102 Lex        De Haan   13-JAN-93 17000
        101 Neena      Kochhar   21-SEP-89 17000
        145 John       Russell   01-OCT-96 14000
        146 Karen      Partners  05-JAN-97 13500
...
```

1-4. Adding Rows to a Table

Problem

You need to add new rows of data to a table. For example, a new employee joins the company, requiring his data to be added to the HR.EMPLOYEES table.

Solution

Use the INSERT statement to add new rows to a table. To add a new row to a table, provide values for all mandatory columns, as well as any values for optional columns. Here's a statement to add a new employee:

```
insert into hr.employees
(employee_id, first_name, last_name, email, phone_number, hire_date, job_id,
 salary, commission_pct, manager_id, department_id)
values
(207, 'John ', 'Doe ', 'JDOE ', '650.555.8877 ', '25-MAR-2009 ', 'SA_REP ',
 3500, 0.25, 145, 80);
```

How It Works

The INSERT statement associates a list of values with a list of columns. It creates a row based upon that association, and inserts that row into the target table.

Oracle will check NULL constraints, as well as primary keys, foreign keys, and other defined constraints to ensure the integrity of your inserted data. See Chapter 10 for recipes on determining the state of constraints on your tables, and how they might affect inserting new data.

You can check which fields are mandatory, defined as not null, by examining the description of the table. You can do this from SQL Developer or SQL*Plus by issuing the DESCRIBE command, which you can abbreviate to DESC. For example:

```
desc hr.employees;
```

```
Name                                Null     Type
----------------------------------- -------- ------------
EMPLOYEE_ID                         NOT NULL NUMBER(6)
FIRST_NAME                                   VARCHAR2(20)
LAST_NAME                           NOT NULL VARCHAR2(25)
EMAIL                               NOT NULL VARCHAR2(25)
PHONE_NUMBER                                 VARCHAR2(20)
HIRE_DATE                           NOT NULL DATE
JOB_ID                              NOT NULL VARCHAR2(10)
SALARY                                       NUMBER(8,2)
COMMISSION_PCT                               NUMBER(2,2)
MANAGER_ID                                   NUMBER(6)
DEPARTMENT_ID                                NUMBER(4)

11 rows selected
```

You can write a shorter INSERT statement by not enumerating the list of column names, and providing data for *every* column in the right order for the current table definition. Here's an example:

```
insert into hr.employees
values
(208, 'Jane ', 'Doe ', 'JADOE ', '650.555.8866 ', '25-MAR-2009 ', 'SA_REP ',↵
 3500, 0.25, 145, 80)
```

■ **Caution** It is rarely, if ever, a good idea to omit the list of column names—and this is for some quite serious reasons. You have no idea what changes might be made to the table in future, and you make your SQL brittle to future schema changes by assuming an implicit column order. Perhaps the best example of what can go wrong is silent logical corruption. If someone rebuilds the underlying table with a different column order, but your INSERT statement passes data type and other checks, you could find yourself silently inserting data into the wrong columns, with disastrous consequences. Our strong recommendation is to always enumerate the columns in your INSERT statement.

1-5. Copying Rows from One Table to Another

Problem

You want to copy information from one table to another.

Solution

Use the INSERT statement with the SELECT option to copy data from one table to another. Suppose you have a table of candidates applying for jobs at your company, with many of the same details as the HR.EMPLOYEES table. This INSERT statement will insert into the HR.EMPLOYEES table based on a SELECT statement on the CANDIDATES table.

```
insert into hr.employees
(employee_id, first_name, last_name, email, phone_number, hire_date, job_id, salary, ↵
commission_pct, manager_id, department_id)
select 210, first_name, last_name, email, phone_number, sysdate, 'IT_PROG', 3500, ↵
NULL, 103, 60
from hr.candidates
where first_name = 'Susan'
  and last_name = 'Jones';
```

How It Works

This recipe seeds the values to be inserted into the HR.EMPLOYEES table with the results of a SELECT on a CANDIDATES table. The SELECT statement can be run by itself to see the data passed to the INSERT statement.

```
select 210, first_name, last_name, email, phone_number, sysdate, job_id, 3500, NULL, ↵
'IT_PROG', 103
from hr.candidates
where first_name = 'Susan'
  and last_name = 'Jones';
```

```
210 FIRST_NAME LAST_NAME EMAIL  PHONE_NUMBER SYSDATE    'IT_PRO 3500 N 103 60
--- ---------- --------- ------ ------------ ---------- ------- ---- - --- --
210 Susan      Jones      SJONES 650.555.9876 30-MAR-09 IT_PROG 3500   103 60
```

We use literal (hard-coded) values for EMPLOYEE_ID, SALARY, and DEPARTMENT_ID. We also use the NULL place-holder to indicate that Susan has no COMMISSION_PCT—that is, she's not a sales person and therefore isn't part of a sales commission scheme. We want the HIRE_DATE to reflect the day on which we run the INSERT statement, so we use the built-in SYSDATE function to return the current system date.

1-6. Copying Data in Bulk from One Table to Another

Problem

You want to copy multiple rows from one table to another.

Solution

The INSERT INTO … SELECT … approach is capable of inserting multiple rows. The key is using desired criteria in the SELECT statement to return the rows you wish to insert. We can amend our previous recipe to handle multiple rows. Here's is an example of multi-row INSERT in action.

```
select candidate_id, first_name, last_name, email, phone_number, sysdate, job_id, 3500, ↵
NULL, 'IT_PROG', 103
from hr.candidates;
```

This recipe relies on the existence of the same HR.CANDIDATES table used in the previous recipe. If you're playing along at home, be sure you create this table first.

How It Works

This recipe also seeds the values to be inserted from the HR.CANDIDATES table. As there is no WHERE clause in the SELECT portion of the statement, all the rows in the CANDIDATES table will be selected, and thus all have equivalent rows inserted into the HR.EMPLOYEES table.

1-7. Changing Values in a Row

Problem

You want to change some of the data in one or more rows of a table.

Solution

The UPDATE statement is designed to change data, as its name suggests. For this problem, let's assume we want to increase the salaries of everyone in department 50 by five percent. This UPDATE statement achieves the change:

```
update hr.employees
set salary = salary * 1.05
where department_id = 50;
```

How It Works

The basic design of the UPDATE statement starts with the UPDATE clause itself

```
update hr.employess
```

This tells Oracle what table is to have its rows updated. The SET clause then specifies which columns are to change and how they are to be updated—either by a literal value, calculation, function result, subselect, or other method.

```
set salary = salary * 1.05
```

In this case, we're using a self-referencing calculation. The new SALARY value will be 1.05 times the existing value, relative to each row (that is, Oracle will perform this calculation for each row affected). Finally, the WHERE clause acts to provide the normal filtering predicates you're already familiar with from the SELECT statement. Only those rows that match a DEPARTMENT_ID of 50 will be affected.

1-8. Updating Multiple Fields with One Statement

Problem

You want to change multiple columns for one or more rows of a table.

Solution

The update statement is designed to update as many rows as you need in one statement. This means you can use multiple column = value clauses in the UPDATE statement to change as many fields as you wish in one statement. For example, to change the phone number, job role, and salary of James Marlow, EMPLOYEE_ID 131, we can use a single UPDATE statement.

```
update hr.employees
set job_id = 'ST_MAN',
  phone_number = '650.124.9876',
  salary = salary * 1.5
where employee_id = 131;
```

How It Works

Oracle evaluates the predicates of the UPDATE statement normally. In this case, it targets the row with the EMPLOYEE_ID of 131. It then changes each field based on the SET criteria given. It performs this action in one pass of the row.

Oracle also supports the grouping the columns and values for updates in parenthesis, in a similar fashion to other databases, but with one quirk.

```
update hr.employees
set (job_id,Phone_number,Salary)
 = (select 'ST_MAN','650.124.9876',salary * 1.5 from dual)
where employee_id = 131;
```

■ **Note** If the subquery returns no data, the values specified in the set clause will be set to null.

Note that the value group has to be specified as a well-formed SELECT—other databases would let you get away in this instance with the shortened form like this.

```
Set (job_id,Phone_number,Salary) = ('ST_MAN','650.124.9876',salary * 1.5)
```

This style of value grouping won't work with Oracle, so remember to use a well-formed SELECT.

1-9. Removing Unwanted Rows from a Table

Problem

An employee has taken a job with another company and you need to remove his details from the HR.EMPLOYEE table.

Solution

Let's assume that James Landry, EMPLOYEE_ID 127, has taken a job with another company. You can use the DELETE statement to remove James' details.

```
delete
from hr.employees
where employee_id = 127;
```

How It works

This recipe illustrates the basic DELETE statement, targeting the table HR.EMPLOYEES in the FROM clause. A WHERE clause provides the predicates to use to affect only those rows that match the specified criteria.

It's possible to construct the DELETE statement with no WHERE clause, in effect matching all rows of the table. In that case, all the table's rows are deleted.

```
delete
from hr.employees;
```

■ **Caution** If you do run either of those DELETE statements, don't forget to roll back if you want to continue using HR.EMPLOYEES data for the following recipes.

1-10. Removing All Rows from a Table

Problem

You want to remove all of the data for a given table.

Solution

Deleting all rows from a table using the DELETE statement allows Oracle to fully log the action, so that you can roll back if you issue this statement by accident. But that same logging, and the time it takes, means that using the DELETE statement is sometimes too slow for the desired result.

Oracle provides a complementary technique for removing all data from a table, called TRUNCATE. To truncate the HR.EMPLOYEES table, let's use the SQL statement:

```
truncate table hr.employees;
```

How It Works

No WHERE clause predicates or other modifiers are used when issuing the TRUNCATE statement. This statement is treated as DDL (Data Definition Language) SQL, which has other implications for transactions, such as implicitly committing other open transactions. See Chapter 9 for more details on recipes for transaction control and monitoring.

Using the TRUNCATE command also resets the high-water mark for a table, which means when Oracle does optimizer calculations that include judging the effect of the used capacity in a table, it will treat the table as if it had never had data consume any space.

1-11. Selecting from the Results of Another Query

Problem

You need to treat the results of a query as if they were the contents of a table. You don't want to store the intermediate results as you need them freshly generated every time you run your query.

Solution

Oracle's inline view feature allows a query to be included in the FROM clause of a statement, with the results referred to using a table alias.

```
select d.department_name
from
 (select department_id, department_name
  from hr.departments
  where location_id != 1700) d;
```

The results will look like this.

```
DEPARTMENT_NAME
----------------
Marketing
Human Resources
Shipping
IT
Public Relations
Sales

6 rows selected.
```

How It Works

This recipe treats the results of a SELECT statement on the HR.DEPARTMENTS table as an inline view, giving it the name "d". Though providing an alias in this case is optional, it makes for more readable, testable, and standards-compliant SQL. You can then refer to the results of that statement as if it were a normal statement in almost all ways. Here are the results of the inline view's SELECT statement.

```
DEPARTMENT_ID DEPARTMENT_NAME
------------- -----------------
           20 Marketing
           40 Human Resources
           50 Shipping
           60 IT
           70 Public Relations
           80 Sales

6 rows selected.
```

The inline view now acts as if you had a table, D, defined with this structure.

```
Name             Null      Type
---------------- --------  -------------
DEPARTMENT_ID    NOT NULL  NUMBER(4)
DEPARTMENT_NAME  NOT NULL  VARCHAR2(30)
```

These are the definitions from the underlying HR.DEPARTMENTS table, which are implicitly inherited by our inline view. The outer SELECT statement queries the result set, just as if there were a real table d and you'd written this statement against it.

```
select department_name
from d;
```

1-12. Basing a Where Condition on a Query

Problem

You need to query the data from a table, but one of your criteria will be dependent on data from another table at the time the query runs—and you want to avoid hard-coding criteria. Specifically, you want to find all departments with offices in North America for the purposes of reporting.

Solution

In the HR schema, the DEPARTMENTS table lists departments, and the LOCATIONS table lists locations.

```
select department_name
from hr.departments
where location_id in
  (select location_id
   from hr.locations
   where country_id = 'US'
     or country_id = 'CA');
```

Our results are as follows:

```
DEPARTMENT_NAME
---------------
IT
Shipping
Administration
Purchasing
Executive
...
```

How It Works

The right-hand side of our in predicate reads the results of the sub-SELECT to provide values to drive the comparison with the LOCATION_ID values from the HR.DEPARTMENTS table. You can see what values are generated by running the sub-SELECT query itself.

```
select location_id
from hr.locations
where country_id = 'US'
  or country_id = 'CA';
```

Here are the results:

```
LOCATION_ID
-----------
       1400
       1500
       1600
       1700
       1800
       1900
```

6 rows selected.

The outer SELECT compares LOCATION_ID values against this dynamically queried list. It is similar to running this static query.

```
select department_name
from hr.departments
where location_id in (1400,1500,1600,1700,1800,1900);
```

The key advantage of this recipe is that, should we open new offices and change all our LOCATION_ID's for North America, we don't have to rewrite our query: the sub-select will output the necessary new values dynamically.

1-13. Finding and Eliminating NULLs in Queries

Problem

You need to report how many of your employees have a commission percentage as part of their remuneration, together with the number that get only a fixed salary. You track this using the COMMISSION_PCT field of the HR.EMPLOYEES table.

Solution

The structure of the HR.EMPLOYEE tables allows the COMMISSION_PCT to be NULL. Two queries can be used to find those whose commission percent is NULL and those whose commission percent is non-NULL. First, here's the query that finds employees with NULL commission percent:

```
select first_name, last_name
from hr.employees
where commission_pct is null;
```

```
FIRST_NAME           LAST_NAME
-------------------- -------------------------
Donald               OConnell
Douglas              Grant
Jennifer             Whalen
Michael              Hartstein
Pat                  Fay
…
```

```
72 rows selected.
```

Now here's the query that finds non-NULL commission-percentage holders:

```
select first_name, last_name
from hr.employees
where commission_pct is not null;
```

```
FIRST_NAME           LAST_NAME
-------------------- -------------------------
John                 Russell
Karen                Partners
Alberto              Errazuriz
Gerald               Cambrault
Eleni                Zlotkey
…
```

```
35 rows selected.
```

How It Works

Our first SELECT statement uses the COMMISSION_PCT IS NULL clause to test for NULL entries. This has only two outcomes: either the column has a NULL entry, thus possessing no value, and satisfies the test; or it has some value.

The second statement uses the COMMISSION_PCT IS NOT NULL clause, which will find a match for any employee with an actual value for COMMISSION_PCT.

Oracle's Non-standard Treatment of the Empty String

Oracle deviates from the SQL standard in implicitly treating an empty, or zero-length, string as a surrogate for NULL. This is for a range of historical and pragmatic reasons, but it's important to remember. Almost all other implementations of SQL treat the empty string as a separate, known value.

Those of you with a programming background will find analogous the idea of a zero length string being well defined, with the memory for the string having a string terminator (\0) as its only component. In contrast, an uninstantiated string has no known state … not even a terminator. You wouldn't use zero-length and uninstantiated strings interchangeably, but this is analogous to what Oracle does with NULLs.

NULL Has No Equivalents

One aspect of recipes (and indeed day-to-day work) involving NULL in SQL often stumps people. SQL expressions are tri-valued, meaning every expression can be true, false, or NULL. This affects all kinds of comparisons, operators, and logic as you've already seen. But a nuance of this kind of logic is occasionally forgotten, so we'll repeat it explicitly. NULL has no equivalents. No other value is the same as NULL, *not even other NULL values*. If you run the following query, can you guess your results?

```
select first_name, last_name
from hr.employees
where commission_pct = NULL;
```

The answer is no rows will be selected. Even though you saw from the above SELECT statement in this recipe that 72 employees have a NULL COMMISSION_PCT, no NULL value equals another, so the COMMISSION_PCT = NULL criterion will never find a match, and you will never see results from this query. Always use IS NULL and IS NOT NULL to find or exclude your NULL values.

1-14. Sorting as a Person Expects

Problem

Your textual data has been stored in a mix of uppercase, lowercase, and sentence case. You need to sort this data alphabetically as a person normally would, in a case-insensitive fashion.

Solution

To introduce some mixed case data into our HR.EMPLOYEES table, let's run the following UPDATE to uppercase William Smith's last name.

```
update hr.employees
set last_name = 'SMITH'
where employee_id = 171;
```

This select statement shows Oracle's default sorting of employee last names.

```
select last_name
from hr.employees
order by last_name;

LAST_NAME
---------
...
Rogers
Russell
SMITH
Sarchand
Sciarra
Seo
Sewall
Smith
Stiles
Sullivan
...
```

Astute readers will have anticipated these results. Oracle, by default, sorts using a binary sort order. This means that in a simple example like this one, text is sorted according to the numeric equivalent on the code page in use (US7ASCII, WEISO8859P1, and so on). In these code pages, upper- and lowercase letters have different values, with uppercase coming first. This is why the uppercase SMITH has sorted before all other names starting with a capital S.

What most people would expect to see are the two "Smith" values sorted together, regardless of case. This NLS directive achieves that result.

```
alter session set NLS_SORT='BINARY_CI';

select last_name
from hr.employees
order by last_name;

LAST_NAME
---------
...
Rogers
Russell
Sarchand
Sciarra
Seo
Sewall
Smith
SMITH
Stiles
Sullivan
...
```

How It Works

Oracle supports both case-sensitive and case-insensitive sort orders. By default, you operate in a case-sensitive sort environment called BINARY. For every such sort order, an equivalent insensitive order exists using a suffix of _CI. We changed to using the BINARY_CI sort order, and reran the query to see results in the order a normal user would expect.

As the name suggests, the NLS_SORT option affects sorting only. It doesn't affect some other aspects of case sensitivity. With NLS_SORT='BINARY_CI', attempts to compare data in a case-insensitive fashion still exhibit Oracle's default behavior.

```
select first_name, last_name
from hr.employees
where last_name like 's%';
```

```
no rows selected
```

Don't despair. Oracle provides a similar option to allow case-insensitive comparisons just like this.

■ **Tip** A more traditional approach tackles this problem without changing any NLS parameters. You can cast the column name, literals, or both to upper- or lowercase for comparison using Oracle's UPPER and LOWER functions. This has the disadvantage of preventing the optimizer from using standard indexes, but you can also create function-based indexes to counter this.

1-15. Enabling Other Sorting and Comparison Options

Problem

You need to perform case-insensitive comparisons and other sorting operations on textual data that has been stored in an assortment of uppercase, lowercase, and sentence case.

Solution

By activating Oracle's linguistic comparison logic, you can use the same statement to retrieve the data a human would expect to see, without the burden of artificial case sensitivity.

```
alter session set NLS_COMP='LINGUISTIC';
```

```
select first_name, last_name
from hr.employees
where last_name = 'smith';
```

```
FIRST_NAME           LAST_NAME
-------------------- -------------------------
William              SMITH
Lindsey              Smith
```

This recipe relies on the same case-altering statements used in the previous recipes. Be sure to run those statements prior to testing this recipe in action.

How It Works

Historically, there were two ways to treat Oracle's normal case-sensitive handling of text when designing applications. One approach was to design the application logic to ensure data would be stored in a consistent fashion, such as the initial-caps data you see in the HR.EMPLOYEES table we've used in several recipes. The other approach allowed data to be stored as users liked, with database and application logic used to hide any case differences from users where they wouldn't be expected.

This once took a great deal of effort, but you can now achieve it with remarkably little fuss. The following statement will retrieve no rows, because no LAST_NAME entered in the HR.EMPLOYEES table is recorded in lowercase.

```
Select first_name, last_name
From hr.employees
Where last_name = 'smith';

no rows selected
```

But our recipe manages to return the right data because it changes the session settings, instructing Oracle to perform comparisons in linguistic fashion. Neither version of *Smith* is stored in the lowercase form we specified in the query, but the NLS_COMP parameter controls comparison and other behaviors in Oracle, and set to LINGUISTIC induces what the typical person would consider normal comparison behavior.

1-16. Conditional Inserting or Updating Based on Existence

Problem

You want to insert rows into a table with a key identifier that may already be present. If the identifier is not present, a new row should be created. If the identifier is present, the other columns for that row should be updated with new data, rather than a new row created.

Solution

The MERGE statement provides the ability to insert new data into a table, and if the proposed new primary key does not already exist in the table, a newly created row is inserted. If the primary key matches an existing row in a table, the statement instead updates that row with the additional details matching that key.

For our recipe, we'll assume the `HR.COUNTRIES` table is to be loaded with amended country details sourced from a NEW_COUNTRIES table.

```
merge into hr.countries c
using
  (select country_id, country_name
   from hr.new_countries) nc
on (c.country_id = nc.country_id)
when matched then
  update set c.country_name = nc.country_name
when not matched then
  insert (c.country_id, c.country_name)
  values (nc.country_id, nc.country_name);
```

How It Works

Rather than simply inserting the source data from the `HR.NEW_COUNTRIES` table directly into the target `HR.COUNTRIES` table—and potentially failing on a primary key duplication error—the `MERGE` statement sets up a logic branch to handle matched and unmatched rows based on the `ON` clause.

Typically, the `ON` clause specifies how to match primary or unique key data between the source and target. In this recipe, that's the matching of `COUNTRY_ID` values like this.

```
on (c.country_id = nc.country_id)
```

This is followed by two additional clauses, the `WHEN MATCHED THEN` clause for values that match the `ON` clause, and the `WHEN NOT MATCHED THEN` clause, for unmatched new rows that need to be treated as new data to be inserted.

The matched and not-matched clauses can also include further filtering criteria, and even criteria that when satisfied result in rows being deleted.

```
merge into hr.countries c
using
  (select country_id, country_name, region_id
   from hr.new_countries) nc
on (c.country_id = nc.country_id)
when matched then
  update set c.country_name = nc.country_name,
    c.region_id = nc.region_id
  delete where nc.region_id = 4
when not matched then
  insert (c.country_id, c.country_name, c.region_id)
  values (nc.country_id, nc.country_name, nc.region_id)
  where (nc.region_id != 4);
```

In this modified version of the recipe, matched rows will have their `COUNTRY_NAME` updated unless the `REGION_ID` of the new data is equal to 4, in which case the row in `HR.COUNTRIES` will ultimately be deleted. Unmatched rows will be inserted into `HR.EMPLOYEES` unless their `REGION_ID` is 4, in which case they will be ignored.

■ ■ ■

Summarizing and Aggregating Data

In this chapter we'll introduce recipes for working with your data at a higher level, where grouping, summaries, and the bigger picture are important. Many of the recipes we'll explore cover common or tricky reporting scenarios, the kind you encounter in a business or professional setting. Most organizations ask for reports about who sold what to whom, how many people, sales, or activities happened in a given time frame, trends across regions or customer groups, and the like.

Many people are familiar with some of the basic methods Oracle provides for performing summaries and aggregates. But often developers and DBAs will try to execute more complex calculations in their applications—and tie themselves in knots. You can spot this in your own work if you see any combination of duplicating database capabilities in code, shuffling temporary data and results around needlessly, and similar less-than-efficient tasks.

Oracle is exploding with this kind of functionality now, especially with the introduction of On-Line Analytical Processing capabilities (OLAP) over the last few major versions. After you've explored these recipes for summarizing and aggregating data, you'll realize that Oracle is the number one tool at your disposal to satisfy a huge range of reporting and other requirements.

2-1. Summarizing the Values in a Column

Problem

You need to summarize data in a column in some way. For example, you have been asked to report on the average salary paid per employee, as well as the total salary budget, number of employees, highest and lowest earners, and more.

Solution

You don't need to calculate a total and count the number of employees separately to determine the average salary. The AVG function calculates average salary for you, as shown in the next SELECT statement.

```
select avg(salary)
from hr.employees;

AVG(SALARY)
-----------
 6473.36449
```

Note there is no WHERE clause in our recipe, meaning all rows in the HR.EMPLOYEES table are assessed to calculate the overall average for the table's rows.

Functions such as AVG are termed *aggregate functions*, and there are many such functions at your disposal. For example, to calculate the total salary paid, use the SUM function, as shown here:

```
select sum(salary)
from hr.employees;

SUM(SALARY)
-----------
     692650
```

To tally the number of people receiving a salary, you can simply count the number of rows in the table using the COUNT function.

```
Select count(salary)
From hr.employees;

COUNT(SALARY)
-------------
          107
```

Maximum and minimum values can be calculated using the MAX and MIN functions. By now you're probably thinking Oracle uses very simple abbreviated names for the statistical functions, and by and large you are right. The MAX and MIN functions are shown next.

```
select min(salary), max(salary)
from hr.employees;

MIN(SALARY) MAX(SALARY)
----------- -----------
       2100       24000
```

How It Works

Oracle has numerous built-in statistical and analytic functions for performing common summarizing tasks, such as average, total, and minimum and maximum value. There's no need for you to manually perform the intermediate calculations, though you can do so if you want to confirm Oracle's arithmetic.

The following statement compares Oracle's average calculation for salary with our own explicit total divided by the number of employees.

```
select avg(salary), sum(salary)/count(salary)
from hr.employees;
```

```
AVG(SALARY) SUM(SALARY)/COUNT(SALARY)
----------- -------------------------
 6473.36449                6473.36449
```

It's pleasing to know Oracle gets this right. To complete the picture on Oracle's aggregation capabilities, we need to consider what happens when our data includes NULL data. Our current recipe aggregates employee's salaries, and it so happens that every employee has a salary. But only sales people have a commission for their sales efforts, reflected in the HR.EMPLOYEES table by a value in the COMMISSION_PCT. Non-sales staff have no commission, reflected by a NULL value in COMMISSION_PCT. So what happens when we try to average or count the COMMISSION_PCT values? The next SQL statement shows both of these aggregates.

```
select count(commission_pct), avg(commission_pct)
from hr.employees;
```

```
COUNT(COMMISSION_PCT) AVG(COMMISSION_PCT)
--------------------- -------------------
                   38                .225
```

Even though we saw 107 employees with a salary, the COUNT function has ignored all NULL values for COMMISSION_PCT, tallying only the 38 employees with a commission. Equally, when calculating the average for the employees' commissions, Oracle has again only considered those rows with a real value, ignoring the NULL entries.

There are only two special cases where Oracle considers NULL values in aggregate functions. The first is the GROUPING function, used to test if the results of an analytic function that includes NULL values generated those values directly from rows in the underlying table or as a final aggregate "NULL set" from the analytic calculation. The second special case is the COUNT(*)function. Because the asterisk implies all columns within the table, Oracle handles the counting of rows independently of any of the actual data values, treating NULL and normal values alike in this case.

To illustrate, the next SQL statement shows the difference between COUNT(*) and COUNT(COMMISSION_PCT) side by side.

```
select count(*), count(commission_pct)
from hr.employees;
```

```
  COUNT(*) COUNT(COMMISSION_PCT)
---------- ---------------------
       107                    38
```

Our use of COUNT(*) tallies all rows in the table, whereas COUNT(COMMISSION_PCT) counts only the non-NULL values for COMMISSION_PCT.

2-2. Summarizing Data for Different Groups

Problem

You want to summarize data in a column, but you don't want to summarize over all the rows in a table. You want to divide the rows into groups, and then summarize the column separately for each group. For example, you need to know the average salary paid per department.

Solution

Use SQL's GROUP BY feature to group common subsets of data together to apply functions like COUNT, MIN, MAX, SUM, and AVG. This SQL statement shows how to use an aggregate function on subgroups of your data with GROUP BY.

```
select department_id, avg(salary)
from hr.employees
group by department_id;
```

Here are the results showing averages by DEPARTMENT_ID.

```
DEPARTMENT_ID AVG(SALARY)
------------- -----------
          100        8600
           30        4150
                      7000
           20        9500
           70       10000
           90  19333.3333
          110       10150
           50  3503.33333
           40        6500
           80  8955.88235
           10        4400
           60        5760
```

`12 rows selected.`

Note that the third result row indicates a null DEPARTMENT_ID.

How It Works

The GROUP BY clause determines what groups the target table's rows should be put into for any subsequence aggregate functions. For performance reasons, Oracle will implicitly sort the data to match the grouping desired. From the first line of the SELECT statement, you can normally glean the columns that will be required in the GROUP BY clause.

```
select department_id, avg(salary)
```

We've told Oracle that we want to aggregate individual salary data into an average, but we haven't told it what to do with the individual DEPARTMENT_ID values for each row. Should we show every DEPARTMENT_ID entry, including duplicates, with the average against each one? Obviously, this would result in wasted, duplicate output—and also leave you wondering if there was something more complex you needed to understand. By using the "unaggregated" fields in the GROUP BY clause, we instruct Oracle how to collapse, or group, the singular row values against the aggregated values it has calculated.

```
group by department_id
```

This means that all values in our SELECT statement are either aggregates or covered by the GROUP BY clause. The key to writing syntactically correct GROUP BY statements is to always remember, values are either grouped or aggregated—no "stragglers" are allowed. You can see this clearly in a query that groups by multiple values.

2-3. Grouping Data by Multiple Fields

Problem

You need to report data grouped by multiple values simultaneously. For example, an HR department may need to report on minimum, average, and maximum SALARY by DEPARTMENT_ID and JOB_ID.

Solution

Oracle's GROUP BY capabilities extend to an arbitrary number of columns and expressions, so we can extend the previous recipe to encompass our new grouping requirements. We know what we want aggregated: the SALARY value aggregated three different ways. That leaves the DEPARTMENT_ID and JOB_ID to be grouped. We also want our results ordered so we can see different JOB_ID values in the same department in context, from highest SALARY to lowest. The next SQL statement achieves this by adding the necessary criteria to the GROUP BY and ORDER BY clauses.

```
Select department_id, job_id, min(salary), avg(salary), max(salary)
From hr.employees
Group by department_id, job_id
Order by department_id, max(salary) desc;
```

DEPARTMENT_ID	JOB_ID	MIN(SALARY)	AVG(SALARY)	MAX(SALARY)
10	AD_ASST	4400	4400	4400
20	MK_MAN	13000	13000	13000
20	MK_REP	6000	6000	6000
30	PU_MAN	11000	11000	11000
30	PU_CLERK	2500	2780	3100

```
...

20 rows selected.
```

How It Works

When ordering by aggregate or other functions, you can take advantage of Oracle's shorthand notation for ordering columns. Thus you can write the statement to order by the column-based positions of your data, rather than having to write the cumbersome full text of the aggregate expression.

```
Select department_id, job_id, min(salary), avg(salary), max(salary)
From hr.employees
Group by department_id, job_id
Order by 1, 5 desc;
```

You can mix column names, aggregate expressions, numeric positions, and even column aliases in the SELECT clause within your ordering when working with grouped results, as shown in the next SQL statement.

```
Select department_id, job_id, min(salary), avg(salary), max(salary) Max_Sal
From hr.employees
Group by department_id, job_id
Order by 1, job_id, Max_Sal desc;
```

Flexibility is the key here, and as you create and use more complex expressions for ordering and grouping, you'll find aliases and ordinal notation helpful. However, for readability's sake, you should try to stay consistent.

2-4. Ignoring Groups in Aggregate Data Sets

Problem

You want to ignore certain groups of data based on the outcome of aggregate functions or grouping actions. In effect, you'd really like another WHERE clause to work after the GROUP BY clause, providing criteria at the group or aggregate level.

Solution

SQL provides the HAVING clause to apply criteria to grouped data. For our recipe, we solve the problem of finding minimum, average, and maximum salary for people performing the same job in each of the departments in the HR.EMPLOYEES table. Importantly, we only want to see these aggregate values where more than one person performs the same job in a given department. The next SQL statement uses an expression in the HAVING clause to solve our problem.

```
select department_id, job_id, min(salary), avg(salary), max(salary), count(*)
from hr.employees
group by department_id, job_id
having count(*) > 1;
```

Our recipe results in the following summary.

```
DEPARTMENT_ID JOB_ID      MIN(SALARY) AVG(SALARY) MAX(SALARY)  COUNT(*)
------------- ----------  ----------- ----------- ----------- ----------
           90 AD_VP            17000       17000       17000          2
           50 ST_CLERK          2100        2800        3600         19
           80 SA_REP            6100  8396.55172       11500         29
           50 ST_MAN            3750  6691.66667        8200          6
           80 SA_MAN           10500       12200       14000          5
           50 SH_CLERK          2500        3215        4200         20
           60 IT_PROG           4200        5760        9000          5
           30 PU_CLERK          2500        2780        3100          5
          100 FI_ACCOUNT        6900        7920        9000          5

9 rows selected.
```

How It Works

You can immediately see that we have results for only nine groups of employees. Compared with the 20 groups returned in the previous recipe, it's obvious the HAVING clause has done something—but what?

The HAVING clause is evaluated after all grouping and aggregation has taken place. Internally, Oracle will first generate results like this:

```
DEPARTMENT_ID JOB_ID      MIN(SALARY) AVG(SALARY) MAX(SALARY)  COUNT(*)
------------- ----------  ----------- ----------- ----------- ----------
          110 AC_ACCOUNT        8300        8300        8300          1
           90 AD_VP            17000       17000       17000          2
           50 ST_CLERK          2100        2800        3600         19
           80 SA_REP            6100  8396.55172       11500         29
          110 AC_MGR           12000       12000       12000          1
...
```

This, in effect, is our recipe without the HAVING clause. Oracle then applies the HAVING criteria

```
having count(*) > 1
```

The bolded rows in the previous results have a count of 1 (there's only one employee of that JOB_ID in the respective DEPARTMENT_ID), which means they fail the HAVING clause criterion and are excluded from the final results, leaving us with the solution we saw above.

The HAVING clause criteria can be arbitrarily complex, so you can use multiple criteria of different sorts.

```
select department_id, job_id, min(salary), avg(salary), max(salary), count(*)
from hr.employees
group by department_id, job_id
having count(*) > 1
and min(salary) between 2500 and 17000
and avg(salary) != 5000
and max(salary)/min(salary) < 2
;
```

DEPARTMENT_ID	JOB_ID	MIN(SALARY)	AVG(SALARY)	MAX(SALARY)	COUNT(*)
90	AD_VP	17000	17000	17000	2
80	SA_REP	6100	8396.55172	11500	29
80	SA_MAN	10500	12200	14000	5
50	SH_CLERK	2500	3215	4200	20
30	PU_CLERK	2500	2780	3100	5
100	FI_ACCOUNT	6900	7920	9000	5

6 rows selected.

2-5. Aggregating Data at Multiple Levels

Problem

You want to find totals, averages, and other aggregate figures, as well as subtotals in various dimensions for a report. You want to achieve this with as few statements as possible, preferably just one, rather than having to issue separate statements to get each intermediate subtotal along the way.

Solution

You can calculate subtotals or other intermediate aggregates in Oracle using the CUBE, ROLLUP and grouping sets features. For this recipe, we'll assume some real-world requirements. We want to find average and total (summed) salary figures by department and job category, and show meaningful higher-level averages and subtotals at the department level (regardless of job category), as well as a grand total and company-wide average for the whole organization.

```
select department_id, job_id, avg(salary), sum(salary)
from hr.employees
group by rollup (department_id, job_id);
```

Our results (partial output shown) include sum and average by DEPARTMENT_ID and JOB_ID, rolled-up aggregates by DEPARTMENT_ID, and grand totals across all data.

DEPARTMENT_ID	JOB_ID	AVG(SALARY)	SUM(SALARY)
...			
80	SA_MAN	12200	61000
80	SA_REP	8396.55172	243500
80		**8955.88235**	**304500**
90	AD_VP	17000	34000
90	AD_PRES	24000	24000
90		**19333.3333**	**58000**
100	FI_MGR	12000	12000
100	FI_ACCOUNT	7920	39600
100		**8600**	**51600**

```
       110 AC_MGR          12000       12000
       110 AC_ACCOUNT       8300        8300
       110                 10150       20300
                      6473.36449      692650
```

33 rows selected.

How It Works

The ROLLUP function performs grouping at multiple levels, using a right-to-left method of rolling up through intermediate levels to any grand total or summation. In our recipe, this means that after performing normal grouping by DEPARTMENT_ID and JOB_ID, the ROLLUP function rolls up all JOB_ID values so that we see an average and sum for the DEPARTMENT_ID level across all jobs in a given department. ROLLUP then rolls up to the next (and highest) level in our recipe, rolling up all departments, in effect providing an organization-wide rollup. You can see the rolled up rows in bold in the output.

Performing this rollup would be the equivalent of running three separate statements, such as the three that follow, and using UNION or application-level code to stitch the results together.

```
select department_id, job_id, avg(salary), sum(salary)
from hr.employees
group by department_id, job_id;
select department_id, avg(salary), sum(salary)
from hr.employees
group by department_id;
select avg(salary), sum(salary)
from hr.employees;
```

Of course, in doing this, you're responsible for your own interspersing of subtotals at the intuitive points in the output. You could try writing a three-way UNION subselect with an outer SELECT to do the ordering. If this sounds more and more complicated, be thankful the ROLLUP command, and its associated command CUBE, have displaced the need to perform such awkward computations.

Careful observers will note that because ROLLUP works from right to left with the columns given, we don't see values where departments are rolled up by job. We could achieve this using this version of the recipe.

```
select department_id, job_id, avg(salary), sum(salary)
from hr.employees
group by rollup (job_id, department_id);
```

In doing so, we get the DEPARTMENT_ID intermediate rollup we want, but lose the JOB_ID intermediate rollup, seeing only JOB_ID rolled up at the final level. To roll up in all dimensions, change the recipe to use the CUBE function.

```
Select department_id, job_id, min(salary), avg(salary), max(salary)
From hr.employees
Group by cube (department_id, job_id);
```

The results show our rollups at each level, shown in bold in the partial results that follow.

```
DEPARTMENT_ID JOB_ID     MIN(SALARY) AVG(SALARY) MAX(SALARY)
------------- ---------- ----------- ----------- -----------
                             7000        7000        7000
                             2100   6392.27273      24000
              AD_VP         17000       17000       17000
              AC_MGR        12000       12000       12000
              FI_MGR        12000       12000       12000
...
           10               4400        4400        4400
           10 AD_ASST       4400        4400        4400
           20               6000        9500       13000
           20 MK_MAN       13000       13000       13000
           20 MK_REP        6000        6000        6000
...
```

The power of both the ROLLUP and CUBE functions extends to as many "dimensions" as you need for your query. Admittedly, the term *cube* is meant to allude to the idea of looking at intermediate aggregations in three dimensions, but your data can often have more dimensions than that. Extending our recipe, we could "cube" a calculation of average salary by department, job, manager, and starting year.

```
Select department_id, job_id, manager_id,
   extract(year from hire_date) as "START_YEAR", avg(salary)
From hr.employees
Group by cube (department_id, job_id,  manager_id, extract(year from hire_date));
```

This recipe results in an examination of average salary in four dimensions!

2-6. Using Aggregate Results in Other Queries

Problem

You want to use the output of a complex query involving aggregates and grouping as source data for another query.

Solution

Oracle allows any query to be used as a subquery or inline view, including those containing aggregates and grouping functions. This is especially useful where you'd like to specify group-level criteria compared against data from other tables or queries, and don't have a ready-made view available.

For our recipe, we'll use an average salary calculation with rollups across department, job, and start year, as shown in this SELECT statement.

```
select * from (
   select department_id as "dept", job_id as "job", to_char(hire_date,'YYYY') as
   "Start_Year", avg(salary) as "avsal"
   from hr.employees
```

```
  group by rollup (department_id, job_id, to_char(hire_date,'YYYY'))) salcalc
where salcalc.start_year > '1990'
or salcalc.start_year is null
order by 1,2,3,4;
```

Our recipe results in the following (abridged) output:

```
    dept job        Start    avsal
---------- ---------- ----- ----------
        10 AD_ASST             4400
        10                     4400
        20 MK_MAN      1996   13000
        20 MK_MAN             13000
        20 MK_REP      1997    6000
        20 MK_REP              6000
...
                            6473.36449
                                 7000

79 rows selected.
```

How It Works

Our recipe uses the aggregated and grouped results of the subquery as an inline view, which we then select from and apply further criteria. In this case, we could avoid the subquery approach by using a more complex HAVING clause like this.

```
having to_char(hire_date,'YYYY') > '1990'
or to_char(hire_date,'YYYY') is null
```

Avoiding a subquery here works only because we're comparing our aggregates with literals. If we wanted to find averages for jobs in departments where someone had previously held the job, we'd need to reference the HR.JOBHISTORY table. Depending on the business requirement, we might get lucky and be able to construct our join, aggregates, groups, and having criteria in one statement. By treating the results of the aggregate and grouping query as input to another query, we get better readability, and the ability to code even more complexity than the HAVING clause allows.

2-7. Counting Members in Groups and Sets

Problem

You need to count members of a group, groups of groups, and other set-based collections. You also need to include and exclude individual members and groups dynamically based on other data at the same time. For instance, you want to count how many jobs each employee has held during their time at the organization, based on the number of promotions they've had within the company.

Solution

Oracle's COUNT feature can be used to count materialized results as well as actual rows in tables. The next SELECT statement uses a subquery to count the instances of jobs held across tables, and then summarizes those counts. In effect, this is a count of counts against data resulting from a query, rather than anything stored directly in Oracle.

```
select jh.JobsHeld, count(*) as StaffCount
from
  (select u.employee_id, count(*) as JobsHeld
   from
    (select employee_id from hr.employees
     union all
     select employee_id from hr.job_history) u
   group by u.employee_id) jh
group by jh.JobsHeld;
```

From that SELECT statement, we get the following concise summary.

```
JOBSHELD STAFFCOUNT
---------- ----------
         1         99
         2          5
         3          3
```

Most staff have had only one job, five have held two positions, and three have held three positions each.

How It Works

The key to our recipe is the flexibility of the COUNT function, which can be used for far more than just physically counting the number of rows in a table. You can count anything you can represent in a *result*. This means you can count derived data, inferred data, and transient calculations and determinations. Our recipe uses nested subselects and counts at two levels, and is best understood starting from the inside and working out.

We know an employee's current position is tracked in the HR.EMPLOYEES table, and that each instance of previous positions with the organization is recorded in the HR.JOB_HISTORY table. We can't just count the entries in HR.JOB_HISTORY and add one for the employees' current positions, because staff who have never changed jobs don't have an entry in HR.JOB_HISTORY.

Instead, we perform a UNION ALL of the EMPLOYEE_ID values across both HR.EMPLOYEES and HR.JOB_HISTORY, building a basic result set that repeats an EMPLOYEE_ID for every position an employee has held. Partial results of just the inner UNION ALL statement are shown here to help you follow the logic.

```
EMPLOYEE_ID
-----------
        100
        101
        101
        101
```

```
        102
        102
        103
...
```

It's useful to remember the difference between UNION and UNION ALL. UNION will remove duplicate entries in result sets (and perform a sort on the data as part of deduplication), whereas UNION ALL preserves all values in all source sets, even the duplicates. In our recipe, the use of UNION would have resulted in a count of one job for every employee, regardless of how many promotions or jobs they'd actually had.

You'll be pleased to know UNION operators are useful ingredients for many recipes in other chapters of the book.

The next subselect aggregates and groups the values derived in our innermost subselect, counting the occurrences of each EMPLOYEE_ID to determine how many jobs each person has held. This is the first point where we use the COUNT function on the results of another query, rather than raw data in a table. Partial output at this subselect would look like this.

```
EMPLOYEE_ID   JOBSHELD
-----------   ----------
        100          1
        101          3
        102          2
        103          1
        104          1
...
```

Our outermost query also performs straightforward aggregation and grouping, once again employing the COUNT function on the results of a subselect—which itself was producing counts of derived data.

2-8. Finding Duplicates and Unique Values in a Table

Problem

You need to test if a given data value is unique in a table—that is, it appears only once.

Solution

Oracle supports the standard HAVING clause for SELECT statements, and the COUNT function, which together can identify single instances of data in a table or result. The following SELECT statement solves the problem of finding if the surname Fay is unique in the HR.EMPLOYEES table.

```
select last_name, count(*)
from hr.employees
where last_name = 'Fay'
group by last_name
having count(*) = 1;
```

   With this recipe, we receive these results:

```
LAST_NAME                  COUNT(*)
------------------------ ----------
Fay                               1
```

   Because there is exactly one LAST_NAME value of Fay, we get a count of 1 and therefore see results.

How It Works

Only unique combinations of data will group to a count of 1. For instance, we can test if the surname King is unique:

```
select last_name, count(*)
from hr.employees
where last_name = 'King'
group by last_name
having count(*) = 1;
```

   This statement returns no results, meaning that the count of people with a surname of King is not 1; it's some other number like 0, 2, or more. The statement first determines which rows have a LAST_NAME value of King. It then groups by LAST_NAME and counts the hits encountered. Lastly, the HAVING clause tests to see if the count of rows with a LAST_NAME of King was equal to 1. Only those results are returned, so a surname is unique only if you see a result.

   If we remove the HAVING clause as in the next SELECT statement, we'll see how many Kings are in the HR.EMPLOYEES table.

```
select last_name, count(*)
from hr.employees
where last_name = 'King'
group by last_name;
```

```
LAST_NAME                  COUNT(*)
------------------------ ----------
King                              2
```

Two people have a surname of King, thus it isn't unique and didn't show up in our test for uniqueness.

The same technique can be extended to test for unique combinations of columns. We can expand our recipe to test if someone's complete name, based on the combination of FIRST_NAME and LAST_NAME, is unique. This SELECT statement includes both columns in the criteria, testing to see if Lindsey Smith is a unique full name in the HR.EMPLOYEES table.

```
select first_name, last_name, count(*)
from hr.employees
where first_name = 'Lindsey'
and last_name = 'Smith'
group by first_name, last_name
having count(*) = 1;
```

```
FIRST_NAME           LAST_NAME                 COUNT(*)
-------------------- ------------------------- ----------
Lindsey              Smith                            1
```

You can write similar recipes that use string concatenation, self-joins, and a number of other methods.

2-9. Calculating Totals and Subtotals

Problem

You need to calculate totals and subtotals in a variety of environments, using the lowest common denominator of SQL. For instance, you need to count the number of people in each department, as well as a grand total, in a way that can run across a variety of editions of Oracle without change.

Solution

In situations where you feel you can't use analytic functions like ROLLUP and CUBE, or are restricted by licensing or other factors, you can use traditional aggregation and grouping techniques in separate SQL statements, and combine the results with a UNION to fold all the logic into a single statement. This SELECT combines counts of employees by department in one query, with the count of all employees in another query.

```
select nvl(to_char(department_id),'-') as "DEPT.", count(*) as "EMP_COUNT"
from hr.employees
group by department_id
union
select 'All Depts.', count(*)
from hr.employees;
```

The recipe results appear as follows, with abridged output to save space.

```
DEPT.        EMP_COUNT
----------- ----------
-                    1
10                   1
100                  6
110                  2
...
90                   3
All Depts.     107
```

13 rows selected.

How It Works

This recipe uses separate queries to calculate different aggregates and different levels, combining the results into a report-style output using UNION. In effect, two distinct sets of results are generated. First, the count of employees by department is accomplished using this SELECT statement.

```
select nvl(to_char(department_id),'-') as "DEPT.", count(*) as "EMP_COUNT"
from hr.employees
group by department_id;
```

Note that the TO_CHAR function is used to convert the integer DEPARTMENT_ID values to character equivalents. This is to ensure the eventual UNION is not plagued by implicit casting overhead, or even casting errors. In this recipe, we know we're going to want to use the literal phrase "All Depts." in conjunction with the overall employee count, and have it appear in line with the DEPARTMENT_ID values. Without casting, this results in an attempt to form a union from a column defined as an integer and a literal string. We'll receive this error if we don't perform the casting.

```
ORA-01790: expression must have same datatype as corresponding expression
```

Obviously not a useful outcome. You will often see this error when dealing with unions that must handle NULL values.

We also need the TO_CHAR conversion to work in conjunction with the NVL null-testing function, to map the employees with a null DEPARTMENT_ID to a "-" to indicate no department. This is for purely cosmetic reasons, but you can see how it can provide clarity for people reading your recipe results. This way, they don't have to wonder what a blank or null DEPARTMENT_ID means.

The second query in the union calculates only the total count of employees in the HR.EMPLOYEES table, and utilizes the flexible literal handling Oracle provides to implicitly group the full count with the value "All Depts."

```
select 'All Depts.', count(*)
from hr.employees
```

The UNION clause then simply stitches the two results together, giving the output you see. This is equivalent to using the ROLLUP clause covered in the recipe *Aggregating Data at Multiple Levels* earlier in this chapter.

2-10. Building Your Own Aggregate Function

Problem

You need to implement a custom aggregation to work in conjunction with Oracle's existing aggregate functions and grouping mechanisms. You specifically want to aggregate strings in multiple rows to one row so that the text from each row is concatenated, one after the other. You've seen this supported in other databases but you can't find an equivalent Oracle function.

Solution

Oracle provides a framework for writing your own aggregate functions, either to provide an aggregation not otherwise available in Oracle or to develop your own custom version of a common aggregate function with differing behavior. Our recipe creates a new aggregate function, STRING_TO_LIST, and the supporting type definition and type body based on Oracle's template for custom aggregates.

The following type definition defines the mandatory four functions Oracle requires for a custom aggregate type.

```
create or replace type t_list_of_strings as object (
  string_list varchar2(4000),

  static function odciaggregateinitialize
    (agg_context in out t_list_of_strings)
    return number,

  member function odciaggregateiterate
    (self in out t_list_of_strings,
     next_string_to_add in varchar2 )
    return number,

  member function odciaggregatemerge
    (self in out t_list_of_strings,
     para_context in t_list_of_strings)
    return number,

  member function odciaggregateterminate
    (self in t_list_of_strings,
     final_list_to_return out varchar2,
     flags in number)
    return number
);
/
```

We've limited the STRING_LIST parameter to 4000, even though PL/SQL supports up to 32000, to ensure we don't pass the threshold supported by plain SQL in Oracle. Each of the four required functions implements the various stages of our aggregation of a set of strings into one list.

```
create or replace type body t_list_of_strings is
  static function odciaggregateinitialize
    (agg_context in out t_list_of_strings)
    return number is
  begin
    agg_context := t_list_of_strings(null);
    return odciconst.success;
  end;

  member function odciaggregateiterate
    (self in out t_list_of_strings,
     next_string_to_add in varchar2 )
    return number is
  begin
    self.string_list := self.string_list || ' , ' || next_string_to_add;
    return odciconst.success;
  end;

  member function odciaggregatemerge
    (self in out t_list_of_strings,
     para_context in t_list_of_strings)
    return number is
  begin
    self.string_list := self.string_list || ' , ' || para_context.string_list;
    return odciconst.success;
  end;

  member function odciaggregateterminate
    (self in t_list_of_strings,
     final_list_to_return out varchar2,
     flags in number)
    return number is
  begin
    final_list_to_return := ltrim(rtrim(self.string_list, ' , '), ' , ');
    return odciconst.success;
  end;
end;
/
```

With the type and type body in place, we build the function we'll use in our actual SQL statements to produce custom aggregated data.

```
create or replace function string_to_list
  (input_string varchar2)
  return varchar2
  parallel_enable
  aggregate using t_list_of_strings;
/
```

We can now use our custom aggregate function to compose a list from any set or subset of strings that we generate in a query. In this recipe, we want to return the surnames of all the employees assigned to a given manager.

```
select manager_id, string_to_list (last_name) as employee_list
from hr.employees
group by manager_id;
```

Our new custom aggregation function does the trick, producing the surnames in a list-like output along with the manager's ID.

```
MANAGER_ID EMPLOYEE_LIST
---------- ------------------------------------------------------------
       100 Hartstein , Kochhar , De Haan , Fripp , Kaufling , Weiss ...
       101 Whalen , Greenberg , Higgins , Baer , Mavris
       102 Hunold
       103 Ernst , Pataballa , Lorentz , Austin
       108 Faviet , Chen , Sciarra , Urman , Popp
...
```

How It Works

Don't let the jump to PL/SQL, or the length of the recipe, scare you away. In fact, the majority of the code above is boiler-plate template offered by Oracle to assist with building custom aggregates quickly and easily.

This recipe builds the three components necessary to create a custom aggregation, and then uses it in a SQL statement to list the employee surnames by manager. First it defines a custom type defining the four prescribed functions Oracle requires for a custom aggregate. These are:

ODCIAggregateInitialize: This function is called at the very beginning of processing and sets up the new instance of the aggregate type—in our case, T_LIST_OF_STRINGS. This new instance has its member variables (if any) and is ready for the main aggregation phase

ODCIAggregateIterate: This holds the core functionality of your custom aggregation. The logic in this function will be called for each data value passed over in your driving query. In our case, this is the logic that takes each string value and appends it to the existing list of strings.

ODCIAggregateMerge: This is the semi-optional function that controls Oracle's behavior, if Oracle decides to perform the aggregation in parallel, using multiple parallel slaves working against portions of the data. While you don't have to enable the parallel option (see below), you still need to include this function. In our case, should our list creation be split into parallel tasks, all we need to do is concatenate the sublists at the end of the parallel process.

ODCIAggregateTerminate; This is the final function and is required to return the result to the calling SQL function. In our case, it returns the global variable STRING_LIST that has been built up in the iteration and parallel merging stages.

We now have the mechanics of aggregation built. The next part of the recipe builds the function that you can call to actually get your great new aggregation feature working on data. We create a function that has many of the normal features you'd expect:

```
create or replace function string_to_list
  (input_string varchar2)
  return varchar2
  parallel_enable
  aggregate using t_list_of_strings;
/
```

The function gets a name, STRING_TO_LIST, and it takes a VARCHAR2 string as input and returns one as output. So far, very mundane. It's the next two lines that are key to our recipe's aggregation behavior.

The PARALLEL_ENABLE clause is entirely optional, and instructs Oracle that it is safe to perform the underlying aggregation logic in parallel if the optimizer decides to take that path. Depending on the logic in your ODCIAGGREGATEITERATE function, you may have particular actions that must happen in a particular order and thus want to avoid parallelism. Enabling parallel processing also implies that logic is in place in the ODCIAGGREGATEMERGE member function to deal with merged subsets of results.

The AGGREGATE USING T_LIST_OF_STRINGS clause is where all the magic happens. This line instructs the function that it is aggregate in nature, and an object of type T_LIST_OF_STRINGS should be instantiated with the input parameter, kicking off the actual aggregation work.

■ **Note** Oracle only supports the creation of custom aggregate functions that take exactly one input parameter, and return exactly one output parameter. That's why you don't see any explicit instruction in our recipe to pass the INPUT_STRING parameter to the instantiated T_LIST_OF_STRINGS type, nor one mapping the return value from the T_LIST_OF_STRINGS.ODCIAGGREGATETERMINATE member function back to the return value of the STRING_TO_LIST function. They are the only things Oracle can do when it sees the aggregate clause, so they are implicit when you use the aggregate feature.

From there, calling and use of the new STRING_TO_LIST function behaves much like any other aggregate function, like AVG, MAX, MIN, and so on.

2-11. Accessing Values from Subsequent or Preceding Rows

Problem

You would like to query data to produce an ordered result, but you want to include calculations based on preceding and following rows in the result set. For instance, you want to perform calculations on event-style data based on events that occurred earlier and later in time.

Solution

Oracle supports the LAG and LEAD analytical functions to provide access to multiple rows in a table or expression, utilizing preceding/following logic—and you won't need to resort to joining the source data to itself. Our recipe assumes you are trying to tackle the business problem of visualizing the trend in hiring of staff over time. The LAG function can be used to see which employee's hiring followed another, and also to calculate the elapsed time between hiring.

```
select first_name, last_name, hire_date,
  lag(hire_date, 1, '01-JUN-1987') over (order by hire_date) as Prev_Hire_Date,
  hire_date - lag(hire_date, 1, '01-JUN-1987') over (order by hire_date)
    as Days_Between_Hires
from hr.employees
order by hire_date;
```

Our query returns 107 rows, linking the employees in the order they were hired (though not necessarily preserving the implicit sort for display or other purposes), and showing the time delta between each joining the organization.

```
FIRST_NAME  LAST_NAME   HIRE_DATE PREV_HIRE DAYS_BETWEEN
----------- ----------- --------- --------- ------------
Steven      King        17-JUN-87 01-JUN-87           16
Jennifer    Whalen      17-SEP-87 17-JUN-87           92
Neena       Kochhar     21-SEP-89 17-SEP-87          735
Alexander   Hunold      03-JAN-90 21-SEP-89          104
Bruce       Ernst       21-MAY-91 03-JAN-90          503
...
David       Lee         23-FEB-00 06-FEB-00           17
Steven      Markle      08-MAR-00 23-FEB-00           14
Sundar      Ande        24-MAR-00 08-MAR-00           16
Amit        Banda       21-APR-00 24-MAR-00           28
Sundita     Kumar       21-APR-00 21-APR-00            0

107 rows selected.
```

You can calculate for yourself the day differences to confirm the LAG function and difference arithmetic are indeed working as claimed. For instance, there really are 503 days between January 3, 1990 and May 21, 1991.

How It Works

The LAG and LEAD functions are like most other analytical and windowing functions in that they operate once the base non-analytic portion of the query is complete. Oracle performs a second pass over the intermediate result set to apply any analytical predicates. In effect, the non-analytic components are evaluated first, as if this query had been run.

```
select first_name, last_name, hire_date
  -- placeholder for Prev_Hire_Date,
  -- placehodler for Days_Between_Hires
from hr.employees;
```

The results at this point would look like this if you could see them:

```
FIRST_NAME   LAST_NAME   HIRE_DATE  PREV_HIRE DAYS_BETWEEN
----------   ---------   ---------  --------- ------------
Steven       King        17-JUN-87  ( To Be Determined )
Jennifer     Whalen      17-SEP-87  ( To Be Determined )
Neena        Kochhar     21-SEP-89  ( To Be Determined )
Alexander    Hunold      03-JAN-90  ( To Be Determined )
Bruce        Ernst       21-MAY-91  ( To Be Determined )
...
```

The analytic function(s) are then processed, providing the results you've seen. Our recipe uses the LAG function to compare the current row of results with a preceding row. The general format is the best way to understand LAG, and has the following form.

```
lag (column or expression, preceding row offset, default for first row)
```

The *column or expression* is mostly self-explanatory, as this is the table data or computed result over which you want LAG to operate. The *preceding row offset* portion indicates the relative row prior to the current row the LAG should act against. In our case, the value '1' means the row that is one row before the current row. The default for LAG indicates what value to use as a precedent for the first row, as there is no row *zero* in a table or result. We've chosen the arbitrary date of 01-JUN-1987 as a notional date on which the organization was founded. You could use any date, date calculation, or date-returning function here. Oracle will supply a NULL value if you don't specify the first row's precedent value.

The OVER analytic clause then dictates the order of data against which to apply the analytic function, and any partitioning of the data into windows or subsets (not shown in this recipe). Astute readers will realize that this means our recipe could have included a general ORDER BY clause that sorted the data for presentation in a different order from the HIRE_DATE ordering used for the LAG function. This gives you the most flexibility to handle general ordering and analytic lag and lead in different ways for the same statement. We'll show an example of this later in this chapter. And remember, you should never rely on the implicit sorting that analytic functions use. This can and will change in the future, so you are best advised to always include ORDER BY for sorting wherever explicitly required.

The LEAD function works in a nearly identical fashion to LAG, but instead tracks following rows rather than preceding ones. We could rewrite our recipe to show hires along with the HIRE_DATE of the next employee, and a similar elapsed-time window between their employment dates, as in this SELECT statement.

```
select first_name, last_name, hire_date,
  lead(hire_date, 1, sysdate) over (order by hire_date) as Next_Hire_Date,
  lead(hire_date, 1, sysdate) over (order by hire_date) - hire_date
    as Days_Between_Hires
from hr.employees;
```

The pattern of dates is very intuitive now that you've seen the LAG example. With LEAD, the key difference is the effect of the default value in the third parameter.

```
FIRST_NAME   LAST_NAME   HIRE_DATE  NEXT_HIRE DAYS_BETWEEN
----------   ---------   ---------  --------- ------------
Steven       King        17-JUN-87  17-SEP-87           92
Jennifer     Whalen      17-SEP-87  21-SEP-89          735
Neena        Kochhar     21-SEP-89  03-JAN-90          104
Alexander    Hunold      03-JAN-90  21-MAY-91          503
```

```
Bruce       Ernst       21-MAY-91 13-JAN-93          603
...
David       Lee         23-FEB-00 08-MAR-00           14
Steven      Markle      08-MAR-00 24-MAR-00           16
Sundar      Ande        24-MAR-00 21-APR-00           28
Amit        Banda       21-APR-00 21-APR-00            0
Sundita     Kumar       21-APR-00 21-APR-09      3287.98

107 rows selected.
```

In contrast to LAG, where the default provides a notional starting point for the first row's comparison, LEAD uses the default value to provide a hypothetical end point for the last row in the forward-looking chain. In this recipe, we are comparing how many days have elapsed between employees being hired. It makes sense for us to compare the last employee hired (in this case, Sundita Kumar) with the current date using the SYSDATE function. This is a quick and easy finishing flourish to calculate the days that have elapsed since hiring the last employee.

2-12. Assigning Ranking Values to Rows in a Query Result

Problem

The results from a query need to be allocated an ordinal number representing their positions in the result. You do not want to have to insert and track these numbers in the source data.

Solution

Oracle provides the RANK analytic function to generate a ranking number for rows in a result set. RANK is applied as a normal OLAP-style function to a column or derived expression. For the purposes of this recipe, we'll assume that the business would like to rank employees by salary, from highest-paid down. The following SELECT statement uses the rank function to assign these values.

```
select employee_id, salary, rank() over (order by salary desc) as Salary_Rank
from hr.employees;
```

Our query produces results from the highest earner at 24000 per month, right down to the employee in 107th place earning 2100 per month, as these abridged results show.

```
EMPLOYEE_ID     SALARY SALARY_RANK
----------- ---------- -----------
        100      24000           1
        101      17000           2
        102      17000           2
        145      14000           4
        146      13500           5
        201      13000           6
        205      12000           7
        108      12000           7
```

```
    147        12000              7
...
    132        2100             107
```

107 rows selected.

How It Works

RANK acts like any other analytic function, operating in a second pass over the result set once non-analytic processing is complete. In this recipe, the EMPLOYEE_ID and SALARY values are selected (there are no WHERE predicates to filter the table's data, so we get everyone employed in the organization). The analytic phase then orders the results in descending order by salary, and computes the rank value on the results starting at 1.

Note carefully how the RANK function has handled equal values. Two employees with salary of 17000 are given equal rank of 2. The next employee, at 14000, has a rank of 4. This is known as *sparse* ranking, where tied values "consume" place holders. In practical terms, this means that our equal second-place holders consume both second and third place, and the next available rank to provide is 4.

You can use an alternative to sparse ranking called *dense* ranking. Oracle supports this using the DENSE_RANK analytical function. Observe what happens to the recipe when we switch to dense ranking.

```
select employee_id, salary, dense_rank() over (order by salary desc)
  as Salary_Rank
from hr.employees;
```

We now see the "missing" consecutive rank values.

EMPLOYEE_ID	SALARY	SALARY_RANK
100	24000	1
101	17000	2
102	17000	2
145	14000	3
146	13500	4
201	13000	5
205	12000	6
108	12000	6
147	12000	6
168	11500	7
...		
132	2100	58

107 rows selected.

The classic examples of when the different kinds of ranking are used are in sporting competitions. Football and other sports typically use sparse ranking when tracking team win/loss progress on a ladder or table. The Olympic Games, on the other hand, tend to use dense ranking when competitors tie in events like swimming and others. They like to ensure that there are always gold, silver, and bronze medalists, even if there are tied entries and they have to give out more medals.

> ■ **Note** The authors live in hope that, one day, writing SQL statements will be an Olympic event. We'll be sure to use a dense ranking approach to maximize our chance of getting a medal.

Our recipe uses a simple ranking across all employees to determine salary order. Both RANK and DENSE_RANK support normal analytic extensions, allowing us to partition our source data so we can generate a rank for each subset of data. Continuing our recipe's theme, this means we could allocate a rank for salary earners from highest to lowest within each department. Introducing that partitioning to the query looks like this:

```
Select department_id, employee_id, salary, rank() over
  (partition by department_id order by salary desc) as Salary_Rank
From hr.employees
;
```

Our results now show per-department ranking of employees by salary.

DEPARTMENT_ID	EMPLOYEE_ID	SALARY	SALARY_RANK
10	200	4400	1
20	201	13000	1
20	202	6000	2
30	114	11000	1
30	115	3100	2
30	116	2900	3
30	117	2800	4
30	118	2600	5
30	119	2500	6
40	203	6500	1

...

As the DEPARTMENT_ID value ticks over, the PARTITION clause drives the RANK function to start its calculation again for the next subset of results.

2-13. Finding First and Last Values within a Group

Problem

You want to calculate and display aggregate information like minimum and maximum for a group, along with detail information for each member. You want don't want to repeat effort to display the aggregate and detail values.

Solution

Oracle provides the analytic functions FIRST and LAST to calculate the leading and ending values in any ordered sequence. Importantly, these do not require grouping to be used, unlike explicit aggregate functions such as MIN and MAX that work without OLAP features.

For our recipe, we'll assume the problem is a concrete one of displaying an employee's salary, alongside the minimum and maximum salaries paid to the employee's peers in their department. This SELECT statement does the work.

```
select department_id, first_name, last_name,
  min(salary)
    over (partition by department_id) "MinSal",
  salary,
  max(salary)
    over (partition by department_id) "MaxSal"
from hr.employees
order by department_id, salary;
```

This code outputs all employees and displays their salaries between the lowest and highest within their own department, as shown in the following partial output.

```
DEPARTMENT_ID FIRST_NAME LAST_NAME     MinSal     SALARY     MaxSal
------------- ---------- ----------  ---------- ---------- ----------
           10 Jennifer   Whalen           4400       4400       4400
           20 Pat        Fay              6000       6000      13000
           20 Michael    Hartstein        6000      13000      13000
           30 Karen      Colmenares       2500       2500      11000
           30 Guy        Himuro           2500       2600      11000
           30 Sigal      Tobias           2500       2800      11000
           30 Shelli     Baida            2500       2900      11000
           30 Alexander  Khoo             2500       3100      11000
           30 Den        Raphaely         2500      11000      11000
           40 Susan      Mavris           6500       6500       6500
...
107 rows selected.
```

How It Works

The key to both the FIRST and LAST analytic functions is their ability to let you perform the grouping and ordering on one set of criteria, while leaving you free to order differently in the main body of the query, and optionally group or not as desired by other factors.

The OLAP window is partitioned over each department with the OVER clause

```
over (partition by department_id) "MinSal"
```

2-14. Performing Aggregations over Moving Windows

Problem

You need to provide static and moving summaries or aggregates based on the same data. For example, as part of a sales report, you need to provide a monthly summary of sales order amounts, together with a moving three- month average of sales amounts for comparison.

Solution

Oracle provides moving or rolling window functions as part of the analytical function set. This gives you the ability to reference any number of preceding rows in a result set, the current row in the result set, and any number of following rows in a result set. Our initial recipe uses the current row and the three preceding rows to calculate the rolling average of order values.

```
select to_char(order_date, 'MM') as OrderMonth, sum(order_total) as MonthTotal,
avg(sum(order_total))
   over
     (order by to_char(order_date, 'MM') rows between 3 preceding and current row)
     as RollingQtrAverage
from oe.orders
where order_date between '01-JAN-1999' and '31-DEC-1999'
group by to_char(order_date, 'MM')
order by 1;
```

We see the month, the associated total, and the calculated rolling three-month average in our results.

```
OR MONTHTOTAL ROLLINGQTRAVERAGE
-- ---------- -----------------
02   120281.6          120281.6
03   200024.1         160152.85
04       1636          107313.9
05   165838.2        121944.975
06   350019.9         179379.55
07   280857.1          199587.8
08   152554.3        237317.375
09   460216.1         310911.85
10    59123.6        238187.775
11   415875.4         271942.35
12     338672        318471.775

11 rows selected.
```

You might notice January (OrderMonth 01) is missing. This isn't a quirk of this approach: rather it's because the OE.ORDERS table has no orders recorded for this month in 1999.

How It Works

Our SELECT statement for a rolling average starts by selecting some straightforward values. The month number is extracted from the ORDER_DATE field using the TO_CHAR() function with the MM format string to obtain the month's number. We choose the month number rather than the name so that the output is sorted as a person would expect.

Next up is a normal aggregate of the ORDER_TOTAL field using the traditional SUM function. No magic there. We then introduce an OLAP AVG function, which is where the detail of our rolling average is managed. That part of the statement looks like this.

```
avg(sum(order_total)) over (order by to_char(order_date, 'MM')
  rows between 3 preceding and current row) as RollingQtrAverage
```

All of that text is to generate our result column, the ROLLINGQTRAVERAGE. Breaking the sections down will illustrate how each part contributes to the solution. The leading functions, AVG(SUM(ORDER_TOTAL)), suggest we are going to sum the ORDER_TOTAL values and then take their average. That is correct to an extent, but Oracle isn't just going to calculate a normal average or sum. These are OLAP AVG and SUM functions, so their scope is governed by the OVER clause.

The OVER clause starts by instructing Oracle to perform the calculations based on the order of the formatted ORDER_DATE field—that's what ORDER BY TO_CHAR(ORDER_DATE, 'MM') achieves—effectively ordering the calculations by the values 02 to 12 (remember, there's no data for January 1999 in the database). Finally, and most importantly, the ROWS element tells Oracle the size of the window of rows over which it should calculate the driving OLAP aggregate functions. In our case, that means over how many months should the ORDER_TOTAL values be summed and then averaged. Our recipe instructs Oracle to use the results from the third-last row through to the current row. This is one interpretation of three-month rolling average, though technically it's actually generating an average over four months. If what you want is really a three-month average —the last two months plus the current month—you'd change the ROWS BETWEEN element to read

```
rows between 2 preceding and current row
```

This brings up an interesting point. This recipe assumes you want a rolling average computed over historic data. But some business requirements call for a rolling window to track trends based on data not only prior to a point in time, but also after that point. For instance, we might want to use a three-month window but base it on the previous, current, and following months. The next version of the recipe shows exactly this ability of the windowing function, with the key changes in bold.

```
select to_char(order_date, 'MM') as OrderMonth, sum(order_total) as MonthTotal,
avg(sum(order_total)) over (order by to_char(order_date, 'MM')
  rows between 1 preceding and 1 following) as AvgTrend
from oe.orders
where order_date between '01-JAN-1999' and '31-DEC-1999'
group by to_char(order_date, 'MM')
order by 1
/
```

Our output changes as you'd expect, as the monthly ORDER_TOTAL values are now grouped differently for the calculation.

```
OR MONTHTOTAL    AVGTREND
-- ----------  ----------
02   120281.6   160152.85
03   200024.1    107313.9
04       1636  122499.433
05   165838.2  172498.033
06   350019.9  265571.733
07   280857.1  261143.767
08   152554.3  297875.833
09   460216.1  223964.667
10    59123.6  311738.367
11   415875.4  271223.667
12     338672    377273.7

11 rows selected.
```

The newly designated AVGTREND value is calculated as described, using both preceding and following rows. Both our original recipe and this modified version are rounded out with a WHERE clause to select only data from the OE.ORDERS table for the year 1999. We group by the derived month number so that our traditional sum of ORDER_TOTAL in the second field of the results aggregates correctly, and finish up ordering logically by the month number.

2-15. Removing Duplicate Rows Based on a Subset of Columns

Problem

Data needs to be cleansed from a table based on duplicate values that are present only in a subset of rows.

Solution

Historically there were Oracle-specific solutions for this problem that used the ROWNUM feature. However, this can become awkward and complex if you have multiple groups of duplicates and want to remove the excess data in one pass. Instead, you can use Oracle's ROW_NUMBER OLAP function with a DELETE statement to efficiently remove all duplicates in one pass.

To illustrate our recipe in action, we'll first introduce several new staff members that have the same FIRST_NAME and LAST_NAME as some existing employees. These INSERT statements create our problematic duplicates.

```
insert into hr.employees
(employee_id, first_name, last_name, email, phone_number, hire_date, job_id,
 salary, commission_pct, manager_id, department_id)
Values
(210, 'Janette', 'King', 'JKING2', '650.555.8880', '25-MAR-2009', 'SA_REP',
 3500, 0.25, 145, 80);
```

```
Insert into hr.employees
(employee_id, first_name, last_name, email, phone_number, hire_date, job_id,
 salary, commission_pct, manager_id, department_id)
Values
(211, 'Patrick', 'Sully', 'PSULLY2', '650.555.8881', '25-MAR-2009', 'SA_REP',
 3500, 0.25, 145, 80);

Insert into hr.employees
(employee_id, first_name, last_name, email, phone_number, hire_date, job_id,
 salary, commission_pct, manager_id, department_id)
Values
(212, 'Allen', 'McEwen', 'AMCEWEN2', '650.555.8882', '25-MAR-2009', 'SA_REP',
 3500, 0.25, 145, 80);

commit;
```

To show that we do indeed have some duplicates, a quick SELECT shows the rows in question.

```
select employee_id, first_name, last_name
from hr.employees
where first_name in ('Janette','Patrick','Allan')
and last_name in ('King','Sully','McEwen')
order by first_name, last_name;

EMPLOYEE_ID FIRST_NAME  LAST_NAME
----------- ----------- ----------
        158 Allan       McEwen
        212 Allan       McEwen
        210 Janette     King
        156 Janette     King
        211 Patrick     Sully
        157 Patrick     Sully
```

If you worked in HR, or were one of these people, you might be concerned with the unpredictable consequences and want to see the duplicates removed. With our problematic data in place, we can introduce the SQL to remove the "extra" Janette King, Patrick Sully, and Allen McEwen.

```
delete from hr.employees
where rowid in
  (select rowid
   from
     (select first_name, last_name, rowid,
      row_number() over
        (partition by first_name, last_name order by employee_id)
        staff_row
      from hr.employees)
   where staff_row > 1);
```

When run, this code does indeed claim to remove three rows, presumably our duplicates. To check, we can repeat our quick query to see which rows match those three names. We see this set of results.

```
EMPLOYEE_ID FIRST_NAME  LAST_NAME
----------- ----------- -------------------------
        158 Allan       McEwen
        156 Janette     King
        157 Patrick     Sully
```

Our DELETE has succeeded, based on finding duplicates for a subset of columns only.

How It Works

Our recipe uses both the ROW_NUMBER OLAP function and Oracle's internal ROWID value for uniquely identifying rows in a table. The query starts with exactly the kind of DELETE syntax you'd assume.

```
delete from hr.employees
where rowid in
  (… nested subqueries here …)
```

As you'd expect, we're asking Oracle to delete rows from HR.EMPLOYEES where the ROWID value matches the values we detect for duplicates, based on criteria evaluating a subset of columns. In our case, we use subqueries to precisely identify duplicates based on FIRST_NAME and LAST_NAME.

To understand how the nested subqueries work, it's easiest to start with the innermost subquery, which looks like this.

```
select first_name, last_name, rowid,
  row_number() over
  (partition by first_name, last_name order by employee_id)
  staff_row
      from hr.employees
```

We've intentionally added the columns FIRST_NAME and LAST_NAME to this innermost subquery to make the recipe understandable as we work through its logic. Strictly speaking, these are superfluous to the logic, and the innermost subquery could be written without them to the same effect. If we execute just this innermost query (with the extra columns selected for clarity), we see these results.

```
FIRST_NAME  LAST_NAME    ROWID               STAFF_ROW
----------- ------------ ------------------- ----------
...
Alexander   Khoo         AAARAgAAFAAAABYAAP           1
Janette     King         AAARAgAAFAAAABXAAD           1
Janette     King         AAARAgAAFAAAABYAA4           2
Steven      King         AAARAgAAFAAAABYAAA           1
...
Samuel      McCain       AAARAgAAFAAAABYABe           1
Allan       McEwen       AAARAgAAFAAAABXAAF           1
Allan       McEwen       AAARAgAAFAAAABYAA6           2
Irene       Mikkilineni  AAARAgAAFAAAABYAAa           1
...
```

```
Martha      Sullivan     AAARAgAAFAAAABYABS         1
Patrick     Sully        AAARAgAAFAAAABXAAE         1
Patrick     Sully        AAARAgAAFAAAABYAA5         2
Jonathon    Taylor       AAARAgAAFAAAABYABM         1
...
```

110 rows selected.

All 110 staff from the HR.EMPLOYEES table have their FIRST_NAME, LAST_NAME and ROWID returned. The ROW_NUMBER() function then works over sets of FIRST_NAME and LAST_NAME driven by the PARTITION BY instruction. This means that for every unique FIRST_NAME and LAST_NAME, ROW_NUMBER will start a running count of rows we've aliased as STAFF_ROW. When a new FIRST_NAME and LAST_NAME combination is observed, the STAFF_ROW counter resets to 1.

In this way, the first Janette King has a STAFF_ROW value of 1, the second Janette King entry has a STAFF_ROW value of 2, and if there were a third and fourth such repeated name, they'd have STAFF_ROW values of 3 and 4 respectively. With our identically-named staff now numbered, we move to the next outermost subselect, which queries the results from above.

```
select rowid
from select
  (select first_name, last_name, rowid,
    row_number() over
    (partition by first_name, last_name order by first_name, last_name)
    staff_row
  from hr.employees)
where staff_row > 1
```

This outer query looks simple, because it is! We simply SELECT the ROWID values from the results of our innermost query, where the calculated STAFF_ROW value is greater than 1. That means that we only select the ROWID values for the second Janette King, Allan McEwen, and Patrick Sully, like this.

```
ROWID
------------------
AAARAgAAFAAAABYAA4
AAARAgAAFAAAABYAA6
AAARAgAAFAAAABYAA5
```

Armed with those ROWID values, the DELETE statement knows exactly which rows are the duplicates, based on only a comparison and count of FIRST_NAME and LAST_NAME.

The beauty of this recipe is the basic structure translates very easily to deleting data based on any such column-subset duplication. The format stays the same, and only the table name and a few column names need to be changed. Consider this a pseudo-SQL template for all such cases.

```
delete from <your_table_here>
where rowid in
  (select rowid
  from
    (select rowid,
     row_number() over
      (partition by <first_duplicate_column>, <second_duplicate_column>, <etc.>
       order by <desired ordering column>)
```

```
      duplicate_row_count
    from <your_table_here>)
  where duplicate_row_count > 1)
/
```

Simply plug in the value for your table in place of the marker *<your_table_here>*, and the columns you wish to use to determine duplication in place of equivalent column placeholders, and you're in business!

2-16. Finding Sequence Gaps in a Table

Problem

You want to find all gaps in the sequence of numbers or in dates and times in your data. The gaps could be in dates recorded for a given action, or in some other data with a logically consecutive nature.

Solution

Oracle's LAG and LEAD OLAP functions let you compare the current row of results with a preceding row. The general format of LAG looks like this

```
Lag (column or expression, preceding row offset, default for first row)
```

The *column or expression* is the value to be compared with lagging (preceding) values. The *preceding row offset* indicates how many rows prior to the current row the LAG should act against. We've used '1' in the following listing to mean the row one prior to the current row. The default for LAG indicates what value to use as a precedent for the first row, as there is no row zero in a table or result. We instruct Oracle to use 0 as the default anchor value, to handle the case where we look for the day prior to the first of the month.

The WITH query alias approach can be used in almost all situations where a subquery is used, to relocate the subquery details ahead of the main query. This aids readability and refactoring of the code if required at a later date.

This recipe looks for gaps in the sequence of days on which orders were made for the month of November 1999:

```
with salesdays as
  (select extract(day from order_date) next_sale,
   lag(extract(day from order_date),1,0)
     over (order by extract(day from order_date)) prev_sale
   from oe.orders
   where order_date between '01-NOV-1999' and '30-NOV-1999')
select prev_sale, next_sale
from salesdays
where next_sale - prev_sale > 1
order by prev_sale;
```

Our query exposes the gaps, in days, between sales for the month of November 1999.

```
PREV_SALE   NEXT_SALE
----------  ----------
         1          10
        10          14
        15          19
        20          22
```

The results indicate that after an order was recorded on the first of the month, no subsequent order was recorded until the 10th. Then a four-day gap followed to the 14th, and so on. An astute sales manager might well use this data to ask what the sales team was doing on those gap days, and why no orders came in!

How It Works

The query starts by using the WITH clause to name a subquery with an alias in an out-of-order fashion. The subquery is then referenced with an alias, in this case SALESDAYS.

The SALESDAYS subquery calculates two fields. First, it uses the EXTRACT function to return the numeric day value from the ORDER_DATE date field, and labels this data as NEXT_SALE. The lag OLAP function is then used to calculate the number for the day in the month (again using the EXTRACT method) of the ORDER_DATE of the preceding row in the results, which becomes the PREV_SALE result value. This makes more sense when you visualize the output of just the subquery select statement

```
select extract(day from order_date) next_sale,
  lag(extract(day from order_date),1,0)
    over (order by extract(day from order_date)) prev_sale
from oe.orders
where order_date between '01-NOV-1999' and '30-NOV-1999'
```

The results would look like this if executed independently.

```
NEXT_SALE   PREV_SALE
----------  ----------
         1           0
        10           1
        10          10
        10          10
        14          10
        14          14
        15          14
        19          15
...
```

Starting with the anchor value of 0 in the lag, we see the day of the month for a sale as NEXT_SALE, and the day of the previous sale as PREV_SALE. You can probably already visually spot the gaps, but it's much easier to let Oracle do that for you too. This is where our outer query does its very simple arithmetic.

The driving query over the SALESDAYS subquery selects the PREV_SALE and NEXT_SALE values from the results, based on this predicate.

```
where next_sale - prev_sale > 1
```

We know the days of sales are consecutive if they're out by more than one day. We wrap up by ordering the results by the PREV_SALE column, so that we get a natural ordering from start of month to end of month.

Our query could have been written the traditional way, with the subquery in the FROM clause like this.

```
select prev_sale, next_sale
from (select extract(day from order_date) next_sale,
  lag(extract(day from order_date),1,0)
    over (order by extract(day from order_date)) prev_sale
  from oe.orders
  where order_date between '01-NOV-1999' and '30-NOV-1999')
where next_sale - prev_sale > 1
order by prev_sale
/
```

The approach to take is largely a question of style and readability. We prefer the WITH approach on those occasions where it greatly increases the readability of your SQL statements.

CHAPTER 3

■ ■ ■

Querying from Multiple Tables

Querying data from Oracle tables is probably the most common task you will perform as a developer or data analyst, and maybe even as a DBA—though probably not as the ETL (Extraction, Transformation, and Loading) tool expert. Quite often, you may query only one table for a small subset of rows, but sooner or later you will have to join multiple tables together. That's the beauty of a relational database, where the access paths to the data are not fixed: you can join tables that have common columns, or even tables that do not have common columns (at your own peril!).

In this chapter we'll cover solutions for joining two or more tables and retrieving the results based on the existence of desired rows in both tables (equi-join), rows that may exist only in one table or the other (left or right outer joins), or joining two tables together and including all rows from both tables, matching where possible (full outer joins).

But wait, there's more! Oracle (and the SQL language standard) contains a number of constructs that help you retrieve rows from tables based on the existence of the same rows in another table with the same column values for the selected rows in a query. These constructs include the INTERSECT, UNION, UNION ALL, and MINUS operators. The results from queries using these operators can in some cases be obtained using the standard table-join syntax, but if you're working with more than just a couple of columns, the query becomes unwieldy, hard to read, and hard to maintain.

You may also need to update rows in one table based on matching or non-matching values in another table, so we'll provide a couple of recipes on correlated queries and correlated updates using the IN/EXISTS SQL constructs as well.

Of course, no discussion of table manipulation would be complete without delving into the unruly child of the query world, the Cartesian join. There are cases where you want to join two or more tables without a join condition, and we'll give you a recipe for that scenario.

Most of the examples in this chapter are based on the schemas in the EXAMPLE tablespace created during an Oracle Database installation when you specify "Include Sample Schemas." Those sample schemas aren't required to understand the solutions in this chapter, but they give you the opportunity to try out the solutions on a pre-populated set of tables and even delve further into the intricacies of table joins.

3-1. Joining Corresponding Rows from Two or More Tables

Problem

You want to return rows from two or more tables that have one or more columns in common. For example, you may want to join the EMPLOYEES and the DEPARTMENTS table on a common column, but not all common columns, and return a list of employees and their department names.

Solution

If you are using Oracle Database 9*i* or later, you can use the ANSI SQL 99 join syntax with the USING clause. For example, the EMPLOYEES and DEPARTMENTS table in the Oracle sample schemas have the DEPARTMENT_ID column in common, so the query looks like this:

```
select employee_id, last_name, first_name, department_id, department_name
from employees
    join departments using(department_id)
;
```

EMPLOYEE_ID	LAST_NAME	FIRST_NAME	DEPARTMENT_ID	DEPARTMENT_NAME
200	Whalen	Jennifer	10	Administration
201	Hartstein	Michael	20	Marketing
202	Fay	Pat	20	Marketing
114	Raphaely	Den	30	Purchasing
115	Khoo	Alexander	30	Purchasing
. . .				
113	Popp	Luis	100	Finance
205	Higgins	Shelley	110	Accounting
206	Gietz	William	110	Accounting

```
106 rows selected
```

The query retrieves most of the results from the EMPLOYEES table, and the DEPARTMENT_NAME column from the DEPARTMENTS table.

How It Works

The sample schemas supplied with a default installation of Oracle Database 11*g* provide a good starting point for trying out some Oracle features. Oracle Database comes with several sample schemas such as HR, OE, and BI to show not only the relationships between database schemas, but also to show some of the varied features such as index-organized tables (IOTs), function-based indexes, materialized views, large objects (BLOBs and CLOBs), and XML objects.

Here is the structure of the EMPLOYEES and DEPARTMENTS tables:

CHAPTER 3 ■ QUERYING FROM MULTIPLE TABLES

```
describe employees
```

Name	Null	Type
EMPLOYEE_ID	NOT NULL	NUMBER(6)
FIRST_NAME		VARCHAR2(20)
LAST_NAME	NOT NULL	VARCHAR2(25)
EMAIL	NOT NULL	VARCHAR2(25)
PHONE_NUMBER		VARCHAR2(20)
HIRE_DATE	NOT NULL	DATE
JOB_ID	NOT NULL	VARCHAR2(10)
SALARY		NUMBER(8,2)
COMMISSION_PCT		NUMBER(2,2)
MANAGER_ID		NUMBER(6)
DEPARTMENT_ID		NUMBER(4)

```
11 rows selected
```

```
describe departments
```

Name	Null	Type
DEPARTMENT_ID	NOT NULL	NUMBER(4)
DEPARTMENT_NAME	NOT NULL	VARCHAR2(30)
MANAGER_ID		NUMBER(6)
LOCATION_ID		NUMBER(4)

```
4 rows selected
```

There are three other basic ways to join these two tables on the DEPARTMENT_ID column. One of them is pre-ANSI SQL 99, one is more suitable when the column names in the joined tables are not identical, and one is outright dangerous, as you will see.

Using the "old style" join syntax, you include the join condition in the WHERE clause, like this:

```
select employee_id, last_name, first_name, e.department_id, department_name
from employees e, departments d
where e.department_id = d.department_id
;
```

While this approach works and is as efficient from an execution plan point of view, the older syntax can be hard to read, as you are mixing the table-join conditions with any filter conditions. It also forces you to specify a qualifier for the join columns in the SELECT clause.

Another ANSI SQL 99 method for joining tables uses the ON clause as follows:

```
select employee_id, last_name, first_name, e.department_id, department_name
from employees e
   join departments d
      on e.department_id = d.department_id
;
```

■ **Note** You can also use the INNER JOIN keywords instead of just JOIN in a multi-table query if you want to be more verbose or want to make it very clear that the query is an equi-join instead of an outer join or Cartesian product.

The ON clause is less readable (and usually requires more typing!) compared to the USING clause when the joined columns have the same name. It has the same downside as using the pre-ANSI SQL 99 syntax in that you must qualify the join columns or any other columns with the same name with an alias.

Finally, you can make the syntax for the EMPLOYEE/DEPARTMENTS query even simpler by using the NATURAL JOIN clause instead of the JOIN . . . USING clause, as in this example:

```
select employee_id, last_name, first_name, department_id, department_name
from employees natural join departments
;
```

When you use NATURAL JOIN, Oracle automatically joins the two tables on columns with the same name, which in this case is the DEPARTMENT_ID column. This makes the query even simpler and more readable, but has a very dark side in some circumstances. Here's an example. The query we've just shown with NATURAL JOIN returns 32 rows, while the earlier queries that used USING or ON each return 106 rows. What happened? Why the difference?

If you look closely at the table definitions, you'll see another common column called MANAGER_ID. NATURAL JOIN includes that column in the join criteria. Thus, the preceding query is really equivalent to the following:

```
select employee_id, last_name, first_name, department_id, department_name
from employees join departments using(department_id, manager_id)
;
```

This join is almost certainly not what you want, as the MANAGER_ID in the EMPLOYEES table has a slightly different meaning than the MANAGER_ID in the DEPARTMENTS table: EMPLOYEES.MANAGER_ID is the employee's manager, whereas DEPARTMENTS.MANAGER_ID is the manager of the entire department. As a result, the query does not return employees and their managers. Instead, it produces a list of employees whose department has the same manager as they do, which will not be the case in many organizations. Furthermore, a large number of departments in the DEPARTMENTS table do not have a manager assigned, thus the query using NATURAL JOIN will leave out employees who do have a reporting manager, but whose department does not have a manager assigned. Use NATURAL JOIN with caution!

Later in this chapter, we'll look at two techniques that can help you uncover these logical errors: using optional joins and dealing with NULL values in queries.

3-2. Stacking Query Results Vertically

Problem

You want to combine the results from two SELECT statements into a single result set.

Solution

Use the UNION operator. UNION combines the results of two or more queries and removes duplicates from the entire result set. In Oracle's mythical company, the employees in the EMPLOYEES_ACT table need to be merged with employees from a recent corporate acquisition. The recently acquired company's employee table EMPLOYEES_NEW has the same exact format as the existing EMPLOYEES_ACT table, so it should be easy to use UNION to combine the two tables into a single result set as follows:

```
select employee_id, first_name, last_name from employees_act;

EMPLOYEE_ID           FIRST_NAME            LAST_NAME
--------------------- --------------------- -------------------------
102                   Lex                   De Haan
105                   David                 Austin
112                   Jose Manuel           Urman
118                   Guy                   Himuro
119                   Karen                 Colmenares
205                   Shelley               Higgins

6 rows selected
```

```
select employee_id, first_name, last_name from employees_new;

EMPLOYEE_ID           FIRST_NAME            LAST_NAME
--------------------- --------------------- -------------------------
101                   Neena                 Kochhar
105                   David                 Austin
112                   Jose Manuel           Urman
171                   William               Smith
201                   Michael               Hartstein

5 rows selected
```

```
select employee_id, first_name, last_name from employees_act
union
select employee_id, first_name, last_name from employees_new
order by employee_id
;

EMPLOYEE_ID           FIRST_NAME            LAST_NAME
--------------------- --------------------- -------------------------
101                   Neena                 Kochhar
102                   Lex                   De Haan
105                   David                 Austin
112                   Jose Manuel           Urman
118                   Guy                   Himuro
119                   Karen                 Colmenares
171                   William               Smith
201                   Michael               Hartstein
205                   Shelley               Higgins

9 rows selected
```

Using UNION removes the duplicate rows. You can have one ORDER BY at the end of the query to order the results. In this example, the two employee tables have two rows in common (some people need to work two or three jobs to make ends meet!), so instead of returning 11 rows, the UNION query returns nine.

How It Works

Note that for the UNION operator to remove duplicate rows, all columns in a given row must be equal to the same columns in one or more other rows. When Oracle processes a UNION, it must perform a sort/merge to determine which rows are duplicates. Thus, your execution time will likely be more than running each SELECT individually. If you know there are no duplicates within and across each SELECT statement, you can use UNION ALL to combine the results without checking for duplicates.

If there are duplicates, it will not cause an error; you will merely get duplicate rows in your result set.

3-3. Writing an Optional Join

Problem

You are joining two tables by one or more common columns, but you want to make sure to return all rows in the first table regardless of a matching row in the second. For example, you are joining the employee and department tables, but some employees lack department assignments.

Solution

Use an outer join. In Oracle's sample database, the HR user maintains the EMPLOYEES and DEPARTMENTS tables; assigning a department to an employee is optional. There are 107 employees in the EMPLOYEES table. Using a standard join between EMPLOYEES and DEPARTMENTS only returns 106 rows, however, since one employee is not assigned a department. To return all rows in the EMPLOYEES table, you can use LEFT OUTER JOIN to include all rows in the EMPLOYEES table and matching rows in DEPARTMENTS, if any:

```
select employee_id, last_name, first_name, department_id, department_name
from employees
    left outer join departments using(department_id)
;
```

```
EMPLOYEE_ID  LAST_NAME       FIRST_NAME      DEPARTMENT_ID      DEPARTMENT_NAME
-----------  --------------  --------------  -----------------  -------------------
200          Whalen          Jennifer        10                 Administration
202          Fay             Pat             20                 Marketing
201          Hartstein       Michael         20                 Marketing
119          Colmenares      Karen           30                 Purchasing
. . .
206          Gietz           William         110                Accounting
205          Higgins         Shelley         110                Accounting
178          Grant           Kimberely

107 rows selected
```

There are now 107 rows in the result set instead of 106; Kimberely Grant is included even though she does not currently have a department assigned.

How It Works

When two tables are joined using LEFT OUTER JOIN, the query returns all the rows in the table to the left of the LEFT OUTER JOIN clause, as you might expect. Rows in the table on the right side of the LEFT OUTER JOIN clause are matched when possible. If there is no match, columns from the table on the right side will contain NULL values in the results.

As you might expect, there is a RIGHT OUTER JOIN as well (in both cases, the OUTER keyword is optional). You can rewrite the solution as follows:

```
select employee_id, last_name, first_name, department_id, department_name
from departments
    right outer join employees using(department_id)
;
```

The results are identical, and which format you use depends on readability and style.

The query can be written using the ON clause as well, just as with an equi-join (inner join). And for versions of Oracle before 9*i*, you must use Oracle's somewhat obtuse and proprietary outer-join syntax with the characters (+) on the side of the query that is missing rows, as in this example:

```
select employee_id, last_name, first_name, e.department_id, department_name
from employees e, departments d
where e.department_id = d.department_id (+)
;
```

Needless to say, if you can use ANSI SQL-99 syntax, by all means do so for clarity and ease of maintenance.

3-4. Making a Join Optional in Both Directions

Problem

All of the tables in your query have at least a few rows that don't match rows in the other tables, but you still want to return all rows from all tables and show the mismatches in the results. For example, you want to reduce the number of reports by including mismatches from both tables instead of having one report for each scenario.

Solution

Use FULL OUTER JOIN. As you might expect, a full outer join between two or more tables will return all rows in each table of the query and match where possible. You can use FULL OUTER JOIN with the EMPLOYEES and DEPARTMENTS table as follows:

```
select employee_id, last_name, first_name, department_id, department_name
from employees
    full outer join departments using(department_id)
;
```

```
EMPLOYEE_ID  LAST_NAME          FIRST_NAME     DEPARTMENT_ID     DEPARTMENT_NAME
-----------  -----------------  -------------  ----------------  --------------------
100          King               Steven         90                Executive
101          Kochhar            Neena          90                Executive
102          De Haan            Lex            90                Executive
. . .
177          Livingston         Jack           80                Sales
178          Grant              Kimberely
179          Johnson            Charles        80                Sales
. . .
206          Gietz              William        110               Accounting
                                               180               Construction
                                               190               Contracting
                                               230               IT Helpdesk

123 rows selected
```

■ **Note** The OUTER keyword is optional when using a FULL, LEFT, or RIGHT join. It does add documentation value to your query, making it clear that mismatched rows from one or both tables will be in the results.

Using FULL OUTER JOIN is a good way to view, at a glance, mismatches between two tables. In the preceding output, you can see an employee without a department as well as several departments that have no employees.

How It Works

Trying to accomplish a full outer join before Oracle9*i* was a bit inelegant: you had to perform a UNION of two outer joins (a left and a right outer join) using the proprietary Oracle syntax as follows:

```
select employee_id, last_name, first_name, e.department_id, department_name
from employees e, departments d
where e.department_id = d.department_id (+)
union
select employee_id, last_name, first_name, e.department_id, department_name
from employees e, departments d
where e.department_id (+) = d.department_id
;
```

Running two separate queries, then removing duplicates, takes more time to execute than using the FULL OUTER JOIN syntax, where only one pass on each table is required.

You can tweak the FULL OUTER JOIN to produce only the mismatched records as follows:

```
select employee_id, last_name, first_name, department_id, department_name
from employees
    full outer join departments using(department_id)
where employee_id is null or department_name is null
;
```

3-5. Removing Rows Based on Data in Other Tables

Problem

You want to delete rows from a table if corresponding rows exist in a second table. For example, you want to delete rows from the EMPLOYEES_RETIRED table for any employees that exist in the EMPLOYEES table.

Solution

Use the IN or EXISTS clause with a subquery. You have a table called EMPLOYEES_RETIRED that should contain only—you guessed it—retired employees. However, the EMPLOYEES_RETIRED table erroneously includes some active employees, so you want to remove any active employees from the EMPLOYEES_RETIRED table. Here's how you can do that:

```
delete from employees_retired
where employee_id
    in (select employee_id from employees)
;
```

How It Works

When you use SELECT, you have the relative luxury of using a join condition to return results. When deleting rows, you can't perform an explicit join unless the join conditions are in a subquery or you use an inline view as follows:

```
delete (
        select employee_id
        from employees_retired join employees using(employee_id)
        );
```

The SQL standard treats views much like tables, in that you can not only run a SELECT statement against a view, but also INSERT, UPDATE and DELETE under certain circumstances. If these circumstances are met (for example, you have a key-preserved table, no aggregates, and so forth), DELETE will delete only from the first table in the FROM clause. Be careful: if your DELETE looks like the following, you will not get the intended results:

```
delete (
      select employee_id
      from employees join employees_retired using(employee_id)
      );
```

The rows will be deleted from the EMPLOYEES table instead, and that is not the desired result!

Another potential solution to the problem uses an EXISTS clause to determine which rows to delete:

```
delete from employees_retired er
where exists (
            select 1 from employees e
            where er.employee_id = e.employee_id
            )
;
```

This is not as elegant as the first solution, but might be more efficient. It appears contrived, and it is, because Oracle never uses the results of the query anywhere. It only uses the subquery to verify the existence of a match, and then deletes the corresponding row(s). You can use a "1", an "X", or even NULL; internally, Oracle translates the result to a zero and does not use it.

Whether you use IN or EXISTS depends on the sizes of the driving table (the outer table referenced in the SELECT, UPDATE, or DELETE) and the size of the result set in the subquery. Using IN is most likely better if the results of the subquery are small or is a list of constants. However, using EXISTS may run a lot more efficiently since the implicit JOIN may take advantage of indexes. The bottom line is, it depends. Look at the execution plans for each method (IN versus EXISTS), and if the relative row counts remain stable whenever the query is run, you can use whichever method is faster.

3-6. Finding Matched Data Across Tables

Problem

You want to find the rows in common between two or more tables or queries.

Solution

Use the INTERSECT operator. When you use INTERSECT, the resulting row set contains only rows that are in common between the two tables or queries:

```
select count(*) from employees_act;

COUNT(*)
----------------------
6

select count(*) from employees_new;

COUNT(*)
----------------------
5
```

```
select * from employees_act
intersect
select * from employees_new
;

EMPLOYEE_ID            FIRST_NAME            LAST_NAME                       . . .
--------------------   --------------------  ------------------------
105                    David                 Austin
112                    Jose Manuel           Urman

2 rows selected
```

How It Works

The INTERSECT operator, along with UNION, UNION ALL, and MINUS, joins two or more queries together. As of Oracle Database 11g, these operators have equal precedence, and unless you override them with parentheses, they are evaluated in left-to-right order. Or, more intuitively since you usually don't have two queries on one line, top-to-bottom order!

■ **Tip** Future ANSI SQL standards give the INTERSECT operator higher precedence than the other operators. Thus, to "bulletproof" your SQL code, use parentheses to explicitly specify evaluation order where you use INTERSECT with other set operators.

To better understand how INTERSECT works, Figure 3-1 shows a Venn diagram representation of the INTERSECT operation on two queries.

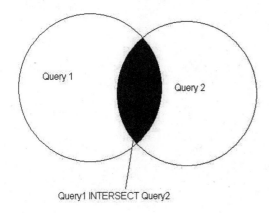

Figure 3-1. An Oracle INTERSECT operation

Finally, for an INTERSECT operation to return the intended results, the corresponding columns in each query of the INTERSECT operation should have data types within the same class: numbers, characters, or date/time. For example, a NUMBER column and a BINARY_DOUBLE column will compare correctly if the conversion of the NUMBER column value to a BINARY_DOUBLE produces the same result. So, a NUMBER(3) column containing the value 250 will compare exactly to a BINARY_DOUBLE having the value 2.5E2.

Using set operators is one of the rare cases where a value of NULL in one column is considered equal to another column containing a NULL. Therefore, running this query returns one row:

```
select 'X' C1, NULL C2 from DUAL
intersect
select 'X' C1, NULL C2 from DUAL
;
```

3-7. Joining on Aggregates

Problem

You want to compare values in individual rows to aggregate values computed from the same table; you also want to filter rows that are used for the aggregate. For example: you want to find all employees whose salary is 20% less than the average salary for the company, except for employees who are in the executive department.

Solution

Use a subquery with an aggregate, and compare the employee's salary to the average salary retrieved in the aggregate. For example, this query uses a subquery to calculate the average salary for employees outside of department 90, and compares every employee's salary to 80% of the result from the subquery:

```
select employee_id, last_name, first_name, salary
from employees
where salary < 0.8 * (
                  select avg(salary)
                  from employees
                  where department_id != 90
                  )
;
```

EMPLOYEE_ID	LAST_NAME	FIRST_NAME	SALARY
105	Austin	David	4800
106	Pataballa	Valli	4800
107	Lorentz	Diana	4200
115	Khoo	Alexander	3100
. . .			
198	OConnell	Donald	2600
199	Grant	Douglas	2600
200	Whalen	Jennifer	4400

```
49 rows selected
```

How It Works

The presented solution returns one row in the subquery. The Oracle optimizer calculates the average salary once, multiplies it by 0.8, and compares it to the salary of all other employees in the EMPLOYEE table other than those in department 90 (the executive group).

If your subquery returns more than one row, the main query will return an error since you are using the < operator; operators such as <, >, =, >=, <=, and != compare a column's or expression's value to another single value. To compare a value in the main query to a list of one or more values in a subquery, you can use the ANY or SOME operator (they are equivalent) in the WHERE clause. For example, if you wanted to return all employees whose salary matches any of the employees in the executive department, you can do this:

```
select employee_id, last_name, first_name, salary
from employees
where salary = any (
                select salary
                from employees
                where department_id = 90
                )
;
```

You can also use subqueries in the HAVING clause of a query that uses aggregates. In this example, you can retrieve all departments and average salaries whose average salary is greater than the average salary of the IT department:

```
select department_id, avg(salary) avg_salary
from employees
group by department_id
having avg(salary) > (
                select avg(salary)
                from employees
                where department_id = 60
                )
;
```

3-8. Finding Missing Rows

Problem

You have two tables, and you must find rows in the first table that are not in the second table. You want to compare all rows in each table, not just a subset of columns.

Solution

Use the MINUS set operator. The MINUS operator will return all rows in the first query that are not in the second query. The EMPLOYEES_BONUS table contains employees who have been given bonuses in the past, and you need to find employees in the EMPLOYEES table who have not yet received bonuses. Use the MINUS operator as follows to compare three selected columns from two tables:

```
select employee_id, last_name, first_name from employees
minus
select employee_id, last_name, first_name from employees_bonus
;
```

```
EMPLOYEE_ID             LAST_NAME                 FIRST_NAME
----------------------  ------------------------  --------------------
100                     King                      Steven
109                     Faviet                    Daniel
110                     Chen                      John
120                     Weiss                     Matthew
140                     Patel                     Joshua

5 rows selected
```

How It Works

Note that unlike the INTERSECT and UNION operators, the MINUS set operator is not commutative: the order of the operands (queries) is important! Changing the order of the queries in the solution will produce very different results.

If you wanted to note changes for the entire row, you could use this query instead:

```
select * from employees
minus
select * from employees_bonus
;
```

A Venn diagram may help to show how the MINUS operator works. Figure 3-2 shows the result of Query1 MINUS Query2. Any rows that overlap between Query1 and Query2 are removed from the result set along with any rows in Query2 that do not overlap Query1. In other words, only rows in Query1 are returned less any rows in Query1 that exist in Query2.

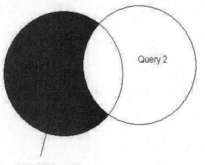

Figure 3-2. *An Oracle MINUS operation*

Rows in Query2 that do not exist in Query1 can be identified by reversing the order of the operands in the query:

```
select * from employees_bonus
minus
select * from employees
;
```

What if Query2 is a proper subset of Query1? In other words, all the rows in Query2 are already in Query1? The query still works as advertised; MINUS only removes rows from Query1 that are in common with Query2, and never returns any rows in Query2 that are not in Query1. Figure 3-3 shows the Venn diagram for the scenario where Query2 is a proper subset of Query1.

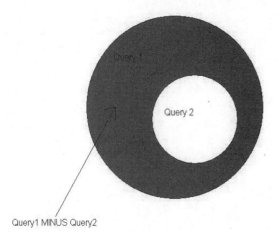

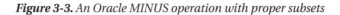

Figure 3-3. An Oracle MINUS operation with proper subsets

You may ask why an outer join or an IN/EXISTS query might solve most problems like this. For sets of tables with a single primary key, it may be more efficient to use a join. However, for query results with a large number of columns or for comparing entire rows of data even when the primary keys match, MINUS is the more appropriate operator to use.

3-9. Finding Rows that Tables Do Not Have in Common

Problem

You want to find rows from two queries or tables that the two queries or tables do NOT have in common. The analysts have provided you with Venn diagrams and the set notation for retrieving the required data, so you must use a combination of Oracle set operators to retrieve the desired result.

Solution

Use aggregate functions and the UNION ALL operator together in a compound query, parenthesizing for clarity and correctness. For example, you want to find the list of employees that are in the EMPLOYEES_ACT table but not in the EMPLOYEES_NEW table, and vice versa. Execute the following queries to show the contents of each table and the results of using Oracle set operators to find the unique rows in each table:

```
select employee_id, first_name, last_name from employees_act
order by employee_id;
```

EMPLOYEE_ID	FIRST_NAME	LAST_NAME
102	Lex	De Haan
105	David	Austin
112	Jose Manuel	Urman
118	Guy	Himuro
119	Karen	Colmenares
205	Shelley	Higgins

6 rows selected

```
select employee_id, first_name, last_name from employees_new
order by employee_id;
```

EMPLOYEE_ID	FIRST_NAME	LAST_NAME
101	Neena	Kochhar
105	David	Austin
112	Jose Manuel	Urman
171	William	Smith
201	Michael	Hartstein

5 rows selected

```
select employee_id, first_name, last_name,
   count(act_emp_src) act_emp_row_count,
   count(new_emp_src) new_emp_row_count
from
   (
   select ea.*, 1 act_emp_src, to_number(NULL) new_emp_src
   from employees_act ea
   union all
   select en.*, to_number(NULL) act_emp_src, 1 new_emp_src
   from employees_new en
   )
group by employee_id, first_name, last_name
having count(act_emp_src) != count(new_emp_src)
;
```

```
EMPLOYEE_ID FIRST_NAME   LAST_NAME        ACT_EMP_ROW_COUNT NEW_EMP_ROW_COUNT
----------- ----------   ---------------- ----------------- -----------------
101         Neena        Kochhar          0                 1
205         Shelley      Higgins          1                 0
102         Lex          De Haan          1                 0
171         William      Smith            0                 1
201         Michael      Hartstein        0                 1
118         Guy          Himuro           1                 0
119         Karen        Colmenares       1                 0

7 rows selected
```

How It Works

To get the correct result, you must first combine both result sets using UNION ALL in the subquery, assigning a "tag" column to indicate where the row came from—the first table or the second. Here, we use a "1", but it would work fine with a "2", or an "X".

The GROUP BY and HAVING clauses pick out the common rows. If a given row exists in both tables once, or several times, the count for that row will be the same, and thus will be excluded by the condition in the HAVING clause. If the counts are not the same, the row will show up in the result along with how many times it appears in one table but not the other, and vice versa. Because we are including primary keys in this query, you will not see more than one non-common row in each table.

Figure 3-4 shows the Venn diagram for the result set.

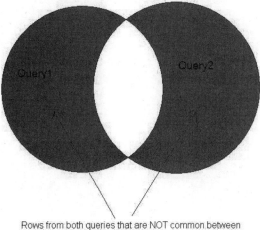

Rows from both queries that are NOT common between
Query1 and Query2

Figure 3-4. *An Oracle set operation to find unique rows between component queries*

Using standard set notation, the result you are looking for can be more succinctly expressed as follows:

```
NOT (Query1 INTERSECT Query2)
```

Although Oracle syntax does have NOT and INTERSECT, NOT is not supported for use with Oracle set operators. Thus, you must write the query as shown in the solution with UNION ALL and GROUP BY to provide the result identified in Figure 3-4. Even if Oracle supported NOT with set operators, you would still have to use the solution provided to identify how many of each non-common row exists in each component query.

3-10. Generating Test Data

Problem

You want to combine two or more tables without common columns to generate test data or a template for all possible combinations of values from two or more tables.

For example, you are writing an embedded Oracle database application to help you count cards at the next blackjack game, and you want to generate the template table for the 52-card deck with a minimum of effort.

Solution

Use a CROSS JOIN construct between the set of four suits (hearts, clubs, diamonds, and spades) and the 13 rank values (Ace, 2-10, Jack, Queen, and King). For example:

```
create table card_deck
    (suit_rank        varchar2(5),
     card_count       number)
;

insert into card_deck
     select rank || '-' || suit, 0 from
        (select 'A' rank from dual
         union all
         select '2' from dual
         union all
         select '3' from dual
         union all
         select '4' from dual
         union all
         select '5' from dual
         union all
         select '6' from dual
         union all
         select '7' from dual
         union all
         select '8' from dual
         union all
         select '9' from dual
         union all
```

```
        select '10' from dual
        union all
        select 'J' from dual
        union all
        select 'Q' from dual
        union all
        select 'K' from dual)
    cross join
        (select 'S' suit from dual
        union all
        select 'H' from dual
        union all
        select 'D' from dual
        union all
        select 'C' from dual)
;

select suit_rank from card_deck;

SUIT_RANK
---------
A-S
2-S
3-S
4-S
5-S
6-S
. . .
10-C
J-C
Q-C
K-C

52 rows selected
```

The Dual Table

The DUAL table comes in handy in many situations. It is available in every version of Oracle from the last 20 years, and contains one row and one column. It is handy when you want to return a row when you don't have to retrieve data from any particular table—you just want to return a value. You would also use the DUAL table to perform an ad-hoc calculation using a built-in function, as in this example:

```
select sqrt(144) from dual;

SQRT(144)
-------------------
12
```

This SQL statement would work just as well if you already had the suits and ranks in two existing tables. In that case, you would reference the two tables rather than write those long subqueries involving UNION operations against the DUAL table. For example:

```
select rank || '-' || suit, 0 from
    card_ranks
cross join
    card_suits
;
```

How It Works

Using a CROSS JOIN, otherwise known as a Cartesian product, is rarely intentional. If you specify no join conditions between two tables, the number of rows in the results is the product of the number of rows in each table. Usually this is not the desired result! As a general rule, for a query with *n* tables, you need to specify at least *n-1* join conditions to avoid a Cartesian product.

If your card games usually involve using one or two jokers in the deck, you can tack them onto the end as easily as this:

```
select rank || '-' || suit, 0 from
    (select 'A' rank from dual
    union all
    select '2' from dual
. . .
    select 'C' from dual)
union (select 'J1', 0 from dual)
union (select 'J2', 0 from dual)
;
```

Using the pre-Oracle9*i* syntax (Oracle proprietary syntax), you can rewrite the original query as follows:

```
select rank || '-' || suit, 0 from
    card_ranks, card_suits
;
```

It's odd to see a multi-table join using the proprietary Oracle syntax and no WHERE clause, but it produces the results you want!

3-11. Updating Rows Based on Data in Other Tables

Problem

You want to update some or all rows in your table based on individual values or aggregates in the same or another table. The values used to update the query are dependent on column values in the table to be updated.

Solution

Use a correlated update to link the values in the subquery to the main table in the UPDATE clause. In the following example, you want to update all employee salaries to 10% more than the average salary for their department:

```
update employees e
   set salary = (select avg(salary)*1.10
                   from employees se
                   where se.department_id = e.department_id)
;

107 rows updated
```

How It Works

For each row in the EMPLOYEES table, the current salary is updated with 10% more than the average salary for their department. The subquery will always return a single row since it has an aggregate with no GROUP BY. Note that this query shows Oracle's read consistency feature in action: Oracle preserves the original salary value for each employee to compute the average while updating each employee's salary in the same UPDATE statement.

Correlated updates are much like correlated subqueries (discussed elsewhere in this chapter): you link one or more columns in the main part of the query with the corresponding columns in the subquery. When performing correlated updates, take special note of how many rows are updated; coding the subquery incorrectly can often update most values in the table with NULL or incorrect values!

In fact, the solution provided will fail if an employee does not have a department assigned. The correlated subquery will return NULL in this scenario because a NULL department value will never match any other department values that are NULL, and thus the employee will be assigned a SALARY of NULL. To fix this problem, add a filter in the WHERE clause:

```
update employees e
   set salary = (select avg(salary)*1.10
                   from employees se
                   where se.department_id = e.department_id)
where department_id is not null
;

106 rows updated
```

All employees without an assigned department will keep their existing salary. Another way to accomplish the same thing is by using the NVL function in the SET clause to check for NULL values:

```
update employees e
   set salary = nvl((select avg(salary)*1.10
                       from employees se
                       where se.department_id = e.department_id),salary)
;

107 rows updated
```

This option may not be as desirable from an I/O perspective or in terms of redo log file usage, since all rows will be updated whether they have a department assigned or not.

3-12. Manipulating and Comparing NULLs in Join Conditions

Problem

You want to map NULL values in a join column to a default value that will match a row in the joined table, thus avoiding the use of an outer join.

Solution

Use the NVL function to convert NULL values in the foreign key column of the table to be joined to its parent table. In this example, holiday parties are scheduled for each department, but several employees do not have a department assigned. Here is one of them:

```
select employee_id, first_name, last_name, department_id
from employees
where employee_id = 178
;
```

EMPLOYEE_ID	FIRST_NAME	LAST_NAME	DEPARTMENT_ID
178	Kimberely	Grant	

1 rows selected

To ensure that each employee will attend a holiday party, convert all NULL department codes in the EMPLOYEES table to department 110 (Accounting) in the query as follows:

```
select employee_id, first_name, last_name, d.department_id, department_name
from employees e join departments d
   on nvl(e.department_id,110) = d.department_id
;
```

EMPLOYEE_ID	FIRST_NAME	LAST_NAME	DEPARTMENT_ID	DEPARTMENT_NAME
200	Jennifer	Whalen	10	Administration
201	Michael	Hartstein	20	Marketing
202	Pat	Fay	20	Marketing
114	Den	Raphaely	30	Purchasing
115	Alexander	Khoo	30	Purchasing
. . .				

113	Luis	Popp	100	Finance
178	**Kimberely**	**Grant**	**110**	**Accounting**
205	Shelley	Higgins	110	Accounting
206	William	Gietz	110	Accounting

```
107 rows selected
```

How It Works

Mapping columns with NULLs to non-NULL values in a join condition to avoid using an OUTER JOIN might still have performance problems, since the index on EMPLOYEES.DEPARTMENT_ID will not be used during the join (primarily because NULL columns are not indexed). You can address this new problem by using a function-based index (FBI). An FBI creates an index on an expression, and may use that index if the expression appears in a join condition or a WHERE clause. Here is how to create an FBI on the DEPARTMENT_ID column:

```
create index employees_dept_fbi on employees(nvl(department_id,110));
```

■ **Tip** As of Oracle Database 11*g*, you can now use *virtual columns* as an alternative to FBIs. Virtual columns are derived from constants, functions, and columns from the same table. You can define indexes on the virtual columns, which the optimizer will use in any query as it would a regular column index.

Ultimately, the key to handling NULLs in join conditions is based on knowing your data. If at all possible, avoid joining on columns that may have NULLs, or ensure that every column you will join on has a default value when it is populated. If the column must have NULLs, use functions like NVL, NVL2, and COALESCE to convert NULLs before joining; you can create function-based indexes to offset any performance issues with joining on expressions. If that is not possible, understand the business rules about what NULLs mean in your database columns: do they mean zero, unknown, or not applicable? Your SQL code must reflect the business definition of columns that can have NULLs.

■ ■ ■

CHAPTER 4

Creating and Deriving Data

Storing your data in the database is only half the story. The other half is making that data available to users in ways they can comprehend. When you extract data from the database, either in a report format or one row at a time on a data maintenance page, the values in each row are often not suitable for display for a number of reasons. Usually, your data is highly normalized for performance and maintenance reasons—storing each part of a name in a different column or using a numeric code set that references the full text descriptions in another table. Other normalization-related scenarios include storing numeric quantities or prices across several rows or within several columns in the same row, and not storing a sum or other transformations within the table.

As a result of a highly normalized database, you often must perform some transformations to make it easy for end-users to interpret the results of a report by creating new values on the fly. You may want to perform transformations on single columns, on several columns within a single row, or on one or more columns across multiple rows within one or many tables. This chapter has recipes to cover all of these scenarios.

Also, your data might not be in the correct format or have erroneous values; you are obligated as a DBA or data analyst to ensure that the data is clean when it is entered into your database. Thus, there are some recipes in this chapter that will help you cleanse the data before it is stored in your database, or transform it to a format suitable for export to a downstream system.

Finally, this chapter will provide some insight on how to generate random data for your database. For load testing, it is often useful to create a random distribution of data to thoroughly test execution paths in your application before going live.

4-1. Deriving New Columns

Problem

You don't want to store redundant data in your database tables, but you want to be able to create totals, derived values, or alternate formats for columns within a row.

Solution

In your SELECT statements, apply Oracle built-in functions or create expressions on one or more columns in the table, creating a virtual column in the query results. For example, suppose you want to summarize total compensation for an employee, combining salary and commissions.

In the sample tables included for the OE user from a default installation of Oracle, the ORDER_ITEMS table contains UNIT_PRICE and QUANTITY columns as follows:

```
select * from order_items;
```

ORDER_ID	LINE_ITEM_ID	PRODUCT_ID	UNIT_PRICE	QUANTITY
2423	7	3290	65	33
2426	5	3252	25	29
2427	7	2522	40	22
2428	11	3173	86	28
2429	10	3165	36	67
. . .				
2418	6	3150	17	37
2419	9	3167	54	81
2420	10	3171	132	47
2421	9	3155	43	185
2422	9	3167	54	39

```
665 rows selected
```

To provide a line-item total in the query results, add an expression that multiplies unit price by quantity, as follows:

```
select order_id, line_item_id, product_id,
   unit_price, quantity, unit_price*quantity line_total_price
from order_items;
```

ORDER_ID	LINE_ITEM_ID	PRODUCT_ID	UNIT_PRICE	QUANTITY	LINE_TOTAL_PRICE
2423	7	3290	65	33	2145
2426	5	3252	25	29	725
2427	7	2522	40	22	880
2428	11	3173	86	28	2408
2429	10	3165	36	67	2412
. . .					
2418	6	3150	17	37	629
2419	9	3167	54	81	4374
2420	10	3171	132	47	6204
2421	9	3155	43	185	7955
2422	9	3167	54	39	2106

```
665 rows selected
```

How It Works

In a SELECT statement (or any DML statement, such as INSERT, UPDATE, or DELETE), you can reference any Oracle built-in function (or one of your own functions) on any or all columns in the statement. You can include aggregate functions such as SUM() and AVG() as well, as long as you include the non-aggregated columns in a GROUP BY clause.

You can also nest your functions within a SELECT statement. The column LINE_TOTAL_PRICE contains the desired result, but is not formatted appropriately for displaying to a customer service representative or a customer. To improve the readability of the output, add the TO_CHAR function to the calculation already in the query as follows:

```
select order_id, line_item_id, product_id,
   unit_price, quantity,
   to_char(unit_price*quantity,'$9,999,999.99') line_total_price
from order_items;
```

ORDER_ID	LINE_ITEM_ID	PRODUCT_ID	UNIT_PRICE	QUANTITY	LINE_TOTAL_PRICE
2423	7	3290	65	33	$2,145.00
2426	5	3252	25	29	$725.00
2427	7	2522	40	22	$880.00
2428	11	3173	86	28	$2,408.00
2429	10	3165	36	67	$2,412.00
. . .					
2418	6	3150	17	37	$629.00
2419	9	3167	54	81	$4,374.00
2420	10	3171	132	47	$6,204.00
2421	9	3155	43	185	$7,955.00
2422	9	3167	54	39	$2,106.00

```
665 rows selected
```

The TO_CHAR function can also be used to convert date or timestamp columns to a more readable or non-default format; you can even use TO_CHAR to convert data types in the national character set (NCHAR, NVARCHAR2, NCLOB) and CLOBs to the database character set, returning a VARCHAR2.

If your users need to run this query often, you might consider creating a database *view*, which will make it even easier for your analysts and other end-users to access the data. The new view will look like another table with one more column than the original table. Use the CREATE VIEW statement to create a view on the ORDER_ITEMS table, including the derived column:

```
create view order_items_subtotal_vw as
select order_id, line_item_id, product_id,
   unit_price, quantity,
   to_char(unit_price*quantity,'$9,999,999.99') line_total_price
from order_items
;
```

To access the table's columns and the derived column from the view, use this syntax:

```
select order_id, line_item_id, product_id,
```

```
    unit_price, quantity, line_total_price
from order_items_subtotal_vw;
```

The next time you need to access the derived LINE_TOTAL_PRICE column, you don't need to remember the calculations or the function you used to convert the total price to a currency format!

Using a database view in this scenario is useful, but adds another object to the data dictionary and thus creates another maintenance point if the base table changes, as when you modify or remove the UNIT_PRICE or QUANTITY columns. If you are using Oracle Database 11*g* or later, you can use a feature called *virtual columns*, which essentially creates the metadata for a derived column within the table definition itself. You can create a virtual column when you create a table, or add it later as you would any other column. The virtual column definition takes up no space in the table itself; it is calculated on the fly when you access the table containing the virtual column. To add the virtual column LINE_TOTAL_PRICE to ORDER_ITEMS, use this syntax:

```
alter table order_items
    add (line_total_price as (to_char(unit_price*quantity,'$9,999,999.99')));
```

The virtual column appears to be a regular column like any of the real columns in the table:

```
describe order_items;
```

Name	Null	Type
ORDER_ID	NOT NULL	NUMBER(12)
LINE_ITEM_ID	NOT NULL	NUMBER(3)
PRODUCT_ID	NOT NULL	NUMBER(6)
UNIT_PRICE		NUMBER(8,2)
QUANTITY		NUMBER(8)
LINE_TOTAL_PRICE		VARCHAR2(14)

```
6 rows selected
```

The data type of the virtual column is implied by the result of the calculation in the virtual column definition; the result of the expression in the LINE_TOTAL_PRICE virtual column is a character string with a maximum width of 14, thus the data type of the virtual column is VARCHAR2(14).

■ **Tip** To find out if a column is a virtual column, you can query the VIRTUAL_COLUMN column of the *_TAB_COLS data dictionary views.

There are a number of advantages to using virtual columns, such not having to create a view on the table, as we did in the previous example. In addition, you can create indexes on virtual columns and collect statistics on them. Here is an example of creating an index on the virtual column from the previous example:

```
create index ie1_order_items on order_items(line_total_price);
```

> ■ **Note** For versions of Oracle that do not support virtual columns (before Oracle Database 11*g*), you can somewhat simulate the indexing feature of a virtual column by creating a function-based index on the expression used in the virtual column.

There are a few restrictions on virtual columns, some of them obvious, some not so much. If your virtual column contains a built-in or user function, the referenced function must be declared as DETERMINISTIC; in other words, the function must return the same results for the same set of input values (for example, other columns in the row). Therefore, you can't use functions such as SYSDATE or SYSTIMESTAMP in a virtual column, as they will almost always return different results every time the row is retrieved (unless the results are retrieved within the same second for SYSDATE or millionth of a second for SYSTIMESTAMP!). If you declare a user function to be DETERMINISTIC when it's not and reference it in a virtual column, you are asking for trouble; your query results that include the virtual column will most likely be incorrect or will produce different results depending on when you run it, who is running it, and so forth.

Other restrictions on virtual columns are not so obvious. A virtual column can't reference another virtual column in the table (although you can certainly include one virtual column's definition within the definition of the second virtual column). In addition, the virtual column can only reference columns within the same table. Overall, virtual columns can enhance your database usability while somewhat reducing the amount of metadata you might otherwise have to maintain in a database view.

4-2. Returning Nonexistent Rows

Problem

You have gaps in the sequence numbers used for a table's primary key, and you want to identify the intermediate sequence numbers.

Solution

Although primary keys are generally (and preferably) invisible to the end user, there are times you may want to reuse sequence numbers where the number of digits in the sequence number must be kept as low as possible to satisfy the requirements of downstream systems or processes. For example, the company baseball team uses the number in EMPLOYEE_ID column as the number on the back of the uniform jersey. The manager wants to reuse old jersey numbers if possible, since the number on the back of the jersey is limited to three digits.

To find the employee numbers that were skipped or are currently not in use, you can use a query with two embedded subqueries as follows:

```
with all_used_emp_ids as
    (select level poss_emp_id from (select max(employee_id) max_emp_num
                                    from employees)
    connect by level <= max_emp_num)
select poss_emp_id
from all_used_emp_ids
```

```
where poss_emp_id not in (select employee_id from employees)
order by poss_emp_id
;

POSS_EMP_ID
----------------------
1
2
3
4
5
. . .
99
179
183

101 rows selected
```

The query retrieves any unused employee numbers up to the highest existing employee number currently in the EMPLOYEES table.

How It Works

The solution uses subquery factoring and two explicit subqueries to find the list of skipped employee numbers. The query in the WITH clause creates a series of numbers (with no gaps) from one to the value of the highest employee number in the EMPLOYEES table. The highlighted part of the subquery that follows retrieves the highest number:

```
(select level poss_emp_id from (select max(employee_id) max_emp_num
                                        from employees)
      connect by level <= max_emp_num)
```

The rest of the query in the WITH clause generates the gapless sequence of numbers. It leverages a subtle feature of Oracle's hierarchical query features (the CONNECT BY clause and the LEVEL pseudo-column) to generate each number in the sequence. See Chapter 13 for other useful recipes that require traversing hierarchical data.

Here is the main part of the SELECT query:

```
select poss_emp_id
from all_used_emp_ids
where poss_emp_id not in (select employee_id from employees)
```

It retrieves all rows from the gapless sequence with possible employee numbers that do not already exist in the EMPLOYEES table. The final result set is ordered by POSS_EMP_ID to make it easy to assign the lowest available number to the next employee. If you want to always exclude one- or two-digit numbers, you can add another predicate to the WHERE clause as follows:

```
with all_used_emp_ids as
   (select level poss_emp_id from (select max(employee_id) max_emp_num
                                          from employees)
      connect by level <= max_emp_num)
```

```
select poss_emp_id
from all_used_emp_ids
where poss_emp_id not in (select employee_id from employees)
  and poss_emp_id > 99
order by poss_emp_id
;

POSS_EMP_ID
----------------------
179
183

2 rows selected
```

In the revised query's results, the only three-digit numbers that can be reused below the highest employee number currently in use are 179 and 183.

4-3. Changing Rows into Columns

Problem

Your transaction data is in a highly normalized database structure, and you want to easily create crosstab-style reports for the business analysts, returning totals or other aggregate results as multiple columns within a single row.

Solution

Use the PIVOT keyword in your SELECT statement to spread values (in one or many columns) from multiple rows aggregated into multiple columns in the query output. For example, in the Oracle order entry sample schema, OE, you want to pick five key products from all orders and find out which customers are buying these products, and how many they bought.

The ORDERS table and ORDER_ITEMS table are defined as follows:

```
describe orders;
```

Name	Null	Type
ORDER_ID	NOT NULL	NUMBER(12)
ORDER_DATE	NOT NULL	TIMESTAMP(6) WITH LOCAL TIME ZONE
ORDER_MODE		VARCHAR2(8)
CUSTOMER_ID	NOT NULL	NUMBER(6)
ORDER_STATUS		NUMBER(2)
ORDER_TOTAL		NUMBER(8,2)
SALES_REP_ID		NUMBER(6)
PROMOTION_ID		NUMBER(6)

```
8 rows selected
```

```
describe order_items;
```

Name	Null	Type
ORDER_ID	NOT NULL	NUMBER(12)
LINE_ITEM_ID	NOT NULL	NUMBER(3)
PRODUCT_ID	NOT NULL	NUMBER(6)
UNIT_PRICE		NUMBER(8,2)
QUANTITY		NUMBER(8)
LINE_TOTAL_PRICE		VARCHAR2(14)

```
6 rows selected
```

Here is the pivot query to retrieve quantity totals for the top five products by customer:

```
with order_item_query as
    (select customer_id, product_id, quantity
     from orders join order_items using(order_id))
select * from order_item_query
pivot (
        sum(quantity) as sum_qty
          for (product_id) in (3170 as P3170,
                               3176 as P3176,
                               3182 as P3182,
                               3163 as P3163,
                               3165 as P3165)
      )
order by customer_id
;
```

CUSTOMER_ID	P3170_SUM_QTY	P3176_SUM_QTY	P3182_SUM_QTY	P3163_SUM_QTY	P3165_SUM_QTY
101				208	
102					
103					
104	70	72	77	61	64
105					
106		62		55	
107					76
108				45	31
109			115		112
116	48	24		5	10
117				63	67
118	42				
119	36			30	
. . .					
167					
168					
169					
170			92		

```
47 rows selected
```

From the results of this query, you can easily see that customer number 104 is the top buyer of all of the products specified in the PIVOT clause.

How It Works

The PIVOT operator, as the name implies, pivots rows into columns. In the solution, you will notice a few familiar constructs, and a few not so familiar. First, the solution uses the WITH clause (subquery factoring) to more cleanly separate the base query from the rest of the query; here is the WITH clause used in the solution:

```
with order_item_query as
   (select customer_id, product_id, quantity
    from orders join order_items using(order_id))
```

Whether you use the WITH clause or an inline view is a matter of style. In either case, be sure to only include columns that you will be grouping by, aggregate columns, or columns used in the PIVOT clause. Otherwise, if you have any extra columns in the query, your results will have a lot more rows than you expected! This is much like adding extra columns to a GROUP BY clause in a regular SELECT statement with aggregates, typically increasing the number of rows in the result.

The PIVOT clause itself generates the additional columns in the query results. Here is the first part of the PIVOT clause in the solution:

```
sum(quantity) as sum_qty
```

You specify one or more aggregates that you want to appear in the new columns and assign a label suffix that Oracle will use for each new column. (We'll show you how to pivot on more than one column or aggregate more than one column later in this section.) In this case, all of the derived columns will end in SUM_QTY.

The column or columns in the FOR clause filter the rows that are used to aggregate the results. Each value of the column in the FOR clause, or each specified combination of two or more columns, will produce an additional derived column in the results. The FOR clause in the solution is as follows:

```
for (product_id) in (3170 as P3170,
                     3176 as P3176,
                     3182 as P3182,
                     3163 as P3163,
                     3165 as P3165)
```

The query will only use rows whose PRODUCT_ID is in the list, and thus acts like a WHERE clause to filter the results before aggregation. The text string specified after each pivoted value is used as the prefix for the new column name, as you can see in the solution query's results.

Finally, the ORDER BY clause does the same thing as it would in any other query—order the final result set by the columns specified.

4-4. Pivoting on Multiple Columns

Problem

You have implemented the solution shown in the previous recipe. Now you wish to pivot not only on the total quantity of products, but also on the total dollar value purchased.

Solution

The following query extends the previous recipe's solution to add a total dollar amount column for each product number:

```
with order_item_query as
   (select customer_id, product_id, quantity, unit_price
    from orders join order_items using(order_id))
select * from order_item_query
pivot (
      sum(quantity) as sum_qty,
      sum(quantity*unit_price) as sum_prc
         for (product_id) in (3170 as P3170,
                              3176 as P3176,
                              3182 as P3182,
                              3163 as P3163,
                              3165 as P3165)
      )
order by customer_id
;
```

CUSTOMER_ID	P3170_SUM_QTY	P3170_SUM_PRC	P3176_SUM_QTY	P3176_SUM_PRC	. . .
101					
102					
103					
104	70	10164	72	8157.6	
105					
106			62	7024.6	
107					
108					
109					
116	48	6969.6	24	2719.2	
117					
118	42	6098.4			
119	36	5227.2			
. . .					

This report further reinforces the findings from the original solution: customer number 104 is a big buyer in terms of total dollars paid as well.

How It Works

Once you've mastered the basics of the PIVOT clause, taking it a step further is easy. Just add as many additional aggregates to your PIVOT clause as you need. Remember, though, that adding a second aggregate doubles the number of derived columns, adding a third triples it, and so forth.

Let's extend the solution even more, adding another pivot column. In the ORDERS table, the column ORDER_MODE contains the string direct if the sale was over the phone and ONLINE if the order was placed on the company's Internet site. To pivot on ORDER_MODE, just add the column to the FOR clause and specify pairs of values instead of single values in the FOR list as follows:

```
with order_item_query as
    (select customer_id, product_id, quantity, unit_price, order_mode
     from orders join order_items using(order_id))
select * from order_item_query
pivot (
        sum(quantity) as sum_qty,
        sum(quantity*unit_price) as sum_prc
            for (product_id, order_mode) in ((3170,'direct') as P3170_DIR,
                                             (3170,'online') as P3170_ONL,
                                             (3176,'direct') as P3176_DIR,
                                             (3176,'online') as P3176_ONL,
                                             (3182,'direct') as P3182_DIR,
                                             (3182,'online') as P3182_ONL,
                                             (3163,'direct') as P3163_DIR,
                                             (3163,'online') as P3163_ONL,
                                             (3165,'direct') as P3165_DIR,
                                             (3165,'online') as P3165_ONL)
    )
order by customer_id
;


CUSTOMER_ID P3170_DIR_SUM_QTY P3170_DIR_SUM_PRC P3170_ONL_SUM_QTY P3170_ONL_SUM_PRC
----------- ----------------- ----------------- ----------------- -----------------
101
102
103
104              70                10164
105
106
107
108
109
116              24                3484.8            24                3484.8
117
118              42                6098.4
119
. . .
```

The output has been truncated horizontally for readability. There is one column for each combination of product number, order mode, and the two aggregates. Looking at the breakdown by order mode, it appears that the company could save money by shifting some or all of customer 104's orders to Internet orders.

Finally, you might not know your pivot criteria ahead of time, as new products may appear on a daily basis, making maintenance of your queries an issue. One possible solution is to dynamically build your queries using Java or PL/SQL, though this solution may have potential security and performance issues. However, if the consumer of your query output can accept XML output, you can use the PIVOT XML clause instead of just PIVOT, and include filtering criteria in the IN clause as in this example, revising the original solution:

```
with order_item_query as
   (select customer_id, product_id, quantity
    from orders join order_items using(order_id))
select * from order_item_query
pivot xml (
          sum(quantity) as sum_qty
             for (product_id) in (any)
          )
order by customer_id
;
```

```
CUSTOMER_ID          PRODUCT_ID_XML
--------------------- --------------------------------------------------------------
101                       <PivotSet><item><column name =
      "PRODUCT_ID">2264</column><column name = "SUM_QTY">29</column></item> . . .
102                       <PivotSet><item><column name =
      "PRODUCT_ID">2976</column><column name = "SUM_QTY">5</column></item> . . .
103                       <PivotSet><item><column name =
      "PRODUCT_ID">1910</column><column name = "SUM_QTY">6</column></item> . . .
. . .
170                       <PivotSet><item><column name =
       "PRODUCT_ID">3106</column><column name = "SUM_QTY">170</column></item>
```

```
47 rows selected
```

The ANY keyword is shorthand for SELECT DISTINCT PRODUCT_ID FROM ORDER_ITEM_QUERY. Instead of ANY, you can put in just about any SQL statement that returns values in the domain you're pivoting on, as in this example where you only want to display results for products that are currently orderable:

```
with order_item_query as
   (select customer_id, product_id, quantity
    from orders join order_items using(order_id))
select * from order_item_query
pivot xml (
          sum(quantity) as sum_qty
             for (product_id) in (select distinct product_id
                                  from product_information
                                  where product_status = 'orderable')
          )
order by customer_id
;
```

Note that you need to include the DISTINCT keyword in your IN clause to ensure that you have only unique values on the pivot columns. Otherwise, the pivot operation will return an error.

4-5. Changing Columns into Rows

Problem

You have a table with multiple columns containing data from the same domain, and you want to convert these columns into rows of a table with a more normalized design.

Solution

Use the UNPIVOT operator after the FROM clause to convert columns into rows.

In the following example, a web form allows a registered account user to sign up for a free vacation holiday with up to three friends. As you might expect, the direct marketing department wants to use the e-mail addresses for other promotions as well. The format of the table (designed by analysts with minimal database design skills!) is as follows:

```
create table email_signup
    (user_account      varchar2(100),
     signup_date       date,
     user_email        varchar2(100),
     friend1_email     varchar2(100),
     friend2_email     varchar2(100),
     friend3_email     varchar2(100))
;
```

The registration data in the first two rows of the table looks like this:

```
USER_ACCOUNT  SIGNUP_DATE  USER_EMAIL     FRIEND1_EMAIL   FRIEND2_EMAIL   FRIEND3_EMAIL
------------  -----------  -------------  --------------  --------------  --------------

rjbryla       21-AUG-09    rjbryla@       rjbdba@         pensivepenman@  unclebob@
                           example.com    example.com     example.com     example.com

johndoe       22-AUG-09    janedoe@                       dog@
                           example.com                    example.com

2 rows selected
```

Unfortunately, the direct marketing application needs the e-mail address list in a more normalized format as follows:

```
REQUEST_ACCOUNT | REQUEST_DATE | EMAIL_ADDRESS
```

To generate the e-mail list in the format that the direct marketing group needs, you can use the UNPIVOT command like so:

```
select user_account, signup_date, src_col_name, friend_email
from email_signup
unpivot (
        (friend_email) for src_col_name
              in (user_email, friend1_email, friend2_email, friend3_email)
        )
;
```

```
USER_ACCOUNT SIGNUP_DATE  SRC_COL_NAME      FRIEND_EMAIL
------------ ------------ ----------------- -------------------------
rjbryla      21-AUG-09    USER_EMAIL        rjbryla@example.com
rjbryla      21-AUG-09    FRIEND1_EMAIL     rjbdba@example.com
rjbryla      21-AUG-09    FRIEND2_EMAIL     pensivepenman@example.com
rjbryla      21-AUG-09    FRIEND3_EMAIL     unclebob@example.com
johndoe      22-AUG-09    USER_EMAIL        janedoe@example.com
johndoe      22-AUG-09    FRIEND2_EMAIL     dog@example.com
```

6 rows selected.

How It Works

In contrast to the PIVOT operator, the UNPIVOT operator changes columns into multiple rows, although you can't reverse engineer any aggregated column totals without the original data—and if you had the original data, you would not need to UNPIVOT! There are many uses for UNPIVOT, as in converting data in a denormalized table or spreadsheet to individual rows for each column or set of columns.

The direct marketing department does not need the column SRC_COL_NAME, but it can come in handy when you want to find out which source column the e-mail address came from. You can also use UNPIVOT to create more than one destination column; for example, the web form may include a field for each friend's name in addition to their e-mail address:

```
select user_account, signup_date, src_col_names, friend_email, friend_name
from email_signup
unpivot (
        (friend_email,friend_name) for src_col_names
            in ((user_email,user_name),
                (friend1_email,friend1_name),
                (friend2_email,friend2_name),
                (friend3_email,friend3_name))
        )
;
```

Before Oracle Could PIVOT and UNPIVOT

Before Oracle Database 11*g*, your options were somewhat limited and painful, as the PIVOT and UNPIVOT clauses did not exist! To perform a PIVOT query, you had to use a series of DECODE statements or make a very complicated foray into the MODEL analytical clause.

Performing an UNPIVOT operation before Oracle Database 11*g* was nearly as painful. Here is a pre-Oracle Database 11*g* UNPIVOT operation on the e-mail address list processing table from the previous section:

```
select user_account, signup_date,
    'USER_EMAIL' as src_col_name, user_email as friend_email
from email_signup
where user_email is not null
union
select user_account, signup_date, 'FRIEND1_EMAIL', friend1_email
from email_signup
where friend1_email is not null
union
select user_account, signup_date, 'FRIEND2_EMAIL', friend2_email
from email_signup
where friend2_email is not null
union
select user_account, signup_date, 'FRIEND3_EMAIL', friend3_email
from email_signup
where friend3_email is not null
;
```

The maintenance cost of this query is much higher and the execution time much longer due to the sorting and merging required with the series of UNION statements and multiple passes over the same table.

4-6. Concatenating Data for Readability

Problem

For reporting and readability purposes, you want to combine multiple columns into a single output column, eliminating extra blank space and adding punctuation where necessary.

Solution

Use Oracle string concatenation functions or operators to save space in your report and make the output more readable. For example, in the EMPLOYEES table, you can use the || (two vertical bars) operator or the CONCAT function to combine the employee's first and last name:

```
select employee_id, last_name || ', ' || first_name full_name, email
from employees
;
```

```
EMPLOYEE_ID      FULL_NAME                         EMAIL
---------------  --------------------------------  ------------------
100              King, Steven                      SKING
101              Kochhar, Neena                    NKOCHHAR
102              De Haan, Lex                      LDEHAAN
103              Hunold, Alexander                 AHUNOLD
104              Ernst, Bruce                      BERNST
```

```
105              Austin, David            DAUSTIN
. . .
204              Baer, Hermann            HBAER
205              Higgins, Shelley         SHIGGINS
206              Gietz, William           WGIETZ
```

107 rows selected

The query concatenates the last name, a comma, and the first name into a single string, aliased as FULL_NAME in the results. If your platform's character set does not support using || as a concatenation operator (as some IBM mainframe character sets do), or you might soon migrate your SQL to such a platform, you can make your code more platform-independent by using the CONCAT functions instead:

```
select employee_id, concat(concat(last_name,', '),first_name) full_name, email
from employees
;
```

Because the CONCAT function only supports two operands as of Oracle Database 11g, concatenating more than two strings can make the code unreadable very fast!

How It Works

You can apply a number of different Oracle built-in functions to make your output more readable; some Oracle shops I've worked in relied solely on SQL*Plus for their reporting. Applying the appropriate functions and using the right SQL*Plus commands makes the output extremely readable, even with queries returning Oracle objects, currency columns, and long character strings.

If your text-based columns have leading or trailing blanks (which of course should have been cleaned up on import or by the GUI form), or the column is a fixed-length CHAR column, you can get rid of leading and trailing blanks using the TRIM function, as in this example:

```
select employee_id, trim(last_name) || ', ' || trim(first_name) full_name, email
from employees
;
```

If you only want to trim leading or trailing blanks, you can use LTRIM or RTRIM respectively. If some of your employees don't have first names (or last names), your output using any of the previous solutions would look a little odd:

```
select employee_id, last_name || ', ' || first_name full_name, email
from celebrity_employees
;
```

```
EMPLOYEE_ID      FULL_NAME                          EMAIL
---------------- ---------------------------------- --------------------
1001             Cher,                              CHER
1021             Kajol,                             KAJOL
1032             Madonna,                           MADONNA
2033             Bono,                              BONO
1990             Yanni,                             YANNI
```

5 rows selected

To remedy this situation, you can add the NVL2 function to your SELECT statement:

```
select employee_id,
   trim(last_name) ||
   nvl2(trim(first_name),', ','') ||
   trim(first_name) full_name,
   email
from employees
;
```

The NVL2 function evaluates the first argument TRIM(FIRST_NAME). If it is not NULL, it returns ', ', otherwise it returns a NULL (empty string), so that our celebrity employees won't have a phantom comma at the end of their name:

```
EMPLOYEE_ID     FULL_NAME                         EMAIL
---------------- --------------------------------- -------------------
1001            Cher                              CHER
1021            Kajol                             KAJOL
1032            Madonna                           MADONNA
2033            Bono                              BONO
1990            Yanni                             YANNI

5 rows selected
```

Finally, you can also take advantage of the INITCAP function to fix up character strings that might have been entered in all caps or have mixed case. If your EMPLOYEES table had some rows with last name and first name missing, you could derive most of the employee names from the e-mail address by using a combination of SUBSTR, UPPER, and INITCAP as in this example:

```
select employee_id, email,
   upper(substr(email,1,1)) || ' ' || initcap(substr(email,2)) name
from employees
;
```

```
EMPLOYEE_ID          EMAIL                   NAME
-------------------- ----------------------- ---------------------------
100                  SKING                   S King
101                  NKOCHHAR                N Kochhar
102                  LDEHAAN                 L Dehaan
103                  AHUNOLD                 A Hunold
104                  BERNST                  B Ernst
105                  DAUSTIN                 D Austin
106                  VPATABAL                V Patabal
. . .
```

This solution is not ideal if the e-mail address does not contain the complete employee name or if the employee's last name has two parts, such as McDonald, DeVry, or DeHaan.

4-7. Translating Strings to Numeric Equivalents

Problem

In an effort to centralize your domain code management and further normalize the structure of your database tables, you want to clean up and convert some text-format business attributes to numeric equivalents. This will enhance reporting capabilities and reduce data entry errors in the future.

Solution

Use the CASE function to translate business keys or other intelligent numeric keys to numeric codes that are centrally stored in a domain code table. For example, the ORDERS table of the OE schema contains a column ORDER_MODE that currently has four possible values, identified in Table 4-1.

Table 4-1. *Mapping the Text in the ORDER_MODE Column to Numeric Values*

Text (source column)	Numeric (destination column)
Direct	1
Online	2
Walmart	3
Amazon	4

The second column of Table 4-1 contains the numeric value we want to map to for each of the possible values in the ORDER_MODE column. Here is the SQL you use to add the new column to the table:

```
alter table orders add (order_mode_num    number);
```

Oracle versions 9*i* and later include the CASE statement, which is essentially a way to more easily execute procedural code within the confines of the typically non-procedural SQL command language. The CASE statement has two forms: one for simpler scenarios with a single expression that is compared to a list of constants or expressions, and a second that supports evaluation of any combination of columns and expressions. In both forms, CASE returns a single result that is assigned to a column in the SELECT query or DML statement.

The recipe solution using the simpler form of the CASE statement is as follows:

```
update orders
set order_mode_num =
    case order_mode
        when 'direct' then 1
        when 'online' then 2
        when 'walmart' then 3
```

```
    when 'amazon' then 4
    else 0
  end
;
```

Once you run the UPDATE statement, you can drop the ORDER_MODE column after verifying that no other existing SQL references it.

How It Works

The CASE statement performs the same function as the older (but still useful in some scenarios) DECODE function, and is a bit more readable as well. For more complex comparisons, such as those evaluating more than one expression or column, you can use the second form of the CASE statement. In the second form, the CASE clause does not contain a column or expression; instead, each WHEN clause contains the desired comparison operation. Here is an example where we want to assign a special code of 5 when the order is an employee order (the CUSTOMER_ID is less than 102):

```
update orders
set order_mode_num =
  case
    when order_mode = 'direct' and
         customer_id < 102 then 5
    when order_mode = 'direct' then 1
    when order_mode = 'online' then 2
    when order_mode = 'walmart' then 3
    when order_mode = 'amazon' then 4
    else 0
  end
;
```

Note that in this scenario you need to check for the employee order first in the list of WHEN clauses, otherwise the ORDER_MODE column will be set to 1 and no customer orders will be flagged, since both conditions check for ORDER_MODE = 'direct'. For both DECODE and CASE, the evaluation and assignment stops as soon as Oracle finds the first expression that evaluates to TRUE.

In the solution, the string 'direct' is translated to 1, 'online' is translated to 2, and so forth. If the ORDER_MODE column does not contain any of the strings in the list, the ORDER_MODE_NUM column is assigned 0.

Finally, reversing the mapping in a SELECT statement for reporting purposes is very straightforward: we can use CASE or DECODE with the text and numeric values reversed. Here is an example:

```
select order_id, customer_id, order_mode_num,
  case order_mode_num
    when 1 then 'Direct, non-employee'
    when 2 then 'Online'
    when 3 then 'WalMart'
    when 4 then 'Amazon'
    when 5 then 'Direct, employee'
    else 'unknown'
  end order_mode_text
```

```
from orders
where order_id in (2458,2397,2355,2356)
;

ORDER_ID       CUSTOMER_ID      ORDER_MODE_NUM     ORDER_MODE_TEXT
-------------- ---------------- ------------------ --------------------
2355           104              2                  Online
2356           105              2                  Online
2397           102              1                  Direct, non-employee
2458           101              5                  Direct, employee

4 rows selected
```

The older DECODE statement is the most basic of the Oracle functions that converts one set of values to another; you can convert numeric codes to human-readable text values or vice versa, as we do in the previous solutions. DECODE has been available in Oracle since the earliest releases. DECODE has a variable number of arguments, but the arguments can be divided into three groups:

- The column or expression to be translated

- One or more pairs of values; the first value is the existing value and the second is the translated value

- A single default value if the column or expression to be translated does not match the first value of any of the specified pairs

Here is the UPDATE statement using DECODE:

```
update orders
set order_mode_num =
   decode(order_mode,
            'direct',1,
            'online',2,
            'walmart',3,
            'amazon',4,
         0)
;

105 rows updated
```

DECODE translates the ORDER_MODE column just as CASE does. If the values in the column do not match any of the values in the first of each pair of constants, DECODE returns 0.

4-8. Generating Random Data

Problem

You need to generate random numbers to simulate real-world events that do not follow a discernible pattern.

Solution

Use the Oracle built-in PL/SQL package DBMS_RANDOM. The RANDOM function returns an integer in the range $[-2^{31}, 2^{31})$ (-2^{31} can be returned, but 2^{31} will not), and the VALUE function returns a decimal number in the range $[0,1)$ with 38 digits of precision.

For example, the merchandising department wants to lower pricing below list price on catalog items on a daily basis to potentially stimulate sales from customers who perceive a bargain when the price is at least 10 percent below list price. However, the merchandising analysts want to vary the discount from 10 percent to 20 percent on a random basis. To do this, first create a DAILY_PRICE column in the PRODUCT_INFORMATION table as follows:

```
alter table product_information add (daily_price  number);
```

Next, use the DBMS_RANDOM.VALUE function to adjust the DAILY_PRICE to a value between 10 percent and 20 percent below the list price:

```
update product_information
set daily_price =
   round(list_price*(0.9-(dbms_random.value*0.1)))
;
```

```
288 rows updated.
```

Here is the query to retrieve the calculated daily price:

```
select product_id, list_price, daily_price
from product_information
;
```

PRODUCT_ID	LIST_PRICE	DAILY_PRICE
1772	456	380
2414	454	379
2415	359	293
2395	123	99
1755	121	104
2406	223	200
2404	221	182
. . .		

Running the UPDATE statement a second time will adjust the prices randomly again, with a different discount for each product, but still ranging from 10 to 20 percent off:

```
update product_information
set daily_price =
   round(list_price*(0.9-(dbms_random.value*0.1)))
;
```

```
select product_id, list_price, daily_price
from product_information
;
```

103

```
PRODUCT_ID              LIST_PRICE              DAILY_PRICE
----------------------  ----------------------  ----------------------
1772                    456                     383
2414                    454                     378
2415                    359                     319
2395                    123                     111
1755                    121                     107
2406                    223                     193
2404                    221                     184
. . .
```

The random number value returned is multiplied by 0.1 (10 percent), subtracted from 0.9 (90 percent of the list price is 10 percent off), resulting in a discount of between 10 and 20 percent. The final result is rounded to the nearest dollar.

How It Works

Most, if not all, random number generators start generating the results with a *seed* value, in other words, a value that the random number generator uses to calculate a starting place in the random number sequence. The DBMS_RANDOM package is no exception. If you do not specify a seed value, Oracle uses the current date, user ID, and process ID to calculate the seed. To reproduce a sequence of random numbers from the same starting point, you can specify your own seed, as in this example:

```
begin
    dbms_random.seed(40027);
end;
```

The DBMS_RANDOM.SEED procedure will also accept a string value to initialize the random number sequence:

```
begin
    dbms_random.seed('The Rain in Spain');
end;
```

The DBMS_RANDOM.VALUE function has even a bit more flexibility: you can specify that the random number fall within the specified range. For example, if you only want random numbers between 50 and 100, you can do this:

```
select dbms_random.value(50,100) from dual;

DBMS_RANDOM.VALUE(50,100)
-------------------------
95.2813813550075919354971754613182604395

1 rows selected
```

As a result, you can modify the recipe solution a bit as follows to take advantage of the range specification:

```
update product_information
```

```
set daily_price =
   round(list_price*(0.9-(dbms_random.value(0.0,0.1))))
;
```

Finally, the DBMS_RANDOM package also includes the STRING function so you can retrieve random string values. You specify two parameters: the type of string returned, and the length. Here is an example:

```
select dbms_random.string('U',20) from dual;

DBMS_RANDOM.STRING('U',20)
--------------------------
FTFGYZPCYWNCOKYCKDJI

1 rows selected
```

The first parameter can be one of these string constants:

- 'u' or 'U': uppercase alpha
- 'l' or 'L': lowercase alpha
- 'a' or 'A': mixed case alpha
- 'x' or 'X': upper case alphanumeric
- 'p' or 'P': any printable characters

Thus, to generate a very cryptic and random set of 25 characters, you can do this:

```
select dbms_random.string('p',25) from dual;

DBMS_RANDOM.STRING('P',25)
--------------------------
n!Wuew+R$$Qhf^mbGR,2%tr@a

1 rows selected
```

4-9. Creating a Comma-Separated Values File

Problem

You need to export an Oracle table or view to CSV (Comma-Separated Values) for import into Microsoft Excel or another application that can import data in CSV format.

Solution

Use SQL*Plus, a custom query against one or more tables, and a set of carefully selected SQL*Plus commands to create a text file that will need no further processing before import into Microsoft Excel.

The query you use to retrieve the data returns the first line with the column names, then the rows in the table with commas separating each column and double quotes around each string. Here is the query along with the required SQL*Plus commands that you can store in a file called emp_sal.sql, for example:

```
-- suppress sql output in results
set echo off
-- eliminate row count message at end
set feedback off
-- make line long enough to hold all row data
set linesize 1000
-- suppress headings and page breaks
set pagesize 0
-- eliminate SQL*Plus prompts from output
set sqlprompt ''
-- eliminate trailing blanks
set trimspool on
-- send output to file
spool emp_sal.csv
select '"EMPLOYEE_ID","LAST_NAME","FIRST_NAME","SALARY"' from dual
union all
select employee_id || ',"' ||
       last_name || '","' ||
       first_name || '",' ||
       salary
from employees
;
spool off
exit
```

The output from running this script looks like this:

```
C:\>sqlplus hr/hr@recipes @emp_sal.sql

SQL*Plus: Release 11.1.0.6.0 - Production on Sun Sep 27 22:12:01 2009

Copyright (c) 1982, 2007, Oracle.  All rights reserved.


Connected to:
Oracle Database 11g Enterprise Edition Release 11.1.0.6.0 - Production
With the Partitioning, OLAP, Data Mining and Real Application Testing options

"EMPLOYEE_ID","LAST_NAME","FIRST_NAME","SALARY"
100,"King","Steven",21266.67
101,"Kochhar","Neena",44098.56
102,"De Haan","Lex",21266.67
. . .
203,"Mavris","Susan",7150
204,"Baer","Hermann",11000
205,"Higgins","Shelley",11165
206,"Gietz","William",11165
```

```
Disconnected from Oracle Database 11g Enterprise Edition
    Release 11.1.0.6.0 - Production
With the Partitioning, OLAP, Data Mining and Real Application Testing options

C:\>
```

How It Works

Many ETL (Extract, Transform, and Load) tools include an option to read from an Oracle database and create an output file in CSV format. If your data movement needs are rather modest and a six-figure ETL tool license is not within your budget, the SQL*Plus version may suffice. Even SQL*Developer, a free tool from Oracle, will export the results of a query or a table to a number of formats including Microsoft Excel, but SQL*Plus is more amenable to scripting and scheduling within a batch job.

The SQL*Plus commands ensure that the default column headers are off, the output width is sufficient, and so forth. The `SPOOL` and `SPOOL OFF` commands send the output to a file on disk that can be read by Microsoft Excel or another program that can read CSV files.

When you open the file `emp_sal.csv` generated in the recipe solution with Microsoft Excel, it looks much like any spreadsheet, as you can see in Figure 4-1.

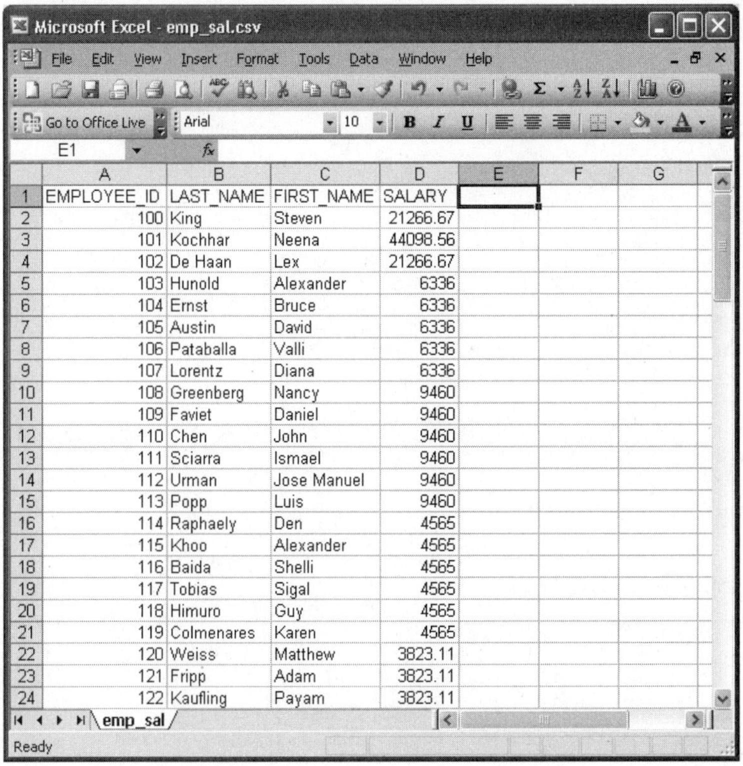

EMPLOYEE_ID	LAST_NAME	FIRST_NAME	SALARY
100	King	Steven	21266.67
101	Kochhar	Neena	44098.56
102	De Haan	Lex	21266.67
103	Hunold	Alexander	6336
104	Ernst	Bruce	6336
105	Austin	David	6336
106	Pataballa	Valli	6336
107	Lorentz	Diana	6336
108	Greenberg	Nancy	9460
109	Faviet	Daniel	9460
110	Chen	John	9460
111	Sciarra	Ismael	9460
112	Urman	Jose Manuel	9460
113	Popp	Luis	9460
114	Raphaely	Den	4565
115	Khoo	Alexander	4565
116	Baida	Shelli	4565
117	Tobias	Sigal	4565
118	Himuro	Guy	4565
119	Colmenares	Karen	4565
120	Weiss	Matthew	3823.11
121	Fripp	Adam	3823.11
122	Kaufling	Payam	3823.11

Figure 4-1. *A SQL*Plus-generated CSV file opened in Microsoft Excel*

CHAPTER 5

■ ■ ■

Common Query Patterns

In this chapter we introduce recipes to handle many common query patterns, often for the sort of problems that you know should have an elegant solution, but for which no obvious SQL command or operator exists. Whether it's predicting the trend in data for extrapolation and planning purposes, paginating your data for display on a web site, or finding lost text in your database, you'll find a recipe to suit you in this chapter.

Many of the problems we address here have multiple solutions. Where space allows, we've tried to cover as many options as possible. Having said that, if you invent or know of a different approach, consider yourself a budding SQL chef too!

5-1. Changing Nulls into Real Values

Problem

You want to substitute null values in a table or result with a meaningful alternative.

Solution

Oracle provides several functions to allow manipulation and conversion of null values into arbitrary literals, including NVL, NVL2, COALESCE, and CASE-based tests. Each of these allows for different logic when handling null values, translating their inclusion in results in different ways. The goal is to turn NULL values into something more meaningful to the non-database professional, or more appropriate to the business context in which the data will be used.

Our recipe's first SELECT statement uses the NVL function to return an employee's id and surname, and either the commission percentage or the human-readable "no commission" for staff with a null COMMISSION_PCT.

```
select employee_id, last_name,
  nvl(to_char(commission_pct), 'No Commission') as COMMISSION
from hr.employees;
```

```
EMPLOYEE_ID                    LAST_NAME              COMMISSION
-----------                    -----------            -------------
...
        177                    Livingston                    .2
        178                    Grant                         .15
        179                    Johnson                       .1
        180                    Taylor                 No Commission
        181                    Fleaur                 No Commission
        182                    Sullivan               No Commission
...
```

The second version of our recipe targets the same information, but uses the NVL2 function to split the employees into those that are paid a commission and those that aren't.

```
select employee_id, last_name,
  nvl2(commission_pct, 'Commission Based', 'No Commission') as COMMISSION
from hr.employees;
```

```
EMPLOYEE_ID               LAST_NAME            COMMISSION
-----------               ----------           ----------------
...
        177               Livingston           Commission Based
        178               Grant                Commission Based
        179               Johnson              Commission Based
        180               Taylor               No Commission
        181               Fleaur               No Commission
        182               Sullivan             No Commission
...
```

Our third recipe returns the product of the COMMISSION_PCT and SALARY for commission-based employees, or the SALARY value for those with NULL COMMISSION_PCT, using the COALESCE function.

```
select employee_id, last_name,
  coalesce((1 + commission_pct) * salary, salary) as SAL_INC_COMM
from hr.employees;
```

```
EMPLOYEE_ID               LAST_NAME            COMM_OR_SAL
-----------               ---------            -----------
...
        210               King                 4375
        211               Sully                4375
        212               McEwen               4375
        100               King                 24000
        101               Kochhar              17000
        102               De Haan              17000
...
```

Our fourth recipe uses the CASE feature to return the salary of non-commissioned employees.

```
select employee_id, last_name,
case
  when commission_pct is null then salary
  else (1 + commission_pct) * salary
  end total_pay
from hr.employees;
```

The results are the same as our recipe code using the COALESCE function.

How It Works

Each of the NVL, NVL2, and COALESCE functions let you handle NULL values in different ways, depending on requirements. Our recipe using NVL selects the EMPLOYEE_ID and LAST_NAME in basic fashion, and then uses NVL to identify whether COMMISSION_PCT has a value or is NULL. Those rows with a genuine value have that value returned, and those rows with NULL return the text "No Commission" instead of nothing at all.

The general structure of the NVL function takes this basic form.

```
nvl(expression, <value to return if expression is null>)
```

By contrast, the second recipe takes the NULL handling slightly further using the NVL2 function. Instead of just substituting a placeholder value for NULL, the NVL2 function acts as a switch. In our example, NVL2 evaluates the value of COMMISSION_PCT. If a real value is detected, the second expression is returned. If a NULL is detected by NVL2, the third expression is returned.

The general form of the NVL2 function is shown next.

```
nvl(expression,
      <value to return if expression is not null>,
      <value to return if expression is null>)
```

Third, we used the COALESCE function to find the first non-NULL value among COMMISSION_PCT and SALARY for each employee. The COALESCE function can take an arbitrary number of expressions, and will return the first expression that resolves to a non-NULL value. The general form is:

```
coalesce(expression_1, expression_2, expression_3 … expression_n)
```

Lastly, we use the CASE expression to evaluate the COMMISSION_PCT field and to switch logic if the value found is NULL. The general form of the CASE expression is:

```
case
  when <expression> then <value, expression, column>
  <optional additional when clauses>
  else <some default value, expression, column>
end
```

5-2. Sorting on Null Values

Problem

Results for a business report are sorted by department manager, but you need to find a way to override the sorting of nulls so they appear where you want at the beginning or end of the report.

Solution

Oracle provides two extensions to the ORDER BY clause to enable SQL developers to treat NULL values separately from the known data, allowing any NULL entries to sort explicitly to the beginning or end of the results.

For our recipe, we'll assume that the report desired is based on the department names and manager identifiers from the HR.DEPARTMENTS table. This SQL selects this data and uses the NULLS FIRST option to explicitly control NULL handling.

```
select department_name, manager_id
from hr.departments
order by manager_id nulls first;
```

The results present the "unmanaged" departments first, followed by the departments with managers by MANAGER_ID. We've abbreviated the results to save trees.

```
DEPARTMENT_NAME                  MANAGER_ID
--------------------             ----------
Control And Credit
Recruiting

...
Shareholder Services
Benefits
Executive                             100
IT                                    103
...
Public Relations                      204
Accounting                            205

27 rows selected.
```

How It Works

Normally, Oracle sorts NULL values to the end of the results for default ascending sorts, and to the beginning of the results for descending sorts. The NULLS FIRST ORDER BY option, together with its complement, NULLS LAST, overrides Oracle's normal sorting behavior for NULL values and places them exactly where you specify: either at the beginning or end of the results.

Your first instinct when presented with the problem of NULL values sorting to the "wrong" end of your data might be to simply switch from ascending to descending sort, or vice versa. But if you think about more complex queries, subselects using ROWNUM or ROWID tricks, and other queries that need to preserve data order while getting NULL values moved, you'll see that NULLS FIRST and NULLS LAST have real utility. Using them *guarantees* where the NULL values appear, regardless of how the data values are sorted.

5-3. Paginating Query Results

Problem

You need to display query results on web pages, showing a subset of results on each page. Users will be able to navigate back and forth through the pages of results.

Solution

Solving pagination problems requires thinking of the process in more generic terms—and using several fundamental Oracle features in combination to tackle problems like this. What we're really attempting to do is find a *defined subset* of a set of results, whether we display this subset on a web page or report, or feed it in to some subsequent process. There is no need to alter your data to add explicit page numbers or partitioning details. Our solutions will use Oracle's ROWNUM pseudo-column and ROW_NUMBER OLAP function to handle implicit page calculations, and nested subselects to control which page of data we see.

We'll use the OE.PRODUCT_INFORMATION table as the source for our solution, supposing we'll use the data therein to publish an online shopping web site. In the sample schema Oracle provides, the OE.PRODUCT_INFORMATION table holds 288 rows. That's too many for a single web page aesthetically, even though you could technically display a list that long. Your poor customers would tire of scrolling before they bought anything!

Thankfully, we can save our clients with the next SELECT statement. We'll control our SELECT statement to return 10 results only.

```
select product_id, product_name, list_price from
  (select prodinfo.*, rownum r
   from
     (select product_id, product_name, list_price
      from oe.product_information
      order by product_id) prodinfo
   where rownum <= 10)
where r >= 1;
```

For once, we won't abbreviate the results the solution so you can see we have 10 rows of results for display on our hypothetical web page.

PRODUCT_ID	PRODUCT_NAME	LIST_PRICE
1726	LCD Monitor 11/PM	259
1729	Chemicals - RCP	80
1733	PS 220V /UK	89
1734	Cable RS232 10/AM	6
1737	Cable SCSI 10/FW/ADS	8

1738	PS 110V /US	86
1739	SDRAM - 128 MB	299
1740	TD 12GB/DAT	134
1742	CD-ROM 500/16x	101
1743	HD 18.2GB @10000 /E	800

10 rows selected.

An alternative technique is to use the ROW_NUMBER OLAP function to perform equivalent row numbering, and similarly filter by a predicate on the numbers it produces.

```
select product_id, product_name, list_price from
  (select product_id, product_name, list_price,
    row_number() over (order by product_id) r
  from oe.product_information)
where r between 1 and 10
```

The results are the same, including the historical artifacts like 18 gigabyte hard disk drives for $800! Those were the days.

How It Works

Let's examine the ROWNUM technique first. The core of this solution is using ROWNUM in a subselect to tag the data we really want with a handy number that controls the pagination. The ROWNUM values aren't stored anywhere: they're not a column in your table or hidden somewhere else. ROWNUM is a pseudo-column of your *results*, and it only comes into being when your results are gathered, but before any sorting or aggregation.

Looking at the subselects at the heart of our recipe, you'll see the format has this structure.

```
select <columns I actually want>, rownum r
from
  (select <columns I actually want>
  from oe.product_information
  order by product_id)
where rownum <= 10
```

We select the actual data and columns we want and wrap those in a similar SELECT that adds the ROWNUM value. We give this an alias for later use in the outer SQL statement, which we'll explain shortly. The FROM and ORDER BY clauses are self-explanatory, leaving us the ROWNUM predicate. In this case, we look for ROWNUM values less than 10, because ultimately we want to show the rows from 1 to 10. In its general form, we are really asking for all matching result rows with a ROWNUM up to the end point we want for our page. So if we wanted to show items 41 to 50 on page 5 of our hypothetical web site, this clause would read WHERE ROWNUM <= 50. In your application code or stored procedure, it's natural to replace this with a bind variable.

```
where rownum <= :page-end-row
```

This means the subselect will actually produce results for all rows up to the last row you intend to use in pagination. If we use our query to ultimately display the page for items 41 to 50 with the WHERE

`ROWNUM <= 50` option, the subselect will gather the results for 50 rows, not just the 10 you intend to display. At this point, the outer query comes in to play.

The structure of the outer query has this general form:

```
select <columns I actually want> from
  (<rows upto the end-point of pagination provided by subselect>)
where r >= 1;
```

We're performing a quite normal subselect, where we take the meaningful columns from the subselect for display in the SELECT portion of the statement, and use our WHERE predicate to lop off any unnecessary leading rows from the results of the subselect, leaving us with the perfect set of data for pagination. For our recipe modification targeting rows 41 to 50, this predicate would change to WHERE R >= 41. Again, using this in a prepared fashion or through a stored procedure would typically be done with a bind variable, giving this general form of the WHERE clause.

```
where r >=  :page-start-row
```

At this point, we hope you find yourself with two lingering questions. Why did we introduce the column alias "r" for ROWNUM in the subselect rather than just using the ROWNUM feature again in the outer SELECT statement, and why didn't we just use a BETWEEN clause to simplify the whole design? The alias is used to preserve the ROWNUM values from the subselect for use in the outer select. Suppose instead we'd tried to use ROWNUM again as in the next SQL statement.

```
-- Note!  Intentionally flawed rownum logic
select product_id, product_name, list_price from
  (select prodinfo.*, rownum from
     (select product_id, product_name, list_price
     from oe.product_information
     order by product_id) prodinfo
   where rownum <= 50)
where rownum >= 41;
```

Try running that yourself and you'll be surprised to find no rows returned. Equally, if we stripped out the subselect constructs and just tried a BETWEEN clause, we'd construct SQL like the next example.

```
-- Note!  Intentionally flawed rownum logic
select product_id, product_name, list_price
from oe.product_information
where rownum between 41 and 50;
```

Oops! Once again, no rows returned. Why are these failing? It's because the ROWNUM mechanism only assigns a value after the basic (non-sorting/aggregating) criteria are satisfied, and always starts with a ROWNUM value of 1. Only after that value is assigned does it increment to 2, and so on. By removing the alias, we end up generating *new* ROWNUM values in the outer SELECT and then asking if the first candidate value, 1, is greater than or equal to 41. It's not, so that row is discarded and our ROWNUM value doesn't increment. No subsequent rows satisfy the same predicate—and you end up with no results. Using the BETWEEN variant introduces the same problem. That's why we use the alias in the first place, and why we refer to the preserved "r" values in our successful recipe.

■ **Caution** Developers often fail to test non-obvious cases when using this style of logic. There is one subset of data where our problematic examples would return results. This would be for the first page of data, where the page starting row does have a ROWNUM value of 1. This is a classic case of the boundary condition working but all other possible data ranges failing. Make sure your testing covers both the natural end points of your data, as well as ranges in between, to save yourself from such pitfalls.

Our second recipe takes a different tack. Using the ROW_NUMBER OLAP function, we achieve the same outcome in one pass over the data. Like all OLAP functions, the ROW_NUMBER function is applied to the query after the normal predicates, joins, and the like are evaluated. For the purposes of pagination, this means that the subquery effectively queries all of the data from the OE.PRODUCT_INFORMATION table, and ROW_NUMBER then applies an incrementing number by the order indicated, in this case by PRODUCT_ID.

```
select product_id, product_name, list_price,
  row_number() over (order by product_id) r
from oe.product_information
```

If we evaluated the subquery by itself, we'd see results like this (abbreviated to save paper).

PRODUCT_ID	PRODUCT_NAME	LIST_PRICE	R
1726	LCD Monitor 11/PM	259	1
1729	Chemicals - RCP	80	2
1733	PS 220V /UK	89	3
...			
3511	Paper - HQ Printer	9	287
3515	Lead Replacement	2	288

```
288 rows selected.
```

Every row of the table is returned, as our SELECT statement hasn't qualified the data with any filtering predicates. The ROW_NUMBER function has numbered all 288 rows, from 1 to 288.

At this point, the outer query comes into play and its role is very straightforward. Our recipe uses an outer query statement that looks like the next SQL snippet.

```
select product_id, product_name, list_price from
  (<subselect returning desired columns and row number "r">)
where r between 1 and 10
```

This outer SQL is as obvious as it looks. Select the desired columns returned from the subselect, where the r value (generated by the subselect's ROW_NUMBER function) is between 1 and 10. In comparison to our other solution that used ROWNUM, if we wanted to represent a different page of results for products 41 to 50, the outer query's WHERE clause would simply change to WHERE R BETWEEN 41 AND 50. In the general form, we'd recommend parameterizing the page-start-row and page-end-row, as illustrated in the following SQL pseudo code.

```
select <desired columns>
```

```
(select <desired columns>,
    row_number() over (order by <ordering column>) r
  from <source table, view, etc.>)
where r between :page-start-row and :page-end-row
```

By now you're probably asking yourself which of the two methods, ROWNUM and ROW_NUMBER, you should use. There's no clear-cut answer to that question. Instead, it's best to remember some of the qualities of both recipes. The ROWNUM approach enjoys historical support and has built-in optimization in Oracle to make the sort induced by the ordering faster than a normal sort. The ROW_NUMBER approach is more versatile, enabling you to number your rows in an order different from the order produced by a standard ORDER BY clause. You can also alter the recipe to use other OLAP functions like RANK and DENSE_RANK to handle different paging requirements, such as needing to show items in "tied" positions.

Pagination Outside the Database

Our recipe drives the pagination of data where it is generally best handled—in the database! You may have used or experienced other techniques, such as cursor-driven pagination and even result-caching at the application tier, with data discarded or hidden to provide pagination.

Our advice is to eschew those techniques in pretty much all cases. The application caching technique inevitably requires excessive network traffic with associated performance delay and cost, which the end user won't appreciate. Cursor-driven approaches do work at the database tier to minimize the network issue, but you are always susceptible to "stale" pagination with cursor techniques. Don't be in any doubt: use the database to paginate for you—and reap the benefits!

5-4. Testing for the Existence of Data

Problem

You would like to compare the data in two related tables, to show where matching data exists, and to also show where matching data doesn't exist.

Solution

Oracle supports the EXISTS and NOT EXISTS predicates, allowing you to correlate the data in one table or expression with matching or missing data in another table or expression. We'll use the hypothetical situation of needing to find which departments currently have managers. Phrasing this in a way that best illustrates the EXISTS solution, the next SQL statement finds all departments where a manager is known to exist.

```
select department_name
from hr.departments d
where exists
  (select e.employee_id
```

```
from hr.employees e
where d.manager_id = e.employee_id);
```

The complement, testing for non-existence, is shown in the next statement. We ask to find all departments in HR.DEPARTMENTS with a manager that does not exist in the data held in HR.EMPLOYEES.

```
select department_name
from hr.departments d
where not exists
 (select e.employee_id
  from hr.employees e
  where d.manager_id = e.employee_id);
```

How It Works

In any database, including Oracle, the EXISTS predicate answers the question, "Is there a relationship between two data items, and by extension, what items in one set are related to items in a second set?" The NOT EXISTS variant tests the converse, "Can it definitively be said that no relationship exists between two sets of data, based on a proposed criterion?" Each approach is referred to as correlation or a correlated subquery (literally, co-relation, sharing a relationship).

Interestingly, Oracle bases its decision on whether satisfying data exists solely on this premise: was a matching row found that satisfied the subquery's predicates? It's almost too subtle, so we'll point out the obvious thing Oracle isn't seeking. What you select in the inner correlated query doesn't matter—it's only the criteria that matter. So you'll often see versions of existence tests that form their subselect by selecting the value 1, the entire row using an asterisk, a literal value, or even NULL. Ultimately, it's immaterial in this form of the recipe. The key point is the correlation expression. In our case, it's WHERE D.MANAGER_ID = E.EMPLOYEE_ID.

This also helps explain what Oracle is doing in the second half of the recipe, where we're looking for DEPARTMENT_NAME values for rows where the MANAGER_ID doesn't exist in the HR.EMPLOYEES table. Oracle drives the query by evaluating, for each row in the outer query, whether no rows are returned by the inner correlated query. Oracle doesn't care what data exists in other columns not in the correlation criteria. It pays to be careful using such NOT EXISTS clauses on their own—not because the logic won't work but because against large data sets, the optimizer can decided to repeatedly scan the inner data in full, which might affect performance. In our example, so long as a manager's ID listed for a department is not found in the HR.EMPLOYEES table, the NOT EXISTS predicate will be satisfied, and department included in the results.

▨ **Caution** Correlated subqueries satisfy an important problem-solving niche, but it's crucial to remember the nature of NULL values when using either EXISTS or NOT EXISTS. NULL values are not equivalent to any other value, including other NULL values. This means that a NULL in the outer part of a correlated query will never satisfy the correlation criterion for the inner table, view, or expression. In practice, this means you'll see precisely the opposite effect as the one you might expect because the EXISTS test will always return false, even if both the inner and outer data sources have NULL values for the correlation, and NOT EXISTS will always return true. Not what the lay person would expect.

5-5. Conditional Branching In One SQL Statement

Problem

In order to produce a concise result in one query, you need to change the column returned on a row-by-row basis, conditional on a value from another row. You want to avoid awkward mixes of unions, subqueries, aggregation, and other inelegant techniques.

Solution

For circumstances where you need to conditionally branch or alternate between source data, Oracle provides the CASE statement. CASE mimics the traditional switch or case statement found in many programming languages like C or Java.

To bring focus to our example, we'll assume our problem is far more tangible and straightforward. We want to find the date employees in the shipping department (with the DEPARTMENT_ID of 50) started their current job. We know their initial hire date with the firm is tracked in the HIRE_DATE column on the HR.EMPLOYEES table, but if they've had a promotion or changed roles, the date when they commenced their new position can be inferred from the END_DATE of their previous position in the HR.JOB_HISTORY table. We need to branch between HIRE_DATE or END_DATE for each employee of the shipping department accordingly, as shown in the next SQL statement.

```
select e.employee_id,
  case
    when old.job_id is null then e.hire_date
    else old.end_date end
  job_start_date
from hr.employees e left outer join hr.job_history old
  on e.employee_id = old.employee_id
where e.department_id = 50
order by e.employee_id;
```

Our results are very straightforward, hiding the complexity that went into picking the correct JOB_START_DATE.

```
EMPLOYEE_ID         JOB_START
-----------         ---------
        120         18-JUL-96
        121         10-APR-97
        122         31-DEC-99
        123         10-OCT-97
        124         16-NOV-99
...
```

How It Works

Our recipe uses the CASE feature, in Search form rather than Simple form, to switch between HIRE_DATE and END_DATE values from the joined tables. In some respects, it's easiest to think of this CASE operation as a combination of two SELECT statements in one. For employees with no promotions, it's as if we were selecting as follows:

```
select e.employee_id, e.hire_date…
```

Whereas for employees that have had promotions, the CASE statement switches the SELECT to the following form:

```
select e.employee_id, old.end_date…
```

The beauty is in not having to explicitly code these statements yourself, and for far more complex uses of CASE, not having to code many dozens or hundreds of statement combinations.

To explore the solution from the data's perspective, the following SQL statement extracts the employee identifier and the hire and end dates using the same left outer join as our recipe.

```
select e.employee_id, e.hire_date, old.end_date end
from hr.employees e left outer join hr.job_history old
  on e.employee_id = old.employee_id
where e.department_id = 50
order by e.employee_id;
```

```
EMPLOYEE_ID            HIRE_DATE           END_DATE
-----------            ---------           ---------
        120            18-JUL-96
        121            10-APR-97
        122            01-MAY-95           31-DEC-99
        123            10-OCT-97
        124            16-NOV-99
...
```

The results show the data that drove the CASE function's decision in our recipe. The values in bold were the results returned by our recipe. For the first, second, fourth, and fifth rows shown, END_DATE from the HR.JOB_HISTORY table is NULL, so the CASE operation returned the HIRE_DATE. For the third row, with EMPLOYEE_ID 122, END_DATE has a date value, and thus was returned in preference to HIRE_DATE when examined by our original recipe. There is a shorthand form of the CASE statement known as the Simple CASE that only operates against one column or expression and has THEN clauses for possible values. This wouldn't have suited us as Oracle limits the use of NULL with the Simple CASE in awkward ways.

5-6. Conditional Sorting and Sorting By Function

Problem

While querying some data, you need to sort by an optional value, and where that value is not present, you'd like to change the sorting condition to another column.

Solution

Oracle supports the use of almost all of its expressions and functions in the ORDER BY clause. This includes the ability to use the CASE statement and simple and complex functions like arithmetic operators to dynamically control ordering. For our recipe, we'll tackle a situation where we want to show employees ordered by highest-paid to lowest-paid.

For those with a commission, we want to assume the commission is earned but don't want to actually calculate and show this value; we simply want to order on the implied result. The following SQL leverages the CASE statement in the ORDER BY clause to conditionally branch sorting logic for those with and without a COMMISSION_PCT value.

```
select employee_id, last_name, salary, commission_pct
from hr.employees
order by
  case
    when commission_pct is null then salary
    else salary * (1+commission_pct)
  end desc;
```

We can see from just the first few rows of results how the conditional branching while sorting has worked.

```
EMPLOYEE_ID        LAST_NAME          SALARY        COMMISSION_PCT
-----------        ---------          ------        --------------
        100        King               24000
        145        Russell            14000             .4
        146        Partners           13500             .3
        101        Kochhar            17000
        102        De Haan             7000
...
```

Even though employees 101 and 102 have a higher base salary, the ORDER BY clause using CASE has correctly positioned employees 145 and 146 based on their included commission percentage.

How It Works

The selection of data for our results follows Oracle's normal approach, so employee identifiers, last names, and so forth are fetched from the HR.EMPLOYEES table. For the purposes of ordering the data using our CASE expression, Oracle performs additional calculations that aren't shown in the results. All the candidate result rows that have a non-NULL commission value have the product of COMMISSION_PCT and SALARY calculated and then used to compare with the SALARY figures for all other employees for ordering purposes.

The next SELECT statement helps you visualize the data Oracle is deriving for the ordering calculation.

```
select employee_id, last_name, commission_pct, salary,
  salary * (1+commission_pct) sal_x_comm
from hr.employees;
```

EMPLOYEE_ID	LAST_NAME	COMMISSION_PCT	SALARY	SAL_X_COMM
100	King		**24000**	
145	Russell	.4	14000	**19600**
146	Partners	.3	13500	**17550**
101	Kochhar		**17000**	
102	De Haan		**17000**	

...

The values in bold show the calculations Oracle used for ordering when evaluating the data via the CASE expression in the ORDER BY clause. The general form of the CASE expression can be expressed simply as follows.

```
case
    when <expression, column, etc.> then <expression, column, literal, etc.>
    when <expression, column, etc.> then <expression, column, literal, etc.>
    ...
    else <default expression for unmatched cases>
end
```

We won't needlessly repeat what the Oracle manual covers in plenty of detail. In short, the CASE expression evaluates the first WHEN clause for a match and if satisfied, performs the THEN expression. If the first WHEN clause isn't satisfied, it tries the second WHEN clause, and so on. If no matches are found, the ELSE default expression is evaluated.

5-7. Overcoming Issues and Errors when Subselects Return Unexpected Multiple Values

Problem

In working with data from a subselect, you need to deal with ambiguous situations where in some cases the subselect will return a single (scalar) value, and in other cases multiple values.

Solution

Oracle supports three expressions that allow a subselect to be compared based on a single column of results. The operators ANY, SOME, and ALL allow one or more single-column values from a subselect to be compared to data in an outer SELECT. Using these operators allows you to deal with situations where you'd like to code your SQL to handle comparisons with flexible set sizes.

Our recipe focuses on using these expressions for a concrete business problem. The order-entry system tracks product information in the OE.PRODUCT_INFORMATION table, including the LIST_PRICE value. However, we know discounts are often offered, so we'd like to get an approximate idea of which items have never sold at full price. To do this, we could do a precise correlated subquery of every sale against list price. Before doing that, a very quick approximation can be done to see if any LIST_PRICE value is

higher than any known sale price for any item, indicated by the UNIT_PRICE column of the
OE.ORDER_ITEMS table. Our SELECT statement takes this form.

```
select product_id, product_name
from oe.product_information
where list_price > ALL
  (select unit_price
   from oe.order_items);
```

From this query, we see three results:

```
PRODUCT_ID          PRODUCT_NAME
----------          ------------------------
      2351          Desk - W/48/R
      3003          Laptop 128/12/56/v90/110
      2779          Desk - OS/O/F
```

These results mean at least three items—two desks and a laptop—have never sold a full price.

How It Works

Our example's use of the ALL expression allows Oracle to compare the UNIT_PRICE values from every sale,
to see if any known sale price was greater than the LIST_PRICE for an item. Breaking down the steps that
make this approach useful, we can first look at the subselect.

```
select unit_price
from oe.order_items
```

This is a very simple statement that returns a single-column result set of zero or more items, shown
next in abbreviated form.

```
UNIT_PRICE
----------
        13
        38
        43
        43
     482.9
...
665 rows selected.
```

Based on those results, our outer SELECT statement compares each LIST_PRICE from the
OE.PRODUCTION_INFORMATION table with every item in the list, as we are using the ALL expression. If the
LIST_PRICE is greater than all of the returned values, the expression resolves to true, and the product is
included in the results. Where even one of the UNIT_PRICE values returned exceeds the LIST_PRICE of an
item, the expression is false and that row is discarded from further consideration.

If you review that logic, you'll realize this is not a precise calculation of every item that didn't sell for
full price. Rather, it's just a quick approximation, though one that shows off the ALL technique quite well.

The alternatives SOME and ANY, which are effectively synonyms, resolve the true/false determination
based on only needing one item in the subselect to satisfy the SOME/ANY condition. Oracle will happily

accept more than one item matching the SOME/ANY criteria, but only needs to determine one value to evaluate the subselect.

5-8. Converting Numbers Between Different Bases

Problem

You need to find a generic way to turn decimal representations of numbers such as IP addresses and MAC addresses into hexadecimal, octal, binary, and other unusual number bases.

Solution

Oracle ships with a small number of base-conversion features, the most notable of which is the TO_CHAR function's ability to convert from decimal to hexadecimal. We can convert an arbitrary value, such as 19452, to hexadecimal using the next SELECT statement:

```
select to_char(19452,'xxxxx')-oi-Oij
from dual;
```

Our output shows the correctly calculated value of 4BFC. Run that query yourself to confirm Oracle's accuracy at hexadecimal conversion. While this is useful for this specific case, often we'll want to see decimals converted to binary, octal, and other uncommon bases.

■ **Tip** You may ask yourself, what other bases might possibly be used? One of the authors once worked on software that stored all numbers in base 36, using the digits 0 to 9 and the letters A to Z to deal with limitations in certain hardware products that could only store strings. You may find yourself needing number conversion to unusual bases when you least expect it!

Other base conversions are not natively addressed out of the box by Oracle, so we'll create our own generic decimal-conversion function that can take a given number and convert it to any base from 2 to 36! We'll build our REBASE_NUMBER function using the fundamental arithmetic operations that do ship with Oracle, as shown here.

```
create or replace function rebase_number
  (starting_value in integer, new_base in number)
return varchar2
is
  rebased_value varchar2(4000) default NULL;
  working_remainder integer default starting_value;
  char_string varchar2(36) default '0123456789ABCDEFGHIJKLMNOPQRSTUVWXYZ';
  sign varchar2(1) default '';
begin
```

```
  if (starting_value < 0) then
    sign := '-';
    working_remainder := abs(working_remainder);
  end if;
  loop
    rebased_value := substr(char_string, mod(working_remainder,new_base)+1, 1)
      || rebased_value;
    working_remainder := trunc(working_remainder/new_base);
    exit when (working_remainder = 0);
  end loop;
  rebased_value := sign || rebased_value;
  return rebased_value;
end rebase_number;
/
```

With the REBASE_NUMBER function now available, we can perform conversions of our original test number, 19452, to a variety of bases. The first example shows conversion to hexadecimal, to prove we're getting the same result as Oracle.

```
select rebase_number(19452,16) as DEC_TO_HEX
from dual;
```

We successfully calculate the correct result.

```
DEC_TO_HEX
----------
4BFC
```

The same number converted to octal also succeeds.

```
select rebase_number(19452,8) as DEC_TO_OCTAL
from dual;
```

```
DEC_TO_OCTAL
------------
45774
```

A final example converting to binary similarly produces the correct result.

```
select rebase_number(19452,2) as DEC_TO_BINARY
from dual;
```

```
DEC_TO_BINARY
---------------
100101111111100
```

How It Works

Our function models the classic discrete mathematics used to perform a conversion between two bases for any number. The basic algorithm takes this form: For each significant digit in the original number (thousands, hundreds, and so forth)

- Perform modulo division on that part of the number using the new base.

- Use the whole part of the result as the new "digit" in the converted number.

- Take the remainder, and repeat until the remainder is less than the new base.

Return the new digits and the last remainder as the converted number.

There are two not-so-obvious aspects of our implementation of this logic that warrant further explanation. The first involves dealing with negative numbers. Our function sets up various local variables, some of which we'll discuss shortly, the last of which is called SIGN. We set this to an empty string, which implicitly means a positive outcome reported to the caller unless we detect that a negative number is passed to the function for conversion. In the first part of the logic body of our function, we test for the sign of the STARTING_VALUE and change the SIGN value to '-' for any negative values detected.

```
if (starting_value < 0) then
  sign := '-';
  working_remainder := abs(working_remainder);
end if;
```

Detecting negative numbers and switching the WORKING_NUMBER to positive using the ABS function isn't part of normal decimal-to-hexadecimal conversion. In fact, we don't use it in our arithmetic either! It exists purely to help with the second non-obvious aspect of our implementation, a trick we utilize in our function that we'll cover in a moment. At the end of our function, we reinstate the SIGN as it should be, so that the user doesn't notice this data massaging happening.

```
rebased_value := sign || rebased_value;
```

So why the two-step with the number's sign in the first place? It's because we use a trick to "look up" the conversion of a decimal digit (or digits) into its new base by finding how the whole part of our modulo division maps to a position in a string. In this case, the string is the unusual local variable you see at the start of the function, CHAR_STRING.

```
char_string varchar2(36) default '0123456789ABCDEFGHIJKLMNOPQRSTUVWXYZ';
```

You may have thought, why are the authors practicing their typing in this book? But we're not! The trick is to use the SUBSTR function to walk this string to find the matching value for our conversion. Here's how it works at its basic level. We take a source number, like 13, and the desired base, like 16, and plug it into our SUBSTR call, as shown in the next fragment.

```
substr(char_string, mod(13 /* our remainder */, 16 /* our new base */)+1, 1)
```

Performing the arithmetic is easy. 13 modulo 16 gives 0 with a remainder of 13. We add one to this value, because our string is zero-based, so we need to account for the "zeroth" position, giving us a value of 14. We then take the substring of the CHAR_STRING starting at this position (14), for 1 character. The 14th character in the string is D. Voilà: we have converted the decimal number 13 to its hexadecimal equivalent, D. From there, it's just a case of repeating the process for successive modulo division results.

The reverse logic can also be incorporated into a function, so values in any base can be converted to decimal. We can also wrap these functions in a helper function that would allow the conversion from any arbitrary base to any other arbitrary base. These functions are available at www.oraclesqlrecipes.com.

5-9. Searching for a String Without Knowing the Column or Table

Problem

You need to find where in the database a particular text value is stored, but don't have access to the application code or logic that would let you determine this from seeing the data via the application. You have only the Oracle catalog tables and SQL to find what you seek.

Solution

No database currently available includes an omniscient "search everywhere for what I'm seeking" operator. However, using the basic building blocks of Oracle's string-searching LIKE operator, and the ability to output one SELECT statement as the result of another, we can execute a series of steps that will automatically track down the schema, table, and column holding the text data we seek.

To give our recipe a concrete flavor, we'll assume that we're looking for the text "Greene" somewhere in the database, but we don't know—and can't find any documentation that would tell us—if this text is a person's name, a supplier or client company name, part of a product name, or part of some other text.

Our solution works in two parts. The first SELECT statement, shown next, produces as results individual SELECT queries to search all columns of all tables in all schemata for our unidentified text, Greene.

```
Select
  'select ''' || owner || ''',
  ''' || table_name || ''',
  ''' || column_name || ''',
  ' || column_name ||
  ' from ' ||
  owner ||
  '.' ||
  table_name ||
  ' where ' ||
  column_name || '
  like ''%Greene%'';' as Child_Select_Statements
from all_tab_columns
where owner in ('BI', 'HR', 'IX', 'OE', 'PM', 'SH')
and data_type in ('VARCHAR2','CHAR','NVARCHAR2','NCHAR')
and data_length >= length('Greene');
```

In our example, the output of this command is a list of 271 SELECT statements, one for each text-like column in each of the tables in Oracle's sample schemata. A subset is shown here, with formatting to make the output readable on this printed page.

```
CHILD_SELECT_STATEMENTS
--------------------------------------------------------------------------------
...
select 'HR','COUNTRIES','COUNTRY_NAME', COUNTRY_NAME
  from HR.COUNTRIES
  where COUNTRY_NAME like '%Greene%';
select 'HR','DEPARTMENTS','DEPARTMENT_NAME', DEPARTMENT_NAME
  from HR.DEPARTMENTS
  where DEPARTMENT_NAME like '%Greene%';
select 'HR','EMPLOYEES','FIRST_NAME', FIRST_NAME
  from HR.EMPLOYEES
 where FIRST_NAME like '%Greene%';
select 'HR','EMPLOYEES','LAST_NAME', LAST_NAME
  from HR.EMPLOYEES
  where LAST_NAME like '%Greene%';
select 'HR','EMPLOYEES','EMAIL', EMAIL
  from HR.EMPLOYEES
  where EMAIL like '%Greene%';
...
```

As you're looking at these output statements, first stop and think if there are performance implications to running statements across many (if not all) of your tables. If your database is multi-terabyte in size, it might be worth some planning to execute these when you won't affect performance. Once you're happy with the logistics of when it's best to use them, run them against the database. They will elicit the schema, table, and column name, plus the column data, where the sought-after text resides. A portion of the results are shown next.

```
select 'HR','EMPLOYEES','FIRST_NAME', FIRST_NAME
  from HR.EMPLOYEES
  where FIRST_NAME like '%Greene%';

no rows selected

select 'HR','EMPLOYEES','LAST_NAME', LAST_NAME
  from HR.EMPLOYEES
  where LAST_NAME like '%Greene%';

'H 'EMPLOYEE 'LAST_NAM LAST_NAME
-- --------- --------- -------------------------
HR EMPLOYEES LAST_NAME Greene
```

```
select 'HR','EMPLOYEES','EMAIL', EMAIL
  from HR.EMPLOYEES
  where EMAIL like '%Greene%';
```

```
no rows selected
```

With the completion of the second set of statements, we've found the text "Greene" in the LAST_NAME column of the HR.EMPLOYEES table.

How It Works

This solution takes a two-pass approach to the problem. When you run the first query, it searches for all the columns in the ALL_TAB_COLUMNS system view to find the schema names, table names, and column names for columns that have a textual data type, such as VARCHAR2 or CHAR. It's a little hard to see the logic through all the literal formatting and string concatenation, so it's best thought of using this general structure.

```
select
  <escaped column, table and schema names for later presentation>,
  <actual column name for later querying>,
  <escaped from clause for later querying >
  <escaped where clause for later querying >
from all_tab_columns
where owner in (<list of schemata in which we're interested>)
and data_type in ('VARCHAR2','CHAR','NVARCHAR2','NCHAR')
and data_length >= <length of text sought>;
```

For each table with at least one relevant textual data type, this query will emit a result that takes the form of a SELECT statement that generally looks like this:

```
select
  <literal schema name>,
  <literal table name>,
  <literal column name>,
  <column_name>
where <column_name> like '%<text sought>%';
```

It's then just a matter of running those SELECT statements and noting which ones actually produce results. All of the elaborate literal escaping and quoting is used to preserve the object names right down to this level, so the results include not only the text you seek in context, but also the human-readable data for schema, table, and column, as you can see in this example row.

```
HR EMPLOYEES LAST_NAME Greene
```

At least one instance of the text "Greene" can be found in HR.EMPLOYEES, in the LAST_NAME column.

ALL_TAB_COLUMNS versus ALL_TAB_COLS

Careful observers will note that we've crafted our solution to work with the ALL_TAB_COLUMNS system view. Oracle also includes a system view named ALL_TAB_COLS. The two seem almost identical, having the same fields, but slightly different row counts. So why choose ALL_TAB_COLUMNS in this recipe?

The answer has to do with the slightly different definitions Oracle uses in defining the two views. The ALL_TAB_COLS system view includes hidden columns not normally visible to users or developers. As our recipe seeks ordinary data used every day by end-users, we rightly assume that the developers have not played tricks by either hiding columns of their own or abusing Oracle's system-controlled hidden columns.

The recipe so far has not made any assumptions about the tool or tools you'll use when working with the solution. You can happily run the first statement in SQL*Plus, SQL Developer, or through a programmable API, and retrieve the second set of statements to run. Similarly, you can use any tool to then execute those statements and view the results revealing the hiding place of your lost text. But some extra niceties are possible. For instance, you could wrap much of the logic in a PL/SQL function or stored procedure, or use the formatting capabilities of a query tool like SQL*Plus to make the solution even more elegant.

5-10. Predicting Data Values and Trends Beyond a Series End

Problem

From a large set of data, you need to predict the behavior or trend of the information beyond the bounds of your current data set.

Solution

Predicting trends and extrapolating possibilities based on patterns in the data, such as relationships between two values, can be addressed in many ways. One of the most popular techniques is linear regression analysis, and Oracle provides numerous linear regression functions for many contemporary trending and analysis algorithms.

As part of the sample schemata included with the Oracle database, a Sales History data warehouse example is provided in the SH schema. This includes a fact table of around a million entries of individual items sold with dimensions for time, sales channel, and so on, and the item price for a given sale.

Our recipe supposes that we're solving the problem of predicting what would happen if we introduced more expensive items than those currently sold. In effect, we'd like to extrapolate beyond the current most expensive item, based on the current sales trend of volume sold compared with item price. We're answering the fundamental question, would we actually sell an item if it were more expensive, and if so, how many of those items would we sell?

The following SELECT statement uses three Oracle linear regression functions to help guide our extrapolation. We're asking what's likely to happen if we start selling items in the Electronics category at higher prices, will we sell more or fewer, and how quickly will sales volume change with price.

```
select
  s.channel_desc,
  regr_intercept(s.total_sold, p.prod_list_price)  total_sold_intercept,
  regr_slope (s.total_sold, p.prod_list_price)  trend_slope,
  regr_r2(s.total_sold, p.prod_list_price)  r_squared_confidence
from sh.products p,
  (select c.channel_desc, s.prod_id, s.time_id, sum(s.quantity_sold) total_sold
   from sh.sales s inner join sh.channels c
     on s.channel_id = c.channel_id
   group by c.channel_desc, s.prod_id, s.time_id) s
where s.prod_id=p.prod_id
and p.prod_category='Electronics'
and s.time_id between to_date('01-JAN-1998') and to_date('31-DEC-1999')
group by s.channel_desc
order by 1;
```

CHANNEL_DESC	TOTAL_SOLD_INTERCEPT	TREND_SLOPE	R_SQUARED_CONFIDENCE
Direct Sales	24.2609713	-.02001389	.087934647
Internet	6.30196312	-.00513654	.065673194
Partners	11.738347	-.00936476	.046714001
Tele Sales	36.1015696	-.11700913	.595086378

For those unfamiliar with interpreting linear regressions, the extrapolated trends can be read in the general form:

```
Y = Intercept + Slope(X)
```

For our data, Y is the total number of items sold and X is the list price. We can see that for Direct Sales, Internet, and Partners, there's a gentle decrease in sales as price increases, whereas sales volume plummets dramatically for Tele Sales as cost increases. However, our confidence values suggest the first three predictions are a poorly fit extrapolation for these channels. The R-squared confidence value indicates how well the extrapolated line of fit suits the data (also known as goodness of fit), where a value of 1.0 means "perfect fit", and 0 means "absolutely no correlation".

How It Works

To feed data to our linear regression functions, such as REGR_SLOPE, we need to ensure we are providing the actual values we want to compare. Our recipe compares the total number of items sold to the list price of an item. The SH.SALES table tracks the sale of each individual item, with one entry per item sold. It's for this reason that we use the inline view to aggregate all of these individual sale entries into aggregate number of sales for a certain product, date, and channel. You can run the subselect by itself, as shown in the next SQL statement.

```
select c.channel_desc, s.prod_id, s.time_id, sum(s.quantity_sold) total_sold
from sh.sales s inner join sh.channels c
  on s.channel_id = c.channel_id
group by c.channel_desc, s.prod_id, s.time_id;
```

No surprises there, and the results provide a simple rolled-up summary ready for use in our linear regression functions.

CHANNEL_DESC	PROD_ID	TIME_ID	TOTAL_SOLD
...			
Direct Sales	30	24-OCT-01	1
Internet	32	30-NOV-01	4
Direct Sales	35	28-OCT-01	12
Partners	47	09-NOV-01	1
Direct Sales	14	06-OCT-01	5
...			

Our results provide this summary for every type of item we sell. We join the inline view to the SH.PRODUCTS table, and then we filter by PROD_CATEGORY of Electronics and a two-year date range to focus on our supposed problem. The fun then starts with the linear regression functions in the SELECT clause.

Each of the three statistical functions takes the calculated TOTAL_SOLD amounts and LIST_PRICE values for each channel (thanks to the GROUP BY clause), and performs the relevant calculations. A good statistics textbook will tell you how these formulae were derived, but Table 5-1 shows you each formula's method.

Table 5-1. *Oracle Statistical Methods Supporting Linear Regression Analysis*

Function	Formula
REGR_INTERCEPT	$(\Sigma y)/n - (\Sigma xy - (\Sigma x)(\Sigma y)/n)/(\Sigma x^2 - (\Sigma x)^2/n) (\Sigma x)/n$
REGR_SLOPE	$(\Sigma xy - (\Sigma x)(\Sigma y)/n)/(\Sigma x^2 - (\Sigma x)^2/n)$
REGR_R2	$(\Sigma xy - (\Sigma x)(\Sigma y)/n)^2/(\Sigma x^2 - (\Sigma x)^2/n)(\Sigma y^2 - (\Sigma y)^2/n)$

Just looking at those formulae should make you glad you don't have to code the calculations yourself. Just call the appropriate function and Oracle does the hard work for you. Armed with the data returned by those functions, you can then visualize how the sales volume changes with price. Figure 5-1 shows our linear regression data expressed as hypothetical extrapolated lines showing the relationship between sales volume and list price.

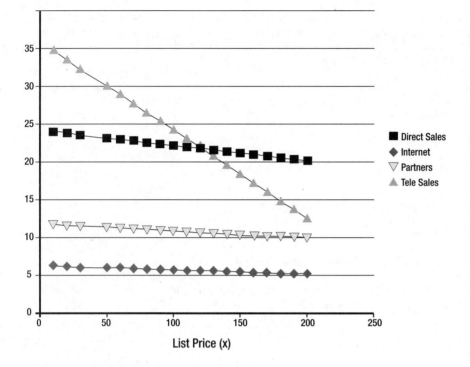

Figure 5-1. *An extrapolation of sales volume and list price using linear regression*

This gives you a clear indication of how your sales volume might change as you alter price. Missing from this is an indication of goodness of fit: literally, how reliable is the estimated relationship between the data and the extrapolation taken from it. This is the r-squared value calculated using the `REGR_R2` function.

5-11. Explicitly (Pessimistically) Locking Rows for an Update

Problem

To protect a particularly sensitive and special business case, you have been asked to ensure that updates to employee salaries are protected from lost updates, and also asked not to use an optimistic locking approach.

Solution

Our problem models one of the classic issues faced by developers and DBAs. While Oracle provides excellent concurrency control and locking mechanisms and supports both optimistic and pessimistic design approaches, often a political or business decision forces you to use one technique.

At some stage in your work with Oracle, you may find your most coherent arguments about Oracle's excellent concurrency technology brushed aside by a manager who says "That's all well and good, but I want to grant pay rises once, and *I don't want to see* any messages indicating another manager updated the same employee's salary and I should try again."

Faced with such a career-threatening imperative, you'll be glad to know Oracle provides the SELECT … FOR UPDATE option to explicitly lock data and provide pessimistic concurrency control. For our recipe, we'll use the next SELECT statement to find the salary data for employee 200, Jennifer Whalen, in preparation for a later update.

```
select employee_id, last_name, salary
from hr.employees
where employee_id = 200
for update;
```

```
EMPLOYEE_ID              LAST_NAME              SALARY
-----------              ---------              ------
        200              Whalen                 4400
```

So far, so good. If a second user (or the same user via a different connection) attempts to perform a SELECT, UPDATE, or DELETE of this row, that user will be blocked. Try issuing the same SELECT statement from another connection and you'll see no results as the session waits for the locks related to the SELECT … FOR UPDATE pessimistic locking to be released.

```
select employee_id, last_name, salary
from hr.employees
where employee_id = 200
for update;
```

```
(no results yet … waiting on blocking exclusive lock)
```

From the first session, we complete our update.

```
update hr.employees
set salary = salary * 1.1
where employee_id = 200;
```

```
commit;
```

Upon commit from the first session, the second session's SELECT statement finally runs, returning these results.

```
EMPLOYEE_ID              LAST_NAME              SALARY
-----------              ---------              ------
        200              Whalen                 4840
```

Note the second session did not interrupt the update, and never saw the pre-updated data.

How It Works

The key to the pessimistic locking effect of the FOR UPDATE clause is in the way it forces Oracle to take locks on the data covered by the SELECT query. Oracle attempts to take a mode X (exclusive) transaction row-level lock on each row that satisfies a SELECT … FOR UPDATE query.

When the first connection issues the SELECT … FOR UPDATE statement, we can query the V$LOCK dynamic view or use a graphical tool like SQL Developer to see the lock taken, as in Figure 5-2.

Username	PID	SID	SERIAL#	SPID	ORA	VLOCK	TYPE	LMODE	WAIT
SYSTEM	23	144	182 3540	SYSMAN	AE	AE	S	(null)	
SYSTEM	24	132	168 5644	DBSNMP	AE	AE	S	(null)	
SYSTEM	25	130	23 624	SYSTEM	AE	AE	S	(null)	
SYSTEM	26	140	37 4648	SYSTEM	AE	AE	S	(null)	
SYSTEM	29	134	5 2548	SYSTEM	AE	AE	S	(null)	
SYSTEM	30	143	194 5324	DBSNMP	AE	AE	S	(null)	
SYSTEM	31	145	28 3008	SYSMAN	AE	AE	S	(null)	
SYSTEM	32	135	165 4664	SYSTEM	AE	AE	S	(null)	
SYSTEM	32	135	165 4664	SYSTEM	TO	TO	RX	(null)	
SYSTEM	33	136	35 4504	SYSMAN	AE	AE	S	(null)	
SYSTEM	34	133	2 3240	SYSMAN	AE	AE	S	(null)	
SYSTEM	35	129	4 1780	SYSMAN	AE	AE	S	(null)	
SYSTEM	36	142	174 372	SYSMAN	AE	AE	S	(null)	
SYSTEM	37	128	21 1496	SYSMAN	AE	AE	S	(null)	
SYSTEM	38	127	33 696	SYSMAN	AE	AE	S	(null)	
SYSTEM	40	123	1 4588	SYSMAN	AE	AE	S	(null)	
SYSTEM	41	125	43 1904	SYSMAN	AE	AE	S	(null)	
SYSTEM	42	120	3575 2584	SYSMAN	AE	AE	S	(null)	
SYSTEM	42	120	3575 2584	SYSTEM	TRANSACTION ROW-LEVEL	DML LOCK	X	(null)	

Figure 5-2. *Select for update explicit locks for first session in SQL Developer*

The highlighted row shows the lock on the row of the HR.EMPLOYEES table for EMPLOYEE_ID 200. As soon as the second connection attempts the same statement, it tries to acquire the same exclusive lock, even though the first consequence of doing so would normally only be to select the data. Figure 5-3 shows how Oracle's normal "writes don't block reads" behavior has been overridden by the FOR UPDATE technique.

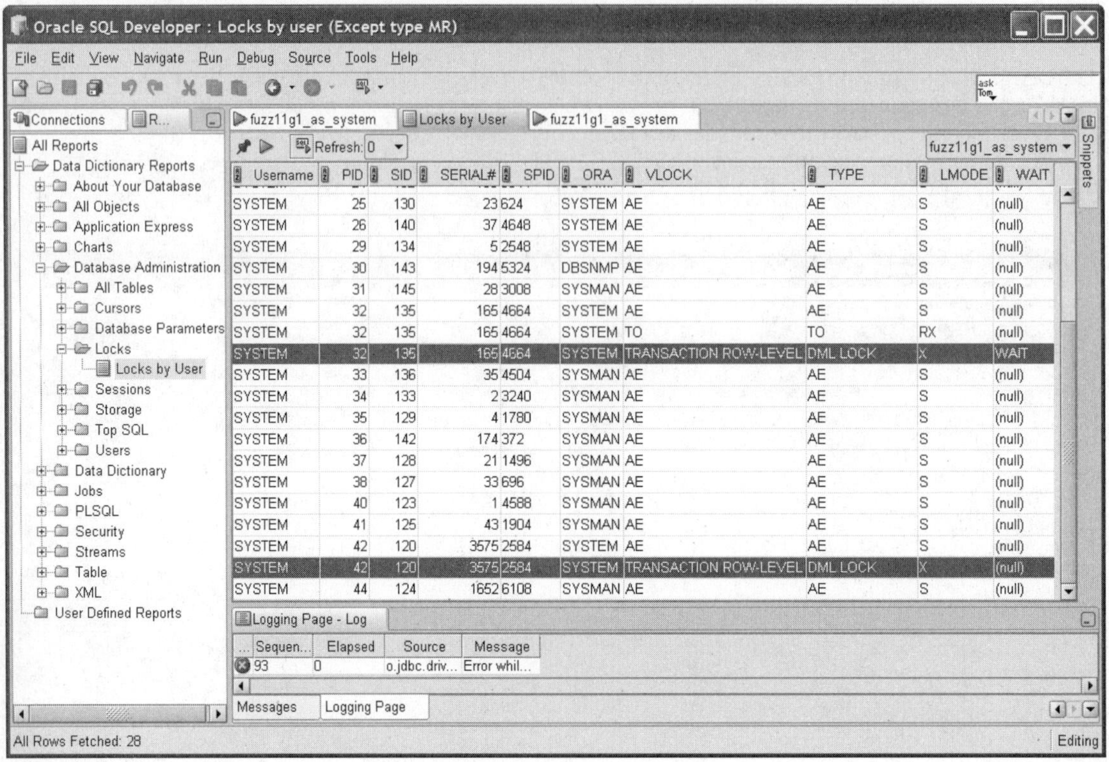

Figure 5-3. *The second select for update blocked, waiting for session 1*

The highlighted row shows the second session in a WAIT state, blocked from taking any action until the first session commits or rolls back its work. As soon as we perform our update and commit the results from session 1, our blocking condition clears and the second session takes the exclusive row-level transaction lock it wanted, and can in turn perform its desired update. Figure 5-4 shows the cleared WAIT state and the second session now holding the lock.

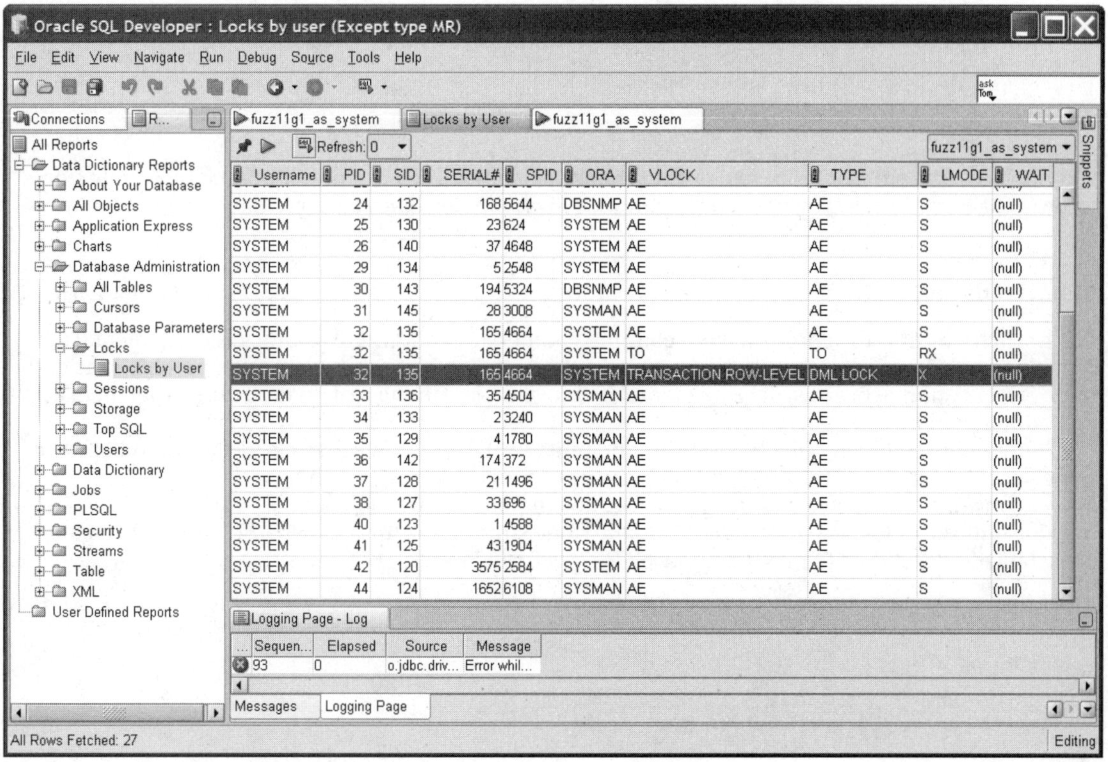

Figure 5-4. *Cleared from the wait state, the second select for update now holds an exclusive lock*

In this way, you can take explicit pessimistic control of locking in Oracle in those specific circumstances where you can't avoid it.

■ **Caution** While this approach might keep your boss happy, you might want to gently educate him or her over time to the great technology in Oracle, especially the non-blocking capabilities where readers don't block writers and everyone gets a consistent view of the data. They may not want to hear it the first time, but keep dropping it into conversations using the phrase, "You were so clever to buy a database that can do this, Boss." That way, their ego starts to work for you rather than against you, and you can avoid these pessimistic locking techniques as much as possible.

5-12. Synchronizing the Contents of Two Tables

Problem

You manage a system that keeps two or more tables with identical structures, but each table only stores some of the other's rows. You need to synchronize these tables so they each contain the full set of rows.

Solution

Table synchronization is a problem with countless potential solutions. All of Oracle's fundamental SQL capabilities can be used to compare, insert, or delete rows. For our recipe, we'll attempt to use one of the more elegant approaches to synchronization, often overlooked in the rush to tackle the problem in a procedural fashion.

Rather than code elaborate loops, tests, and more in SQL or PL/SQL, Oracle's MINUS union operator can be used to determine the difference in two sets of data in a set-wise fashion.

To illustrate our recipe, we'll imagine that our company has two subsidiaries, each of which is tracking a subset of employees in tables with the same structure as the HR.EMPLOYEES table. We create these tables, EMPA and EMPB, with the next CREATE TABLE statements.

```
create table hr.empa
as
select *
from hr.employees
where employee_id < 175;

create table hr.empb
as
select *
from hr.employees
where employee_id > 125;
```

The EMPLOYEE_ID cutoff chosen is arbitrary and was selected only to ensure there were not only some duplicates in the two tables, but also some rows unique to each table. We can quickly prove that our tables have different data with the next two SQL statements.

```
select min(employee_id), max(employee_id), count(*)
from hr.empa;
```

MIN(EMPLOYEE_ID)	MAX(EMPLOYEE_ID)	COUNT(*)
100	174	75

```
select min(employee_id), max(employee_id), count(*)
from hr.empb;
```

MIN(EMPLOYEE_ID)	MAX(EMPLOYEE_ID)	COUNT(*)
126	212	84

So we've established our subsidiary tables and can see they have overlapping, but in places different, data. Our solution uses the MINUS operation to bring the tables in to synchronization in the next two statements.

```
insert into hr.empa
select *
from hr.empb
minus
select *
from hr.empa;

insert into hr.empb
select *
from hr.empa
minus
select *
from hr.empb;
```

With our synchronization performed, a quick check shows we seem to now have identical sets of data.

```
select min(employee_id), max(employee_id), count(*)
from hr.empa;
```

MIN(EMPLOYEE_ID)	MAX(EMPLOYEE_ID)	COUNT(*)
100	212	110

```
select min(employee_id), max(employee_id), count(*)
from hr.empb;
```

MIN(EMPLOYEE_ID)	MAX(EMPLOYEE_ID)	COUNT(*)
100	212	110

Naturally, you are welcome to browse the entire set of data in both tables, but you'll be glad to know you won't be disappointed and all of the data will show as synchronized.

How It Works

This recipe uses the MINUS operation twice, once in each direction. First, we work on the table HR.EMPA, using an INSERT INTO … SELECT method. It's the SELECT that is key, as shown in the next statement fragment.

```
select *
from hr.empb
minus
select *
from hr.empa;
```

You can run this in isolation, to see how the contents of HR.EMPA itself are "subtracted" from the contents of HR.EMPB to leave us with the rows unique to HR.EMPB. These sample results are abbreviated to save space.

```
EMPLOYEE_ID          FIRST_NAME          AST_NAME          EMAIL    ...
-----------          ----------          --------          --------
        175          Alyssa              Hutton            AHUTTON  ...
        176          Jonathon            Taylor            JTAYLOR  ...
        177          Jack                Livingston        JLIVINGS ...
        178          Kimberely           Grant             KGRANT   ...
        179          Charles             Johnson           CJOHNSON ...
...
```

These results from the MINUS operation are then fed into the INSERT, and HR.EMPA then has all of its original rows, plus all those rows HR.EMPB had that were not present in HR.EMPA.

We then simply reverse the order of data flow in the second statement, using the MINUS operation to select only those rows in HR.EMPA that were missing from HR.EMPB, and insert them appropriately. It doesn't matter in which order these two INSERT statements are performed, so long as they both complete successfully.

You can also replace the second SQL statement with an alternative. Because we know HR.EMPA has the complete set of data after the first INSERT, we can remove all the data from HR.EMPB and copy everything over from HR.EMPA without the need for any predicates or union operators. The next code shows the necessary statements for the second step.

```
truncate table HR.EMPB;
insert into HR.EMPB select * from HR.EMPA;
```

This can sometimes be faster, as you avoid the implied sort that using the MINUS operator means.

PART 2

Data Types
and Their Problems

■ ■ ■

CHAPTER 6

Working with Date and Time Values

This chapter deals with recipes for date, time, and related temporal datatypes. Queries involving dates and times are very common in almost all databases. Working with dates and times is also very strange when compared to other forms of data, due to the long history (pardon the pun) of how our concepts of dates, hours, minutes, seconds, days, months and years came about. For instance, our division of minutes into 60 seconds, hours into sixty minutes, and days into two 12-hour blocks is derived from ancient Sumerian and Babylonian tradition. And they got the notion of a base-12 for counting hours and other things by using the segments of the four fingers (not the thumb) of one hand.

Calendars around the world stem from various religious influences, the whims of emperors and kings in different regions, and more. To put the icing on the cake, when you think you understand dates and times at a fundamental level, just ask astronomers for their perspective. They'll tell you there are at least three different measurements for the length of a day—depending on whether you're measuring rotation of the Earth; the Earth's time to return to point to the same fixed stars in the night sky; and, strangest of all, simply considering the day as an equation relating to angles in space.

It is therefore no surprise that dealing with date and time values, performing temporal arithmetic, and answering supposedly simple date and time questions can often lead to very tricky problems—with or without Oracle.

One of the key aspects of this chapter is to get you thinking about your own date and time problems and queries in a new light, and to spark your imagination as to how Oracle's many and varied date and time functions and tools can solve some of your trickiest chronological problems.

6-1. Converting Datetime Values into Readable Strings

Problem

You want to convert the short dates provided by Oracle's default date format into a full date for inclusion in a form letter or report.

Solution

Use Oracle's `TO_CHAR` function to format date, time, and other temporal data in the desired format. The `TO_CHAR` function supports a wide range of date-specific formatting options that handle day and month names, number notation and formatting, and similar tasks. Our recipe assumes you want to display the date on which employees were hired in a fully descriptive format. Specifically, you'd want 1/1/2009 reported as Thursday, January 1st, 2009.

The next SQL statement performs the relevant calculations and formatting for all employees.

```
select first_name, last_name,
  to_char(hire_date, 'Day, Month DDTH, YYYY') formatted_hire_date
from hr.employees;
```

Results from our `TO_CHAR` formatting appear with the correct day name, month name and other desired formatting in place.

```
FIRST_NAME           LAST_NAME            FORMATTED_ HIRE_DATE
-------------------- -------------------- ----------------------------------------
Donald               OConnell             Monday,    June       21ST, 1999
Douglas              Grant                Thursday,  January    13TH, 2000
Jennifer             Whalen               Thursday,  September  17TH, 1987
Michael              Hartstein            Saturday,  February   17TH, 1996
Pat                  Fay                  Sunday,    August     17TH, 1997
...
```

How It Works

Our recipe uses a very straightforward structure to select the `FIRST_NAME` and `LAST_NAME` values from the `HR.EMPLOYEE` table. When selecting the `HIRE_DATE`, we employ the `TO_CHAR` function with specific formatting codes to change the default format of the data, instructing Oracle to emit the full day and month name, ordinal date number, and full year.

The general format of the `TO_CHAR` function for converting dates takes this form.

```
to_char(<date/time expression>, '<format options>')
```

In our recipe, we used several options to format the day. We led with the `Day` option, which returns the full day name, such as Monday. We also use `DD`, together with the ordinal formatting code `TH`, to return the ordinal day number, such as 21st and 17th. The `MONTH` code returns the full month name, such as January. The year is returned by the `YYYY` code, which instructs Oracle to return the full four-digit year. We assume a future upgrade of Oracle will support five Y formatting characters here at some point before the year 10000.

Oracle includes numerous other day, month, year, and other formatting options to return date and time information in digits, words, and regionally sensitive strings (although the key words that are used in formatting commands are always in English). There are five more formatting characters in the string, though they may not be immediately obvious. The two comma characters and three spaces are themselves included as format options. These, together with other common punctuation such as dashes and colons, are all valid options in the `TO_CHAR` format string.

■ **Note** It's comforting to know that Oracle supports all manner of formatting codes and options in TO_CHAR for dates and times. However, there is a 22-character limit on the formatting options passed to the TO_CHAR function. This can frustrate your attempts to format dates and times in elaborate fashion. Don't despair if you run into this limit. You can always combine multiple calls to TO_CHAR, with other string functions, such as those shown in Chapter 7, to produce your desired output.

6-2. Converting Strings to Datetime Values

Problem

You need to convert date information provided in textual form to Oracle's DATE format.

Solution

Just as Oracle supports the TO_CHAR function to convert dates and times to text, it supports an equivalent function TO_DATE to perform the complementary process of converting text into dates and times.

Suppose you are given a date in written form, like January 17, 2009. Oracle expects dates to appear in a default format depending on the NLS regional settings. Oracle defaults to expecting one of DD-MMM-YY or DD-MMM-YYYY as the date format. You can use the TO_DATE function to convert January 17, 2009 to one of these formats, as shown in the next SQL statement.

```
select to_date('January 17, 2009', 'Month DD, YYYY') formatted_date
from dual;

FORMATTED_DATE
--------------
17-JAN-09
```

How It Works

The TO_DATE function is designed to interpret dates and times in textual and numeric form and uses a formatting pattern to apply translation rules to produce a result cast to the DATE datatype. The general form of the TO_DATE function is shown next.

```
to_date(<string>, <format options>)
```

The string parameter to the function is the textual words, numbers, and punctuation you wish converted to an Oracle DATE datatype. The format parameter is a string composed of formatting options. Oracle uses the formatting options to parse the textual string in a "parse and match" fashion. The key to successfully converting your text to a meaningful date is to find the format option that matches the text you need to convert.

Table 6-1 shows some of the most common formatting options used for the TO_DATE function (this is by no means an exhaustive list). These are also used in the TO_CHAR function when converting from dates and times to text.

Table 6-1. *Common Date and Time Formatting Options*

Code	Format
Day	Day of week in full written form (for example, Wednesday)
DD	Day of month in numeric form, 1 to 31
DY	Day of week in abbreviated written form (for example, Mon for Monday)
HH	Hour of the day in numeric form, 1 to 12
HH12	Hour of the day in numeric form, 1 to 12
HH24	Hour of the day in 24-hour clock numeric form, 0 to 23
MI	Minute of the hour in numeric form, 0 to 59
MM	Month in numeric form, 01 to 12
Mon	Month in abbreviated written form (for example, Apr for April)
Month	Month in full written form (for example, September)
RR	Year from the previous (20th) century in two-byte notation
YYYY	Numeric year, expressed with four digits.

Oracle even includes formatting codes to deal with such complexities as the day of the month, expressed in numeric ordinal form in words rather than numbers. So you can successfully convert the string January Seventeenth if you need to.

6-3. Detecting Overlapping Date Ranges

Problem

You need to find where start and end date ranges overlap for some of the data modeled in your system.

Solution

Oracle supports all of the typical comparison operators for query criteria and predicates with the DATE, TIMESTAMP and other temporal datatypes. This means you can test if dates are greater than others, less than others, equal to others, in a given list, not found in a given list, and so on. The concepts of greater and lesser dates translate to earlier and later points in time.

Our recipe will focus on the SH.PROMOTIONS table, which tracks what promotional offers like coupons and discount codes have been recorded and used as part of sales over time. The next SQL statement determines which promotions began while an existing promotion was still running, for the Ad News subcategory within the Newspaper promotional category.

```
select p2.promo_name || ' started before ' || p1.promo_name || ' ended.'
  as "Promotion Overlap"
from sh.promotions p1 inner join sh.promotions p2 on
  (p1.promo_category = p2.promo_category and
   p1.promo_subcategory = p2.promo_subcategory and
   p1.promo_id != p2.promo_id)
where p1.promo_category = 'newspaper'
and p1.promo_subcategory = 'ad news'
and p2.promo_begin_date >= p1.promo_begin_date
and p2.promo_begin_date <= p1.promo_end_date;
```

The results provide details of the overlapping promotions in plain English language.

```
Promotion Overlap
------------------------------------------------------------------------------
newspaper promotion #16-108 started before newspaper promotion #16-441 ended.
newspaper promotion #16-349 started before newspaper promotion #16-216 ended.
newspaper promotion #16-349 started before newspaper promotion #16-512 ended.
newspaper promotion #16-349 started before newspaper promotion #16-345 ended.
newspaper promotion #16-327 started before newspaper promotion #16-330 ended.
...
```

A concrete example of the usefulness of calculating such overlaps is to dynamically determine what promotion codes or coupon codes are operating concurrently, and preventing people from using multiple codes simultaneously.

How It Works

Our recipe works by finding pairs of rows in the SH.PROMOTIONS table, where the date of PROMO_BEGIN_DATE for the second row falls in the date window between PROMO_BEGIN_DATE and PROMO_END_DATE for the first row.

The SELECT portion of the recipe is straightforward. We concatenate the two promotions we find that overlap, P1.PROMO_NAME and P2.PROMO_NAME, with text so that our results show as a succinct human-readable summary of overlapping promotions. The FROM clause is the key to our logic. Here we join the SH.PROMOTIONS table to itself and refer to each copy in the join as P1 and P2. We join based on PROMO_CATEGORY and PROMO_SUBCATEGORY to meet our original recipe criteria for finding overlapping promotions within the same category and subcategory, so we only join rows with matching values for these fields. Importantly, we include the additional join criteria P1.PROMO_ID != P2.PROMO_ID, because we don't want to join a promotion to itself—it would be nonsensical to try to determine if a promotion overlapped itself.

With the SH.PROMOTIONS table self-joined using our join criteria, our WHERE clause then filters to only target Newspaper promotions in the Ad News subcategory. Again, this is to ensure we match our hypothetical criteria outlined in the recipe problem (these criteria could have been included in the join conditions instead).

The last two criteria work to find where the start of a second promotion occurs during the active window of a first promotion. The criterion P2.PROMO_BEGIN_DATE >= P1.PROMO_BEGIN_DATE finds joined pairs where the second promotion begins on or after the date of the first promotion. The criterion P2.PROMO_BEGIN_DATE <= P1.PROMO_END_DATE then discards all of those matches except the ones where the start of the second promotion also occurs before the first promotion finishes.

6-4. Automatically Tracking Date and Time for Data Changes

Problem

You want to track when changes to data occur for auditing purposes, but your current table design hasn't incorporated any dedicated fields for this purpose. You want to determine the date and time of historic changes if possible, and provide a mechanism to track future changes.

Solution

Use Oracle's ORA_ROWSCN pseudo-column and the SCN_TO_TIMESTAMP function to find approximate or exact times that rows were changed.

The next SQL illustrates the SCN_TO_TIMESTAMP function using the ORA_ROWSCN pseudo-column to determine the TIMESTAMP value at which rows in the HR.EMPLOYEES table were changed.

```
select employee_id, last_name, salary,
  scn_to_timestamp(ora_rowscn) Change_Timestamp
from hr.employees;
```

EMPLOYEE_ID	LAST_NAME	SALARY	CHANGE_TIMESTAMP
210	King	3510	12-SEP-09 03.54.55.000000000 PM
211	Sully	3510	12-SEP-09 03.54.55.000000000 PM
212	McEwen	3510	12-SEP-09 03.54.55.000000000 PM
100	King	24000	08-AUG-09 11.06.28.000000000 PM
101	Kochhar	17000	08-AUG-09 11.06.28.000000000 PM
102	De Haan	17000	08-AUG-09 11.06.28.000000000 PM

...

How It Works

The ORA_ROWSCN is a pseudo-column Oracle has supported since the release of Oracle 10g. By default, its value is taken from the block-level System Change Number (SCN) on the block storing the row or rows in question. This SCN can be seen directly with the next SQL that returns the SCN for the rows in our `HR.EMPLOYEES` table.

```
select employee_id, ora_rowscn
from hr.employees;
```

```
EMPLOYEE_ID ORA_ROWSCN
----------- ----------
        210    7824020
        211    7824020
        212    7824020
        100    7824148
        101    7824148
        102    7824148
...
```

The SCN value is passed to the `SCN_TO_TIMESTAMP` function, which determines at what time the relevant SCN was generated by Oracle. This value is of type `TIMESTAMP`, although Oracle states that the `TIMESTAMP` returned is only accurate to within 3 seconds, rather than the microsecond accuracy a `TIMESTAMP` can store. Where the SCN is older than the oldest SCN still tracked by the instance, you will receive a "ORA-08181: specified number is not a valid system change number" error message. This means that SCN values months or years in the past may not be translatable using this technique.

▓ **Tip** You can find the `TIMESTAMP` to SCN relationship independently of any given row or block of data, by looking at the `SYS.SMON_SCN_TIME` table.

One limitation of our recipe might have struck you from the description of the SQL used, or the results. Our use of the `ORA_ROWSCN` pseudo-column is returning the block-level SCN, which is Oracle's default level of SCN tracking. This means that any value updated for a row on a given block, or any new row inserted into the block, will set the `ORA_ROWSCN` value to the SCN of the relevant transaction. Because of this, it will appear that all rows stored on a given block were changed at the same time. You can see this in the sample results where several rows appear to have been updated simultaneously at `12-SEP-09 03.54.55.000000000 PM`.

Oracle provides a table option called `ROWDEPENDENCIES` to enable tracking of SCNs at the row level. This option can only be chosen at table creation time—it can't be activated once a table already exists. With `ROWDEPENDENCIES` in place, Oracle will use an additional six bytes of storage for row-based SCNs. We could adapt our `HR.EMPLOYEES` table by creating a new table based on its contents with `ROWDEPENDENCIES` enabled, and then use it to track when desired data like salary changed, by using our recipe's `SCN_TO_TIMESTAMP` approach.

6-5. Generating a Gapless Time Series from Data with Gaps

Problem

You would like to report business activity on each day of the month, but only store data on dates on which actions like launching a new promotion occur. You'd like to generate data for all the dates in a month, filling in the gaps in your records and showing zero activity on days for which no data was recorded.

Solution

Use Oracle's CONNECT BY LEVEL functionality and an OUTER JOIN to join date and time data with gaps to a reference table representing all dates and/or times you want to cover.

Our recipe SQL, shown next, uses this approach to fill in the gaps in promotions recorded in the SH.PROMOTIONS table for the month of June 1998.

```
select Day_Source.Day_Row Promotion_Date,
   count(sh.promotions.promo_begin_date) Promotions_Launched
from
  (select to_date('01-JUN-98') + rownum - 1 as Day_Row
   from dual
   connect by level <= 30)
Day_Source left outer join sh.promotions
  on Day_Source.Day_Row = sh.promotions.promo_begin_date
group by Day_Source.Day_Row
order by Day_Source.Day_Row;
```

Even though there were 14 days in June 1998 when no data was recorded in the SH.PROMOTIONS table, our recipe can report full results for each day of the month, showing zero promotions for those "missing" days.

```
PROMOTION_DATE PROMOTIONS_LAUNCHED
-------------- -------------------
01-JUN-98                        3
02-JUN-98                        6
03-JUN-98                        7
04-JUN-98                        0
05-JUN-98                        0
06-JUN-98                        1
07-JUN-98                        0
08-JUN-98                        0
09-JUN-98                        0
10-JUN-98                        0
11-JUN-98                        6
12-JUN-98                        0
13-JUN-98                        6
14-JUN-98                        0
15-JUN-98                        1
```

```
16-JUN-98                        1
17-JUN-98                        1
18-JUN-98                        0
19-JUN-98                        0
20-JUN-98                        6
21-JUN-98                        0
22-JUN-98                        1
23-JUN-98                        0
24-JUN-98                        1
25-JUN-98                        1
26-JUN-98                        0
27-JUN-98                        1
28-JUN-98                        1
29-JUN-98                        0
30-JUN-98                        1

30 rows selected.
```

How It Works

Our recipe works by creating an inline view, DAY_SOURCE, that comprises every day in the month of June 1998, and uses that as the outer table in a LEFT OUTER JOIN with the SH.PROMOTIONS table.

We can examine the recipe from the inside out to gain some understanding. The inner SELECT statement uses the DUAL table and CONNECT BY LEVEL to create a very simple virtual table. If we run the inner SELECT statement in isolation, as shown next, you'll immediately see how simple this construct is.

```
select to_date('01-JUN-98') + rownum - 1 as Day_Row
from dual
connect by level <= 30
```

The SELECT clause may look complex at first, but it's actually quite simple. We use TO_DATE to turn the string 01-JUN-98 into a valid Oracle DATE datatype. Then we perform simple date arithmetic to add the number from the pseudo-column ROWNUM to the date, and subtract one. Our recipe does this so the first date generated isn't the second of the month. We could have used TO_DATE('31-MAY-98') + ROWNUM instead, but casual reading of a function with "May" in the data doesn't immediately suggest one would be generating dates for June. As CONNECT BY LEVEL does its work for each successive row, we build up a complete view of dates, shown in abbreviated form next.

```
DAY_ROW
---------
01-JUN-98
02-JUN-98
03-JUN-98

...

29-JUN-98
30-JUN-98
```

This inline view of all of the dates for the given month is then used to overcome the fact our real data is missing a variety of dates, thanks to no activity happening on a given day. A traditional approach to reporting our promotions starting would be to COUNT the entries and GROUP BY the date, as shown in the next SQL statement.

```
select promo_begin_date, count(*)
from sh.promotions
where promo_begin_date between '01-JUN-98' and '30-JUN-98'
group by promo_begin_date
order by promo_begin_date;
```

Our results look promising, but we see no value for June 4, or 5, or 7 and other dates.

```
PROMO_BEGIN_DATE   COUNT(*)
----------------   ----------
01-JUN-98                 3
02-JUN-98                 6
03-JUN-98                 7
06-JUN-98                 1
11-JUN-98                 6
```

At this point, our recipe's use of LEFT OUTER JOIN becomes obvious. We join our inline view of all the relevant dates to the dates that are present in SH.PROMOTIONS. We then COUNT the instances of each PROMO_BEGIN_DATE, which returns the correct number where promotions started on a given date, and zero where no promotions took place.

6-6. Converting Dates and Times Between Time Zones

Problem

You need to convert date and time information stored (implicitly or explicitly) in one time zone to another time zone. For example, you'd like to convert the current date and time in your location to that of another location automatically in your code, and not need to worry about correcting for daylight savings yourself.

Solution

Use Oracle's TIMESTAMP and TIMESTAMP WITH TIME ZONE datatypes to deal with date and time information that needs to track or work with time zones. With the FROM_TZ function, you use TIMESTAMP data to have Oracle perform all the calculations around converting from one zone to another, dealing with daylight savings changes, and even dealing with historic changes to zones and their daylight savings start and end dates.

The next SQL takes a given time in Sydney, Australia and converts it to the time in Los Angeles, USA. It takes into consideration that at the time specified in the SQL, daylight savings was in force in the USA but not in Australia.

```
select
from_tz
  (cast
```

```
(to_date
  ('2009-08-14 11:25:00','YYYY-MM-DD HH:MI:SS')
  as timestamp)
, 'Australia/Sydney')
at time zone 'America/Los_Angeles' "Date and Time in LA"
from dual;

Date and Time in LA
----------------------------------------------
13-AUG-09 06.00.00.000000 PM AMERICA/LOS_ANGELES
```

If you wanted to check Oracle's calculation, you could call the "speaking clock" time service in both cities, or use a web site like www.timeanddate.com to confirm that Oracle does indeed get the calculation right.

How It Works

The recipe is built in three parts, working from the specification of the date and time in question all the way up to a TIMESTAMP WITH TIME ZONE value of our Sydney-derived time as the local Los Angeles equivalent at that moment.

We start by taking our literal representation of 11:25 in the morning of August 14, 2009 (when this recipe was written), and passing it to the TO_DATE function to create a DATE datatype value. We then cast that DATE value to a TIMESTAMP, as that is the required datatype for the final step in the chain.

With our chosen point in time converted to a TIMESTAMP, we can use the FROM_TZ function to convert the result to a TIMESTAMP WITH TIME ZONE based on the time zone we specify. In this case, we use 'Australia/Sydney' to provide the value for our recipe. At this point, we can use the AT TIME ZONE option of a TIMESTAMP WITH TIME ZONE to have Oracle perform the inter-time-zone conversion for us, to determine the moment in Los Angeles based on our Sydney time.

To take our recipe further, we can use the system value SYSTIMESTAMP to convert the current time—whatever it is—into any number of other time zones. The following SQL statement determines the time dynamically in Sydney and Los Angeles.

```
select
  systimestamp at time zone 'Australia/Sydney' "Current Time In Sydney",
  systimestamp at time zone 'America/Los_Angeles' "Current Time In Los Angeles"
from dual;

Current Time In Sydney                    Current Time In Los Angeles
------------------------------------------ -------------------------------------
14-AUG-09 10.06.39.335000 PM AUSTRALIA/SYDNEY
  14-AUG-09 05.06.39.335000 AM AMERICA/LOS_ANGELES
```

Our results have wrapped on the printed page, but the time calculation is clear. This type of dynamic calculation is usually then fed into another query or process, as while the calculation on its own is of some interest, it does turn Oracle into perhaps a very expensive world clock.

6-7. Detecting Leap Years

Problem

You need to determine if any given year is a leap year.

Solution

There are lots of shortcut techniques to finding if a year is a leap year. These include quirky calculations to determine whether February 29 exists in the year, or whether March 1 is the 61st or 62nd day of the year. The SQL we show next uses the classic (and official) definition for leap years.

```
select to_number(to_char(sysdate,'YYYY')) Year,
  case
    when mod(to_number(to_char(sysdate,'YYYY')),400) = 0 then 'Leap Year'
    when mod(to_number(to_char(sysdate,'YYYY')),100) = 0 then 'Not Leap Year'
    when mod(to_number(to_char(sysdate,'YYYY')),4) = 0 then 'Leap Year'
    else 'Not Leap Year'
  end as "Leap Year?"
from dual;
```

For the year of publication, 2009, we can see the results are as expected.

```
YEAR Leap Year?
---- -------------
2009 Not Leap Year
```

We can also use our recipe's general form to replace our year calculation with a literal year value, like 2000, to receive an accurate result.

```
select '2000' Year,
  case
    when mod(2000,400) = 0 then 'Leap Year'
    when mod(2000,100) = 0 then 'Not Leap Year'
    when mod(2000,4) = 0 then 'Leap Year'
    else 'Not Leap Year'
  end as "Leap Year?"
from dual;
```

```
YEAR Leap Year?
---- -------------
2000 Leap Year
```

How It Works

Our solution is based on the standard definition of a leap year, derived from the year number. The standard algorithm holds that if a year is divisible by four, it is a leap year. However, if the year is also divisible by 100, this overrides the divisible-by-four rule and the year it is not a leap year. Finally, if the year is also divisible by 400, then this overrides all other rules, and the year is a leap year.

Translating this to our SQL recipe, we start by echoing the current year back to the caller in the SELECT statement. This is solely to show off the workings of our recipe. In practice, you might turn our recipe components into the logic of a function, and not repeat the year at all.

We use a CASE statement to drive the main body of our leap-year detection logic. We apply the leap year algorithm in reverse within the case statement, to leverage the behavior of the CASE statement. As soon as a matching rule is found, the CASE statement will break. That means we want to evaluate the most important rule first, the one that overrides all others: is the year divisible by 400? Should that be false, we want to evaluate the next most stringent rule–division by 100–and so on.

We perform a modulus division using the MOD function. In the first instance, if the year modulus 400 has no remainder, we know it is exactly divisible by 400, and therefore is a leap year. For this case, we return the string Leap Year, and the CASE statement ends. If our year modulus 400 has a remainder, we know it's not a leap year, and move on to perform modulus division on the year by 100. If there is no remainder, we know the year is perfectly divisible by 100, and therefore isn't a leap year. We know this because we wouldn't have evaluated this part of the CASE expression if the year was also divisible by 400, as the CASE statement would already have terminated.

Similarly, if both modulus divisions have a remainder, we fall through to the third modulus division, which finds the remainder of dividing the year by four. Again, if there's no remainder, we know the prior two rules have not been matched, and therefore the year is a leap year.

At this point, our CASE statement is exhausted, and we know that the year hasn't matched any of the explicit rules for finding a leap year. We can therefore infer that the year isn't a leap year, and return Not Leap Year. We wrap up by giving the evaluated result of the CASE statement a meaningful alias, Leap Year?.

6-8. Computing the Last Date in a Month

Problem

You need to dynamically determine the last date in a given month at runtime.

Solution

Use Oracle's LAST_DAY function to automatically calculate the date for the last day of a given month. We first use LAST_DAY on the current date in the next SQL statement, to mimic how you'd approach dynamically determining the end of the current month at run time.

```
select last_day(sysdate)
from dual;

LAST_DAY
---------
31-MAY-09
```

The typical corner case that worries most developers and data users is ensuring the last day of February is calculated correctly in leap years and non-leap years. The next SQL statement shows the

LAST_DAY function correctly determining the end of February for a range of interesting leap years and non-leap years.

```
select '1900' Year,last_day('01-FEB-1900') End_Of_Feb
from dual
union
select '2000' Year,last_day('01-FEB-2000') End_Of_Feb
from dual
union
select '2010' Year,last_day('01-FEB-2010') End_Of_Feb
from dual;

YEAR END_OF_FEB
---- ---------
1900 28-FEB-00
2000 29-FEB-00
2010 28-FEB-10
```

How It Works

The LAST_DAY function is designed for exactly this calculation, freeing you from the need to do awkward arithmetic on month numbers, or use lookup tables to determine the correct values.

In our recipe, we pass the returned value of SYSDATE to the LAST_DAY function. This means we're providing a date datatype value, as if we'd run this SQL statement on its own.

```
select sysdate
from dual;

LAST_DAY
---------
21-MAY-09
```

The date value, such as 21-MAY-09, is then used by LAST_DAY to extract the month value, and internally then calculates the last day for that month based on the calendar in use. This works for all calendars supported by Oracle, including Gregorian, Royal Thai, Imperial Japanese, and so on.

The LAST_DAY function was originally designed to operate on date datatypes. You can call it using a TIMESTAMP value. In this instance, Oracle will first implicitly cast your TIMESTAMP to a DATE before performing the LAST_DAY calculation.

6-9. Determining the First Date or Day in a Month

Problem

You need to dynamically determine the first date in a given month at runtime.

Solution

Oracle's TRUNC function can be used on dates to perform start-of-period calculations, such as the first day of the month.

```
select trunc(sysdate,'mm')
from dual;

TRUNC(SYS
---------
01-MAY-09
```

Our recipe was written on May 21st. Any arbitrary date, datetime, or timestamp expression can be used.

How It Works

At first, you might be tempted to think that it's just not that hard to determine the first date of a month. It's always going to be the first! But in practice, when you're performing calculations on dates, you want to dynamically determine the full date value representing the first of the month, for the month in which you are interested.

The date-oriented version of the TRUNC function takes any date, datetime or timestamp value (implicitly converting to date before proceeding), and a date format string. The date format string is based on the same date format codes used elsewhere in Oracle, such as MM or MONTH for month, and YY or YYYY for year. Table 6-1 earlier in this chapter highlighted some common options for date format strings.

You can extend this recipe into a more generic form to find the first "date" of a dynamic week, quarter, or other time period for which Oracle has a formatting code. Simply pass the code along with a date to the TRUNC function, and it does the work for you. The next SQL takes our recipe and changes only the formatting option to Q for quarter to get the first day of the quarter.

```
select trunc(sysdate,'q')
from dual;

TRUNC(SYS
---------
01-APR-09
```

6-10. Calculating the Day of the Week

Problem

You want to determine the day of the week, and also indicate whether it's considered a work day or weekend.

Solution

Use Oracle's TO_CHAR function with a DAY format code to retrieve the textual name for the day of the week. To determine working day or weekend day, use the TO_CHAR function with the D format code to retrieve the number of the day of the week, from 1 to 7, and then apply regionally specific conventions to determine the day's status. This is an important consideration, as the working week varies widely all around the world. It could be that your code operates in Saudi Arabia, where the working days are typically Saturday to Wednesday, or various regions in China where it's common to think of the working week running Monday to Saturday.

Our recipe puts TO_CHAR into action to determine both the day name, and workday/weekend status in the next succinct SQL statement, starting with Monday to Friday as the basis for the working week.

```
select to_char(sysdate,'Day') Day_Of_Week,
  case
    when to_char(sysdate,'D') in (1,7) then 'Weekend'
    else 'Weekday'
  end Day_Type
from dual;
```

Running our recipe on a Monday returns the following results.

```
DAY_OF_WEEK DAY_TYPE
----------- --------
Monday      Weekday
```

Conversely, running our recipe on a Saturday shows this output.

```
DAY_OF_WEEK DAY_TYPE
----------- --------
Saturday    Weekend
```

How It Works

Oracle itself does almost all the heavy lifting in this recipe. We leverage the DAY format option when passing the current date returned from SYSDATE to the TO_CHAR function. This automatically returns the name of the day according to the current regional settings. We make the results a little more easily read by providing the alias DAY_OF_WEEK.

Note that the DAY formatting code works on any supplied date, not just the day given by SYSDATE or CURRENT_DATE. We can pass a literal date string that includes the day name, and have DAY extract it for us. We can also pass a calculation or expression that returns a date. This conforms to the general rule of date formatting codes we saw earlier in Table 6-1.

Determining whether the day is a working day or weekend uses a shortcut that can be tailored to suit any region around the world. We use the TO_CHAR function again on our date, but this time we use the formatting code D to return the number of the day of the week, and use this to drive a CASE statement. The D date format defaults to 1 for Sunday, 2 for Monday and so on, through to 7 for Saturday. This correlation between day number and name is dictated by your regional settings, but the logic we use can be adjusted to suit operation in whatever location you find yourself.

We look to see if the day number is in the set (1,7): that is, does the day number equal 1 or 7. The numbers 1 and 7 match Sunday and Saturday respectively.

```
when to_char(sysdate,'D') in (1,7) then 'Weekend'
```

If the day number is not 1 or 7, by implication the day would be Monday through Friday, which in much of the Western world is considered the work week. We give the result of the CASE statement a useful column alias, DAY_TYPE, to complete the logic.

■ **Tip** Where your local definition of the weekend or non-working days differs from our example, simply change the day numbers in the CASE statement to suit.

6-11. Grouping and Aggregating by Time Periods

Problem

You'd like to group date or datetime data by month or year.

Solution

Oracle's grouping functionality supports use of any deterministic function, including the TO_CHAR function for dates. We can use this to extract date information at the level of aggregation in which we're interested, and have a GROUP BY clause handle the necessary grouping.

Let's suppose we want to report how many orders our company receives by month, so we can see when the busy and slow sales periods are throughout the year, and run some promotions to boost the slow months. The next SQL statement counts the orders in the OE.ORDERS table by month.

```
select to_char(order_date, 'MM') Order_Month, count(*) Order_Count
from oe.orders
group by to_char(order_date, 'MM')
order by 1;
```

We see the fluctuations in results across the months of the year, with April being a notably poor month for orders.

```
ORDER_MONTH ORDER_COUNT
----------- -----------
         01           5
         02           9
         03          11
         04           1
         05          10
         06          14
         07          14
         08           5
         09          11
```

```
10           5
11          16
12           4
```

How It Works

Both the SELECT and GROUP BY clauses use the TO_CHAR function to target the desired month portion of the ORDER_DATE field. The MM code extracts the two-digit version of the date, which we've chosen solely so the sorting appears in chronological month order.

This grouping is used by Oracle to determine how to bundle together the different order rows—and specifically the month value calculated—for the COUNT function. This follows the rules highlighted in Chapter 2's recipes to ensure all non-aggregated values in the result are in our GROUP BY clause.

Grouping by time periods is possible on any conceivable result we can achieve using TO_CHAR or other functions on the date. We can perform date arithmetic, timestamp to date, or other datatype conversion, and more. A slight tweak to our recipe produces order counts aggregated at the year level.

```
select to_char(order_date, 'YYYY') Order_Year, count(*) Order_Count
from oe.orders
group by to_char(order_date, 'YYYY')
order by 1;

ORDER_YEAR ORDER_COUNT
---------- -----------
      1990           3
      1996           1
      1997           1
      1998          12
      1999          69
      2000          19
```

The strange gaps in those years, and the dearth of orders since the turn of the millennium relate to Oracle's sample data—any company with no orders for a decade would surely be an *ex*-company.

6-12. Finding the Difference Between Two Dates or Date Parts

Problem

You want to calculate the elapsed time between two dates or datetime values.

Solution

Oracle supports intuitive date and datetime arithmetic using normal operators like the addition and subtraction symbols. Subtracting two dates to find the difference between them works, but produces results that aren't necessarily formatted for easy understanding. For instance, we can use the next SQL statement to find the employment duration for employees in the HR.EMPLOYEES table, but then have to wrestle with part-days represented as fractional numbers.

```
select employee_id, first_name, last_name, sysdate - hire_date Length_of_employment
from hr.employees;
```

```
EMPLOYEE_ID FIRST_NAME  LAST_NAME   LENGTH_OF_EMPLOYMENT
----------- ----------  ---------   --------------------
        198 Donald      OConnell            3636.5341
        199 Douglas     Grant               3430.5341
        200 Jennifer    Whalen              7931.5341
        201 Michael     Hartstein           4856.5341
        202 Pat         Fay                 4309.5341
...
```

If you're calculating date and time differences, you usually want to be precise, down to the second or even smaller time unit. If you're calculating employee duration for a human-readable report, you probably want values in years or years and months. There's little need to be accurate to the fraction of a second in this kind of report. The next SQL statement achieves both precise seconds and human-readable years and months as output.

```
select employee_id, first_name, last_name,
  (sysdate - hire_date)*86400 Emp_Length_Seconds,
  extract(year from (sysdate - hire_date) year to month) || ' years, ' ||
  extract(month from (sysdate - hire_date) year to month) || ' months. '
  Emp_Length_Readable
from hr.employees;
```

```
EMPLOYEE_ID FIRST_NAME  LAST_NAME   EMP_LENGTH_SECONDS EMP_LENGTH_READABLE
----------- ----------  ---------   ------------------ -------------------
        198 Donald      OConnell           314198410  9 years, 11 months.
        199 Douglas     Grant              296400010  9 years,  5 months.
        200 Jennifer    Whalen             685286410  21 years,  9 months.
        201 Michael     Hartstein          419606410  13 years,  4 months.
        202 Pat         Fay                372345610  11 years, 10 months.
...
```

How It Works

It's unlikely that if asked the question, "How long have you worked here?" you'd respond "3636.5341 days". However, if you really do need that kind of value in days and fractions of days, then the default subtraction arithmetic in our recipe's first SQL statement delivers. We select the employee's ID, given name, and surname, and then perform simple date arithmetic using this equation:

```
sysdate - hire_date
```

We give this a more readable alias, LENGTH_OF_EMPLOYMENT. Oracle performs its date difference calculation internally and returns the result.

It's far more likely you'll want either a precise figure that no one will see but will be fed into subsequent processing or calculations, or a human-readable description of time elapsed between two dates. We achieve the precise calculation of number of seconds of employment by multiplying the elapsed time calculated in days by the number of seconds in a day, 86400.

```
(sysdate - hire_date)*86400
```

While we've provided a meaningful name for the results shown, EMP_LENGTH_SECONDS, in all likelihood you'd use this style of calculation unseen in other statements or PL/SQL procedures and functions.

The second calculation performed to return a more English-language style response is more elaborate and deserves a more in-depth explanation.

```
extract(year from (sysdate - hire_date) year to month) || ' years, ' ||
extract(month from (sysdate - hire_date) year to month) || ' months. '
Emp_Length_Readable
```

In this clause, we use the EXTRACT function to first glean the number of years from our base calculation, SYSDATE - HIRE DATE. We use the YEAR TO MONTH interval datatype to accurately cast our base arithmetic result into a form useful for extracting the number of years elapsed. We perform the same calculation a second time, but in the second instance we use EXTRACT to find the remaining month portion of the interval elapsed between the two dates. Finally, we concatenate the calculated year and month intervals with the words "years" and "months" using the || concatenation operator, and give the whole result a meaningful alias, EMP_LENGTH_READABLE.

6-13. Determining the Dates of Easter for Any Year

Problem

You would like to dynamically determine the dates of Easter for a given year.

Solution

Oracle doesn't provide a single, elegant function to perform Easter calculations for you. But Oracle does have robust date arithmetic functions that we can use to build our own Easter calculator. This begs the question, how do we decide the dates of Easter anyway?

For Easter under the Gregorian calendar, Easter Sunday is the Sunday following the first full moon after Lent. Contemporary algorithms translate this to the first Sunday after the first full moon on or after March 21.

The next function returns the date of Easter Sunday for a specified year.

```
create or replace function easter_sunday(given_year number) return date
as
  golden_metonic number;
  century number;
  leap_year_fix number;
  lunar_sync number;
  sunday_date number;
  epact number;
```

```
  day_of_month number;
  easter_offset number;
begin
  golden_metonic := mod(given_year,19) + 1;
  century := (given_year / 100) + 1;
  leap_year_fix := (3 * century / 4) - 12;
  lunar_sync := ((8 * century + 5)/25) - 5;
  sunday_date := (5 * given_year / 4) - leap_year_fix - 3;
  epact := mod((11 * golden_metonic + 20 + lunar_sync - leap_year_fix),30);
  if((epact = 25 and golden_metonic < 11) or (epact = 24)) then
    epact := epact + 1;
  end if;
  day_of_month := 44 - epact;
  if(day_of_month < 21) then
    day_of_month := day_of_month + 30;
  end if;
  easter_offset := (day_of_month + 7 - mod((sunday_date + day_of_month),7)) - 1;
  return to_date('01-MAR-' || to_char(given_year),'DD-MON-YYYY') + easter_offset;
end;
/
```

We could have coded this in pure SQL as one rather large nested set of IF and CASE statements, but this function is both easier to read and easier to use in practice. We can now find Easter for any given year, such as 2000 shown in the next SQL statement.

```
select easter_sunday(2000)
from dual;
```

```
EASTER_SUNDAY
-------------
   23-APR-00
```

We can also dynamically determine Easter Sunday for the current year without needing to explicitly state the year. The next SQL statement illustrates this in action.

```
select easter_sunday(extract(year from (sysdate)))
from dual;
```

```
EASTER_SUNDAY
-------------
   12-APR-09
```

How It Works

Rather than work from the notion of the first Sunday after the full moon following March 21 to derive an algorithm from first principles, we'll turn to the doyen of computer algorithms, Donald Knuth. Knuth provides an excellent algorithm in *The Art Of Computer Programming, Volume 1* (Addison-Wesley) to determine the Sunday of Easter.

Knuth's algorithm takes a year, and calculates a golden "metonic" cycle, the century, leap year offset, lunar synchronization, and an "epact" value to then return the number of days after March 1 for

Easter Sunday. All other days of Easter can then be derived from this. In fact, other dates such as Ash Wednesday, Palm Sunday, and more can then be calculated by fixed offsets.

There are two caveats to using this implementation to find Easter. First, as mentioned, it only deals with the Gregorian calendar. This means that it's not accurate for finding the Orthodox Easter. Secondly, for the same reason, we can't reliably predict Easter for years prior to the adoption of the first adoption of Gregorian calendar in 1582.

6-14. Calculating "X Day Active" Users for a Web Site

Problem

You want to track how many unique web site visitors or customers you've had in the last seven days.

Solution

Oracle's date arithmetic together with the DISTINCT operator for dealing with duplicates are the perfect tools for tracking details like seven-day or one-month active users. In fact, any duration window can be tracked. The main consideration is adapting the technique to the way the visitor or customer data is collected and stored.

For our recipe, we'll use the sales history data collected in the SH.SALES table. This tracks simple data like customer ID, the date and time a purchase was made, and the sales channel used. This mimics what many web sites collect for their shopping cart data. Where you wish to track simple visitors, this kind of data is analogous to a web server log that tracks visitor IP address, page requested, and date and time of request.

Use this SQL statement to show customers making a purchase in the seven days up to December 31, 2001.

```
select count(distinct cust_id) Seven_Day_Customers
from sh.sales
where time_id > to_date('31-DEC-2001') - 7;
```

Our results indicate the number of unique customers who have placed orders in the last seven days.

```
SEVEN_DAY_CUSTOMERS
-------------------
                455
```

How It Works

Oracle supports the COUNT(DISTINCT …) aggregate function to enable you to count distinct rows with data. We use this in our SELECT clause to count our unique customers. The sole criterion in the WHERE clause acts to control our time window. Our use of TIME_ID > TO_DATE('31-DEC-2001') - 7 is a shorthand way of writing this criterion.

```
where time_id between to_date('24-DEC-2001') and to_date('31-DEC-2001')
```

This saves us from having to write a nested subquery to first find the unique values, and then an outer query to count those unique values. That's still perfectly legal SQL, and we could write our recipe to use the nested subquery if required, as shown in the next SQL statement.

```
select count(*) Seven_Day_Customers
from
  (select distinct cust_id
   from sh.sales
   where time_id > to_date('31-DEC-2001') - 7
  );
```

If we had simply counted all the customer IDs noted in the seven-day range, we would have included repeat purchases by the same client, which is not what our problem statement set out to find.

```
select count(cust_id) Seven_Day_Sales
from sh.sales
where time_id > to_date('31-DEC-2001') - 7;

SEVEN_DAY_SALES
---------------
           4807
```

It is good to know we made 4807 sales in that week, but we're missing the vital detail of how many unique clients bought our products.

A more general form of the recipe to find unique seven-day customers would target the most recent data, based on using the current date returned from SYSDATE or CURRENT_DATE. The next statement shows this general form.

```
select count(distinct cust_id) Seven_Day_Customers
from sh.sales
where time_id between sysdate and sysdate - 7;
```

Note that if you run this against the SH.SALES table in the Oracle example SH schema, you won't see any data returned, as there are no sales after 2001 in that table. However, the applicability remains.

■ **Caution** Because we are using the COUNT(DISTINCT …) form of the COUNT aggregate, we do *not* count NULL values encountered in the CUST_ID field. This is a moot point in this instance, as there are no such NULL values in the SH.SALES table for CUST_ID. However, it is important to remember that only the COUNT(*) form of the COUNT function observes NULL values. All other types of COUNT ignore NULL values.

CHAPTER 7

■ ■ ■

Strings

Most likely, at least some of your database tables have some kind of string columns, whether they are CHAR, VARCHAR2, CLOB, or one of the equivalent multibyte versions. Once you have these columns in your tables, you generally have to do more than just display or capture the values in those columns. Thus, the focus of the recipes in this chapter is on searching, concatenating, and splitting string values in database columns.

Oracle has many built-in functions to search and manipulate strings. The INSTR function searches for a specified string within a second string. You can start the search anywhere within the second string, and you can also search for a specific occurrence of the first string as well.

To perform one-to-one substitutions of characters in a string, you can use the TRANSLATE function. The REPLACE function extends the functionality of TRANSLATE to find one or more occurrences of a specified string and replace them with a second string.

To make string manipulation, searching, and extraction even easier for developers who typically use regular expressions in the Unix environment, Oracle provides the REGEXP_REPLACE, REGEXP_SUBSTR, and REGEXP_INSTR functions. They operate the same as the REPLACE, SUBSTR, and INSTR functions except that they allow you to specify the search or replacement pattern as a regular expression.

We'll cover all of these functions in the following recipes. However, no chapter on Oracle string usage would be complete without some tips on how to efficiently find the strings you're looking for across all rows in the table, not just within a column of a single row. Therefore, we'll provide a recipe to help speed up your queries that search for rows containing a string expression or use strings in your join conditions.

7-1. Searching for a Substring

Problem

You want to search a string in a VARCHAR2 or CLOB database table column for one or more occurrences of a specified string.

Solution

Use the INSTR function to find the specified string within the table column. Using INSTR, you can optionally specify a different starting place in the target string, as well as find the second, third, or any occurrence of the search string.

The INSTR function returns the position in the string where the search string starts, otherwise it returns 0. If you want to search for a string represented by a pattern (in other words, a regular expression), you can use REGEXP_INSTR instead.

In this example, you want to search the EMPLOYEES table for any last names containing the string ll (two lowercase "l" characters) after the third position in the string. Here is the solution using INSTR with the position parameter:

```
select employee_id, last_name, first_name
from employees
where instr(last_name,'ll',4) > 0
;
```

```
EMPLOYEE_ID             LAST_NAME                FIRST_NAME
--------------------    ------------------------  --------------------
106                     Pataballa                Valli
145                     Russell                  John
161                     Sewall                   Sarath
198                     OConnell                 Donald

4 rows selected
```

How It Works

For each row in the table, the INSTR function checks for the first occurrence of the string ll starting at the fourth position in the LAST_NAME column. If the return value from INSTR returns 0, then the string ll was not found starting at the fourth position in LAST_NAME.

Oracle typically gives you many ways to solve a problem, and string searching and extraction is no exception. This recipe's problem can also be solved using the LIKE clause as follows:

```
select employee_id, last_name, first_name
from employees
where last_name like '___%ll%'  -- three underscores
;
```

The LIKE clause is a *very* limited implementation of pattern matching. LIKE supports pattern matching with two characters: % and _. The % character represents zero or more characters, and _ represents exactly one character. This solution would return too many results if you left out the underscore characters; in that case, the LIKE clause would return all last names with ll anywhere in the string.

If you wanted to return only employees whose last name ends with ll, you can leave off the last % in the LIKE clause:

```
select employee_id, last_name, first_name
from employees
where last_name like '___%ll'  -- three underscores
;
```

```
EMPLOYEE_ID           LAST_NAME                    FIRST_NAME
--------------------  ---------------------------  --------------------
145                   Russell                      John
161                   Sewall                       Sarath
198                   OConnell                     Donald

3 rows selected
```

■ **Tip** If you want to search for the characters % or _ within a string, you can add the ESCAPE keyword, specifying a character that will interpret the next character in the search string literally. For example, if you want to search for underscores in a column, you could use this syntax:

```
select * from products where product_name like '%\_%' escape '\';
```

If you want to also search for the escape character itself, you specify it twice in the search string, or switch escape characters!

Since you can use both INSTR and LIKE to produce identical results in many cases, which should you use? It depends. From a coding-style standpoint, LIKE can be more readable, and may even use an index if there are no pattern-matching characters at the beginning of the search string. INSTR will never use an existing index unless you have created a function-based index containing the exact INSTR clause that you use in the WHERE clause. (We'll cover function-based indexes in another recipe).

The NOT prefix reverses the logic of the LIKE clause, finding a match if the search string is *not* in the target string. If you wanted to list all employees who do not have ll in their last names starting with the fourth character in the string, you can simply prefix the LIKE clause with NOT, as in this example:

```
select employee_id, last_name, first_name
from employees
where last_name not like '___%ll%'  -- three underscores
;
```

Using INSTR is a better choice than LIKE if you want to use substitution variables at runtime to specify the starting position of the search as well as the occurrence number, as in this example:

```
select employee_id, last_name, first_name
from employees
where instr(last_name,'&srch_str',&start_pos,&occ_num) > 0
;
```

In a few cases, you can do things in INSTR that you can't do in the LIKE clause. For example, you can specify a negative number for the last parameter of the INSTR function to search for the occurrence number starting from the end of the string instead of from the beginning.

If you can't construct a search query using either INSTR or LIKE, you'll almost certainly be able to perform the search using REGEXP_INSTR, which we will cover in another recipe in this chapter. A good rule of thumb is to use INSTR or LIKE when the pattern is simple, and REGEXP_INSTR when the complexity can be encapsulated into a single REGEXP_INSTR call instead of multiple INSTR and SUBSTR calls.

7-2. Extracting a Substring

Problem

You need to split up string values into two or more pieces or extract only the relevant portions of a string column. For example, you want to split up a database column that has two attributes into two separate columns to further normalize the design of the table.

Solution

Use the SUBSTR function to extract a substring from a string. The SUBSTR function has three arguments: the source string, the position in the string to start the extraction, and an optional length component.

For this solution, we'll use the tables included in the EXAMPLE schema, which can be installed when you install the Oracle database software (if not, you can install with the scripts in the $ORACLE_HOME/demo/schema directory). The EMPLOYEES table in the Oracle sample database has a column called JOB_ID in this format:

dd_jjjjjjjjjj

The dd portion of the JOB_ID column is an alphanumeric representation of the department, and jjjjjjjjjj is the job title. This SQL statement uses the SUBSTR function to separate the department identifier from the job title:

```
select employee_id, last_name, job_id,
    substr(job_id,1,2) dept_code,
    substr(job_id,4) job_code
from employees
;
```

EMPLOYEE_ID	LAST_NAME	JOB_ID	DEPT_CODE	JOB_CODE
100	King	AD_PRES	AD	PRES
101	Kochhar	AD_VP	AD	VP
102	De Haan	AD_VP	AD	VP
103	Hunold	IT_PROG	IT	PROG
104	Ernst	IT_PROG	IT	PROG
. . .				
204	Baer	PR_REP	PR	REP
205	Higgins	AC_MGR	AC	MGR
206	Gietz	AC_ACCOUNT	AC	ACCOUNT

107 rows selected

How It Works

In the solution we use the SUBSTR function twice: once with an explicit length and the second time with only the starting position. As a result, the second SUBSTR will start extracting at the third position in the string and return the remaining portion of the string regardless of length.

The SUBSTR function is even more useful in conjunction with other functions, such as INSTR. In the solution for this recipe, you assume that the underscore character is always the third character in the JOB_ID column. If future assignments of the JOB_ID value include a department code that is three characters instead of two, the solution will not return the desired results.

To allow for a department code of any length, you can use the INSTR function to search for the underscore and use the results to determine where in the source string the job code starts, as well as how long the department code is. Here is the revised solution for future expansion of the department code:

```
select employee_id, last_name, job_id,
   substr(job_id,1,instr(job_id,'_')-1) dept_code,
   substr(job_id,instr(job_id,'_')+1) job_code
from employees
;
```

EMPLOYEE_ID	LAST_NAME	JOB_ID	DEPT_CODE	JOB_CODE
100	King	AD_PRES	AD	PRES
101	Kochhar	AD_VP	AD	VP
102	De Haan	AD_VP	AD	VP
103	Hunold	IT_PROG	IT	PROG
104	Ernst	IT_PROG	IT	PROG
. . .				
204	Baer	PR_REP	PR	REP
205	Higgins	AC_MGR	AC	MGR
206	Gietz	AC_ACCOUNT	AC	ACCOUNT

```
107 rows selected
```

Not surprisingly, this query returns the same results as the original solution, but it helps to future-proof the query in case changes are made to the format of the column. The first SUBSTR stops extracting right before the first underscore character in the string, and the second SUBSTR starts extracting the remainder of the string right after the first underscore.

This solution is fairly robust. If there is no underscore in the source string, the first SUBSTR returns NULL and the second SUBSTR returns the entire string. The assumption therefore is that any JOB_ID without an underscore does not include a department code.

In another recipe, you will see how REGEXP_SUBSTR expands the functionality of SUBSTR by allowing you to specify a pattern instead of a starting position to extract the desired string. In other words, you can extract a substring of the source string that matches the pattern without knowing where in the source string the desired substring begins.

7-3. Single-Character String Substitutions

Problem

You want to perform single-character substitutions in string columns. The characters to be substituted can be anywhere in the string, and all other characters not in the substitution list are left as is.

Solution

You can use the built-in TRANSLATE function to perform one-to-one character substitutions within a string. In the HR sample schema, the data-entry person accidentally entered brackets "[]" instead of parentheses "()" and underscores "_" instead of hyphens "-" in some of the street addresses. Here are some rows with incorrect values:

```
select location_id, street_address
from locations
where location_id in (2100,2900)
;

LOCATION_ID            STREET_ADDRESS
---------------------- ----------------------------------------
2100                   1298 Vileparle [E]
2900                   20 Rue des Corps_Saints

2 rows selected
```

To make all substitutions in one pass, you can use the TRANSLATE function, specifying the source string to be translated, the list of characters that need to be translated, and the list of corresponding characters that will replace those characters to be translated. Here is the UPDATE statement you can use to fix the STREET_ADDRESS column in the LOCATIONS table:

```
update locations
    set street_address = translate(street_address,'[]_','()-')
where location_id in (2100,2900)
;

2 rows updated
```

How It Works

The TRANSLATE function checks each character in the source string (in this case, STREET_ADDRESS). For each individual character in the source string, TRANSLATE checks for one of the characters in the second argument; if there is a match, the character is replaced with the corresponding character in the third argument. Thus, "[" is replaced by "(", "]" is replaced by ")", and "_" is replaced by a "-". Any characters in the source string that are not found in the second argument are not replaced.

You can also use TRANSLATE to completely remove characters in the source string. To do this, you specify a single character that will *not* be translated plus the characters to be removed in the second argument, and specify only the single character not to be translated in the third argument. This is best explained by an example. In this UPDATE statement, you want to remove all bracket characters from the source string:

```
update locations
    set street_address = translate(street_address,'X[]','X')
where location_id in (2100,2900)
;
```

2 rows updated

All occurrences of the letter "X" are replaced with an "X", and the bracket characters are removed and not replaced. You must specify at least one character to be replaced because if any argument of TRANSLATE is NULL, then the result is NULL, and that is certainly not the desired result!

Of course, if you want to both replace and remove characters in the source string, you do not need to specify any extra characters. Therefore, if you want to replace the underscore character with a hyphen and remove the brackets completely, the UPDATE statement would look like this:

```
update locations
    set street_address = translate(street_address,'_[]','-')
where location_id in (2100,2900)
;
```

2 rows updated

You must typically use a WHERE clause when you perform conditional updates to columns containing character strings, unless the table is very small. Without the WHERE clause, you will create a lot of unnecessary undo since all rows in a table will be updated. In addition, you may create performance problems and cause unnecessary delays for other sessions that want to update rows that your UPDATE statement does not really need to update.

Finally, you may have a scenario where you do not know which rows need to be updated. In the previous examples, we knew that rows with a LOCATION_ID of 2100 and 2900 needed updating. But what if you know there are more than a few incorrect values for STREET_ADDRESS, but don't know what the values are for LOCATION_ID? In this situation, you can change the WHERE clause to check for the same characters that you're substituting with the TRANSLATE statement, as in this example:

```
update locations
    set street_address = translate(street_address,'[]_','()-')
where instr(street_address,'[') > 0
   or instr(street_address,']') > 0
   or instr(street_address,'_') > 0
;
```

As you will find out in one of the recipes later in this chapter, you can simplify this code even further by using REGEXP_INSTR, the regular expression equivalent of INSTR, in the WHERE clause, as in this example:

```
update locations
    set street_address = translate(street_address,'[]_','()-')
where regexp_instr(street_address,'\[|\]|_') > 0
;
```

The REGEXP_INSTR method is generally preferred when the number of characters to be replaced is large; otherwise, the number of INSTR function calls in your WHERE clause makes the code a bit harder to maintain compared to the REGEXP_INSTR method. However, as is apparent from this example, the syntax for an argument to a regular expression function can become cryptic, especially if you have to use the "\" character to specify a character that otherwise has special meaning within a regular expression function.

7-4. Searching for a Pattern

Problem

Some of the strings you want to search can't be searched using constants; your search criteria include anchoring your search at the beginning or end of a line, ignoring whitespace characters, matching an exact number of appearances of a character or string, or specifying a range of characters in a character list.

Solution

Although INSTR may satisfy some of the requirements in the problem statement, REGEXP_INSTR provides the most flexibility for your string searches. In this example, you want to find all employees in the EMPLOYEES table whose last name satisfies these criteria:

- Begins with the characters A, B, C, or D

- Contains at least two non-consecutive lowercase "a" characters

- Can contain embedded spaces

- Ends in the "t" character

Here is a list of the first 25 names, alphabetically, in the EMPLOYEES table:

```
select employee_id, last_name, first_name from employees order by last_name;
```

EMPLOYEE_ID	LAST_NAME	FIRST_NAME
174	Abel	Ellen
166	Ande	Sundar
130	Atkinson	Mozhe
105	Austin	David
204	Baer	Hermann
116	Baida	Shelli
167	Banda	Amit
172	Bates	Elizabeth
192	Bell	Sarah
151	Bernstein	David
129	Bissot	Laura
169	Bloom	Harrison
185	Bull	Alexis

187	Cabrio	Anthony
154	Cambrault	Nanette
148	Cambrault	Gerald
110	Chen	John
188	Chung	Kelly
119	Colmenares	Karen
142	Davies	Curtis
102	De Haan	Lex
186	Dellinger	Julia
189	Dilly	Jennifer
160	Doran	Louise
104	Ernst	Bruce
147	Errazuriz	Alberto
. . .		

To satisfy the requirements of the solution, you can use this query:

```
select employee_id, last_name, first_name
from employees
where regexp_instr(last_name,'^[A-D][[:alpha:] ]*a[^a]+a[[:alpha:] ]*t$') > 0
order by last_name, first_name
;
```

```
EMPLOYEE_ID          LAST_NAME            FIRST_NAME
-----------------    -----------------    ------------------
148                  Cambrault            Gerald
154                  Cambrault            Nanette
```

```
2 rows selected
```

Although REGEXP_INSTR can perform all tasks that INSTR can, you can still use INSTR if your search does not require pattern matching and you want to make your code more readable. INSTR will also perform a slight bit more efficiently than REGEXP_INSTR, but the performance benefits should be considered only in the most computation-intensive applications where string manipulation is the primary function of the application.

How It Works

Understanding regular expressions may seem daunting at first, until you break the regular expressions down into their individual components. Regular expressions (also known as *patterns*) are the mainstay of the Unix or Linux command line when you use the egrep command or write a PERL script. They consist of two types of characters: regular characters and special *metacharacters*. One or more regular characters match those same characters in the strings to be searched. For example, cat matches the string cat or caterer or scat. Extra characters in the target string don't really matter. As long as the target string (such as "caterer") contains the pattern (for example, "cat"), the result will be a match.

The most common regular expressions you will see include the metacharacters in Table 7-1. For example, ca?t matches cat or cart, cat|dog matches either cat or dog in the string, and d[oi]g matches dog or dig.

Table 7-1. *Regular Expression Metacharacters*

Metacharacter	Operator Name	Description
. (Dot)	Any Character	Matches any character in the database character set.
+	One or More	Matches one or more occurrences of the previous character or subexpression.
?	Zero or One	Matches zero or one occurrence of the previous character or subexpression.
*	Zero or More	Matches zero or more occurrences of the preceding subexpression.
{m}	Exact Count	Matches exactly *m* occurrences of the preceding subexpression.
{m,}	At Least Count	Matches at least *m* occurrences of the preceding subexpression.
{m,n}	Interval Count	Matches at least *m* but not more than *n* occurrences of the preceding subexpression.
[...]	Matching Character	Matches any single character, with dash (-) as the range operator.
[^...]	Nonmatching Character	Matches any single character not in the list, with dash (-) as the range operator.
|	Or	Matches one of the alternatives.
\	Escape	Treats specified character as a literal instead of a metacharacter.
^	Beginning of Line Anchor	Matches the beginning of the string.
$	End of Line Anchor	Matches the end of the string.

If you want to include one of the special characters in your pattern, you can *escape* it by preceding it with a backslash (\). To match a backslash character, you can specify it twice (\\). Adding a backslash to a character that would otherwise not need escaping provides an alternate meaning in regular expression evaluation. For example, \d matches a digit character and \D matches a non-digit character.

Oracle's regular expression support in string functions fully complies with the IEEE Portable Operating System Interface (POSIX) standard, and Oracle extends this support for multilingual data beyond the POSIX standard. Oracle also supports PERL regular expression extensions that do not conflict with the POSIX standard, such as \s for a whitespace character or ?? to match the preceding pattern 0 or 1 time.

Let's break down the regular expression in this recipe piece by piece. An exhaustive review of regular expressions is beyond the scope of this book, but we will be using them in other examples, so it's useful to understand just what the regular expression is doing:

- ^: Start the pattern match at the beginning of the target string.

- [A-D]: Match any single character in the range A-D.

- [[:alpha:]]*: Match zero or more alphabetic characters or spaces.

- a[^a]+a: Match a single "a" character, one or more characters that is not "a", then another "a" character.

- [[:alpha:]]*: Match zero or more alphabetic characters or spaces.

- t: Match a single "t" character.

- $: Finish the pattern match at the end of the target string.

If we did not include the ^ at the beginning of the pattern, you could not guarantee that the first character in the range A-D would be found at the beginning of the string. Similarly, using $ at the end of the pattern right after the "t" ensures that there is a "t" at the end of the string you are searching.

Matching for A-D as the first character eliminates all last names after Doran in the list. Matching two "a" characters with at least one non-"a" character in between eliminates all but Baida, Banda, and the two Cambrault employees. Anchoring the pattern with a "t" at the end eliminates Baida and Banda, leaving us with the two Cambrault employees.

There are five additional parameters for REGEXP_INSTR after the required source string and pattern parameters, all optional:

- **position**: Where to begin the search in the target string (default 1).

- **occurrence**: Which occurrence of the pattern to find in the target string (default is first occurrence).

- **return_option**: 0 = return position of first character in the pattern occurrence (default); 1 = return the position of the first character after the pattern occurrence.

- **match_parameter**: Change the default matching behavior.

- **subexpression**: Specify which subexpression to use when the pattern contains a subexpression.

The match_parameter parameter can be one or more of the following characters:

- i: case-insensitive match

- c: case-sensitive match (the default unless it is overridden by the NLS_SORT initialization parameter)

- n: allow a period "." to match the newline character

- m: treat the target string as multiple lines

- x: ignore whitespace characters, such as a space or tab character

---

■ **Note** You can specify contradictory values in **match_parameter**, but Oracle ignores all conflicting values except for the last one. For example, if you specify both i and c, Oracle considers only the one that comes last.

You want to search for all last names with at least two "s" characters that don't follow a "u" character, and you also want to know the position of the second occurrence of the pattern in the target string, so your SELECT statement would look like this:

```
select employee_id, last_name, first_name,
    regexp_instr(last_name,'[^u]?s',1,2,0,'i') next_char
from employees
where regexp_instr(last_name,'[^u]?s',1,2,0,'i') > 0
order by last_name, first_name
;
```

```
EMPLOYEE_ID   LAST_NAME                 FIRST_NAME             NEXT_CHAR
-------------  ------------------------  --------------------  --------------
129           Bissot                    Laura                 4
138           Stiles                    Stephen               6
120           Weiss                     Matthew               5
```

3 rows selected

The search pattern matches any character except for a "u" followed by a single "s". To match successive "s" characters or an "s" at the beginning of the string, you put a ? after the [^u] to specify zero or one occurrences. The search begins at the first character in the target string, and you're looking for the second occurrence of the search pattern. The function will return the position of the second occurrence of the pattern in the target string. The "i" specifies that the search will be case-insensitive, and thus returns the last name "Stiles". Note that a last name of "Russell" would not be returned because there is a "u" before one of the occurrences of "s."

7-5. Extracting a Pattern

Problem

The SUBSTR function is limited to a starting position and length, and you want instead to extract a substring based on a pattern.

Solution

You can use the REGEXP_SUBSTR function to extract a substring of the target string based on a regular expression. You can optionally specify a starting position for the search, along with many other options found in other built-in functions that manipulate regular expressions such as REGEXP_INSTR.

If you wanted to search for two-part last names (in other words, an embedded space within the last name) that end with the character "n," for example, here's the SELECT statement you'd use:

```
select employee_id, last_name, first_name,
   regexp_substr(last_name,' [a-zA-Z]+n$') second_part
from employees
where regexp_substr(last_name,' [a-zA-Z]+n$') is not null
order by last_name, first_name
;
```

```
EMPLOYEE_ID          LAST_NAME          FIRST_NAME          SECOND_PART
------------         --------------     --------------      ---------------
102                  De Haan            Lex                 Haan
```

For last names that do not have an embedded space and end with an "n," and thus don't match the regular expression, REGEXP_SUBSTR returns NULL. The solution uses the NULL value to filter the results in the WHERE clause.

How It Works

The REGEXP_SUBSTR function has very little in common with the SUBSTR function, other than specifying the string to be searched and a starting position for the search. In fact, REGEXP_SUBSTR has much more in common with REGEXP_INSTR: it has the same arguments, except that REGEXP_INSTR returns the position of the substring that matches the pattern, and REGEXP_SUBSTR returns the substring itself. (The only other difference is that the number REGEXP_INSTR returns can be either the first character of the substring or the first character after the substring). Another recipe in this chapter exercises many of the arguments of REGEXP_INSTR.

The solution could be rewritten using a combination of INSTR and SUBSTR as follows:

```
select employee_id, last_name, first_name,
   substr(last_name,instr(last_name,' ')) second_part
from employees
where instr(last_name,' ') > 0 and substr(last_name,-1,1)  = 'n'
order by last_name, first_name
;
```

It's a slightly less elegant and arguably a less readable alternative to using REGEXP_SUBSTR in this situation. Moreover, other more complex patterns would be difficult or impossible using INSTR and SUBSTR.

7-6. Counting Patterns

Problem

You want to count how many times a pattern defined by a regular expression occurs in a string.

Solution

The built-in function REGEXP_COUNT counts the number of times a pattern occurs in a specified target string. REGEXP_INSTR will tell you whether the pattern occurs 1 or more times, but if you need to know exactly how many times the pattern occurs, use REGEXP_COUNT.

In this example, you want to find out how many street addresses are more than three words. The sample tables included in the HR schema include the LOCATIONS table:

```
select location_id, street_address,
   city, postal_code
from locations;
```

LOCATION_ID	STREET_ADDRESS	CITY	POSTAL_CODE
1000	1297 Via Cola di Rie	Roma	00989
1100	93091 Calle della Testa	Venice	10934
1200	2017 Shinjuku-ku	Tokyo	1689
1300	9450 Kamiya-cho	Hiroshima	6823
1400	2014 Jabberwocky Rd	Southlake	26192
1500	2011 Interiors Blvd	South San Francisco	99236
1600	2007 Zagora St	South Brunswick	50090
1700	2004 Charade Rd	Seattle	98199
1800	147 Spadina Ave	Toronto	M5V 2L7
1900	6092 Boxwood St	Whitehorse	YSW 9T2
2000	40-5-12 Laogianggen	Beijing	190518
2100	1298 Vileparle (E)	Bombay	490231
2200	12-98 Victoria Street	Sydney	2901
2300	198 Clementi North	Singapore	540198
2400	8204 Arthur St	London	
2500	Magdalen Centre, The Oxford Science Park	Oxford	OX9 9ZB
2600	9702 Chester Road	Stretford	09629850293
2700	Schwanthalerstr. 7031	Munich	80925
2800	Rua Frei Caneca 1360	Sao Paulo	01307-002
2900	20 Rue des Corps-Saints	Geneva	1730
3000	Murtenstrasse 921	Bern	3095
3100	Pieter Breughelstraat 837	Utrecht	3029SK
3200	Mariano Escobedo 9991	Mexico City	11932

23 rows selected

To find out which street addresses are more than three words, use the following:

```
select location_id, street_address,
   city, postal_code
from locations
where regexp_count(street_address,'\s') >= 3
;
```

LOCATION_ID	STREET_ADDRESS	CITY	POSTAL_CODE
1000	1297 Via Cola di Rie	Roma	00989
1100	93091 Calle della Testa	Venice	10934
2500	Magdalen Centre, The Oxford Science Park	Oxford	OX9 9ZB
2800	Rua Frei Caneca 1360	Sao Paulo	01307-002
2900	20 Rue des Corps-Saints	Geneva	1730

5 rows selected

The pattern \s matches a whitespace character (a space, tab, or line break, for example) in the target string. Thus, no matches on \s means that the address is one word, one match means the address is two words, and so forth.

How It Works

In cases where you only want to find out if a string matches a pattern, REGEXP_INSTR or even INSTR works fine. You can even find the *n*th occurrence of the string. But before you extract the *n*th occurrence, you often want to know what *n* is! Once you know the count, it makes your looping constructs in PL/SQL or another language a bit simpler. It's also another way to filter the rows in the table: for example, only include rows where the count exceeds a threshold, as in the solution.

■ **Note** There is no equivalent single built-in Oracle function to REGEXP_COUNT that returns the count of a string constant (instead of a pattern) within a target string.

REGEXP_COUNT includes two additional parameters you will see in other Oracle functions that find patterns: one for changing the starting position of the search in the target string and one for changing the matching behavior. For example, you may want your search to start in the fifth position of the target string and perform a case-insensitive match:

```
select location_id, street_address, city
from locations
where regexp_count(street_address,'east [0-9]*',5,'i') > 0
;
```

Regardless of where you start the search in the target string, REGEXP_COUNT starts looking for successive matches at the first character after the end of the previous match.

7-7. Replacing Text in a String

Problem

You need to perform basic address standardization by converting all variations of "Road" to the string "RD" at the end of the string.

Solution

To update substrings within several database columns using a regular expression, you can use the REPLACE function; however REPLACE may be not be suitable or practical for some substring substitutions, such as scenarios where using REPLACE will be tedious, error-prone, or even impossible without using a programming language. Thus, you can use the REGEXP_REPLACE built-in function to extend the functionality of REPLACE to specify a regular expression instead of a constant as the string to replace. This example performs basic address standardization by converting all variations of "Road" to "RD" at the end of the string:

```
update locations
set street_address =
   regexp_replace(street_address,'\s(road|rd|roade)$',' RD',1,0,'i')
where regexp_instr(street_address,'\s(road|rd|roade)$',1,1,0,'i') > 0
;
```

3 rows updated

If you query the table after performing the update, you can see the translated street addresses (including street addresses that already include "RD" in the street address):

```
select location_id, street_address
from locations
where instr(street_address,'RD') > 0
;
```

```
LOCATION_ID            STREET_ADDRESS
---------------------  ----------------------------------------
1400                   2014 Jabberwocky RD
1700                   2004 Charade RD
2600                   9702 Chester RD
```

3 rows selected

The REGEXP_REPLACE starts searching at the first character in the string and replaces all occurrences of any of the strings within the pattern. REGEXP_REPLACE ignores case when performing the substitutions.

Note that you must include the whitespace character \s in the regular expression to make sure you do not match words like "Oxford" or "Broad" or any word ending with one of the options within the regular expression at the end of the street address.

How It Works

The solution uses REGEXP_REPLACE and REGEXP_INSTR to perform the task. To further simplify the task, you could simplify the UPDATE statement to this:

```
update locations
set street_address =
   regexp_replace(street_address,'\s(road|rd|roade)$',' RD',1,0,'i')
;
```

However, there is a significant downside to this UPDATE statement. Regardless of whether there is a match, *every* row will have its STREET_ADDRESS column updated. This will introduce unnecessary row locking on the table, as well as excessive use of the redo log files where it is not necessary. Unless you expect to update all rows in the table, use the WHERE clause. The slight additional CPU cost of running both REGEXP_REPLACE and REGEXP_INSTR for rows that match the WHERE clause is a much better alternative than reducing table availability or unnecessarily using redo and undo space.

You can specify that REGEXP_REPLACE start in a specific position within the target string, match only the nth occurrence, or change matching behavior such as case sensitivity; the solution mapped all variations of "road" using case-insensitivity. These capabilities are common among all of the Oracle REGEXP_ functions. Here is the list of parameters for REGEXP_REPLACE:

- **source_string**: the column or string to be updated.

- **pattern**: the regular expression used to search for the pattern to be replaced one or more times within the source_string.

- **replacement_string**: the string substituted for each occurrence of the substring matched by the pattern.

- **position**: where to begin the search in the target string (default 1).

- **occurrence**: which occurrence of the pattern to find in the target string (defaults to first occurrence).

- **match_parameter**: change the default matching behavior.

All parameters after **pattern** are optional, but you must specify values for the intermediate parameters if you use parameters such as match_parameter, for example. The options for match_parameter are the same as for REGEXP_INSTR and REGEXP_COUNT.

For example, you may only want to change the second occurrence of the pattern in the regular expression, regardless of its position within the string (the recipe solution anchored the search to the occurrence at the end of the string). The UPDATE statement would instead look like this:

```
update locations
set street_address =
   regexp_replace(street_address,'\s(road|rd|roade)',' RD',1,2,'i')
where regexp_instr(street_address,'\s(road|rd|roade)',1,2,1,'i') > 0
;
```

Taking this solution one step further, what if you want to perform a substitution for the *last* occurrence of the regular expression? Use REGEXP_COUNT (see the recipe for REGEXP_COUNT earlier in this chapter) to find the number of occurrences, then use the result of that function to substitute the last occurrence. In this variation, you want to substitute "S" for all occurrences of "South" or "So" anywhere except the beginning or end of the string:

```
update locations
set street_address =
    regexp_replace(street_address,'\s(south|so)\s',' S',1,
      regexp_count(street_address,'\s(south|so)\s',1,'i'),'i')
where regexp_count(street_address,'\s(south|so)\s',1,'i') > 0
;
```

This UPDATE statement only updates rows that have at least one occurrence of the pattern, but uses REGEXP_COUNT in the WHERE clause to determine the number of occurrences instead of using REGEXP_INSTR.

7-8. Speeding Up String Searches

Problem

You need to frequently search a large table on a part of a VARCHAR2 column. The string you are searching for is either a substring or a transformation of a column using another Oracle function that returns a string result.

Solution

When you run a SELECT query with a WHERE clause that contains an Oracle string function returning a VARCHAR2 value, Oracle will perform a full table scan even if there is an index on the column referenced by the string function. To enable Oracle to use an index, create a function-based index (FBI) using the same expression in the WHERE clause as in the CREATE INDEX statement.

The following CREATE INDEX statement creates an FBI on the CITY column that evaluates to a non-zero value if there are at least two whitespace characters in the CITY column:

```
create index ie1_locations on locations(regexp_instr(city,'\s\S+\s'));

create index succeeded.
```

For Oracle to (possibly) utilize the index, your filter criteria in the WHERE clause needs to reference the expression used to create the index, as in this example:

```
select location_id, street_address, city, state_province
from locations
where regexp_instr(city,'\s\S+\s') > 0
;

LOCATION_ID  STREET_ADDRESS         CITY                       STATE_PROVINCE
-----------  ---------------------  -------------------------  ------------------
1500         2011 Interiors Blvd    South San Francisco        California

1 rows selected
```

Oracle may still not use the function-based index, depending on the size of the table and other factors, but for queries that will return a very small number of rows, an FBI will often trigger a range scan instead of a full table scan. The syntax for your SELECT statement is the same whether or not an FBI exists on the columns in the WHERE clause.

How It Works

A function-based index is an index built on an expression and it is applicable to data types other than VARCHAR2, including NUMBER and DATE data types. The decision to create an FBI is much the same as the decision to create a b-tree, bitmap, or even an index-organized table (IOT): will the performance improvements for SELECT statements offset the cost of additional disk space for the index as well as the overhead for maintaining the index during DML statements such as INSERT, DELETE, UPDATE, and MERGE. If the number and frequency of SELECT statements outnumber DML statements in your environment by a wide margin (as in a data warehouse or other types of reporting application), creating another index might be justified.

The solution includes an FBI based on the REGEXP_INSTR function, but the function definition can be as simple as converting the database column to uppercase, as in this example:

```
create index ie1_employees on employees(upper(last_name));

create index succeeded.
```

For searches on employee last names, using upper(last_name) in the WHERE clause will allow Oracle to leverage the FBI.

You can also use numeric operators on NUMBER columns in the arguments to the CREATE INDEX statement for an FBI to leverage an index if the calculation appears in the WHERE clause. If your EMP_SAL_HIST table looks like this:

```
Name                            Null     Type
------------------------------- -------- -----------------
EMPLOYEE_ID                     NOT NULL NUMBER
FISCAL_YEAR                     NOT NULL NUMBER(4)
SALARY                          NOT NULL NUMBER
BONUS                                    NUMBER
```

You can create an FBI that can speed up searches on total compensation with this statement:

```
create index ie1_emp_sal_hist on emp_sal_hist(salary + nvl(bonus,0));

create index succeeded.
```

Thus, if you search for total compensation in 2008 of $200,000.00 or more using this SELECT statement, the Oracle optimizer will likely use the FBI:

```
select employee_id
from emp_sal_hist
where fiscal_year = 2008
  and salary+nvl(bonus,0) >= 200000
;
```

However, the following statement will not use the index, since the expression in the WHERE clause does not exactly match the expression used to create the FBI, even though the WHERE clause specifies the exact same filtering condition:

```
select employee_id
from emp_sal_hist
where fiscal_year = 2008
    and salary+decode(bonus,null,0,bonus) >= 200000
;
```

In addition, the preceding SELECT statement will also most likely produce undesirable results, since the expression in the WHERE clause will return a NULL result for any employees having a NULL value in the BONUS column.

There are a few restrictions on creating and using FBIs. For example, an FBI can't contain an expression with aggregate functions. In addition, for Oracle to use the FBI, the table or index containing the FBI must be analyzed to gather statistics on the result of the calculations in the FBI. Finally, any FBI must return a deterministic value. In other words, the function must return the same value given the same input values. A good example of this restriction is a function that fails this restriction: a function that is dependent on the current date. Therefore, trying to create this index fails:

```
create index ie2_employees on employees(sysdate-hire_date);

Error starting at line 1 in command:
create index ie2_employees on employees(sysdate-hire_date)
Error at Command Line:1 Column:40
Error report:
SQL Error: ORA-01743: only pure functions can be indexed
01743. 00000 -  "only pure functions can be indexed"
*Cause:    The indexed function uses SYSDATE or the user environment.
*Action:   PL/SQL functions must be pure (RNDS, RNPS, WNDS, WNPS).  SQL
           expressions must not use SYSDATE, USER, USERENV(), or anything
           else dependent on the session state.  NLS-dependent functions
           are OK.
```

If you use a built-in or user-written function in an FBI, the function (or the package specification containing the function) must be declared as DETERMINISTIC. This does not ensure that the function returns the same value every time, but it provides another reminder that your index will not find the correct rows in the table if the function does not return the same values for a given set of input values every time. In other words, when you declare a function as DETERMINISTIC, make sure it *is* deterministic! Similarly, if you change the logic in a function and recompile it, you must drop and recreate any indexes or materialized views that depend on the function, since the index entries or materialized view rows are pre-computed based on the previous version of the function.

CHAPTER 8

■ ■ ■

Working with Numbers

When is a number not a number? When it's a string, of course. Throughout the history of databases, developers and DBAs have had to grapple with numeric data that is presented as a string, and with the need to convert digits in text to a number data type. Beyond data type issues, numbers also present interesting problems of precision and size. Contemporary computers are fantastic at dealing with numbers on both a vast or miniscule scale, but at some point you'll likely need to deal with data infinitely larger or smaller than you expected. Perhaps one of the most subtle issues when working with numbers is the tension between humans counting in base 10, and computers using binary.

This chapter introduces a host of recipes to deal with manipulating numeric data, conversion between data types, precision and scale, and strange corner cases that crop up thanks to the nature of relational databases. So, let's get started. Pick a number between 1 and 10.

8-1. Converting Between String and Numeric Data Types

Problem

Users are providing you data in the char or varchar2 data type that you subsequently need to convert to number, integer, or other numeric type.

Solution

Oracle provides the handy TO_NUMBER function to convert a wide variety of textual data to valid numeric form. This function includes not just the ability to convert digits in a textual string to their equivalent number, but also lets you deal with decimal markers, separators, grouping characters, currency symbols, and more.

For our recipe, we'll assume that employees in our HR.EMPLOYEES table have been granted a 100.00 per month salary increase. However, the system flagging the increase is using text for the 100.00, rather than a number. The next SQL statement uses the TO_NUMBER function to correctly interpret that character string and converts it to a numeric type that Oracle can use to perform addition on the underlying SALARY column, which is of data type NUMBER.

```
update hr.employees
set salary = salary +  to_number('100.00');

commit;
```

How It Works

This TO_NUMBER recipe is very straightforward in showing the syntax of the function. We pass the string or expression we want converted to the TO_NUMBER function and the function parses the text, attempting to interpret a valid number from it.

We used the TO_NUMBER function in an UPDATE statement. To see that it really produced the number 100 and added that to the employee salaries, you can run a SELECT statement that shows the existing and new salaries side by side, as shown in the next SQL block.

```
select salary "Existing salary", salary + to_number('100.00') "New Salary"
from hr.employees;
```

```
Existing salary  New Salary
---------------  ----------
           2600        2700
           2600        2700
           4400        4500
          13000       13100
           6000        6100
```

So far, we've displayed the basic form of the TO_NUMBER function. There are also two optional parameters that may be passed to the TO_NUMBER function, giving three different forms of the function overall.

TO_NUMBER(<expression or literal string>): Convert the expression or literal string to an Oracle number using implicit parsing, matching, and conversion rules.

TO_NUMBER(<expression or literal string>, <format mask>): Convert the expression using the provided format mask to match digits, thousands separators, and decimal points.

TO_NUMBER(<expression or literal string>, <format mask>, <'NLS parameters'>): Use the format mask and explicit localization NLS parameters to force a match, especially where foreign currency symbols and different punctuation forms are used.

Where the NLS parameters and format mask are not specified, TO_NUMBER refers to settings such as NLS_NUMERIC_CHARACTERS and NLS_CURRENCY to determine implicit values for use. See section 8-5 for recipes that illustrate the format mask and NLS parameters in action.

8-2. Converting Between Numeric Data Types

Problem

You need to convert numeric data between two Oracle data types. For instance, you have data stored as NUMBER and need to convert it to BINARY_DOUBLE while controlling any loss of accuracy.

Solution

Oracle provides explicit functions to accommodate conversion between numeric data types. While you can often rely on implicit conversion, it can be important to take control of the conversion process explicitly, to handle issues such as rounding, loss of precision, scale differences, and more.

To illustrate these functions, our recipe uses the TO_BINARY_DOUBLE function in the next SQL statement to convert the product of employee salaries and commissions.

```
select to_binary_double(salary*commission_pct)
from hr.employees
where job_id = 'SA_REP';

TO_BINARY_DOUBLE(SALARY*COMMISSION_PCT)
---------------------------------------
            8.75E+002
            8.75E+002
            8.75E+002
            3.0E+003
            2.375E+003
...
```

How It Works

There are many reasons for needing this exact kind of conversion, such as exchanging data with a finance system that requires numeric data in binary form (and with binary precision).

The TO_BINARY_DOUBLE function, like its peer functions that deal with other numeric types, takes a numeric value or expression and performs the necessary conversion to the BINARY_DOUBLE data type. Importantly, this conversion in particular deals with converting data stored with decimal precision (used with the NUMBER data type) to binary precision. As such, there is a chance for minor rounding errors or loss to creep in because certain decimal fractions cannot be precisely represented in binary form.

Other related numeric conversion functions are TO_NUMBER and TO_BINARY_FLOAT.

Binary vs Decimal Precision

When storing any number in Oracle, regardless of type, there are issues related to how much space it takes to store your number, and even whether it can be represented accurately at all. In essence, a number with binary precision is stored as the sum of various powers of two. For instance, 0.5 would be stored as 2^{-1}, and 0.75 would be stores as $2^{-1} + 2^{-2}$. With decimal precision, the same values would be stored as 5×10^{-1}, or $7 \times 10^{-1} + 5 \times 10^{-2}$. The result would be the same number, but the method of storage differs.

This becomes important as the numbers become harder to represent as powers of 2 or powers of 10. Oracle can literally run out of storage to represent a number accurately within a given datatype. We can illustrate this with a table declared as follows:

```
create table numbersize (
  base2number binary_double,
  base10number number);
```

Inserting the same number is easy.

```
Insert into numbersize values (1/3, 1/3);
```

With the value one-third stored in each column, we can use the VSIZE function to show it was much more complicated to store this with decimal precision, taking nearly three times the space.

```
select
  vsize(base2number) size_of_binary_double,
  vsize(base10number) size_of_number
from numbersize;

SIZE_OF_BINARY_DOUBLE SIZE_OF_NUMBER
--------------------- --------------
                    8             21
```

With a little exploration, you'll quickly find values that can't be stored precisely with one data type or the other.

8-3. Choosing Data Type Precision and Scale

Problem

You want to store currency information for prices, order amounts, and sales discounts in an online shopping application. You need to track dollars and cents (or other currencies) accurately.

Solution

Almost all of Oracle's NUMBER-style data types could be used to store prices and sale amounts. To best illustrate the use of precision and scale, we'll use the NUMBER data type itself.

Our recipe will focus on a new table for our order entry system in the OE schema. Let's create a table to track coupons for customer discounts.

```
create table oe.coupons (
  coupon_code number(9,0) not null,
  customer_id number(6,0) not null,
  coupon_value number(5,2) not null,
  restrictions varchar2(100)
);
```

We can now store precise coupon discount amounts using the new OE.COUPON table. The next INSERT statement illustrates adding new data to the table.

```
insert into oe.coupons values
(1, 150, 29.95, 'No restrictions');

commit;
```

Querying the table shows each of our NUMBER values stored with the precision and scale as defined in our CREATE TABLE statement.

```
select * from oe.coupons;
```

COUPON_CODE	CUSTOMER_ID	COUPON_VALUE	RESTRICTIONS
1	150	29.95	No restrictions

How It Works

The best way to think about the format of NUMBER, NUMERIC, and DECIMAL data types is in the general form

```
number(p,s)
```

In this expression, *number* is the name of the data type; you may use numeric or decimal, but know that these are implicitly mapped to the NUMBER data type for storage. The value *p* is the precision, which states the total number of digits of precision the number may have, *including* the fractional (scale) part of the number. The value *s*, scale, indicates how many of the total precision digits are dedicated to the fractional part of the number, that is, the portion to the right of the decimal point.

In our OE.COUPONS table, you can deduce that COUPON_CODE may be up to 9 digits, with no decimal places as the scale value is zero. Similarly, CUSTOMER_ID, the foreign key of the OE.CUSTOMERS table, uses a NUMBER of up to six digits with no allowance for decimal places.

The COUPON_VALUE field introduces a common specification you'll see for currency in dollar-denominated and similar systems. Its precision is five, meaning a total of five digits can be used for the whole and fractional part of the value of a coupon. The scale is two, constraining the COUPON_VALUE to using two of its five digits for decimal places. By implication, this only leaves three digits for whole dollars. You can test this yourself with the next INSERT statement, which attempts to create a coupon with a value beyond the constraints of our COUPON_VALUE column.

```
insert into oe.coupons values
(2, 155, 1000, 'Requires CEO approval');
```

Attempting this INSERT returns an error highlighting the restrictions on COUPON_VALUE.

```
ERROR at line 2:
ORA-01438: value larger than specified precision allowed for this column
```

Note that the error presented specifies it's the precision of the COUPON_VALUE field that prevents the value 1000 being used. Because the column is specified as COUPON_VALUE NUMBER(5,2) NOT NULL, Oracle implicitly can only store three digits of precision, meaning values up to 999, but not 1000, which requires four digits. It's tempting to think that the same style of constraint applies to the scale, should you exceed the specified number of two scale digits. The next INSERT statement attempts to insert a new coupon with a scale specified far more specifically than our table definition allows.

```
insert into oe.coupons values
(3, 160, 0.9950, 'We will see if anyone can spend half a cent!');
```

```
1 row created.
```

If you were expecting to see an error, you've been caught out by Oracle's separate handling of scale beyond the constrained value of the column in question. The next SELECT statement will expose what Oracle has done with our fraction of a cent.

```
select * from oe.coupons;
```

```
COUPON_CODE   CUSTOMER_ID   COUPON_VALUE   RESTRICTIONS
-----------   -----------   ------------   -------------------------
          1           150          29.95   No restrictions
          3           160             1    We will see if anyone can spend half a cent!
```

Where scale is concerned, Oracle will round the fractional part of a number to fit the scale specified by the column. So in our recipe, our attempt to store a coupon value of 0.9950 is rounded to 1, because the scale of two means 0.9950 could not be stored. This is not just rounded for display purposes; the value 1 is what has actually been stored.

8-4. Performing Calculations Correctly with Non-Numbers and Infinite Numbers

Problem

You need to manage numeric data that involves dealing with abnormal results and values not considered numbers. For instance, your calculations may return values larger than can possibly be stored, or need to flag division by zero with something other than an error.

Solution

Use Oracle's BINARY_FLOAT and BINARY_DOUBLE data types to enable the storage and use of the values infinity (INF) and not-a-number (NAN). Our recipe will use a hypothetical requirement to manage the results of probability calculations, as might be used with astronomical calculations.

The next example provides the simplest display of safe division by zero using the BINARY_FLOAT data type.

```
select
  to_binary_float(42) / to_binary_float(0) Div_By_Zero
from dual;
```

Instead of the error you might expect, Oracle returns the following results.

```
DIV_BY_ZERO
-----------
        Inf
```

How It Works

The BINARY_FLOAT and BINARY_DOUBLE data types conform to the IEEE standard for floating point computation. The IEEE standard includes mandated support for the special values infinity and not-a-number. In normal SQL, results from calculations that might return an error, such as division by zero, will provide resilient behavior and return the appropriate special value. This may seem at first like an "escape from your errors for free" recipe—but remember, your code and applications still need to expect this behavior and respond accordingly.

In our recipe, we cast the numbers 42 and zero to BINARY_FLOAT, and then implicitly performed a BINARY_FLOAT division. This returned the value INF. If we had attempted this with NUMBER or INTEGER values, the result would have been quite different. The next SQL statement shows the results you probably expect to see when dividing by zero.

```
select 42 / 0
from dual;

select 42 / 0
         *
ERROR at line 1:
ORA-01476: divisor is equal to zero
```

This means you can define columns of a desired data type, such as BINARY_DOUBLE and avoid the need to wrap your division in a helper PL/SQL function or case statement to trap the division by zero. Ask yourself, what is easier: our recipe using BINARY_DOUBLE, or the next PL/SQL and SQL that historically might have been used to avoid the ORA-01476 error.

```
create or replace procedure safediv (op1 number, op2 number) is
  result number;
begin
  result := op1 / op2;
  -- more logic
  -- ...
exception
  when zero_divide then
    -- throw a catchable error, or attempt some other resolution
    -- ...
end;
/

select safediv(42, 0) from dual;
```

We know which option appeals when a problem calls for handling infinity and not-a-number. However, it is important to note that there are consequences to using BINARY_FLOAT and BINARY_DOUBLE. Principal among these is their use of binary precision, not decimal precision. This means that values that can be precisely stored in a NUMBER or FLOAT may not be precisely stored in BINARY_FLOAT and BINARY_DOUBLE. Conversely, some values can be stored precisely that NUMBER or FLOAT would implicitly round.

The other major consideration is whether your development environment and/or programming language support IEEE data types. There's little point in going to the effort of using these data types if you then have to discard useful features like not-a-number and infinity because your programming language doesn't understand them.

> **Bigger Than Infinity?**
>
> One interesting consequence of the IEEE standard— and its implementation in Oracle— is that the value not-a-number, NAN, is considered larger than infinity, INF. You can check this yourself using some quick SQL to test which is the largest value. The following code does just such a comparison.
>
> ```
> select
>   case
>     when to_binary_float('nan') > to_binary_float('inf')
>       then 'Nan is greater than Inf'
>       else 'Inf is greater than Nan'
>   end Largest_Value
> from dual;
>
> LARGEST_VALUE
> -----------------------
> Nan is greater than Inf
> ```
>
> This means that your arithmetic needs to account for NULL, NAN, and INF values and their quirks if you use the BINARY_DOUBLE or BINARY_FLOAT data types.

8-5. Validating Numbers in Strings

Problem

You need to parse, validate, and convert a number presented as fully formatted text. For example, you need to take a string representation of a sales figure in a foreign currency and validate and convert it for further processing as an Oracle NUMBER.

Solution

Oracle's TO_NUMBER function can convert textual representations of numbers to the NUMBER data type, and includes the ability to handle regional formatting preferences, currency symbols, and punctuation.

For this recipe, we'll tackle the problem of receiving a currency figure from a European partner, customer, or supplier, formatted according to the customs of the country of origin. Fifteen European countries use the Euro, typically written with its own symbol €. Some European locations use the comma as the decimal separator, and the period as a thousands separator. The figure €12.345.687,90 can be converted using the TO_NUMBER function, illustrated with the next SQL statement.

```
select to_number
('€12.345.687,90',
 'L99G999G999D99',
 ' nls_currency = ''€'' nls_numeric_characters = '',.'' ') Profit
from dual;
```

```
     PROFIT
----------
12345687.9
```

Note that the loss of the trailing zero is normal `NUMBER` data type behavior in trimming trailing zeros of no significance, not a special feature of this formatting example.

How It Works

Our recipe uses two of the major optional parameters with the `TO_NUMBER` function, the format mask and the `NLS_LANGUAGE` string. These parameters work in tandem to allow Oracle to parse the provided string and correctly convert it to numeric form. Here's the general form of the `TO_NUMBER` function for cases such as this:

```
to_number
(<string representation or expression>,
 <format mask>,
 <nls_language options>)
```

For our recipe, the string is the figure €12.345.687,90. Naturally, this can be a string literal, a value returned from a table, a view, or any other string expression.

Our format mask has the value `L99G999G999D99`. To save you from having to wade through pages of Oracle documentation, a shorthand way of remembering these values is to keep in mind that the letters stand for substitution options that are provided by the `NLS_LANGUAGE` options string, as follows:

L: Local currency symbol

G: Grouping character (such as the thousands separator)

D: Decimal symbol

`NLS_LANGUAGE` is a `STRING` whose options are parsed; it does not mean that multiple parameters are passed to `TO_NUMBER`. The options are embedded in the string and sent as one paramter. This is very quirky behavior and can lead to frustrating debugging to determine where exactly quotes for string formatting and escaping are needed. In our recipe, you'll see that the options string is enclosed in single quotes.

```
' nls_currency = ''€'' nls_numeric_characters = '',.'' '
```

We've even added extra spaces so you can easily see the quotes and escaping. You only need to specify options in this string to match the format mask characters used. In our case, we need to specify `NLS_CURRENCY` to identify what character will replace L to represent the currency symbol. In our case, that's the Euro symbol, €. We then use the `NLS_NUMERIC_CHARACTERS` option to specify both the grouping separator G and the decimal character D.

Oracle requires grouping and decimal symbols appear in the order GD, and accidentally reversing these normally results in ORA-01722 Invalid Number errors as Oracle tries to understand why you have multiple decimal "point" symbols in your numbers. This kind of transposition mistake can be really hard to spot, especially if your source data has used a decimal point as a group separator, and a comma as a decimal symbol, just as our example does. Here's an example to give you practice spotting the error.

```
select to_number
('€12.345.687,90',
 'L99G999G999D99',
 ' nls_currency = ''€'' nls_numeric_characters = ''.,'' ') Profit
from dual;

('€12.345.687,90',
 *
ERROR at line 2:
ORA-01722: invalid number
```

If you had only seen this SQL statement and not the preceding description, tracking down the transposed period and comma (in bold) could be a very frustrating experience.

8-6. Generating Consecutive Numbers

Problem

You need to generate numbers in a consecutive fashion, according to a set of business rules. For example, you have decided to use surrogate or synthetic keys for your primary key data, and need a way to reliably generate unique incrementing or decrementing values.

Solution

Oracle provides the sequence as a dedicated object to enable number generation, freeing you from the need to craft your own arithmetic, number tracking, and contention-management arrangements. Here's the basic sequence-creation SQL:

```
create sequence hr.employee_num;
```

To use the sequence, include a reference to the pseudocolumns CURRVAL and NEXTVAL wherever you require a new consecutive number. The following statement simply returns the next sequence value available.

```
select hr.employee_num.nextval
from dual;

   NEXTVAL
----------
         1
```

The same pseudocolumn naming can be used in INSERT, UPDATE, and other statements. The following code automatically generates a key for a hypothetical NEW_EMPLOYEE table.

```
insert into hr.new_employee
(employee_pk, last_name, first_name)
values
(hr.employee_num.nextval, 'Green', 'Sally');
```

The CURRVAL pseudocolumn can be similarly referenced. The next statement retrieves the last value provided by the sequence.

```
select hr.employee_num.currval from dual;

   CURRVAL
----------
         2
```

■ **Tip** CURRVAL always gives you the current value of the sequence used in your session, which means that awkward programming that selects the NEXTVAL and concatenates it into a string (or uses INTO to store the value into a temporary variable) is totally unnecessary. You can rely on CURRVAL to provide a consistent current value in your session for a given sequence. This will make your code much cleaner, more reliable, and easier to test.

How It Works

A sequence in Oracle tracks and distributes integers according to a few rules. First and foremost, a sequence guarantees that each new person or application that requests a number receives a unique number, normally the next logical number according to the sequence's rules.

Our recipe creates a new sequence named HR.EMPLOYEE_NUM, with no visible additional criteria. We then immediately used the sequence to return the first available number by issuing the next SQL command.

```
select hr.employee_num.nextval
from dual;
```

We received the number 1, then moved on to test an insert that (apparently) received the number 2. Under the hood, Oracle picked up numerous defaults to control the numbers it generated.

The most noticeable default is Oracle's choice for starting the sequence at the number 1. Our first call to the NEXTVAL pseudocolumn returned this to confirm 1 as the default initial value. Oracle defaults to incrementing subsequent calls to our sequence by 1 as well. Our mock insert grabbed the number 2, and subsequent calls would return 3, then 4, and so on.

Some of the not-so-obvious defaults are still important to know about. Oracle created the sequence with no upper (or lower) limit to the numbers generated. This implicitly means we can create numbers based on our HR.EMPLOYEE_NUM sequence up to the largest supported NUMBER value: a 1 followed by 38 digits! Oracle also used the NOCYCLE default, to indicate that when we hit this upper threshold, we won't "wrap around" and start issuing numbers from one again.

The final two implicit defaults cause Oracle to cache 20 values, and not force strict first-come, first-served ordering on those who call NEXTVAL. Both of these defaults improve performance under heavy concurrent load. Oracle accomplishes this by recording the next uncached value in the SYS.SEQ$ table, and by not logging individual sequence selection. For our recipe, 20 values are cached in memory, and Oracle notes in SYS.SEQ$ that the HR.EMPLOYEE_NUM sequence will be at the value 21 when the current cached values are exhausted. In this way, Oracle avoids contention on both an underlying table and the redo log when dealing with cached sequence values.

8-7. Generating Numbers to a Formula or Pattern

Problem

You need to generate numbers that increase according to a given algorithm. For example, you want to feed odd numbers into one process and even numbers into another process, so that they can be used for job or task selection and control. You want strict control over the order in which numbers are submitted for job processing.

Solution

Sequences in Oracle can be defined with several qualifiers and options to meet more complex generation requirements. The next SQL statement creates a sequence for generating odd numbers, and controls the order and reliability of generation to the best of Oracle's ability.

```
create sequence odd_number_generator
  start with 3
  increment by 2
  maxvalue 999999
  nocycle
  nocache
  order;
```

Using this sequence, our recipe can produce odd numbers for feeding to one of our job control processes, using the NEXTVAL pseudocolumn. The next three SQL statements show our sequence in action.

```
select odd_number_generator.nextval from dual;

   NEXTVAL
----------
         3

select odd_number_generator.nextval from dual;

   NEXTVAL
----------
         5

select odd_number_generator.nextval from dual;

   NEXTVAL
----------
         7
```

We can then create a second sequence with a slightly different starting position, to feed only even numbers to our other job control process.

```
create sequence even_number_generator
  start with 2
  increment by 2
  maxvalue 999999
  nocycle
  nocache
  order;
```

This gives us some simple load balancing without needing external software or monitoring.

How It Works

Our recipe uses many of the optional features of sequences in Oracle, in order to meet our simple job-control and load-balancing requirements. We named our first sequence ODD_NUMBER_GENERATOR, which is nice and descriptive. Then we used sequence options to control many aspects of the sequence's behavior.

The first option, START WITH 3, indicates the starting value generated and returned by the sequence. You'll note the first invocation of ODD_NUMBER_GENERATOR.NEXTVAL returned 3.

The second option, INCREMENT BY 2, instructs Oracle to add two to the sequence every time it is referenced, so that the next value would be 5, and the one following that would be 7, as shown by the second and third calls to ODD_NUMBER_GENERATOR.NEXTVAL.

Our third option is MAXVALUE 999999. We've used this as a purely arbitrary limit to the odd numbers we'll generate. Using the MAXVALUE option is often done to suit particular business requirements.

The fourth option is NOCYCLE. This instructs Oracle to halt issuing any new sequence values once the MAXVALUE threshold is reached. Oracle returns the error shown next when a sequence is exhausted and NOCYCLE has been specified.

```
ORA-08004: sequence ODD_NUMBER_GENERATOR.NEXTVAL exceeds MAXVALUE and cannot be instantiated
```

This would be especially important in cases like our job control process, as we wouldn't necessarily want to resubmit the same job number again.

Our second-last option is NOCACHE, which instructs Oracle not to precalculate and cache any sequence values for this sequence. By default, 20 such values are generated and cached, which helps to speed up concurrent rapid access to sequence values. The downside of caching is that cached values may be lost or discarded if Oracle crashes, causing the sequence to appear to jump a gap and start handing out number beyond the previously cached block. Normally, you should never code your logic to rely on every sequence number being generated. After all, transactions can fail or roll back for many reasons, and Oracle will never try to backtrack and use a sequence value missed due to a lost cache, regardless of the CACHE/NOCACHE setting. By using the NOCACHE option, at least we won't skip values due to recovery processes.

Lastly, we issued the ORDER option when creating our sequence. This means that sequence values will be handed out to callers in order of their execution of the NEXTVAL pseudocolumn. With the ORDER option, Oracle can reorder requests for processing and performance reasons. Again, it makes sense not to rely on this unless strictly necessary: we're using this in our recipe to indicate that you want jobs processed in order.

8-8. Handling Nulls in Numeric Calculations

Problem

You are performing arithmetic and other calculations on data that may contain NULL values. You want to ensure your results are valid and not affected by the NULL data.

Solution

Oracle strictly adheres to ternary logic rules when any arithmetic or mathematical operation involves a NULL value. In lay terms, that means any calculation that operates on an unknown value returns an unknown result. Any addition, subtraction, multiplication, or other calculation involving NULL will always return NULL. When you want to deal with NULL values in another way, the key is to override normal Oracle behavior by intercepting the NULL values and substituting your desired alternative.

For our recipe, we'll tackle the problem of attempting to calculate the total annual salary plus commission for all staff in the HR.EMPLOYEES table. The next SQL statement overrides Oracle's default NULL arithmetic, providing an answer both the business and employees would deem correct.

```
select employee_id, job_id, salary * (1 + nvl(commission_pct,0)) final_pay
from hr.employees;
```

Our results are meaningful for both sales representatives, with a JOB_ID of SA_REP, and for non-sales representatives.

EMPLOYEE_ID	JOB_ID	FINAL_PAY
199	SH_CLERK	2600
200	AD_ASST	4400
201	MK_MAN	13000
...		
210	SA_REP	4375
211	SA_REP	4375
212	SA_REP	4375
...		

How It Works

Our recipe relies on the NVL function to substitute an alternative whenever the expression or column in question evaluates to NULL. For our purposes, we've passed NVL the COMMISSION_PCT column, so that employees who aren't on commission don't receive a final pay of NULL. It would be hard to pay the mortgage or buy groceries with that kind of salary.

Without our intervention, the calculation for FINAL_PAY would sorely disappoint some of the employees. The next SQL statement shows the strict behavior of our calculation if we don't intervene to handle the NULL values.

```
select employee_id, job_id, salary * (1 + commission_pct) final_pay
from hr.employees;

EMPLOYEE_ID             JOB_ID              FINAL_PAY
-----------             ---------           ----------
        199             SH_CLERK            NULL
        200             AD_ASST             NULL
        201             MK_MAN              NULL
...
        210             SA_REP              4375
        211             SA_REP              4375
        212             SA_REP              4375
...
```

To reinforce the strict behavior you will normally see when performing calculations that encounter NULL values, the next SQL tries just about every combination of arithmetic on our SALARY and COMMISSION_PCT values.

```
select
employee_id,
job_id,
salary * commission_pct product,
salary + commission_pct "SUM",
salary - commission_pct difference,
salary / commission_pct quotient
from hr.employees;

EMPLOYEE_ID    JOB_ID       PRODUCT      SUM          DIFFERENCE     QUOTIENT
-----------    ---------    ----------   ----------   -----------    ---------
        199    SH_CLERK
        200    AD_ASST
        201    MK_MAN
...
        210    SA_REP       875          3500.25      3499.75        14000
        211    SA_REP       875          3500.25      3499.75        14000
        212    SA_REP       875          3500.25      3499.75        14000
...
```

If we put the somewhat nonsensical nature of our calculations to the side, you can see that a NULL COMMISSION_PCT translates to NULL results from any calculation.

Oracle's One Exception To NULL Results

Oracle adheres to the "any calculation with NULL equals NULL rule" for any arithmetic calculation. However, there's one non-numeric function where Oracle relaxes the rule: string concatenation.

Joining strings doesn't really fit with a chapter on handling numbers, but this one exception is worth raising here at the end.

8-9. Automatically Rounding Numbers

Problem

You need incoming data to be automatically rounded to a given level, without forcing users or developers to remember to use the ROUND, TRUNC or CEIL functions. For instance, you need to track budget numbers in the thousands, millions, or billions, ignoring much smaller cash amounts.

Solution

Oracle supplies several ways to round numbers automatically. Some people opt for triggers while others choose PL/SQL wrappers and other automatic processing to force the use of the ROUND function or similar approaches. However, Oracle comes with the ability to round numbers to any degree of digits without needing added code or data interception. And Oracle's precision feature for the numeric data types, like NUMBER, allows us to specify negative precision. This will perform the rounding for us.

For our recipe, we'll assume we're calculating the salary budget for all departments, but we aren't interested in the hundreds, tens, or units of dollars at the "small" end of our calculation. Our budget requirements mean we're only interested in increments of a thousand.

The next SQL statement creates our budget tracking table. We use a negative precision for the SALARY_BUDGET to manage our automatic rounding.

```
create table hr.dept_budget
(
  department_id number(4,0),
  salary_budget number(10,-3)
);
```

We use the next INSERT statement to populate our HR.DEPT_BUDGET table with a summary of current salary numbers.

```
insert into hr.dept_budget
select department_id, sum(salary * 12)
from hr.employees
group by department_id;
```

At this point, our desire to round at the thousands level has been processed automatically. Compare the results of the next two SQL statements. First we see our automatic rounding in action by selecting the contents of HR.DEPT_BUDGET.

```
select *
from hr.dept_budget
order by department_id;
```

DEPARTMENT_ID	SALARY_BUDGET
10	53000
20	228000
30	299000

```
         40                    78000
         50                  1892000
...
```

Performing a raw calculation against the base data in the HR.EMPLOYEES table confirms we've achieved our desired outcome.

```
select department_id, sum(salary * 12)
from hr.employees
group by department_id
order by department_id;
```

```
DEPARTMENT_ID            SUM(SALARY*12)
-------------            --------------
         10                    52800
         20                   228000
         30                   298800
         40                    78000
         50                  1891800
...
```

The items in bold show our automatic rounding in action in the first result set, and the raw data in the second result set.

How It Works

It's easy to think of the precision specified for a number as meaning how many significant digits are in the fractional part of a number. However, Oracle actually implements the concept of precision in its entirety. It uses positive and negative precision to track significant digits either side of the decimal point (or decimal symbol for your locale).

The best way to think about the precision element of a number is to remember this basic format.

```
number (<scale>, <where precision ends>)
```

You then interpret <where precision ends> as follows

- **Positive precision:** number of places to the right of the decimal symbol at which precision ends.

- **Negative precision:** number of places to the left of the decimal symbol at which precision ends.

- **Zero precision:** precision ends at the decimal symbol.

With these easy rules in mind, you can rely on Oracle to round your number at the point precision ends, regardless of whether that's to the left or right of the decimal symbol. For our recipe, we defined the SALARY_BUDGET amount like this:

```
salary_budget number(10,-3)
```

Using our simple shorthand, we know Oracle will end its tracking of precision three places to the left of the decimal point. That is, units, tens and hundreds, being the first three places to the left of the decimal point will be *discarded*, and the number rounded up or down appropriately, and *automatically*.

Our first department, number 10, has a raw salary budget of 52800. But we know that the '800' component is beyond the precision of our SALARY_BUDGET field, so the value 52800 is rounded using typical mathematics rules to 53000 automatically. This is repeated for all the values we stored, and we didn't need to force developers or users down the path of building triggers, wrapper functions, or remembering to make this calculation themselves in their code.

8-10. Automatically Generating Lists of Numbers

Problem

You want to generate a list of numbers for a one-time calculation or SQL query. For instance, you need a table or view with the numbers 1 to 1000 for ranking and position calculations, but you don't want to create a sequence and call it 1000 times to populate your table.

Solution

Oracle provides several techniques for spontaneously generating sets of numbers. Our recipe will use Oracle's traditional hierarchy support via the CONNECT BY clause and the ROWNUM pseudocolumn, to build a ready-made list of numbers.

The next SQL statement uses CONNECT BY LEVEL against the dual table, to build a list of the numbers 1 to 1000.

```
select rownum as my_numbers
from dual
connect by level <= 1000;
```

The results are hopefully obvious, but just in case you're wondering, we return the numbers 1 to 1000 (with abridged results shown here to save space).

```
MY_NUMBERS
----------
         1
         2
         3
...
       999
      1000

1000 rows selected.
```

We can use this SQL to act as an inline view or the basis of a CREATE TABLE AS SELECT statement for ranking, counting, and other problems, such as in the recipe *Filtering Results by Relative Rank*, in Chapter 11.

How It Works

In standard use, the CONNECT BY ability in Oracle relies on the user specifying two aspects to drive Oracle to build a hierarchy. You typically tell Oracle how one row is a child or parent of another row using the PRIOR ... notation, and then you tell Oracle how to start the hierarchy by specifying a START WITH clause so it can derive lower tiers or levels in the hierarchy from there.

Our recipe cheats by not doing these things! We start by telling Oracle to simply select the ROWNUM from the table DUAL. The CONNECT BY clause is then left deliberately empty, giving Oracle no instruction how to relate parents to children in the following iterations. At this point, Oracle has no choice but to connect all prior rows to the current result row. It does this for as many times as we specify in the LEVEL clause, which in our recipe is 1000 times.

So to begin with, Oracle links the ROWNUM value 1 to the first row, then links the ROWNUM 2 for level 2, and so on all the way to level 1000. At this point, our inline view has generated 1000 rows, with values from 1 to 1000.

PART 3

Your Development Environment

CHAPTER 9

■ ■ ■

Managing Transactions

A single update or insert to a database table is often part of several other updates, deletes, or inserts (DML statements) within a unit of work for a particular task. Those inserts, updates, or deletes that must all succeed to maintain the integrity of the data must occur as a database *transaction*. Every modern RDBMS supports the concept of transactions by encapsulating one or more DML statements and treating them as an atomic unit of work.

In addition to ensuring that the entire set of operations either succeeds or fails, a transaction also hides the visibility of the changes within a transaction from other database users who may be reading or changing the same data. Once a transaction completes, the changes are visible to any other user sessions that begin their own transaction after the first transaction completes. Note that a single DML statement is also considered a transaction—the changes made during the DML statement are not visible to other sessions until a COMMIT occurs.

The recipes in this chapter will cover several aspects of transactions in the database. First, we'll show you some data dictionary views that will help you identify your own transactions, as well as other active transactions that may be preventing your own transactions from completing.

The dreaded *deadlock*, where two transactions exclusively lock a resource that each transaction needs before it can complete, is automatically resolved by Oracle, which unceremoniously rolls back one of the transactions. However, preventing a deadlock from occurring in the first place saves time and database resources, so we'll also provide a recipe for minimizing the occurrence of a deadlock.

Finally, there's a recipe to change the constraint definition on one or more tables such that the constraint is not checked until you attempt to issue a COMMIT statement. This scenario may occur when you have a third-party application that is not aware of the relational integrity (RI) of the database, or when you receive child rows from an upstream process before you receive the parent rows.

9-1. Partially Rolling Back a Transaction

Problem

You have a group of DML statements that must all complete for your transaction to be successful, but you want the capability to roll back only the most recent statements and not all statements since the beginning of the transaction.

Solution

Use the SAVEPOINT statement to create markers within the transaction. You can undo DML within the
transaction to any SAVEPOINT created since the implicit or explicit beginning of the transaction. For
example, you want to adjust salaries for several employees within department 100. Employee John Chen
will get a raise of $1000 per month, and all other employees in the department will get smaller raises
such that the total monthly salary for the department does not exceed $60,000. Here is the list of
employees and the current total salary for department 100:

```
select employee_id, last_name, first_name, salary
from employees
where department_id = 100
;
```

EMPLOYEE_ID	LAST_NAME	FIRST_NAME	SALARY
108	Greenberg	Nancy	9460
109	Faviet	Daniel	9460
110	Chen	John	9460
111	Sciarra	Ismael	9460
112	Urman	Jose Manuel	9460
113	Popp	Luis	9460

```
6 rows selected
```

The total salary for department 100 before any updates is as follows:

```
select sum(salary)
from employees
where department_id = 100
;
```

```
SUM(SALARY)
-----------
56760
```

```
1 rows selected
```

Next, we will update Chen's salary and create a SAVEPOINT:

```
update employees
set salary = salary + 1000
where employee_id = 110
;
```

```
1 rows updated
```

```
savepoint chen_salary;
```

```
savepoint chen_salary succeeded.
```

Next, we'll update the rest of the salaries in department 100 and see if we're still within the budget guidelines:

```
update employees
set salary = salary + 450
where department_id = 100 and employee_id != 110
;
```

5 rows updated

```
select sum(salary)
from employees
where department_id = 100
;
```

```
SUM(SALARY)
-----------
60010
```

1 rows selected

The total salary is over $60,000, so we need to lower the salary adjustment for all employees except for Chen. We'll roll back the UPDATEs up to but not including the Chen salary adjustment:

```
rollback to savepoint chen_salary;
```

rollback to succeeded.

Updating the remaining employees in department 100 by a lower amount ($400 instead of $450), we find that we're within the total salary guidelines:

```
update employees
set salary = salary + 400
where department_id = 100 and employee_id != 110
;
```

5 rows updated

```
select sum(salary)
from employees
where department_id = 100
;
```

```
SUM(SALARY)
----------------------
59760
```

1 rows selected

Finally, we'll perform a COMMIT and look at the final salary totals:

```
commit;

commit succeeded.

select employee_id, last_name, first_name, salary
from employees
where department_id = 100;

EMPLOYEE_ID            LAST_NAME              FIRST_NAME            SALARY
---------------------  ---------------------  -------------------  -----------
108                    Greenberg              Nancy                9860
109                    Faviet                 Daniel               9860
110                    Chen                   John                 10460
111                    Sciarra                Ismael               9860
112                    Urman                  Jose Manuel          9860
113                    Popp                   Luis                 9860

6 rows selected
```

Note that Chen's salary update remained intact, since we performed a ROLLBACK to a point in time (to a System Change Number or SCN) right after Chen's update.

How It Works

A transaction begins when any of the following occurs:

- A session begins

- A COMMIT is executed

- A ROLLBACK is executed

- Any DDL (Data Definition Language) or DCL (Data Control Language) command is executed

When a ROLLBACK is performed, all DDL commands are reversed to the beginning of the transaction, unless you specify a *savepoint* in the ROLLBACK command. A savepoint is a marker within a transaction that can divide a transaction into smaller parts that can incrementally be reversed, or rolled back, without rolling back the entire transaction.

As mentioned in the recipe solution, a SAVEPOINT command assigns a label to a System Change Number (SCN). An SCN is created in the Oracle database every time any change is made to the database; an SCN is unique across the entire database.

You can specify any name for a SAVEPOINT that follows Oracle object naming conventions. If you re-use a SAVEPOINT name within a transaction, the first SAVEPOINT with the same name is no longer accessible via a ROLLBACK command. After a COMMIT or a ROLLBACK without a SAVEPOINT name, all SAVEPOINTS are cleared and no longer accessible.

9-2. Identifying Blocking Transactions

Problem

When you execute various DML statements, such as UPDATE and DELETE, you often have to wait several seconds or longer for the statement to complete. You suspect that other users are holding locks on rows or waiting too long to perform a COMMIT.

Solution

Use Oracle dynamic performance views to see which objects are being concurrently accessed, along with who is holding the resource and who is waiting on it. For example, you can query dynamic performance views such as V$LOCK and data dictionary tables such as DBA_OBJECTS to retrieve currently locked objects. Here is the SELECT statement:

```
select s1.username blkg_user, s1.machine blkg_ws, s1.sid blkg_sid,
       s2.username wait_user, s2.machine wait_ws, s2.sid wait_sid,
       lo.object_id blkd_obj_id, do.owner, do.object_name
from v$lock l1, v$session s1, v$lock l2, v$session s2,
     v$locked_object lo, dba_objects do
where s1.sid = l1.sid
  and s2.sid = l2.sid
  and l1.id1 = l2.id1
  and s1.sid = lo.session_id
  and lo.object_id = do.object_id
  and l1.block = 1
  and l2.request > 0
;
```

```
BLKG_USER BLKG_WS BLKG_SID WAIT_USER WAIT_WS WAIT_SID BLKD_OBJ_ID OWNER OBJECT_NAME
--------- ------- -------- --------- ------- -------- ----------- ----- -----------
RJB       WRK1    122      HR        WRK87   131      70272       HR    EMPLOYEES

1 rows selected
```

The query retrieves all currently locked objects, which user is holding the lock, which user is waiting for access, and the username and workstation holding the lock. In this example, the user RJB is holding a lock on one or more rows of the EMPLOYEES table, and HR is waiting for the lock to be released. It also lists the session ID and the workstation ID of each user.

How It Works

The solution uses a number of data dictionary views to retrieve the information about who is locking the objects as well as the schema name and object names that are locked:

- V$LOCK: Locks currently held, and requests for a lock. The BLOCK column is 1 if this lock is in effect and is blocking other lock requests, otherwise 0 if this is a request for a lock. The REQUEST column is the type of lock requested; a value of 0 indicates that no lock is requested.

- V$SESSION: Session identifier, user name, status.

- V$LOCKED_OBJECT: Session ID and object ID for locked objects.

- DBA_OBJECTS: All database objects, with object number, object name, owner.

You can use other columns in V$SESSION to further identify which rows are involved in the lock, but typically you only need to know the username, workstation, and the object being locked so you can give the user a call and find out why the rows are locked for an extended period of time!

The only caveat to this method pertains to database security. Typically, a developer or an end user will not have access to data dictionary views or tables. However, in a development environment, the DBA will be more likely to grant such access to help the developers debug the application and identify any transaction-related coding errors before moving to production. Alternatively, the DBA can create a view accessing these dynamic performance views, and grant SELECT access to developers and support personnel.

9-3. Optimizing Row and Table Locking

Problem

DML queries are taking a long time to complete and the DBA suspects that other users or application transactions are holding locks longer than necessary.

Solution

To follow Oracle best practices for application development, use the NOWAIT clause and minimize the use of LOCK statements unless the application requires it. When a DML statement runs, the NOWAIT clause returns immediately if there is already a lock on the resource you require for the DML statement. For example, you want to update a row in the EMPLOYEES table, but you don't want to perform the update if there is already other activity on the row or rows you are trying to update. Here is an example:

```
update employees
set salary = salary * 1.2
where employee_id = 101
;
```

If there is no current lock on the row, the UPDATE statement returns immediately. If a second user runs the same UPDATE statement, the command waits until the first user's UPDATE is committed or rolled back. To avoid the wait during the second UPDATE attempt, use the NOWAIT clause in a SELECT before the UPDATE statement in all sessions, as follows:

```
select * from employees e
where employee_id = 101
  for update of salary nowait
;
```

If another session already has the row locked, you will receive this error message:

```
Error starting at line 1 in command:
select * from employees e
where employee_id = 101
  for update of salary nowait
Error report:
SQL Error: ORA-00054: resource busy and acquire with NOWAIT specified or timeout expired
00054. 00000 -  "resource busy and acquire with NOWAIT specified"
*Cause:    Resource interested is busy.
*Action:   Retry if necessary.
```

How It Works

Concurrent access of Oracle tables is usually hassle-free, as Oracle automatically acquires the appropriate level of locking to minimize contention and maximize throughput. In addition, even if the application supports more than one user at a time, the users are typically not editing the same row or set of rows at the same time. But for those scenarios where you want to alert the user immediately when there is contention on the same rows in a table, you can use the NOWAIT keyword in a SELECT statement.

■ **Note** You can specify explicit locking in a number of ways, such as with SELECT . . . FOR UPDATE. However, Oracle's default locking mechanisms are almost always the most efficient, minimizing the number of rows locked for a particular transaction. There are exceptions, though, such as when you need to ensure consistent data across changes to multiple tables in parent/child relationships.

Queries (SELECT statements) against a table always succeed, even if one or more processes lock some or all rows of the table. A SELECT statement from another session will use the unchanged version of the rows in the undo tablespace until a COMMIT occurs in the session holding the lock.

Rather than retrying a number of times to obtain the lock in an application loop, you can specify the number of seconds to wait to acquire a lock on one or more rows by using the WAIT *n* clause instead of NOWAIT, as in this example:

```
select * from employees e
where employee_id = 101
  for update of salary wait 15
;
```

If the rows are not available for DML statements within 15 seconds, the statement terminates with an error as if NOWAIT was specified, although with a slightly different error message:

```
Error starting at line 1 in command:
select * from employees e
where employee_id = 101
  for update of salary wait 15
Error report:
SQL Error: ORA-30006: resource busy; acquire with WAIT timeout expired
30006. 00000 -  "resource busy; acquire with WAIT timeout expired"
*Cause:    The requested resource is busy.
*Action:   Retry the operation later.
```

If you want to set a global timeout for the instance, you can set the initialization parameter DDL_LOCK_TIMEOUT as follows:

```
SQL> connect / as sysdba
Connected.
SQL> alter system set ddl_lock_timeout = 15 scope=both;

System altered.

SQL>
```

The default value is 0. Even when setting this parameter at the instance or session level, it can still be overridden in a SELECT statement with an explicit value in the WAIT clause.

Two guidelines will help ease any locking issues you may have: first, hold a lock for as little time as possible, especially in a transactional environment. Second, if at all possible, let Oracle manage locks automatically. In the vast majority of scenarios, Oracle will pick the most efficient locking method for the situation.

9-4. Avoiding Deadlock Scenarios

Problem

In your transaction environment, you frequently encounter deadlocks. Although Oracle resolves these deadlocks automatically, the deadlocks cause delays and unnecessarily use extra resources— and must still be handled within your application.

Solution

Deadlocks are a more serious type of locking conflict in that this type of lock cannot be resolved by waiting for one user to COMMIT or ROLLBACK since each session is waiting on a resource held by the other. For example, consider the scenario described in Table 9-1.

Table 9-1. *Typical Deadlock Scenario*

Time	Session A DML	Session B DML
9:55 A.M.	update employees set salary = salary * 1.25 where employee_id = 105;	update employees set job_id = 'IT_WEB' where employee_id = 110;
9:58 A.M.	update employees set salary = salary * 1.35 where employee_id = 110;	
9:59 A.M.		update employees set job_id = 'IT_WEB' where employee_id = 105;

At around 9:55 a.m., two separate sessions run UPDATE statements on employee numbers 105 and 110 in the EMPLOYEES table; they complete successfully but are not yet committed. So far, so good. At 9:58 a.m., session A runs an UPDATE statement on employee 110 and the statement pauses, because session B has that row locked. Still not a major concern. At 9:59 a.m., however, session B tries to update a row (for employee number 105) that is locked by session A. Both sessions are now waiting on the other for the desired resource to become available.

The immediate solution to the problem requires no user intervention: Oracle detects the deadlock and automatically rolls back one of the transactions, releasing one of the sets of row locks so that the other session's DML will complete. The session, however, still waits on the lock already in place. Thus, this is a good scenario for using NOWAIT at the command line or similar logic in the application. The session whose statement was rolled back receives the error message shown in Figure 9-1.

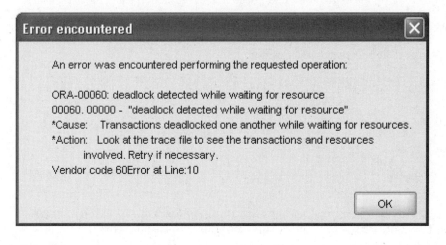

Error encountered

An error was encountered performing the requested operation:

ORA-00060: deadlock detected while waiting for resource
00060. 00000 - "deadlock detected while waiting for resource"
*Cause: Transactions deadlocked one another while waiting for resources.
*Action: Look at the trace file to see the transactions and resources
          involved. Retry if necessary.
Vendor code 60Error at Line:10

OK

Figure 9-1. *Oracle deadlock resolution error message*

The user may then attempt to retry the original DML statement that caused the deadlock, since it is possible that the other session's DML statement has completed and been committed.

How It Works

Although Oracle automatically rolls back one of the statements involved in the deadlock, you still cause delays for users and waste database resources when these deadlocks occur. There are many ways to avoid deadlocks entirely. For instance, for the example in Table 9-1, it appears that the maintenance duties are by column instead of by row. In other words, one user is modifying all salaries, and the other user is modifying job roles. If instead the user maintains all columns for an individual employee, this deadlock situation would most likely be avoided.

Another frequent cause of deadlocks is explicit locking at a level that is unnecessarily high. Oracle will most often lock at the lowest level after analyzing the DML statement, and no explicit locking is typically required.

9-5. Deferring Constraint Validation

Problem

You have many dependencies in your database with foreign keys that enforce referential integrity (RI), commonly known as parent/child relationships, and you want to prevent transactions from failing due to the ordering of the INSERT statements to the parent and child tables.

Solution

Drop and recreate the constraint on the child tables referenced in the transaction using the DEFERRABLE keyword in the constraint definition. For example, the EMPLOYEE table in the HR schema contains a foreign key (FK) constraint on the JOB_ID column called EMP_JOB_FK. This constraint ensures that any job identifier entered into the JOB_ID column in the EMPLOYEES table must exist in the JOBS table as a primary key (PK). Here is the SQL to drop and recreate the constraint:

```
alter table employees drop constraint emp_job_fk;

alter table employees
    add constraint emp_job_fk
    foreign key (job_id)
    references hr.jobs(job_id)
    initially deferred deferrable
    enable
;
```

Future inserts or updates to the EMPLOYEES table will not validate the value inserted into the JOB_ID column against the JOBS table until a COMMIT is issued. If the constraint is not valid at COMMIT time, the entire transaction is rolled back with an error message.

How It Works

For the EMPLOYEES table, you must provide a department identifier (JOB_ID), since that column is not nullable. If the employee is part of a new department and the row in the DEPARTMENTS table is not there yet, but you want to use the employee number for other operations within the transaction before the department row is available, you have a dilemma. You could wait until all information is available in all parent tables, but this might cause a bottleneck when the employee needs her identification badge and the employee number must be printed on the badge. In another scenario, you may get all the employee and department data from a daily feed, but the order of the data is not guaranteed to be the new department before the new employee.

If you try to insert a row into the EMPLOYEES table with a job identifier that is not there yet and the constraint is not deferred, here is what happens when you try to perform the insert:

```
insert into employees
    (employee_id, first_name, last_name, email, hire_date, job_id)
values
    (301, 'Ellen', 'Kruser', 'EKRU', '31-may-1966', 'IT_WEB')
;

Error starting at line 1 in command:
insert into employees
    (employee_id, first_name, last_name, email, hire_date, job_id)
values
    (301, 'Ellen', 'Kruser', 'EKRU', '31-may-1966', 'IT_WEB')
Error report:
SQL Error: ORA-02291: integrity constraint (HR.EMP_JOB_FK) violated - parent key not found
02291. 00000 -  "integrity constraint (%s.%s) violated - parent key not found"
*Cause:    A foreign key value has no matching primary key value.
*Action:   Delete the foreign key or add a matching primary key.
```

If the constraint is set as DEFERRABLE, then the INSERT succeeds. However, if the DEPARTMENTS parent row is not there yet, a COMMIT will result in the following:

```
insert into employees
    (employee_id, first_name, last_name, email, hire_date, job_id)
values
    (301, 'Ellen', 'Kruser', 'EKRU', '31-may-1966', 'IT_WEB')
;

1 rows inserted

commit;

Error starting at line 6 in command:
commit
Error report:
SQL Error: ORA-02091: transaction rolled back
ORA-02291: integrity constraint (HR.EMP_JOB_FK) violated - parent key not found
02091. 00000 -  "transaction rolled back"
*Cause:    Also see error 2092. If the transaction is aborted at a remote
```

```
            site then you will only see 2091; if aborted at host then you will
            see 2092 and 2091.
*Action:    Add rollback segment and retry the transaction.
```

Thus, you must make sure that the parent row (in the DEPARTMENTS table) exists before performing the commit, as in this example:

```
insert into employees
    (employee_id, first_name, last_name, email, hire_date, job_id)
values
    (301, 'Ellen', 'Kruser', 'EKRU', '31-may-1966', 'IT_WEB')
;

1 rows inserted

insert into jobs
    (job_id, job_title)
values
    ('IT_WEB', 'Web Developer')
;

1 rows inserted

commit;

commit succeeded.
```

Note that the INSERT into the DEPARTMENTS table happened after the INSERT into the EMPLOYEES table. Because the constraint on the JOB_ID column was set as DEFERRABLE, the order of the inserts can be arbitrary as long as the data is consistent when the COMMIT is issued.

When you recreate the constraint, you can set the deferred constraint as INITIALLY DEFERRED or INITIALLY IMMEDIATE. In other words, even if the constraint is set to be DEFERRABLE, you can still initially perform immediate constraint checking by default with INITIALLY IMMEDIATE. If the constraint is created as INITIALLY DEFERRED, as in the recipe solution, you can turn on immediate constraint checking with this statement:

```
set constraint emp_job_fk immediate;
```

And of course, you can change it back to the DEFERRED state as follows:

```
set constraint emp_job_fk deferred;
```

The scope of the SET CONSTRAINT statement is for the duration of the transaction (until a COMMIT or ROLLBACK is issued) or until another SET CONSTRAINT command is issued.

■ **Note** You can set all applicable constraints to be deferred by using the SET CONSTRAINTS ALL DEFERRED command.

As you may infer, you cannot create a constraint as INITIALLY DEFERRED NOT DEFERRABLE. Here is the error message you will receive if you dare to try it:

```
Error starting at line 1 in command:
alter table employees
    add constraint emp_job_fk
    foreign key (job_id)
    references hr.jobs(job_id)
    initially deferred not deferrable
    enable
Error report:
SQL Error: ORA-02447: cannot defer a constraint that is not deferrable
02447. 00000 -  "cannot defer a constraint that is not deferrable"
*Cause:    An attempt was made to defer a nondeferrable constraint
*Action:   Drop the constraint and create a new one that is deferrable
```

To be able to recreate the constraint, you must know the name of the constraint to drop. To find the name of the constraint in the child and parent tables, you can look in the data dictionary tables USER_CONSTRAINTS and ALL_CONS_COLUMNS for the constraint name, as in this example:

```
select uc.table_name child_table_name,
       acc1.column_name child_column_name,
       uc.constraint_name child_constraint_name,
       acc2.table_name parent_table_name,
       uc.r_constraint_name parent_constraint_name
from user_constraints uc
   join all_cons_columns acc1
      on uc.table_name = acc1.table_name
         and uc.constraint_name = acc1.constraint_name
   join all_cons_columns acc2
      on uc.r_constraint_name = acc2.constraint_name
where uc.table_name = 'EMPLOYEES'
  and acc1.column_name = 'JOB_ID'
  and uc.constraint_type = 'R' -- foreign key
;
```

CHILD_TABLE	CHILD_COLUMN	CHILD_CONSTRAINT	PARENT_TABLE	PARENT_CONSTRAINT
EMPLOYEES	JOB_ID	EMP_JOB_FK	JOBS	JOB_ID_PK

```
1 rows selected
```

Ideally, however, you will have a data model or the original DDL used to create the tables. This is not always practical, especially when you are working with tables from a third-party package or if you inherit a database with no documentation!

There are other ways to find this information, even without using an expensive, GUI-based third-party tool. You can use Oracle's Enterprise Manager Database Control (EM Database Control), or if you are more of a developer than a DBA, you can use Oracle's free SQL Developer tool to query the tables, columns, constraints, and DDL for any table. As Figure 9-2 shows, you can browse the columns in the table, noting any NOT NULL constraints and other column attributes.

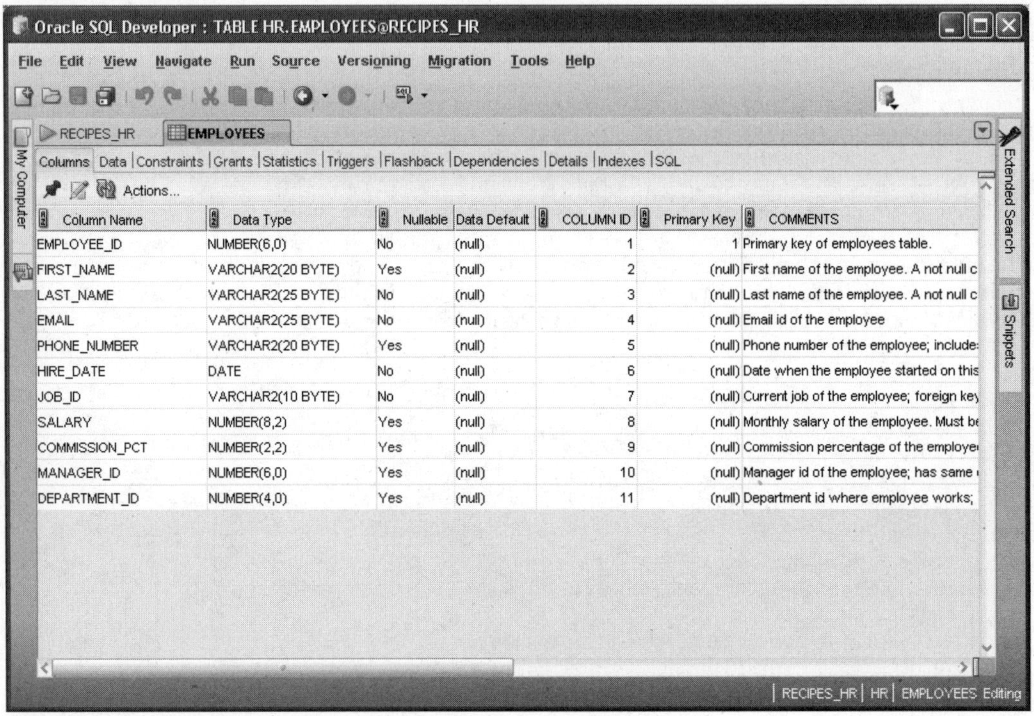

Figure 9-2. *SQL Developer view of the EMPLOYEES table's columns*

In Figure 9-3, you click on the Constraints tab for the table, and you can confirm any check constraints—including the NOT NULL constraints—as well as the names of foreign key constraints.

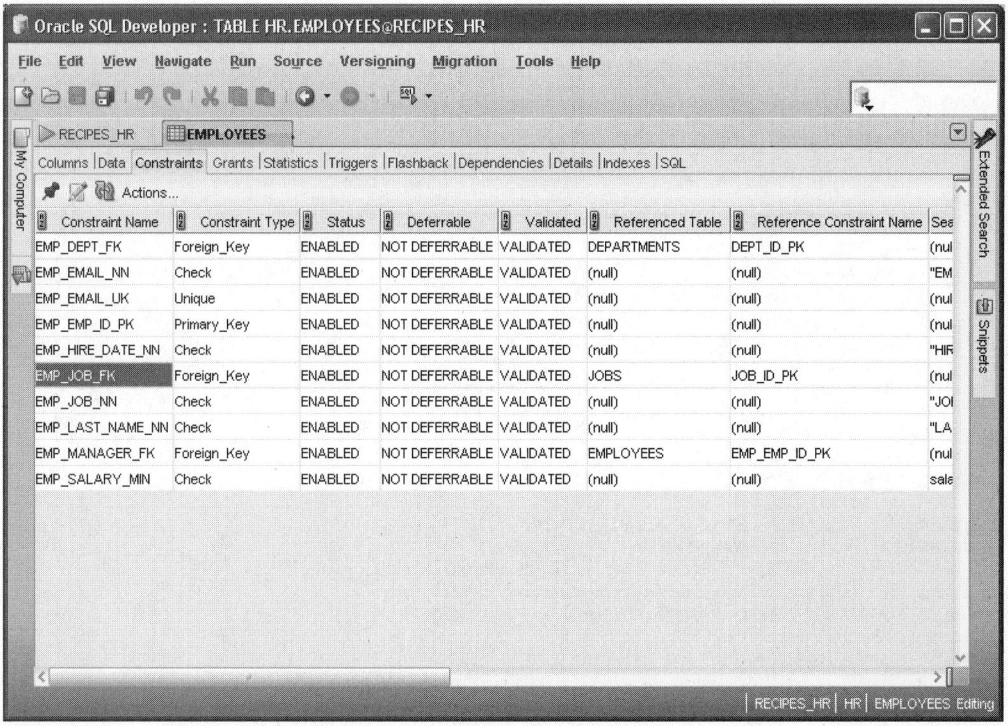

Figure 9-3. *SQL Developer view of the EMPLOYEES table's constraint*

However, you still can't explicitly link the JOB_ID column to the primary key of the parent table; to do this, you click on the SQL column for the EMPLOYEES table and SQL Developer will reverse-engineer the DDL for the EMPLOYEES table, including the foreign key constraint on the JOB_ID column, highlighted in Figure 9-4.

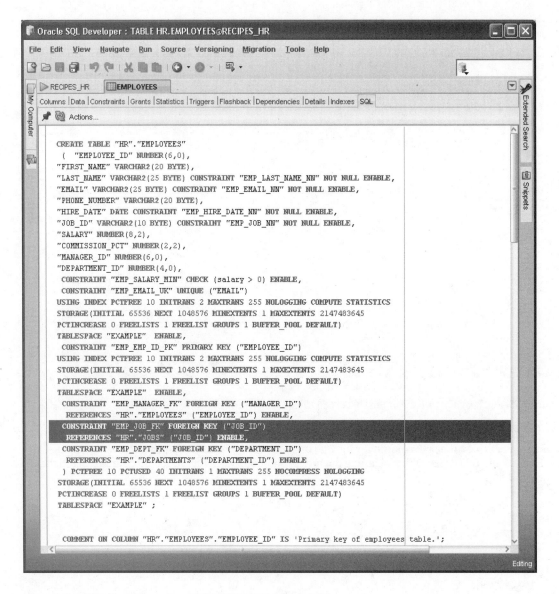

Figure 9-4. SQL Developer view of the EMPLOYEES table's DDL

For those who are GUI-phobic, an anonymous PL/SQL block such as the following will show you the actual referential integrity constraint definitions as they are stored in the data dictionary using the DBMS_METADATA built-in PL/SQL procedure:

```
declare
  v_consdef varchar2(4000);
begin
  for rec in (select constraint_name as name
              from user_constraints
              where constraint_type = 'R'
                and table_name not like 'BIN$%')
  loop
    select dbms_metadata.get_ddl('REF_CONSTRAINT', rec.name)
      into v_consdef from dual;
    dbms_output.put_line(v_consdef);
  end loop;
end;
```

9-6. Ensuring Read-Consistency Across a Transaction

Problem

By default, Oracle provides read-consistency for individual SELECT statements, but you want to ensure that several queries within a transaction maintain read-consistency until the transaction completes.

Solution

Use the SET TRANSACTION command to change the default read-consistency option. In this example, you want to run "what if" scenarios against the EMPLOYEES table, as in this example where you want to see the effects of raising or lowering salaries across a department:

```
select sum(salary+100)
from employees
where department_id = 100
;

select sum(salary-50)
from employees
where department_id = 100
;
```

However, what if another employee changes some of the salaries in department 100 after you run the first SELECT but before you start the second? The results will most likely be inconsistent with your expectations. Thus, you can run this command before starting your analyses:

```
set transaction read only;
```

Once you run this command, the entire transaction will see a read-consistent version of the EMPLOYEES table until you perform a COMMIT or ROLLBACK,

How It Works

Oracle supports *multiversioning* to provide more than one view of a table when there are multiple concurrent readers and writers. The rows returned by a query are always consistent to a single point in time. Writers never block readers and vice versa; two writers will not block each other unless they are accessing the same row in a table.

In the recipe solution, you set the transaction environment to be READ ONLY. By default, Oracle starts a transaction as READ WRITE: queries are read-consistent across a single query only. Any changes committed by another session to a table during a long-running query will not be reflected in the query results. A subsequent query, however, will see those changes. Here is how you can explicitly set the transaction isolation level to read/write:

```
set transaction read write;
```

If you perform any DML against a table in a read/write transaction, any changes against rows that have already been changed but not committed in another transaction will wait until the other transaction completes or is rolled back.

9-7. Managing Transaction Isolation Levels

Problem

You want to provide transaction-level read-consistency as well as be able to perform DML statements within the transaction.

Solution

Set the transaction isolation level to serializable by using the following command:

```
set transaction isolation level serializable;
```

Any SELECT statements throughout the transaction will be read-consistent until a COMMIT or ROLLBACK is performed. You can perform any DML statements during the transaction as long as you do not try to access any table rows that were uncommitted at the beginning of the serialized transaction.

How It Works

The *isolation level* of a transaction defines how transactions containing DML commands are managed in relation to other transactions containing DML commands. Depending on the type of isolation level, your transactions may leave the database in different states. Here are three types of phenomena that are either permitted or not permitted at a specific isolation level:

- Dirty reads: a SELECT in one transaction reads uncommitted data from another transaction.

- Fuzzy (non-repeatable) reads: a transaction reads the same row a second time and returns different data, or no data (the row has been deleted).

- Phantom reads: a transaction re-executes a query and returns more rows that have since been committed by another transaction.

Fuzzy reads and phantom reads are different in that fuzzy reads access changed or deleted rows, and phantom reads access new rows from a transaction. However, and this is a key differentiator from dirty reads, they are the same in that another transaction has committed the new or changed rows. Some databases support dirty reads for performance reasons; Oracle does not support any form of dirty reads, as you will see shortly. Table 9-2 shows the types of isolation levels defined by the ANSI SQL standard that allow these phenomena.

Table 9-2. *Read Anomalies by ANSI SQL Isolation Level*

Isolation Level	Dirty Read	Fuzzy (Non-repeatable) Read	Phantom Read
Read Uncommitted	Allowed	Allowed	Allowed
Read Committed	Not Allowed	Allowed	Allowed
Repeatable Read	Not Allowed	Not Allowed	Allowed
Serializable	Not Allowed	Not Allowed	Not Allowed

For example, if you set the isolation level of your transaction to read-committed, a SELECT statement repeated within a session may see either changed rows or new rows, but will never see uncommitted data from another transaction.

A transaction set to serializable, as in the recipe solution, appears to the session as if no one else is making changes to the database. The read-consistency extends beyond a single SELECT statement to the entire transaction. You can perform DML statements within a serializable transaction just as you can with a read-consistent transaction, with this important difference: if the serializable transaction tries to change a row that has already been changed and committed by another session after the serializable transaction has begun, you will receive this error:

```
ORA-08177: Cannot serialize access for this transaction
```

If this happens, your choices are to roll back the entire transaction or commit the work made up to this point. After a COMMIT or ROLLBACK, you will have access to the changes made by other sessions.

Using serializable isolation avoids the non-repeatable read and phantom read in Table 9-2, but at a high cost. Due to additional locking required, your transaction throughput will suffer. Serializable transactions are also more prone to deadlocks.

You can set the isolation level to read-committed (the default) by using this command:

```
set transaction isolation level read committed;
```

The ISOLATION_LEVEL clause is also available in the ALTER SESSION command.

If you want read-consistency across the entire transaction but you are not going to perform any DML commands, you can use read-only serialization (Oracle's variation from the ANSI standard) by using this command:

```
set transaction read only;
```

The advantage of using this method is that you won't receive any ORA-08177 errors. However, as with single long-running SELECT statements, if your undo retention is not set properly, you can still receive an ORA-01555 snapshot too old error. This isolation level was covered in a previous recipe.

CHAPTER 10

■ ■ ■

Data Dictionary

This chapter focuses on techniques using SQL to display information about database objects. Developers and DBAs frequently access the Oracle data dictionary to view the structure of objects, relationships between objects, frequency of events, and so on.

An effective database engineer must know where to look and how to query the database when resolving security, availability, and performance issues. Using data dictionary posters from your last Oracle conference as office wallpaper isn't enough. When problems arise, you need to know where to look and how to interpret and translate metadata information into solutions.

Graphical Tools vs. SQL

There are several graphical tools available for viewing metadata about your database. Often, a visual image is extremely valuable in troubleshooting issues in your environment. Many people are more comfortable with pointing, clicking, and visually diagnosing problems. Both novice and experienced DBAs understand the power of graphics.

So why bother learning how to use SQL manually to query the database metadata when you have powerful graphical tools that can do the job? Here are a few reasons to ponder:

- You're in a new shop where your favorite graphical tool is not available.

- There's an issue with your high-speed Internet access and you are forced to diagnose remote database issues via a sluggish dial-up connection where using a graphical display is painfully slow.

- The graphical tool won't display additional information, though you know it's available in the data dictionary.

- You're interviewing for a job and the old-school DBA seems obsessed with asking trivia questions about data dictionary views.

- There is no source code available and you want to directly query the data dictionary via SQL for information.

- You understand you'll be a more effective database engineer if you know how to retrieve information directly from the data dictionary.

- You want to attract a potential mate at the Oracle OpenWorld SQL trivia event.

- You see strange results in the graphical tool and want a second opinion.

- There are a few custom database checks you want to automate but they're not available via the visual tool.

These are not reasons to stop using graphical tools like Enterprise Manager, SQL Developer, TOAD, and so on. We fully understand the power and usefulness of these utilities. Graphical tools are invaluable for providing a quick and easy way to view the database metadata. Furthermore, these visual utilities have become ubiquitous and so it's often a job requirement to know how to use them. However, the preceding list does point out some very valid reasons why it is important to know how to use SQL to query the data dictionary. You will be a more effective database engineer if you know which data dictionary views contain the information required to solve the problem at hand.

Data Dictionary Architecture

There are two general categories of Oracle data dictionary views:

- Static USER/ALL/DBA views

- Dynamic V$ and GV$ views

In the following sections we'll discuss the basic architecture of static and dynamic views.

Static Views

Oracle describes a subset of the data dictionary views as *static*. Oracle's documentation states that these views are static in the sense that they change only when certain events transact in the database, such as the creation of a table or the granting of a privilege.

However, in some cases the static name can be something of a misnomer. For example, the DBA_SEGMENTS and DBA_EXTENTS views will change dynamically as the amount of data in your database grows and shrinks. Regardless, Oracle has made the distinction between static and dynamic and it's important to understand this architectural nuance when querying the data dictionary. There are three types or levels of static views:

- USER

- ALL

- DBA

The USER views contain information available to the current user. For example, the USER_TABLES view contains information on tables owned by the current user. No special privileges are required to select from these views.

The next level is the ALL static views. The ALL views show you all object information the current user has access to. For example, the ALL_TABLES view displays all database tables that the current user can select from. No special privileges are required to query from these views.

Next are the DBA static views. The DBA views contain metadata describing all objects in the database (regardless of ownership or access privilege). To access the DBA views you must have a DBA role or SELECT_CATALOG_ROLE granted to the current user.

The static views are based on internal Oracle tables such as USER$, TAB$, and IND$. If you have access to the SYS schema, you can view underlying tables directly via SQL. For most situations, you only need to access the static views that are based on the internal tables.

The data dictionary tables (like USER$, TAB$, and IND$) are created during the execution of the CREATE DATABASE command. As part of creating a database, the sql.bsq file is executed, which builds these internal data dictionary tables. The sql.bsq file is usually located in the ORACLE_HOME/rdbms/admin directory and can be viewed via an operating system editing utility (such as vi in UNIX or notepad in Windows).

The static views are created when you run the catalog.sql script (usually this script is run immediately after the CREATE DATABASE operation succeeds). The catalog.sql script is located in the ORACLE_HOME/rdbms/admin directory. Figure 10-1 shows the process of creating the static data dictionary views.

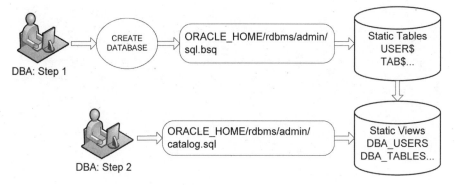

Figure 10-1. *Creating the static data-dictionary views*

Static views such as DBA_USERS, DBA_TABLES, and DBA_INDEXES are built upon the static tables (such as USER$, TAB$ and IND$). You can view the creation scripts of these static views by querying the TEXT column of DBA_VIEWS.

■ **Note** You must be connected as the SYS schema when you run the catalog.sql script. The SYS schema is the owner of all objects in the data dictionary.

Dynamic Performance Views

The dynamic performance data dictionary views are often referred to as the V$ and GV$ views. These views are constantly updated by Oracle and reflect the current condition of the instance and database. The dynamic views are critical for diagnosing real-time performance issues.

The V$ and GV$ views are indirectly based on the underlying X$ tables, which are internal memory structures that are instantiated when you start your Oracle instance. Some of the V$ views are available the moment the Oracle instance is first started. For example, the V$PARAMETER contains meaningful data after the STARTUP NOMOUNT command has been issued, and does not require the database to be mounted or open. Other dynamic views depend on information in the control file and therefore only contain meaningful information after the database has been mounted (like V$CONTROLFILE). Some V$ views provide kernel processing information (like V$BH) and thus only have useful data after the database has been opened.

At the top layer, the V$ views are synonyms that point to underlying SYS.V_$ views. At the next layer down, the SYS.V_$ objects are views created on top of another layer of SYS.V$ views. The SYS.V$ views in turn are based on the SYS.GV$ views. At the bottom layer, the SYS.GV$ views are based on the X$ memory structures.

■ **Tip** You can display the V$ and GV$ view definitions by querying the V$FIXED_VIEW_DEFINITION data dictionary view.

The top level V$ synonyms and SYS.V_$ views are created when you run the catalog.sql script, which is usually run by the DBA after the database is initially created. Figure 10-2 shows the process for creating the V$ dynamic performance views.

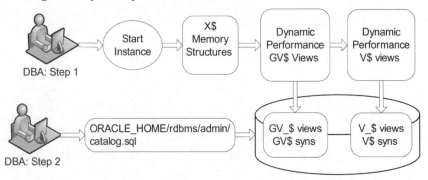

Figure 10-2. *Creating the dynamic* V$ *performance data dictionary views*

Accessing the V$ views through the top-most synonyms will almost always be adequate for your dynamic performance information needs. There will be rare occasions, however, when you'll want to query internal information that may not be available through the V$ views. In these situations, it's critical to understand the underlying X$ underpinnings.

If you work with Oracle Real Application Clusters, you should be familiar with the GV$ global views. These views provide global dynamic performance information regarding all instances in a cluster (whereas the V$ views are instance-specific). The GV$ views contain an INST_ID column for identifying specific instances within a clustered environment.

This chapter does not contain an exhaustive set of SQL scripts for querying data dictionary objects. Rather, we try to show you common (and some not- so-common) techniques for directly querying the data dictionary. You should be able to build upon the concepts in this chapter to fulfill any requirement you have for viewing data dictionary metadata.

Sys vs. System

Oracle novices sometimes ask "what's the difference between the SYS and SYSTEM schemas?" The SYS schema is the super user of the database, owns all internal data dictionary objects, and is used for tasks such as creating a database, starting or stopping the instance, backup and recovery, and adding or moving data files. These types of tasks typically require the SYSDBA or the SYSOPER role. Security for these roles is often controlled through access to the operating system account owner of the Oracle software. Additionally, security for these roles can also be administered via a password file, which allows remote client/server access.

In contrast, the SYSTEM schema isn't very special. It is just a schema that has been granted the DBA role. Many shops simply lock the SYSTEM schema after database creation and never use it because it is often the first schema a hacker will try to access when attempting to break into a database.

Rather than risking an easily guessable entry point to the database, DBAs will create a separate schema (named something other than SYSTEM) that has the DBA role granted to it. This DBA schema is used for administrative tasks such as creating users, changing passwords, granting database privileges, and so on. Having a separate DBA schema(s) for administrators provides more options for security and auditing.

10-1. Displaying User Information

Problem

You want to display information about schemas in the database.

Solution

To quickly display the schema you are currently connected as, use this statement:

```
SQL> show user;
```

To get a quick listing of information about the user you are currently connected as, query the USER_USERS view. The following query will show information like your username and the temporary and default tablespace assigned to your schema:

```
select * from user_users;
```

If you want to view information about all users in the database, use the DBA_USERS view. The following will display information such as when each account was created:

```
select
  username
 ,account_status
 ,created
```

```
,lock_date
from dba_users
order by 1;
```

All_Users and Security

Any schema with the `CREATE SESSION` system privilege can select schema information from the `ALL_USERS` view. For example:

```
select
  username
 ,created
from all_users
order by username;
```

This ability to select from `ALL_USERS` can be a security concern because it allows any user with minimal privileges (like `CREATE SESSION`) to view all user names in the database. Viewing all user information allows a malicious person to start guessing passwords for existing users. If you are a database administrator, ensure that you change the default passwords to well-known accounts and encourage users to use passwords that are not easily guessable.

How It Works

A *schema* is a collection of database objects (such as tables, indexes, and so on). A schema is owned by a database user (and has the same name as the user). A *database user* is an account through which you can log in to the database and establish a connection. A *session* is a connection to the Oracle database through a user operating-system process. Sometimes the terms *account* or *username* are also used when referring to a database user. An account can also refer to an operating system user (such as `oracle`).

When a DBA creates a user (via a `CREATE USER` statement) an entry is added to the data dictionary. You can use views like USER/ALL/DBA_USERS to display information about users in your database. You can also use the SYS_CONTEXT built-in SQL function to display a wide variety of details about your currently connected session. This example displays the user, authentication method, host, and instance:

```
select
 sys_context('USERENV','CURRENT_USER') usr
,sys_context('USERENV','AUTHENTICATION_METHOD') auth_mth
,sys_context('USERENV','HOST') host
,sys_context('USERENV','INSTANCE_NAME') inst
from dual;
```

■ **Note** The SYS_CONTEXT function can be called from either SQL or PL/SQL.

If you want to view dynamic information such as users currently logged onto your database, use the following query:

```
select
  count(*)
 ,username
from v$session
group by username;
```

If you want to see the SQL statements that currently connected users are running, issue this query:

```
select a.sid, a.username, b.sql_text
from v$session a
    ,v$sqltext_with_newlines b
where a.sql_id = b.sql_id
order by a.username, a.sid, b.piece;
```

If you're using an Oracle Database 9*i* or earlier, the previous query won't work because the SQL_ID column is not available. Here is a query that works for older versions of Oracle:

```
select a.sid, a.username, b.sql_text
from v$session a
    ,v$sqltext_with_newlines b
where a.sql_address    = b.address
and   a.sql_hash_value = b.hash_value
order by a.username, a.sid, b.piece;
```

■ **Tip** The V$SQLTEXT_WITH_NEWLINES is identical to V$SQLTEXT with the exception that V$SQLTEXT_WITH_NEWLINES does not replace tabs and newlines with spaces.

10-2. Determining the Tables You Can Access

Problem

The application you have written requires some reference information from another schema and you want to display which tables you have access to.

Solution

Users always have access to their own tables. You can query the USER_TABLES view to display your tables:

```
select table_name, tablespace_name
from user_tables;
```

Use this query to display which tables your user account has select access to:

```
select table_name, tablespace_name
from all_tables;
```

Run the following query to view table privileges that have been granted to your current user account:

```
select grantee, table_name, privilege
from user_tab_privs
where grantee = sys_context('USERENV','CURRENT_USER')
order by table_name, privilege;
```

In the previous lines of code, the SYS_CONTEXT function is used to extract the current username from the session. Without qualifying the GRANTEE to your current username, the query would also display object privileges you have granted and show privileges that have been granted by other users to your objects. The query could have alternatively prompted you for your current username. For example:

```
select grantee, table_name, privilege
from user_tab_privs
where grantee = UPPER('&your_user_name')
order by table_name, privilege;
```

How It Works

Querying the USER_TABLES view is a quick way to determine which tables exist in your current account, whereas the ALL_TABLES view contains every table you have select access to. If you have access to the DBA_TABLES view, you can also query the tables a user has access to via the following query:

```
select table_name
from dba_tables
where owner = upper('&owner');
```

When troubleshooting issues, sometimes DBAs will check columns like CREATED and LAST_DDL_TIME, which tells when the structure of the table was last modified. Use the following query to view this information:

```
select a.table_name, b.created, b.last_ddl_time, a.last_analyzed
from dba_tables  a, dba_objects b
where a.table_name = b.object_name
and    a.owner       = upper('&owner');
```

If you don't have access to the DBA-level data dictionary views, you can access the ALL or USER-level views to display information regarding objects you have privileges on. The following query shows information regarding tables for the user you're connected to the database as:

```
select a.table_name, b.created, b.last_ddl_time, a.last_analyzed
from user_tables  a, user_objects b
where a.table_name = b.object_name;
```

10-3. Displaying a Table's Disk Space Usage

Problem

You're trying to anticipate when to add space to a tablespace that contains several large tables. You want to determine how much space the tables are currently using.

Solution

The next query is handy when you want to view the space consumption of a table:

```
UNDEFINE owner
UNDEFINE tab_name
SET linesize 200
COL table_name       FORMAT A25
COL tablespace_name FORMAT A20
COL partition_name  FORMAT A25
COL file_name        FORMAT A35
COL meg_space_used  FORMAT 999,999,999.999
--
SELECT
  a.table_name
 ,b.tablespace_name
 ,b.partition_name
 ,c.file_name
 ,SUM(b.bytes)/1024/1024 meg_space_used
FROM dba_tables     a
    ,dba_extents    b
    ,dba_data_files c
WHERE a.owner      = UPPER('&&owner')
AND   a.table_name = UPPER('&&tab_name')
AND   a.owner      = b.owner
AND   a.table_name = b.segment_name
AND   b.file_id    = c.file_id
GROUP BY
  a.table_name
 ,b.tablespace_name
 ,b.partition_name
 ,c.file_name
ORDER BY a.table_name, b.tablespace_name;
```

This script will prompt you for a user and a table name. If the table has partitions, the space per partition will be displayed. You will need access to DBA-level views to run the script. You can modify the script to point at the ALL or USER-level tables to report on tables for the currently connected user account. This query also uses SQL*Plus-specific commands, such as setting the line size and column formatting, which are necessary to make the output readable.

How It Works

Each table in the database consumes some amount of physical disk space. The query in the solution section will display the space consumed in megabytes, the physical data file(s) that the table data exists in, the tablespace name, and partition names (if any).

Managing object space in Oracle starts with understanding how Oracle internally stores information regarding space usage. When a database is created, it contains multiple logical space containers called tablespaces. Each tablespace consists of one or more physical data files. Each data file consists of many operating system blocks.

Each database also contains many users. Each user has a schema that is the logical container for objects such as tables and indexes. Each table or index consists of a segment. If a table or index is partitioned, there will be many partition segments for each partitioned table or partitioned index.

Each segment contains one or more extents. As a segment needs space, it allocates additional extents. Each extent consists of a set of database blocks. A typical database block size for an online transaction processing (OLTP) database is 8K. Each database block contains one or more operating system blocks. Figure 10-3 describes the relationships between logical and physical structures in an Oracle database.

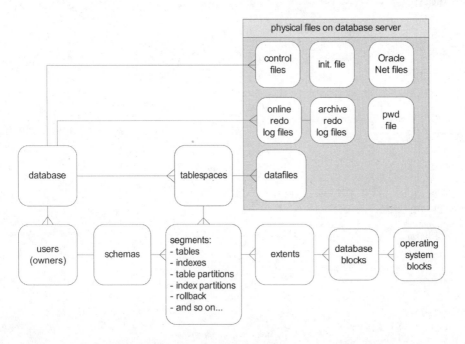

Figure 10-3. *Oracle database logical and physical structure relationships*

Table 10-1 contains a description of some of the views used to report on database physical space management. This is not an exhaustive list; rather this table contains the most commonly used tables for monitoring database space.

Table 10-1. *Overview of Database Space-Management Views*

Data Dictionary View	Purpose
V$DATABASE	Information about the database in the control file.
DBA/ALL/USER_USERS	User account information.
DBA/USER_TABLESPACES	Describes tablespaces.
DBA_DATA_FILES	Describes database datafiles.
DBA/USER_FREE_SPACE	Free extents in tablespaces
V$DATAFILE	Datafile information from the control file.
DBA/ALL/USER_TABLES	Describes table attributes.
DBA/ALL/USER_INDEXES	Describes index attributes.
DBA/USER_SEGMENTS	Storage data for segments.
DBA/ALL/USER_PART_TABLES	Partitioned table data.
DBA/ALL/USER_PART_INDEXES	Partitioned index data.
DBA/ALL/USER_TAB_PARTITIONS	Storage information for partitioned tables.
DBA/ALL/USER_IND_PARTITIONS	Storage information for partitioned indexes.
DBA/USER_EXTENTS	Extent information of each segment.
V$CONTROLFILE	Names and size of control files.
V$LOG	Online redo log file information in the control file.
V$LOG_HISTORY	Online redo log file history information in control file.
V$ARCHIVED_LOG	Archive log file information in the control file.

10-4. Displaying Table Row Counts

Problem

You want to run a report that shows the row counts of tables within a schema.

Solution

Run the following SQL code as a DBA-privileged schema. Notice that this script contains SQL*Plus-specific commands such as UNDEFINE and SPOOL. The script will prompt you each time for a username:

```
UNDEFINE user
SPOOL tabcount_&&user..sql
SET LINESIZE 132 PAGESIZE 0 TRIMSPO OFF VERIFY OFF FEED OFF TERM OFF
SELECT
    'SELECT RPAD(' || '''' || table_name || '''' ||',30)'
    || ',' || ' COUNT(*) FROM &&user..' || table_name || ';'
FROM dba_tables
WHERE owner = UPPER('&&user')
ORDER BY 1;
SPO OFF;
SET TERM ON
@@tabcount_&&user..sql
SET VERIFY ON FEED ON
```

This code will generate a file named tabcount_<user>.sql that contains the SQL statements that select row counts from all tables within the specified schema.

How It Works

Developers and DBAs often use SQL to generate SQL statements. This is a useful technique when you need to apply the same SQL process (repetitively) to many different objects, such as all tables within a schema. The code in the solution section assumes you have access to the DBA_TABLES view. If you don't have access to DBA-level views, you can query the USER_TABLES view. For example:

```
SPO tabcount.sql
SET LINESIZE 132 PAGESIZE 0 TRIMSPO OFF VERIFY OFF FEED OFF TERM OFF
SELECT
    'SELECT RPAD(' || '''' || table_name || '''' ||',30)'
    || ',' || ' COUNT(*) FROM ' || table_name || ';'
FROM user_tables
ORDER BY 1;
SPO OFF;
SET TERM ON
@@tabcount.sql
SET VERIFY ON FEED ON
```

If you have accurate statistics, you can query the ROW_NUM column of the DBA/ALL/USER_TABLES view. This column will normally have a close row count if statistics are generated on a regular basis. This query selects NUM_ROWS from the USER_TABLES view:

```
select table_name, num_rows from user_tables;
```

If you have partitioned tables and want to show row counts by partition, use the next few lines of SQL and PL/SQL code:

```
UNDEFINE user
SET SERVEROUT ON SIZE 1000000 VERIFY OFF
SPO part_count_&&user..txt
DECLARE
  counter  NUMBER;
  sql_stmt VARCHAR2(1000);
  CURSOR c1 IS
  SELECT table_name, partition_name
  FROM dba_tab_partitions
  WHERE table_owner = UPPER('&&user');
BEGIN
  FOR r1 IN c1 LOOP
    sql_stmt := 'SELECT COUNT(*) FROM &&user..' || r1.table_name
      ||' PARTITION ( '||r1.partition_name ||' )';
    EXECUTE IMMEDIATE sql_stmt INTO counter;
    DBMS_OUTPUT.PUT_LINE(RPAD(r1.table_name
      ||'('||r1.partition_name||')',30) ||' '||TO_CHAR(counter));
  END LOOP;
END;
/
SPO OFF
```

10-5. Displaying Indexes for a Table

Problem

You're experiencing some performance problems with a SQL query. You wonder if a table has any indexes.

Solution

First ensure that the object you're dealing with is a table (and not a synonym or a view). Run the following query to check whether an object is a table:

```
select
  object_name
  ,object_type
from user_objects
where object_name=upper('&object_name');
```

The prior query will prompt you for a SQL*Plus ampersand variable (OBJECT_NAME). If you're not using SQL*Plus, you may have to modify the query to explicitly query for a particular object.

Once you have verified that the object is a table, now query the USER_INDEXES view to display indexes for a particular table in your user:

```
select
  a.index_name, a.column_name, b.status, b.index_type, a.column_position
from user_ind_columns a
     ,user_indexes     b
where a.table_name = upper('&table_name')
and    a.index_name = b.index_name
order by a.index_name, a.column_position;
```

The prior query will prompt you for a SQL*Plus ampersand variable (TABLE_NAME). If you're not using SQL*Plus, you may have to modify the query to explicitly query for a specific table. The indexes and the corresponding columns will be displayed for the table you enter.

How It Works

When dealing with performance issues, one of the first items to check is which columns are indexed on a table. The USER_INDEXES view contains the index name information and the USER_IND_COLUMNS view contains the columns that are indexed. If the index is built on more than one column, the COLUMN_POSITION column will provide the order in which the columns appear in the index.

If you use function-based indexes, sometimes it's handy to display the expression used to create those indexes. The function expression is contained in the COLUMN_EXPRESSION column of the DBA/ALL/USER_IND_EXPRESSIONS view. The following script displays that expression, along with the index and table names:

```
SELECT table_name, index_name, column_expression
FROM user_ind_expressions
ORDER BY table_name;
```

10-6. Showing Foreign Key Columns Not Indexed

Problem

You have a standard for your database that all foreign key columns must have indexes created for them. You want to verify that all foreign key columns are indexed.

Solution

The following query will indicate for a schema which table columns have foreign key constraints defined for them but do not have a corresponding index:

```
select
  a.constraint_name cons_name
 ,a.table_name   tab_name
 ,b.column_name cons_column
 ,nvl(c.column_name,'***No Index***') ind_column
from user_constraints  a
     join
     user_cons_columns b on a.constraint_name = b.constraint_name
     left outer join
     user_ind_columns  c on b.column_name = c.column_name
                       and b.table_name   = c.table_name
where constraint_type = 'R'
order by 2,1;
```

Any column that has a foreign key constraint but no corresponding index will be noted in the last column of the output with the text ***No Index***. Here is some sample output:

```
CONS_NAME            TAB_NAME             CONS_COLUMN          IND_COLUMN
-------------------- -------------------- -------------------- ----------------
FK_DEPOSITS          DEPOSITS             BATCH_NO             ***No Index***
```

How It Works

The query in the solution section joins three views. The USER_CONSTRAINTS view contains definitions of all constraints in a user's schema. This is joined to USER_CONS_COLUMNS, which contains information about the columns accessible to the user that are used in constraints. A LEFT OUTER JOIN clause is placed between USER_CONS_COLUMNS and USER_IND_COLUMNS because there might be a case where the view on the left-hand side of the join has rows without corresponding rows on the right. We then apply the condition that any constraints reported by this query are of type R (a referential or foreign key constraint).

The following listing shows the old Oracle syntax style for querying with an outer join. The outer join is specified by the (+) characters.

```
select
  a.constraint_name cons_name
 ,a.table_name   tab_name
 ,b.column_name cons_column
 ,nvl(c.column_name,'***No Index***') ind_column
from user_constraints  a
    ,user_cons_columns b
    ,user_ind_columns  c
```

```
where constraint_type = 'R'
and a.constraint_name = b.constraint_name
and b.column_name      = c.column_name(+)
and b.table_name       = c.table_name(+)
order by 2,1;
```

10-7. Displaying Constraints

Problem

You want to display the constraints associated with a table.

Solution

Query the DBA_CONSTRAINTS view to display constraint information for an owner and table name. The following script will prompt you for two SQL*Plus ampersand variables (OWNER and TABLE_NAME). If you are not using SQL*Plus, you may need to modify the script with the appropriate values before you run the script:

```
select
 (case constraint_type
    when 'P' then 'Primary Key'
    when 'R' then 'Foreign Key'
    when 'C' then 'Check'
    when 'U' then 'Unique'
    when 'O' then 'Read Only View'
    when 'V' then 'Check view'
    when 'H' then 'Hash expression'
    when 'F' then 'REF column'
    when 'S' then 'Supplemental logging'
  end) cons_type
 ,constraint_name cons_name
 ,search_condition check_cons
 ,status
from dba_constraints
where owner      like upper('&owner')
and   table_name like upper('&table_name')
order by cons_type;
```

Here is some sample output:

```
CONS_TYPE         CONS_NAME              CHECK_CONS                      STATUS
---------------   --------------------   -----------------------------   --------
Check             SYS_C0030642           "DOWNLOAD_COUNT" IS NOT NULL    ENABLED
Check             SYS_C0030643           "CREATE_DTT" IS NOT NULL        ENABLED
Foreign Key       F_DOWN_SKUS_FK1                                        ENABLED
Foreign Key       F_DOWN_PRODS_FK1                                       ENABLED
Foreign Key       F_DOWN_PROD_DESC_FK1                                   ENABLED
Foreign Key       F_DOWN_LOCS_FK1                                        ENABLED
```

As you can see from the output, this table has two check constraints and four foreign key constraints enabled. The SEARCH_CONDITION column of DBA_CONSTRAINTS contains the text of the search condition for CHECK type constraints.

How It Works

The DBA/ALL/USER_CONSTRAINTS views document the constraints defined for tables in your database. Integrity constraints allow you to define rules about your data that are verified by the database engine before the data can be successfully added or modified. This ensures that your data has a high degree of quality.

The CONSTRAINT_TYPE column of the DBA/ALL/USER_CONSTRAINTS views is a one character code. There are currently nine different types of constraints. Table 10-2 describes the integrity constraints available.

Table 10-2. *Integrity Constraints*

Constraint Code	Meaning
C	Check for a condition
P	Primary key
U	Unique key
R	Referential integrity (foreign key)
V	With check option on a view
O	With read only on a view
H	Hash expression
F	Constraint with a REF column
S	Supplemental logging

■ **Note** The check constraint types of H, F, and S are available only in Oracle Database 11*g* or higher.

10-8. Showing Primary Key and Foreign Key Relationships

Problem

You know that a child table has foreign key constraints defined on it. You want to show the child table foreign key constraints and its corresponding parent table primary key constraints.

Solution

The following script queries the DBA_CONSTRAINTS view to determine the parent primary key constraints that are related to child foreign key constraints. This script correlates foreign key columns (for the entered table) to any parent key column constraints:

```
select
 a.constraint_type cons_type
,a.table_name      child_table
,a.constraint_name child_cons
,b.table_name      parent_table
,b.constraint_name parent_cons
,b.constraint_type cons_type
from dba_constraints a
    ,dba_constraints b
where a.owner     = upper('&owner')
and a.table_name = upper('&table_name')
and a.constraint_type = 'R'
and a.r_owner = b.owner
and a.r_constraint_name = b.constraint_name;
```

The preceding script will prompt you for two SQL*Plus ampersand variables (OWNER and TABLE_NAME). If you are not using SQL*Plus, you may need to modify the script with the appropriate values before you run the script.

```
C CHILD_TABLE     CHILD_CONS          PARENT_TABLE     PARENT_CONS         C
- --------------- ------------------- ---------------- ------------------- -
R REG_COMPANIES   REG_COMPANIES_FK2   D_COMPANIES      D_COMPANIES_PK      P
R REG_COMPANIES   REG_COMPANIES_FK1   CLUSTER_BUCKETS  CLUSTER_BUCKETS_PK  P
```

This output shows that there are two foreign key constraints and it also shows the parent table primary key constraints.

How It Works

Sometimes when troubleshooting data integrity issues, you'll need to verify how foreign keys are related to primary keys. This usually involves interrogating one of the DBA/ALL/USER_CONSTRAINTS views.

When the CONSTRAINT_TYPE column contains an R value, this indicates that the row describes a referential integrity constraint, which means that the child table constraint references a primary key constraint. We use the technique of joining to the same table twice to retrieve the primary key constraint information. The child constraint columns (R_OWNER and R_CONSTRAINT_NAME) will match with another row in the DBA_CONSTRAINTS view that contains the primary key information.

You can also do the reverse of the problem for this recipe. In other words, for a primary key constraint, find the foreign key columns (if any) that correlate to it. The next script takes the primary key record and looks to see if it has any child records that have a constraint type of R. When you run this script, you will be prompted for the primary key table owner and name:

```
select
  b.table_name          primary_key_table
 ,a.table_name          fk_child_table
 ,a.constraint_name     fk_child_table_constraint
from dba_constraints a
    ,dba_constraints b
where a.r_constraint_name = b.constraint_name
and    a.r_owner          = b.owner
and    a.constraint_type  = 'R'
and    b.owner            = upper('&table_owner')
and    b.table_name       = upper('&table_name');
```

Here is some sample output:

```
PRIMARY_KEY_TABLE    FK_CHILD_TABLE      FK_CHILD_TABLE_CONSTRAINT
-------------------  ------------------  -------------------------------
CLUSTER_BUCKETS      CB_AD_ASSOC         CB_AD_ASSOC_FK1
CLUSTER_BUCKETS      CLUSTER_CONTACTS    CLUSTER_CONTACTS_FK1
CLUSTER_BUCKETS      CLUSTER_NOTES       CLUSTER_NOTES_FK1
CLUSTER_BUCKETS      DOMAIN_NAMES        DOMAIN_NAMES_FK1
CLUSTER_BUCKETS      REG_COMPANIES       REG_COMPANIES_FK1
CLUSTER_BUCKETS      CB_MS_ASSOC         CB_MS_ASSOC_FK2
```

The output indicates that the CLUSTER_BUCKETS table has several foreign key constraints that refer to it.

10-9. Displaying Object Dependencies

Problem

You're about to drop a table and you wonder what other objects may be dependent on it.

Solution

Use the DBA_DEPENDENCIES view to display object dependencies. The following query will prompt you for a user and an object name:

```
select '+' || lpad(' ',level+2) || type || ' ' || owner || '.' || name  dep_tree
from dba_dependencies
connect by prior owner = referenced_owner and prior name = referenced_name
and prior type = referenced_type
start with referenced_owner = upper('&object_owner')
and referenced_name = upper('&object_name')
and owner is not null;
```

In the output, each object listed has a dependency on the object you entered. Lines are indented to show the dependency of an object on the object in the preceding line.

```
DEP_TREE
-----------------------------------------------------------
+    TRIGGER STAR2.D_COMPANIES_BU_TR1
+    MATERIALIZED VIEW CIA.CB_RAD_COUNTS
+    SYNONYM STAR1.D_COMPANIES
+     SYNONYM CIA.D_COMPANIES
+      MATERIALIZED VIEW CIA.CB_RAD_COUNTS
```

In this example, the object being analyzed is a table named D_COMPANIES. There are several synonyms, materialized views, and one trigger that are dependent on this table. For example, the materialized view CB_RAD_COUNTS owned by CIA is dependent on the synonym D_COMPANIES owned by CIA, which in turn is dependent on the D_COMPANIES synonym owned by STAR1.

How It Works

The DBA_DEPENDENCIES view is handy for determining what database objects are dependent on other database objects. For example, you may have a table that has synonyms, views, materialized views, functions, procedures, and triggers that rely on it. You may want to drop or modify a table, and before making the changes you want to review what other objects are dependent on the object you are modifying.

The DBA_DEPENDENCIES view contains a hierarchical relationship between the OWNER, NAME, and TYPE columns and their referenced column names of REFERENCED_OWNER, REFERENCED_NAME, and REFERENCED_TYPE. Oracle provides a number of constructs to perform hierarchical queries. For example, START WITH and CONNECT BY allow you to identify a starting point in a tree and walk either up or down the hierarchical relationship.

■ **Note** See Chapter 13 for a complete discussion of hierarchical queries.

The SQL in the solution section operates on only one object. If you want to inspect every object in a schema, you can use SQL to generate SQL to create scripts that display all dependencies for a schema's objects. The next section of code does that. For formatting and output, we used some constructs specific to SQL*Plus, such as setting the page sizes and line size and spooling the output:

```
UNDEFINE owner
SET LINESIZE 132 PAGESIZE 0 VERIFY OFF FEEDBACK OFF TIMING OFF
SPO dep_dyn_&&owner..sql
SELECT 'SPO dep_dyn_&&owner..txt' FROM DUAL;
--
SELECT
'PROMPT ' || '_____'|| CHR(10) ||
'PROMPT ' || object_type || ': ' || object_name || CHR(10) ||
'SELECT ' || '''' || '+' || '''' || ' ' || '''|| LPAD(' || '''' || ' ' || '''' || ',level+3)'
|| CHR(10) || ' || type || ' ' || '''' || ' ' || '''' ||
' || owner || ' || '''' || '.' || '''' || ' || name' || CHR(10) ||
' FROM dba_dependencies ' || CHR(10) ||
' CONNECT BY PRIOR owner = referenced_owner AND prior name = referenced_name '
|| CHR(10) ||
' AND prior type = referenced_type ' || CHR(10) ||
' START WITH referenced_owner = ' || '''' || UPPER('&&owner') || '''' || CHR(10) ||
' AND referenced_name = ' || '''' || object_name || '''' || CHR(10) ||
' AND owner IS NOT NULL;'
FROM dba_objects
WHERE owner = UPPER('&&owner')
AND object_type NOT IN ('INDEX','INDEX PARTITION','TABLE PARTITION');
--
SELECT 'SPO OFF' FROM dual;
SPO OFF
SET VERIFY ON LINESIZE 80 FEEDBACK ON
```

You should now have a script named dep_dyn_<owner>.sql created in the same directory you ran the script from. This script contains all of the SQL required to display dependencies on objects within the owner you entered. Run the script to display object dependencies. In this example, the owner is CIA:

```
SQL> @dep_dyn_cia.sql
```

When the script runs, it will spool a file with the format of dep_dyn_<owner>.txt. You can open that text file with an operating system editor to view its contents. Here's a sample of the output from this example:

```
TABLE: DOMAIN_NAMES
+      FUNCTION STAR2.GET_DERIVED_COMPANY
+      TRIGGER STAR2.DOMAIN_NAMES_BU_TR1
+      SYNONYM CIA_APP.DOMAIN_NAMES
```

The previous output shows that the table DOMAIN_NAMES has three objects that are dependent on it, a function, a trigger, and a synonym.

Utldtree

Oracle provides a script that will build objects that can be used to display a dependency tree. To install UTLDTREE, run this script in the schema in which you want to analyze dependencies:

```
SQL> @?/rdbms/admin/utldtree
```

Now you can build a dependency tree by executing the DEPTREE_FILL procedure. This procedure accepts three arguments: object type, owner, and object name:

```
SQL> exec deptree_fill('table','inv_mgmt','inv');
```

To display the dependency tree, issue this SQL statement:

```
SQL> select * from ideptree;
```

Be aware that when running the UTLDTREE script, it will drop and create objects within the currently connected user account: therefore we recommend using this utility only in a test or development environment.

10-10. Displaying Synonym Metadata

Problem

You want to display information regarding a synonym.

Solution

Use the following SQL to view synonym metadata for a user:

```
select
  synonym_name, table_owner, table_name, db_link
from user_synonyms
order by 1;
```

The ALL_SYNONYMS view will display all private synonyms, all public synonyms, and also any private synonyms owned by different users where you have select access to the underlying base table. You can display information for all private and public synonyms in your database by querying the DBA_SYNONYMS view.

How It Works

The `TABLE_NAME` column in the `DBA/ALL/USER_SYNONYMS` views is a bit of a misnomer because `TABLE_NAME` can actually reference many types of database objects, such as another synonym, view, package, function, procedure, materialized view, and so on. Similarly, `TABLE_OWNER` refers to the owner of the object (and that object may not necessarily be a table).

You can also use the `GET_DDL` function of the `DBMS_METADATA` package to display synonym metadata. You must pass the `GET_DDL` function the object type, name, and schema, for example:

```
select
  dbms_metadata.get_ddl('SYNONYM','VDB','INV')
from dual;
```

When diagnosing data integrity issues, sometimes you'll first want to identify what table or object is actually being accessed. You can select from what appears to be a table, but in reality it can be a synonym that points to a view that selects from a synonym that in turn points to a table in a different database.

The following query is often a starting point for figuring out if an object is a synonym, view, or a table:

```
select
 owner
,object_name
,object_type
,status
from dba_objects
where object_name like upper('&object_name%');
```

Notice that using the percent sign wildcard character in this query allows you to enter the partial name of the object. Therefore the query has the potential to return information regarding any object that partially matches the text string you enter.

10-11. Displaying View Text

Problem

You want to see the text associated with a view.

Solution

Use the following script to display the text associated with a particular view for a user:

```
select
  view_name
 ,text
```

```
from dba_views
where owner = upper('&owner')
and view_name like upper('&view_name');
```

You can also query from the ALL_VIEWS view for the text of any view you have access to:

```
select text
from all_views
where owner='INV'
and view_name='INV_VIEW';
```

If you want to display the view text that exists within your schema, use the USER_VIEWS view:

```
select text
from user_views where view_name=upper('&view_name');
```

How It Works

The TEXT column of DBA_VIEWS is of data type LONG. The default amount of data in a LONG data type displayed by SQL*Plus is 80 characters. If you don't SET LONG to a length greater than the number of characters in the TEXT column, only part of the view listing will be shown. You can determine the view length by querying the TEXT_LENGTH column of DBA/ALL/USER_VIEWS.

You can also use the DBMS_METADATA package GET_DDL function to display a view's code. The data type returned from GET_DDL is a CLOB, therefore if you run it from SQL*Plus, make sure you first set your LONG variable to a sufficient size to display all of the text. For example, here's how to set LONG to 5000 characters:

```
SQL> set long 5000
```

You need to provide the GET_DDL function the object type, name, and schema respectively. You can display the view code by invoking DBMS_METADATA.GET_DDL with a SELECT statement as follows:

```
select
  dbms_metadata.get_ddl('VIEW','USER_VIEW','INV')
from dual;
```

Oracle Internal View Definitions

You may occasionally need to view the definition of an Oracle internal view. For example, you might be troubleshooting an issue and need to know more details on how Oracle is retrieving information from the data dictionary. Select from the V$FIXED_VIEW_DEFINITION view for definitions of the V$ views. This example selects the text of the V$BH view:

```
select view_definition from v$fixed_view_definition where view_name='V$BH';
```

Here is the corresponding output:

```
select file#, block#, class#, status, xnc, forced_reads,

forced_writes, lock_element, addr, lock_element_name,

lock_element_class, dirty, temp, ping, stale, direct,

new, objd, ts#  from gv$bh where inst_id = USERENV('Instance')
```

Displaying these definitions can also give you a better understanding of the intricacies of Oracle internals.

10-12. Displaying Database Code

Problem

You want to display the code associated with PL/SQL object or a trigger.

Solution

Select from the USER_SOURCE view to see trigger code:

```
select
  text
from user_source
where name like upper('&unit_name%')
and type    = 'TRIGGER'
order by type, name, line;
```

The TYPE column is used because there can be different types of PL/SQL within the USER_SOURCE view, such as procedures, functions, and packages. For example, it's possible that you may have named a trigger with the exact same name as a procedure of function. Therefore you need to use the TYPE column or you could return some confusing results.

How It Works

With the SQL example in the solution section of this recipe, you can type in a partial name of the trigger. The LIKE predicate can be used with wildcard characters such as the percent sign and the underscore. The percent sign instructs LIKE to match on any number of characters you type in, whereas the underscore symbol matches on exactly one character.

The TEXT column in the DBA/ALL/USER_SOURCE views is a VARCHAR2 column (and not a LONG). Therefore you don't need to set the SQL*Plus LONG variable before querying the view.

You can also use the DBMS_METADATA package GET_DDL function to display trigger code. The data type that is returned from GET_DDL is a CLOB, therefore if you run it from SQL*Plus, make sure you first set your LONG variable to a sufficient size to display all of the text. For example, to set LONG to 5000 characters:

```
SQL> set long 5000
```

You need to provide the GET_DDL function the object type, name, and owner respectively. You can display the trigger code by invoking DBMS_METADATA.GET_DDL with a SELECT statement as follows:

```
select
  dbms_metadata.get_ddl('TRIGGER', 'INVTRIG_BU1', 'INV')
from dual;
```

For triggers, you can also view source information in the DBA/ALL/USER_TRIGGERS static views. For example:

```
select
   trigger_name
 ,triggering_event
 ,trigger_type
 ,table_name
 ,trigger_body
from user_triggers
where trigger_name = upper('&trigger_name');
```

The TRIGGER_BODY column is of type LONG, so if you're running this code from SQL*Plus, be sure to use the SET LONG command to make the size large enough to display all of the trigger code.

10-13. Displaying Granted Roles

Problem

You want to display the roles that a user has been granted.

Solution

Use this query to view which roles are granted to the currently connected user:

```
select
  username, granted_role
from user_role_privs;
```

This next query displays the roles that have been granted to a specific user:

```
select
  grantee
 ,granted_role
from dba_role_privs
where grantee = upper('&grantee')
order by grantee;
```

How It Works

A role is a database object that lets you group together system and object privileges and then grant that grouping (the role) to another user or role. Roles help manage database security. For example, DBAs will often use roles in the management and administration of database object privileges and system privileges.

The USER_ROLE_PRIVS and DBA_ROLE_PRIVS views describe roles granted to users. To view roles granted to roles, query the ROLE_ROLE_PRIVS view:

```
select role, granted_role
from role_role_privs;
```

When you create a database, several predefined roles are created for you, including. DBA and SELECT_CATALOG_ROLE. To view all roles in your database (both predefined and user-created), select the ROLE column from DBA_ROLES:

```
select role from dba_roles;
```

Here is some sample output of role names in a typical database:

```
CONNECT
RESOURCE
DBA
SELECT_CATALOG_ROLE
EXECUTE_CATALOG_ROLE
DELETE_CATALOG_ROLE
EXP_FULL_DATABASE
IMP_FULL_DATABASE
```

Roles in USER$

Internally, role names are stored in the data dictionary USER$ table. If you run this SELECT statement you'll see all of the role names in your database:

```
select name

from user$

where type# = 0;
```

Compare that output to the following query:

```
select role

from dba_roles;
```

You'll notice that there are a few roles in the first query that do not appear in the second.

10-14. Displaying Object Privileges

Problem

You want to see what object-level privileges have been granted to a user.

Solution

The following query selects from the USER_TAB_PRIVS_RECD view to display the table privileges that have been granted to the currently connected user:

```
select
  owner
 ,table_name
 ,grantor
 ,privilege
from user_tab_privs_recd;
```

To view privileges that the current user has granted to other users, select from the USER_TAB_PRIVS_MADE view:

```
select
  grantee
 ,table_name
 ,grantor
 ,privilege
from user_tab_privs_made;
```

How It Works

Object privileges are grants that allow you to perform data manipulation (DML) operations (INSERT, UPDATE, and DELETE) on another user's tables. Before you can perform DML operations on another user's objects, you must be granted the appropriate privileges. Object privileges are managed through the GRANT and REVOKE statements.

This next query selects from USER_TAB_PRIVS and ROLE_TAB_PRIVS to check for any object privileges that have been granted directly to the user or granted through a role that has been granted to the user:

```
select
  grantee
 ,owner
 ,table_name
 ,grantor
 ,privilege
from user_tab_privs
union
```

```
select
  role
 ,owner
 ,table_name
 ,'ROLE'
 ,privilege
from role_tab_privs
order by 2, 3;
```

The ROLE_TAB_PRIVS view will show table privileges that have been granted to a role that the current user has access to.

10-15. Displaying System Privileges

Problem

You want to see the database system privileges assigned to a user.

Solution

Query the DBA_SYS_PRIVS view to display which system privileges have been granted to various user. Listed next is a simple script that prompts for the GRANTEE:

```
select
  grantee
 ,privilege
 ,admin_option
from dba_sys_privs
where grantee = UPPER('&grantee')
order by privilege;
```

To view system privileges granted to the currently connected user, run this query:

```
select username, privilege, admin_option
from user_sys_privs;
```

The USERNAME column will show whether the privilege has been granted to the currently connected user or if the privilege has been granted to PUBLIC.

How It Works

The DBA_SYS_PRIVS view displays system privileges granted to database users and roles. System privileges allow you to manage some aspect of the database like creating tables and views. For example, some commonly granted privileges are CREATE TABLE and CREATE VIEW.

The ROLE_SYS_PRIVS view displays what system privileges have been assigned to a role. When querying this view, you will only see roles that have been granted to the currently connected schema:

```
select
  role, privilege
from role_sys_privs
where role = upper('&role');
```

The SQL example in the Solution section displays only database system privileges that have been directly granted to a user. To view any system privileges that have been granted through a role to a user, you have to additionally query a view such as ROLE_SYS_PRIVS. The following query will display system privileges granted either directly to the currently connected user or through any roles granted to the user:

```
select
 privilege
,'DIRECT GRANT'
from user_sys_privs
union
select
privilege
,'ROLE GRANT'
from role_sys_privs;
```

Two roles—CONNECT and RESOURCE—are commonly assigned to newly created accounts. However, Oracle recommends not assigning these roles to users because they may not be available in future releases. Instead, Oracle advises that you create your own roles and assign privileges as required. Run this query to view privileges assigned to these roles:

```
select grantee, privilege
from dba_sys_privs
where grantee IN ('CONNECT','RESOURCE')
order by grantee;
```

Here is the output:

```
ROLE                     PRIVILEGE
------------------------ ------------------------
CONNECT                  CREATE SESSION
RESOURCE                 CREATE CLUSTER
RESOURCE                 CREATE INDEXTYPE
RESOURCE                 CREATE OPERATOR
RESOURCE                 CREATE PROCEDURE
RESOURCE                 CREATE SEQUENCE
RESOURCE                 CREATE TABLE
RESOURCE                 CREATE TRIGGER
RESOURCE                 CREATE TYPE
```

There are a great many data dictionary views that can be used to determine what users and roles have been assigned which system and object privileges. We have touched on just a few examples in this recipe. See Table 10-3 for a description of the various privilege-related data dictionary views and their purposes.

Table 10-3. *Privilege-Related Data Dictionary Views*

Role	Description
DBA_ROLES	All roles in the database.
DBA_ROLE_PRIVS	Roles granted to users and roles.
DBA_SYS_PRIVS	All system privileges granted to users and roles.
DBA_TAB_PRIVS	All object privileges granted to users and roles.
DBA_COL_PRIVS	All column object grants.
ROLE_ROLE_PRIVS	Roles granted to other roles, only for roles that the user has access to.
ROLE_SYS_PRIVS	Privileges granted to other roles, only for roles that the user has access to.
ROLE_TAB_PRIVS	Table privileges granted to roles, only for roles that the user has access to.
ALL_TAB_PRIVS	Object grants for which the user is the object owner, grantor, or grantee; also object grants for which PUBLIC is the grantee.
ALL_TAB_PRIVS_MADE	Object grants where the user is the object owner or grantor.
ALL_TAB_PRIVS_RECD	Object grants where the user is the grantee or where PUBLIC is the grantee.
ALL_COL_PRIVS	Column object grants where the user is the object owner, grantor, or grantee; also column grants where PUBLIC is the grantee.

Table 10-3. *Privilege-Related Data Dictionary Views (continued)*

Role	Description
ALL_COL_PRIVS_MADE	Column object grants where the user is the object owner or grantor.
ALL_COL_PRIVS_RECD	Column object grants where the user is the grantee or PUBLIC is the grantee.
USER_ROLE_PRIVS	Roles granted to the user.
USER_SYS_PRIVS	System privileges granted to the user.
USER_TAB_PRIVS	Object grants for which the user is the object owner, grantor, or grantee.
USER_TAB_PRIVS_MADE	Object grants where the user is the object owner.
USER_TAB_PRIVS_RECD	Object grants where the user is the grantee.
USER_COL_PRIVS	Column object grants where the user is the object owner, grantor, or grantee.
USER_COL_PRIVS_MADE	Column object grants where user it he the object owner.
USER_COL_PRIVS_RECD	Column object grants where the user is the grantee.

PART 4

Special Topics

■ ■ ■

CHAPTER 11

Common Reporting Problems

As a SQL developer, DBA, or power user, at some point you'll have to write reports to share with colleagues, management, clients, or other companies. If you're lucky, you'll be able to concentrate on the logic and presentation of your reports in peace and quiet. Unfortunately, however, you'll almost certainly be confronted with "shoulder surfing" report critics. You know the kind: they stand behind you, gesticulating at the screen, offering helpful advice like "That should be converted to a spreadsheet." or "Can you make it look like the old report? It's easier to read that way."

Many of these demands will have common solutions, to rotate, compress, substitute and otherwise transform perfectly normal report data into a format that's more familiar or suitable for the intended audience. This chapter covers many common styles of reporting, and offers some common and not-so-common solutions to help you meet your immediate needs, as well as equip you with ideas to tackle future reporting scenarios we haven't thought of, but your boss surely has.

11-1. Avoiding Repeating Rows in Reports

Problem

You want to mimic the SQL*Plus BREAK feature to suppress near-identical leading data in rows of data. For instance, in a multi-column report where only the last column differs from one row to the next, you want to blank out the repeated early columns and show only the differing column's data.

Solution

Oracle's SQL*Plus tool has supported the BREAK feature for decades, and many basic text reports rely on this crude but effective formatting approach. Unfortunately, the BREAK command isn't native to SQL, so it can't be used to achieve the same results outside of SQL*Plus. Using Oracle's ROW_NUMBER analytic function and the CASE expression, you can mimic the BREAK behavior from any SQL interface.

For those not familiar with the SQL*Plus BREAK feature, the next commands illustrate it "hiding" identical job identifiers and manager identifiers in a simple SELECT statement's output. Only partial results are shown, but you can clearly see the effect.

```
break on job_id on manager_id
```

```
select job_id, manager_id, employee_id
from hr.employees
order by job_id, manager_id, employee_id;

JOB_ID       MANAGER_ID  EMPLOYEE_ID
------       ----------  -----------
...
AD_VP           100         101
                102
FI_ACCOUNT      108         109
                110
                111
                112
                113
FI_MGR          101         108
HR_REP          101         203
IT_PROG         102         103
                103         104
...
```

We can use Oracle's CASE expression and the ROW_NUMBER analytic function to mimic the BREAK feature from any SQL query interface or programming API. The next SQL statement shows these two features in action, and the identical results generated from any interface.

```
select
  case when job_ctr = 1 then job_id else null end "JOB_ID",
  case when jobman_ctr = 1 then manager_id else null end "MANAGER_ID",
  employee_id
from (
  select job_id,
  row_number() over (partition by job_id order by job_id)
    as job_ctr,
  manager_id,
  row_number() over (partition by job_id, manager_id order by job_id, manager_id)
    as jobman_ctr,
  employee_id
  from hr.employees
);
```

As promised, our results are pleasingly similar to the SQL*Plus approach, with precious ink saved in not printing repeating data.

```
JOB_ID        MANAGER_ID   EMPLOYEE_ID
----------    ----------   -----------
...
AD_VP            100          101
                 102
FI_ACCOUNT       108          109
                 110
                 111
                 112
                 113
FI_MGR           101          108
HR_REP           101          203
IT_PROG          102          103
                 103          104
...
```

How It Works

Our recipe works in two parts. The inner query selects the columns of data in which we are interested, in this case, JOB_ID, MANAGER_ID, and EMPLOYEE_ID. It also adds two further columns computed with the ROW_NUMBER analytic function that we don't see in the final output. These two columns are the JOB_CTR and JOBMAN_CTR values, and are used to number the result rows based on our explicit desire to have JOB_ID displayed first, and MANAGER_ID displayed second. Our partitioning and sorting options for JOB_CTR restarts numbering each time the JOB_ID changes. For JOBMAN_CTR, we restart numbering each time the MANAGER_ID changes within each JOB_ID.

To understand how we then use this data in the outer SELECT, let's look at the results of the subselect in isolation. The next SQL statement is the subselect executed as a stand-alone SELECT statement, followed by partial results.

```
select job_id,
 row_number() over (partition by job_id order by job_id)
    as job_ctr,
  manager_id,
  row_number() over (partition by job_id, manager_id order by job_id, manager_id)
    as jobman_ctr,
  employee_id
from hr.employees;
```

JOB_ID	JOB_CTR	MANAGER_ID	JOBMAN_CTR	EMPLOYEE_ID
...				
AD_VP	**1**	100	**1**	101
AD_VP	2	100	2	102
FI_ACCOUNT	**1**	108	**1**	109
FI_ACCOUNT	2	108	2	110
FI_ACCOUNT	3	108	3	111
FI_ACCOUNT	4	108	4	112
FI_ACCOUNT	5	108	5	113
FI_MGR	**1**	101	**1**	108
HR_REP	**1**	101	**1**	203
IT_PROG	**1**	102	**1**	103
IT_PROG	2	103	**1**	104
...				

The key to understanding our outer SELECT is the test performed by the respective CASE statement on the counters. We've emphasized in bold the values of interest in the above output.

Our outer SELECT statement is designed to test when the counter value equals one, as that signals when the related JOB_ID or MANAGER_ID value changes. Any other value indicates the row we're examining has the same JOB_ID or MANAGER_ID as the previous row. We know we've printed the relevant value already, so we can substitute a NULL that ordinarily won't be displayed. So in our partial results, we have a JOB_ID of AD_VP and MANAGER_ID of 100, both of which were counted as the first instance of those values in that combination by the ROW_NUMBER technique. Our recipe's CASE statements detect that those values should therefore be printed. The next row has the same JOB_ID and MANAGER_ID, and each has a counter value of 2. Our CASE expressions evaluate to NULL, so the final result suppresses these values, printing nothing except the EMPLOYEE_ID.

You can expand this technique to as many columns as you like. All that's needed is to pair the desired result column with a counter determined by the ROW_NUMBER technique, and to craft an identically patterned CASE statement in the outer SELECT block.

11-2. Parameterizing a SQL Report

Problem

You have a variety of SQL statements you'd like to provide to users for reporting purposes, with the ability to let them specify values for various predicates and criteria. For example, you have used SQL*Plus features for parameters, and need similar support in other query tools.

Solution

When composing reporting SQL via a programming language like Java or C#, adding parameters to your SQL statements is fairly straightforward. However, when dealing with "native" SQL and query tools, you don't have the luxury of an object model and well-defined methods for allowing users to simply provide values to parameters in a query. This recipe acts as not quite a SQL recipe, but as a SQL usage recipe.

You may previously have used the ampersand and double-ampersand labeling technique in SQL*Plus to place substitutable parameters into your SQL statements. Our recipe shows that this technique is actually supported across almost all of Oracle's query tool interfaces, such as SQL Developer, SQL Worksheet, and the APEX SQL Command tool. Even better, even some third-party tools such as TOAD support the same syntax.

We'll show our recipe in action by using the following SQL statement to query for all staff with a salary above a certain value. We'll use a parameter for the threshold salary value, to be supplied by the user at runtime.

```
select employee_id, last_name, salary
from hr.employees
where salary > &threshold_salary
```

Executing this query through SQL*Plus gives the familiar prompt for the THRESHOLD_SALARY value:

```
Enter value for threshold_salary: 15000
```

We've entered the value 15000. Our parameter is substituted, and the results are shown.

```
old   3: where salary > &threshold_salary
new   3: where salary > 15000
```

EMPLOYEE_ID	LAST_NAME	SALARY
100	King	24000
101	Kochhar	17000
102	De Haan	17000

But look what happens when we issue the identical SQL through SQL Developer. It understands Oracle's notation for parameters (or substitution variables) in query tools, and prompts you for the parameter in an intuitive dialog box as shown in Figure 11-1.

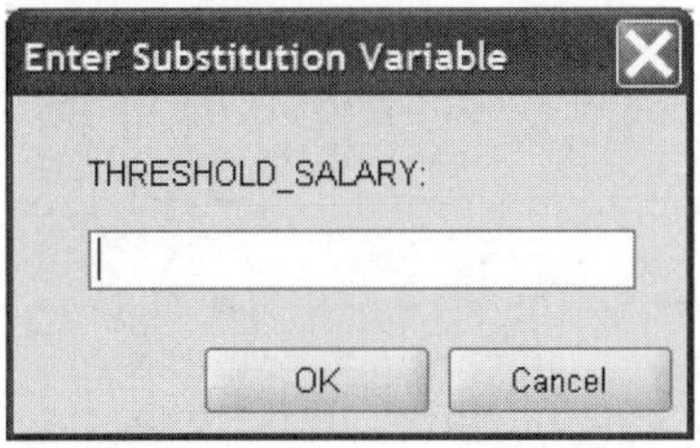

Figure 11-1. SQL Developer prompts for SQL parameters.

As you'd expect, with the value 15000 entered again, SQL Developer performs the identical substitution. Figure 11-2 shows SQL Developer returning the same results, as you'd expect.

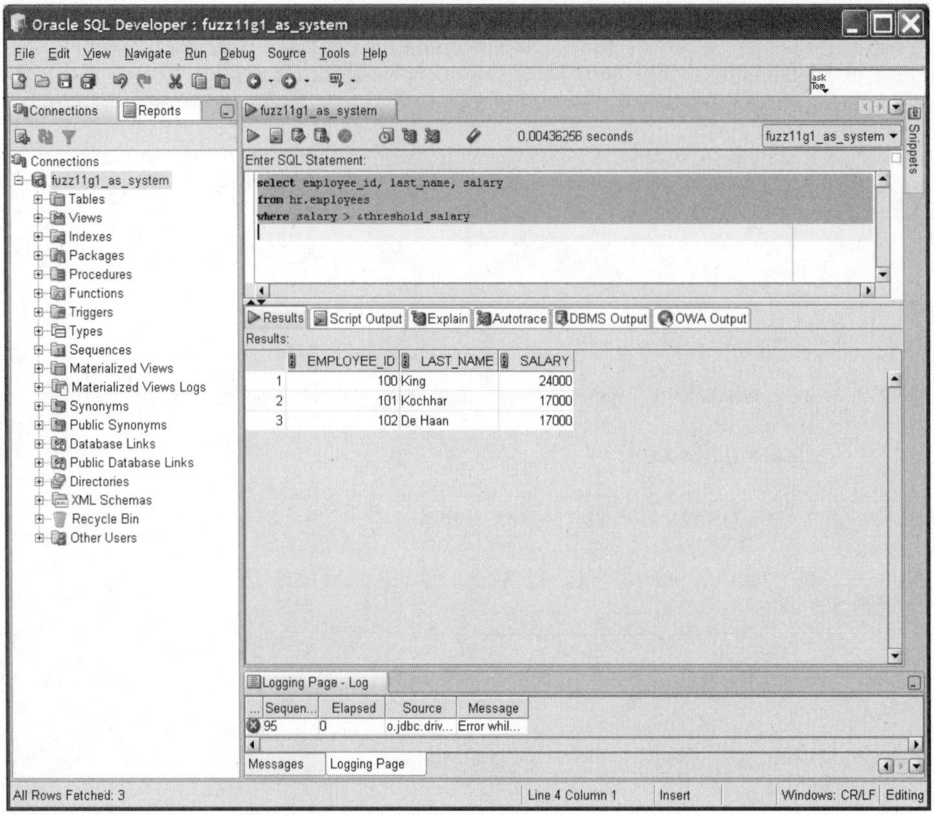

Figure 11-2. SQL Developer accepts and correctly uses Oracle-style SQL parameters.

How It Works

Early in the development of SQL*Plus, support was added for the ampersand-style substitution variables to allow users to pass parameter values to their queries. Oracle has ensured that the same technique can be used with most (if not all) of its subsequent query tools, and other companies' products have followed suit, most notably TOAD.

Both the single-ampersand and double-ampersand style of parameters can be used across all of these tools. For those unfamiliar with the difference between the two, single-ampersand parameters are temporary substitution variables, taking and using a value once for one SQL statement. If you re-execute the statement with a single-ampersand substitution variable, you'll be asked to provide a value again. A double-ampersand parameter creates a permanent substitution variable. The first value you provide will persist as the substituted value for the duration of your session.

There is an important difference between SQL*Plus-style substitution variables and bind variables in prepared statements in application code. Our recipe, and any other SQL you write utilizing substitution variables, works by using client-side string replacement techniques. SQL*Plus, SQL Developer, or your tool of choice, finds the substitution variables in your SQL before passing the statement to the Oracle database. The query tool itself prompts for the values to be substituted, and uses string functions to replace the variable marker with the value you provide. Only then does the SQL statement get sent to Oracle for parsing and execution. This means the database never knows about the substitution variables, or the string manipulation that occurred on the statement it receives.

Bind variables in prepared statements are treated very differently. Any high-level language where you use a bind variable, such as PL/SQL, Java, or C#, passes your SQL including its bind variable markers to Oracle for preparation and execution. Oracle knows the statement has bind variables present, and optimizes the query's execution plan accordingly. As you provided values for the prepared statements with bind variables, the values are sent to Oracle, which deals with the mechanics of correctly substituting them in place of the bind variables, and executing the resulting statement. Where bind variables are concerned, Oracle is fully aware of their existence, and intimately involved in their use at the database level.

11-3. Returning Detail Columns in Grouped Results

Problem

While performing aggregation with various data, you need to include additional result columns on the same line that are not going to be grouped, without changing the degree of aggregation. For example, you need aggregate data on the longest and shortest serving employees in each department, together with more detail columns on those employees without having to included them in the GROUP BY clause.

Solution

Use Oracle's analytic equivalents for functions like MAX and MIN, in conjunction with nested SELECT statements, to add additional detail to aggregate rows without affecting your degree of aggregation.

Our recipe uses the HIRE_DATE for employees within each department, together with useful information like the employee's first and last name and employee identifier. The next SQL block shows the recipe for our particular problem, but can be utilized for every similar demand to return additional detail data combined with aggregation.

```
select department_id, employee_id, first_name, last_name,
case
  when hire_date = first_hire and hire_date = last_hire
    then 'Shortest and Longest Serving'
  when hire_date = first_hire then 'Longest Serving'
  when hire_date = last_hire then 'Shortest Serving'
end Department_Tenure
from (
  select department_id, employee_id, first_name, last_name, hire_date,
  max(hire_date) over(partition by department_id) first_hire,
  min(hire_date) over(partition by department_id) last_hire
  from hr.employees
) Hire_Dates
where hire_date in (first_hire, last_hire)
order by department_id, department_tenure;
```

The results show the aggregation working as desired to return the correct determination of shortest and longest-serving employee, together with additional details about that employee.

```
DEPARTMENT_ID   EMPLOYEE_ID   FIRST_NAME   LAST_NAME   DEPARTMENT_TENURE
-------------   -----------   ----------   ---------   -----------------------------
           10           200   Jennifer     Whalen      Shortest and Longest Serving
           20           202   Pat          Fay         Longest Serving
           20           201   Michael      Hartstein   Shortest Serving
           30           119   Karen        Colmenares  Longest Serving
           30           114   Den          Raphaely    Shortest Serving
           40           203   Susan        Mavris      Shortest and Longest Serving
           50           128   Steven       Markle      Longest Serving
           50           122   Payam        Kaufling    Shortest Serving
...
```

How It Works

If we attempted a normal SELECT that looked for MIN and MAX statement, our SELECT statement would look like the next SQL block.

```
select department_id, employee_id, first_name, last_name,
  min(hire_date),  max(hire_date)
from hr.employees
group by department_id, employee_id, first_name, last_name;
```

We receive totally unhelpful results, because we were forced to group by non-aggregated columns like FIRST_NAME and EMPLOYEE_ID, and some of these are unique!

```
DEPARTMENT_ID   EMPLOYEE_ID   FIRST_NAME   LAST_NAME   MIN(HIRE_DATE)   MAX(HIRE_DATE)
-------------   -----------   ----------   ---------   --------------   --------------
           20           201   Michael      Hartstein   17-FEB-96        7-FEB-96
           20           202   Pat          Fay         17-AUG-97        17-AUG-97
           60           103   Alexander    Hunold      03-JAN-90        03-JAN-90
           60           107   Diana        Lorentz     07-FEB-99        07-FEB-99
          100           113   Luis         Popp        07-DEC-99        07-DEC-99
...
```

We have no grouping for aggregation, and all employees are returned as a detail row with their own HIRE_DATE as both the earliest and latest value—quite meaningless output, even if it is technically accurate.

If we omit the columns in the GROUP BY clause that we want included as details, Oracle quite rightly complains, as in the next SQL block.

```
select department_id, employee_id, first_name, last_name,
  min(hire_date),  max(hire_date)
from hr.employees
group by department_id;

select department_id, employee_id, first_name, last_name,
                      *
ERROR at line 1:
ORA-00979: not a GROUP BY expression
```

Using the analytic versions of MIN and MAX in an inline view, our recipe overcomes this problem. This recipe works by *expecting* many of the rows to be discarded by the outer SELECT statement, and ensures that every row in the inline view has the necessary details. The inline view from our recipe generates results (cropped to save space) that are shown next.

DEPARTMENT_ID	EMPLOYEE_ID	FIRST_NAME	LAST_NAME	HIRE_DATE	FIRST_HIRE	LAST_HIRE
10	200	Jennifer	Whalen	17-SEP-87	17-SEP-87	17-SEP-87
20	201	Michael	Hartstein	17-FEB-96	17-AUG-97	17-FEB-96
20	202	Pat	Fay	17-AUG-97	17-AUG-97	17-FEB-96
30	114	Den	Raphaely	07-DEC-94	10-AUG-99	07-DEC-94
30	119	Karen	Colmenares	10-AUG-99	10-AUG-99	07-DEC-94
30	115	Alexander	Khoo	18-MAY-95	10-AUG-99	07-DEC-94
30	116	Shelli	Baida	24-DEC-97	10-AUG-99	07-DEC-94
30	117	Sigal	Tobias	24-JUL-97	10-AUG-99	07-DEC-94
30	118	Guy	Himuro	15-NOV-98	10-AUG-99	07-DEC-94

...

The analytic MIN and MAX function have effectively recorded the hire date of the first employee and last employee in each department against every employee—even if they were neither the first or last employee themselves. At first, this will seem strange, but this is where the outer SELECT statement comes in to play. Our main SELECT uses this WHERE clause.

```
where hire_date in (first_hire, last_hire)
```

This effectively discards all rows except those where the employee's HIRE_DATE matched the calculated FIRST_HIRE or LAST_HIRE dates. Our CASE statements then simply evaluate whether the remaining rows have a HIRE_DATE that matches FIRST_HIRE or LAST_HIRE, and emits a meaningful string for our report.

11-4. Sorting Results into Equal-Size Buckets

Problem

You need to group data into equal-size buckets for a report. For instance, you want to sort your customers in quartiles based on the value of their orders, so you can identify your big spenders.

Solution

Use Oracle's two bucket-style analytic functions to perform easy bucket sorts. NTILE provides constant-height (equi-height) bucket sorts, and WIDTH_BUCKET provides constant width, histogram-style bucket sorts.

In order to find quartiles among our customers based on spending, we'll use the NTILE function. This will provide equal-sized quartiles for our analysis. The next SQL examines the total order amount by customer, returning the quartiles we seek.

```
select customer_id, order_total,
ntile(4) over (order by order_total desc) as order_quartile
from oe.orders;
```

The abbreviated results give you the feel for how the quartiles break down.

CUSTOMER_ID	ORDER_TOTAL	ORDER_QUARTILE
147	295892	1
150	282694.3	1
149	268651.8	1
...		
168	45175	2
102	42283.2	2
...		
169	15760.5	3
116	14685.8	3
...		
103	78	4
167	48	4

A common sales technique in many companies would see account representatives target the highest quartile, and ensure those customers get special treatment and support to keep the big orders rolling in. Customer 167 is unlikely to get such attention, based on a $48 order.

How It Works

The NTILE function takes the general form of specifying the number of buckets to use for grouping, and the data to use for ordering to determine the groups. In pseudo-SQL, the general form looks like this.

```
NTILE(<number of buckets>) over (<partitioning and ordering to determine bucket>)
```

In our recipe, we've instructed Oracle to create four buckets using NTILE(4), so we can create four groups to satisfy the usual meaning of quartile. The OVER (ORDER BY ORDER_TOTAL DESC) clause directs Oracle to order the data by ORDER_TOTAL in descending order for the purposes of allocating each row to the relevant bucket/quartile. Whatever data is sorted first will be allocated to the first bucket, so the choice of ascending and descending sorts in the analytic function controls whether high or low values are considered to be in the first or last bucket.

Remember, this ordering does not dictate the order in which the data will be finally displayed. It only controls bucket allocation for the NTILE function. The sample results appear to be neatly ordered by bucket, but this is just coincidence. If your data is large, or Oracle uses parallel query execution, you could find the results returned in a different order. The bucket allocation will still be correct, of course. To control the order of presentation, use a normal ORDER BY clause, as shown in the next SQL.

```
select customer_id, order_total,
ntile(4) over (order by order_total desc) as order_quartile
from oe.orders
order by 2 desc, 3;
```

This ordering ensures you will always see the highest-value orders, those in the first quartile, sorted first in the results.

You can satisfy yourself that NTILE has produced equal-size buckets by wrapping the base query into a simple outer SELECT with a COUNT function. The next SQL shows how the customer order data has been balanced across the buckets.

```
select order_quartile, count(*) as bucket_count
from (
  select customer_id, order_total,
  ntile(4) over (order by order_total desc) as order_quartile
  from oe.orders )
group by order_quartile
order by order_quartile;
```

```
ORDER_QUARTILE    BUCKET_COUNT
--------------    ------------
             1              27
             2              26
             3              26
             4              26
```

You can see how Oracle has dealt with the fact that the number of orders is not perfectly divisible into our four buckets, and has approximated a perfect balance as a result.

11-5. Creating Report Histograms

Problem

You want to report customer sales data grouped into a histogram visualization. For instance, you want to report how many customers fall into groups based on their total orders in multiples of $50,000.

Solution

Oracle's WIDTH_BUCKET analytic function generates histograms over your data based on specified grouping requirements. Using WIDTH_BUCKET in conjunction with the regular SUM function lets you form your histogram results into a meaningful report. The next SQL displays the histogram numbers based on customer sales in buckets of $50,000.

```
select count(*) Customer_Count, total_spend_histogram * 50000 Spend_Bucket
from
  (select customer_id, sum(order_total),
     width_bucket(sum(order_total),0,500000,10) as total_spend_histogram
   from oe.orders
   group by customer_id)
group by total_spend_histogram * 50000
order by 2;
```

Sales are dominated by many small customers, with a few big spenders reaching almost half a million in business.

```
CUSTOMER_COUNT  SPEND_BRACKET
--------------  -------------
            27          50000
             7         100000
             3         150000
             5         200000
             1         250000
             2         300000
             1         400000
             1         450000

8 rows selected.
```

How It Works

The WIDTH_BUCKET function splits the source data into a number of buckets based on upper and lower bounds provided to the function. The general structure WIDTH_BUCKET takes looks like this:

```
WIDTH_BUCKET
  (<expression or column>, <lower bound>, <upper bound>, <number of buckets>)
```

Working from the inline view's subquery in our recipe out, we first ask Oracle to use WIDTH_BUCKET to split our data into 10 buckets between the bounds 0 and 500000, based on the SUM or the ORDER_TOTAL values for a customer. If we run the inner SELECT statement on its own, we'd gather these results:

```
select customer_id, sum(order_total),
  width_bucket(sum(order_total),0,500000,10) as total_spend_histogram
from oe.orders
group by customer_id

CUSTOMER_ID  SUM(ORDER_TOTAL)    TOTAL_SPEND_HISTOGRAM
-----------  ----------------    ---------------------
    101          190395.1                4
    102          69211.4                 2
    103          20591.4                 1
    104          146605.5                3
    105          61376.5                 2
...
```

The results of the inline view are easy to interpret. Customer 101 spent a total of $190395.10 across all of its orders. This puts it in the 4th bucket, which would include values between $150001 and $200000. The next customer, 102, is in bucket 2, and so on.

We use the results of the inline view in our outer SQL, to count the number of customers in each bucket. As a final flourish, we multiply the customer group's histogram bucket by the value 50000 to report the histogram in multiples of 50000 as originally sought in our recipe problem.

11-6. Filtering Results by Relative Rank

Problem

You want to filter query results to find rows at an arbitrary position in the sorted results. For instance, you want to mimic the top N or nth result query capabilities of other databases.

Solution

With 11*g* Release 2, Oracle has introduced its new nth result capabilities. Until 11*g* Release 2 is widely deployed, you should use the existing analytic function ROW_NUMBER to determine the nth result, or top N result, of any grouping.

For our recipe, we want to find the employee with the third-highest salary in each department of the business. The next SQL statement uses ROW_NUMBER in a nested subquery to allow us to quickly find the third-highest salary recipient in each area.

```
select department_id, last_name, salary as third_salary
from (
  select department_id, last_name, salary,
    row_number()
      over (partition by department_id order by salary desc) sal_position
    from hr.employees )
    sal_by_dept
where sal_by_dept.sal_position = 3;
```

```
DEPARTMENT_ID    LAST_NAME     THIRD_SALARY
-------------    ---------     -------------
          30     Baida                 2900
          50     Kaufling              7900
          60     Austin                4800
          80     Errazuriz            12000
          90     De Haan              17000
         100     Chen                  8200
```

Each of the third-highest departmental salary earners is listed with the relevant salary.

How It Works

Our recipe uses Oracle's ubiquitous analytic function ROW_NUMBER to help identify which rows should be returned as the nth item in a group. The results of the ROW_NUMBER-based query are then used as an inline view within an outer query. The outer query is crafted with a WHERE clause to find the target rows.

Starting with the inline view, the key component is the OVER clause of the ROW_NUMBER function.

```
row_number()
  over (partition by department_id order by salary desc) sal_position
```

Here, we instruct Oracle to split the source data into subgroups by DEPARTMENT_ID. Within those groups, we order the data by descending salary value so we can then apply the ROW_NUMBER value. We give the resulting number the name SAL_POSITION. Here's the (partial) resulting intermediate working data of this inline view:

```
DEPARTMENT_ID    LAST_NAME    SALARY   SAL_POSITION
-------------    ---------    -------  ------------
...
          30     Raphaely     11000              1
          30     Khoo          3100              2
          30     Baida         2900              3
          30     Tobias        2800              4
...
          50     Fripp         8200              1
          50     Weiss         8000              2
          50     Kaufling      7900              3
          50     Vollman       6500              4
...
```

You can see that the highlighted rows have the third-highest salary for their respective departments and have been given the SAL_POSITION number of 3, derived from our ROW_NUMBER expression.

From this point, the operation of the outer query is clear. We have a simple SELECT of the columns we seek from the inline view, and a WHERE clause that looks for SAL_POSITION equal to 3. This technique is flexible, in that you only need to change the final WHERE clause to use a different value to find a different nth value. Here's the general form of this recipe.

```
select <desired rows from inline view>
from (
  select <desired rows>,
    row_number()
      over (
        partition by <partition column>
        order by <column for n-th detection>)
      <your_column_alias>
    from <target table> )
    <inline_view_alias>
where <inline_view_alias>.<your_column_alias> = <n-th position>;
```

One aspect you may wish to tweak is how ranking is determined. You can substitute the RANK or DENSE_RANK analytic function in place of ROW_NUMBER to control how tied or absent values affect your nth result determination.

11-7. Comparing Hypotheses on Sets of Data

Problem

You have two or more sets of similar data that need comparison at the set level. Specifically, you'd like to use a recognized hypothesis-comparison approach with your data residing in Oracle—without having to move the data to another tool or system—to compare similar purchasing history for the residents of two states.

Solution

Oracle provides a number of recognized hypothesis-testing statistical functions, including functions for F-test, T-test, ANOVA, and numerous others. Many readers will probably be wondering what on earth these types of functions do, and more importantly, why they might be useful in comparing sets of data.

Statistics students in the audience will know that tests like the T-test help in modeling linear regressions and in inferring differences in statistical mean and variance between two groups. In lay terms, a T-test could, for example, help you make decisions about whether you could sell more items online or from direct retail stores, or learn whether a particular income group is affecting your sales. The T-test tells you whether the difference between two groups is real, or an artifact of errors in your sampling or measurement.

Beer And Statistics Do Mix

The T-test was invented by staff at the Guinness Brewery in Ireland, where the proprietor was a firm believer in using statistics to make a better brew. This included examining everything from what a better quality of hops or barley might do to the beer, all the way through to determining whether the brewery would be better off by hiring the greatest minds of Oxford and Cambridge universities.

At the time of its invention, the T-test was considered one of Guinness' best trade secrets, but luckily the passage of time means you can benefit from it, both in your business data management tasks and in any beer drinking you might fancy.

For our recipe, we'll try to determine if the residents of the states of New Jersey and New York in the USA have statistically significant purchasing history for the same income brackets.

The next SQL invokes several different forms of the T-test to assess the sales history data for these two groups.

```
select substr(cust_income_level, 1, 22) income_level,
  avg(case when cust_state_province = 'NJ' then amount_sold else null end) NJ_sales,
  avg(case when cust_state_province = 'NY' then amount_sold else null end) NY_sales,
  stats_t_test_indepu(cust_state_province, amount_sold, 'STATISTIC', 'NY')
    T_observed,
  stats_t_test_indepu(cust_state_province, amount_sold)
    two_sided_p_value
from sh.customers c, sh.sales s
where c.cust_id = s.cust_id
and c.cust_state_province in ('NY','NJ')
group by rollup(cust_income_level)
order by income_level, NJ_sales, NY_sales, t_observed;
```

The results at first seem a little esoteric, but to the trained eye they indicate that our samples of New Jersey and New York residents aren't statistically related, even where they share similar incomes.

INCOME_LEVEL	NJ_SALES	NY_SALES	T_OBSERVED	TWO_SIDED_P_VALUE
A: Below 30,000	355.49			
B: 30,000 - 49,999	69.5092135	76.8800909	.823635357	.410381645
C: 50,000 - 69,999	117.665082	178.304286	2.07992326	.038877289
D: 70,000 - 89,999	87.3445326	88.2114295	.107196057	.914642507
E: 90,000 - 109,999	117.349201	74.2791951	-3.9997919	.000067875
F: 110,000 - 129,999	83.0574793	107.932624	2.10680901	.035346513
G: 130,000 - 149,999	113.41765	107.76663	-.67993691	.496585995
H: 150,000 - 169,999	87.9378656	75.5795925	-1.0492257	.294347158
I: 170,000 - 189,999	61.99	106.499274	.980448064	.422460165
J: 190,000 - 249,999	17.99	104.578557	6.66684928	.008117071
K: 250,000 - 299,999	87.341512	8.7281255	-2.1514597	.032154957
L: 300,000 and above	64.43125	126.332644	2.79656692	.005747719
	98.6444766	95.11524	-.93404774	.350301558

How It Works

The mechanics of our recipe can be split into two areas. The first, selecting the salary brackets and the average purchases using the CASE expression and the grouping and ordering clauses, are typical SQL. The second is the heart of the T-test technique and comes from the two calls to the STATS_T_TEST_INDEPU function.

While statistical definitions of T-test are often quite convoluted, the calculations that Oracle performs can be explained in lay terms. Essentially, the STATS_T_TEST_INDEPU function tests two groups that we know are not equal in number, and for which we expect some significant variance from the mean, *and* the variances are different for both groups.

With those caveats in mind, our test attempts to establish whether the two samples sets are related, and if so, how closely. In plain English, we're trying to determine if the purchasing habits of the residents of New Jersey and New York are similar, even though there are different numbers of buyers in each state, in different income brackets, purchasing different products of different value.

Out resultant observed T values, and the two-sided test P value, differ markedly between each income bracket. To the trained statistician, this suggests that for many of our income groups, the differences in purchasing behavior we see in the base data could be due to sampling errors or the small size of the two income brackets being compared. For example, the 190,000 - 249,999 income bracket has a T value of 6.66684928, suggesting significant sampling issues. Looking at the base data, this is almost certainly because only one purchase was made by a New Jersey resident in this income bracket. We can safely say this group isn't statistically comparable, or related to, the same income bracket in New York.

11-8. Graphically Representing Data Distribution with Text

Problem

You'd like to include simple graphs or histograms with your basic SQL reports. You don't want to export data to a graphing or GUI tool, and would like to use SQL statements and string manipulation to create ASCII-art style graphics in native SQL.

Solution

The need to print ASCII-style art in a report is not necessarily a common one, so when it does crop up, the solution needs a little lateral thinking. One of the best ways to present the magnitude of something is with a bar chart, and with Oracle we can use the RPAD function to print a string of identical characters to a specified length, to mimic the look and feel of a bar chart.

The next SQL statement uses RPAD and simple calculations to print a bar chart of comparative employee salary, using a chart made up of X characters to symbolize the magnitude of a given employee's salary

```
select employee_id, last_name, rpad('X',floor(salary/1000), 'X') salary_graph
from hr.employees
order by salary desc;
```

The results produce exactly the kind of simple graph we want. If it helps, try turning the book sideways to have your graph "rise" from the x-axis at the bottom, rather than the side.

```
EMPLOYEE_ID     LAST_NAME     SALARY_GRAPH
-----------     ---------     ------------------------
        100     King          XXXXXXXXXXXXXXXXXXXXXXXX
        101     Kochhar       XXXXXXXXXXXXXXXX
        102     De Haan       XXXXXXXXXXXXXXXX
        145     Russell       XXXXXXXXXXXXX
        146     Partners      XXXXXXXXXXXX
        201     Hartstein     XXXXXXXXXXXX
        205     Higgins       XXXXXXXXXXX
        108     Greenberg     XXXXXXXXXXX
        147     Errazuriz     XXXXXXXXXXX
        168     Ozer          XXXXXXXXXXX
        148     Cambrault     XXXXXXXXXXX
...
```

We've cut the results at ten lines to save space, but try this recipe for yourself to see what an ASCII graph with a long tail looks like. Other useful implementations of this technique include visualizing overlapping time windows, for instance in project tasks or resource allocation.

How It Works

The key to our recipe's graphical gymnastics is the RPAD function, which simply reproduces the same character—in this case the X character—as many times as instructed. To create a graph that is proportional to an employee's salary, we simply pass RPAD the salary value. In our recipe, we've taken the floor of the salary when divided by 1000, as this provides a graph of the same relative size, without requiring 24000 Xs for the highest-paid employee.

In this recipe, this means someone with a salary between 8000 and 9000 will have eight X's printed, while someone with a salary between 9000 and 10000 will have ten Xs, and so on.

There is one quirk to this recipe. The RPAD function obeys Oracle's NULL handling rules, so we can't start with an empty string (which Oracle considers NULL) and add Xs to that. In practice, this means an RPAD-style graph must have at least one character. If accuracy at this low level is important to you, wrap the RPAD function in a CASE expression to substitute a true NULL value for those rows that should be represented with no characters.

11-9. Producing Web-Page Reports Directly from the Database

Problem

You'd like to produce graphical web-page reports directly from the database, without having to use an additional reporting application to generate HTML. For instance, you'd like a graphical depiction of relative salary across all employees.

Solution

While you may not think of Oracle as a GUI designer for web sites, using simple functions like ROUND, TO_CHAR, || string concatenation, and literal strings can produce all of the textual elements that make up a HTML page or report.

The next SQL statement builds all of the HTML required to represent employee salary in a comparative graph.

```
select
case rownum
  when 1 then
    '<html>' || chr(10) ||
    '<head>' || chr(10) ||
    '<style type="text/css">' || chr(10) ||
    ' body {background-color: Lavender;}' || chr(10) ||
    ' table.outer {width: 80%; border: Black solid 1px;}' || chr(10) ||
    ' table.inner {width: 100%; border: none;}' || chr(10) ||
    ' th {background-color: LightSteelBlue; color: WhiteSmoke;}' || chr(10) ||
    ' .bar {background-color: LightSlateGray;}' || chr(10) ||
    ' .empty {background-color: Lavender;}' || chr(10) ||
    ' .left {text-align: left; padding-left: 5px;}' || chr(10) ||
    ' .right {text-align: right; padding-right: 5px;}' || chr(10) ||
    '</style>' || chr(10) ||
    '</head>' || chr(10) ||
    '<body>' || chr(10) ||
    '<center>' || chr(10) ||
    '<table class="outer">' || chr(10) ||
    '<tr>' || chr(10) ||
    '<th width="15%">Employee ID</th>' || chr(10) ||
    '<th width="20%">Last Name</th>' || chr(10) ||
    '<th>Salary Graph</th>' || chr(10) || '</tr>'
  else ''
end ||
'<tr><td class="right">' || to_char(employee_id) || '</td>' || chr(10) ||
'<td class="left">' || last_name || '</td>' || chr(10) ||
'<td class="left">' ||
  '<table class="inner">' || chr(10) ||
    '<tr><td class="bar" width="' ||
      to_char(round(100 * salary / maxsalary)) ||
      '%">' || chr(38) || 'nbsp;</td>' || chr(10) ||
    '<td class="empty" width="' ||
      to_char(100 - round(100 * salary / maxsalary)) ||
      '%">' || chr(38) || 'nbsp;</td></tr>' || chr(10) ||
  '</table></td></tr>' || chr(10) ||
case rownum
```

```
  when row_count then
     '</table>' || chr(10) ||
     '</center>' || chr(10) ||
     '</body>' || chr(10) ||
     '</html>'
   else ''
end
from
  (select employee_id, last_name, salary,
     count(*) over () as row_count,
     max(salary) over () as maxsalary
   from hr.employees
   order by salary desc);
```

The resultant text is the entire HTML page required to produce the web page. A short sample looks like the following text block:

```
<html>
<head>
<style type="text/css">
 body {background-color: Lavender;}
 table.outer {width: 80%; border: Black solid 1px;}
 table.inner {width: 100%; border: none;}
 th {background-color: LightSteelBlue; color: WhiteSmoke;}
 .bar {background-color: LightSlateGray;}
 .empty {background-color: Lavender;}
 .left {text-align: left; padding-left: 5px;}
 .right {text-align: right; padding-right: 5px;}
</style>
</head>
<body>
<center>
<table class="outer">
<tr>
<th width="15%">Employee ID</th>
<th width="20%">Last Name</th>
<th>Salary Graph</th>
</tr><tr><td class="right">100</td>
<td class="left">King</td>
<td class="left"><table class="inner">
<tr><td class="bar" width="100%"> </td>
<td class="empty" width="0%"> </td></tr>
</table></td></tr>
...
```

Naturally, reading the raw HTML doesn't quite give you the graphical impact, so the results spooled to a file and viewed in a browser are shown in Figure 11-3.

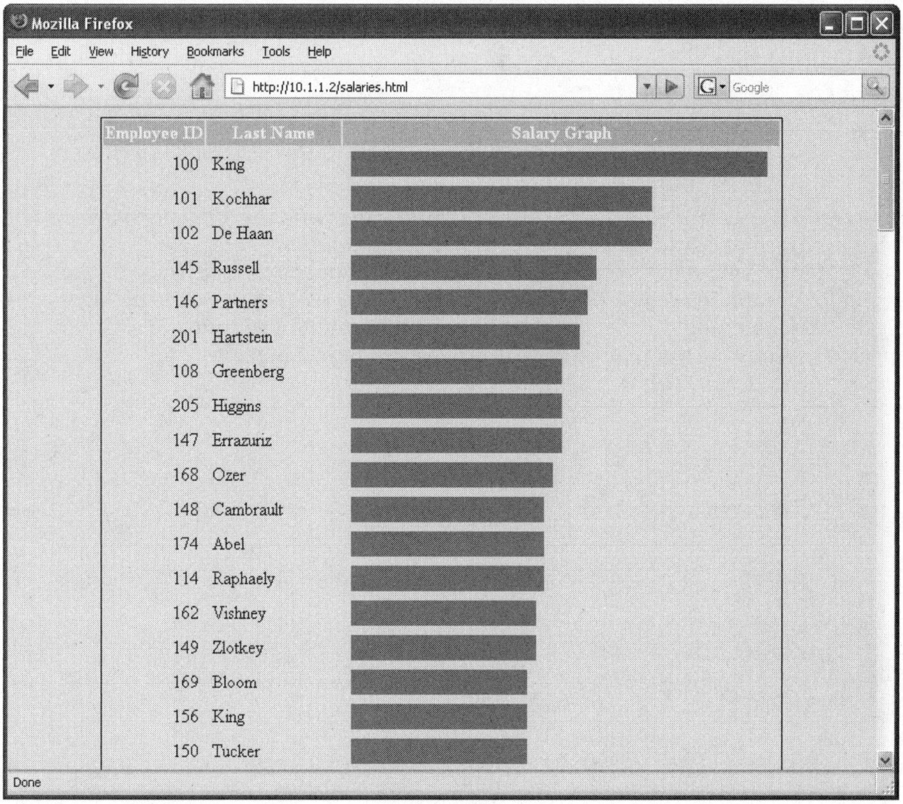

Figure 11-3. *HTML report output for salaries displayed in a browser*

How It Works

Don't be daunted by the size of the SQL statement used to generate our HTML. We can break the statement down into four parts to make it digestible, and from there you'll see how easy it is to create even more complex HTML output.

Starting with the inline view at the end of the recipe, we query our base employee salary data to find several values that help craft our HTML. The SQL for our inline view is shown next, followed by its output if run in isolation.

```
select employee_id, last_name, salary,
  count(*) over () as row_count,
  max(salary) over () as maxsalary
from hr.employees
order by salary desc
```

```
EMPLOYEE_ID    LAST_NAME    SALARY    ROW_COUNT    MAXSALARY
-----------    ---------    ------    ---------    ---------
        100    King         24000          110        24000
        101    Kochhar      17000          110        24000
        102    De Haan      17000          110        24000
        145    Russell      14010          110        24000
        146    Partners     13510          110        24000
...
```

We select the employee's ID, surname, and SALARY, and combine that with the analytic functions to return the total number of rows in the result set, and the maximum salary.

We start using some of these values in the earlier parts of our SQL. Our recipe constructs the full HTML header and footer for our report using string concatenation of literals. It determines the right point to inject the header and footer into the results by evaluating the ROWNUM of the outer SELECT statement. The abbreviated sections of our recipe that control this are shown here.

```
select
case rownum
  when 1 then
    <many literal strings concatenated to form the HTML header>
  else ''
end ||
...
case rownum
  when row_count then
    <literal strings concatenated to form the HTML footer
  else ''
end
...
```

When dealing with the first result row, with ROWNUM of 1, for the body of the HTML report our recipe prefixes all of the HTML header requirements. When it encounters the row with a ROWNUM equal to the ROW_COUNT calculated in the inline view, it knows it has encountered the last row of results. At this point it appends the HTML footer.

The remaining part of our recipe is the section that builds the table rows with colored bars to represent the comparative salary levels. This section of the SELECT statement is shown next.

```
...
'<tr><td class="right">' || to_char(employee_id) || '</td>' || chr(10) ||
'<td class="left">' || last_name || '</td>' || chr(10) ||
'<td class="left">' ||
  '<table class="inner">' || chr(10) ||
    '<tr><td class="bar" width="' ||
to_char(round(100 * salary / maxsalary)) ||
    '%">' || chr(38) || 'nbsp;</td>' || chr(10) ||
```

```
    '<td class="empty" width="' ||
to_char(100 - round(100 * salary / maxsalary)) ||
      '%">' || chr(38) || 'nbsp;</td></tr>' || chr(10) ||
  '</table></td></tr>' || chr(10) ||
...
```

The body of the HTML report is produced as a table whose each row is itself a table. These individual rows have a table structure formed by two table cells. The code shown in bold is the heart of the calculation. First, the left-hand side table cell is given a width proportional to the employee's salary compared to the maximum salary. So for employee King, whose salary of 24000 is the maximum, this table cell is 100% of the width of the outer table. The right-hand cell for the employee is calculated as 100 minus the percentage calculated for the first cell. In King's case, this means the right-hand cell is zero width. The HTML header includes style-sheet information to color the left-hand cell in blue, and the right-hand cell to match the background color so it appears transparent.

As we move through employees in the inline view whose SALARY amounts are a smaller and smaller fraction of the maximum, the size of the left-hand table cell shrinks and the size of the right-hand table cell grows in proportion. This gives the appearance of correctly sized graph bars representing proportional salary.

■ **Note** The authors would like to thank our great technical editor, Stéphane Faroult, for his idea for this recipe.

CHAPTER 12

■ ■ ■

Cleansing Data

Occasionally you'll find yourself working in environments where you are extracting information from some data source and importing it into a relational database. The source of the information could be spreadsheets, CSV files, other databases, and so on. For example, it's common in data warehouse environments to take data from several different database sources and import it into a centralized reporting database.

When moving data from one source to another, there are sometimes conversion issues if the source data types are different from the target data types. In these situations, you'll have to check the source data to make sure it is loadable into the destination database. For example, you could have a character string that needs to be imported into an Oracle database field that is of a `TIMESTAMP` data type. Or you may be transferring data from a system that does not have a primary key defined for a table, and before you load it into a destination database you'll need to detect any duplicate rows.

In some environments you may have an automated ETL (extract, transform, and load) process that performs the data cleansing. However, even if you are using a feature-rich ETL tool, you will still encounter situations in which you need to quickly use SQL to troubleshoot issues with the data. If the ETL process breaks or produces inconsistent results, you will have to use SQL to validate data.

When transferring data, you'll find that you need to use SQL to ensure that data conforms to the business rules for the destination database. These types of activities are broadly referred to as *data cleansing* (or data scrubbing). This chapter shows common SQL techniques that developers and DBAs use when moving data from one data source to another.

12-1. Detecting Duplicate Rows

Problem

You're trying to add a primary key constraint to a table:

```
alter table d_prods add constraint d_prods_pk primary key(d_prod_id);
```

You then receive this error message:

```
ORA-02437: cannot validate (STAR1.D_PRODS_PK) - primary key violated
```

You need to identify which rows are duplicates.

Solution

Use a SELECT statement with a GROUP BY and HAVING COUNT clause. The next listing of code displays duplicate rows in the PARTIES table based on values in the PARTY_ID column:

```
select
  count(*)
 ,party_id
from parties
group by party_id
having count(*) > 1;
```

Here is some sample output for this scenario:

```
  COUNT(*)    PARTY_ID
---------- ----------
         3          69
         2          55
```

How It Works

The query in the solution section using the HAVING clause reports only when there is more than one record with the same PARTY_ID. You can think of the HAVING clause as a WHERE clause for the GROUP BY clause.

If you have a primary key that is composed of multiple columns, you'll need to use all of these columns in the SELECT and GROUP BY clauses. For example, say your primary key consists of the FIRST_NAME and LAST_NAME columns; to find duplicate values, use both columns as shown in the next code listing:

```
select
  count(*)
 ,first_name
 ,last_name
from parties
group by first_name, last_name
having count(*) > 1;
```

12-2. Removing Duplicate Rows

Problem

You want to remove duplicate rows from a table.

Solution

Use a correlated subquery to remove duplicate rows from a table. The following example removes duplicate rows from the PARTIES table where there are duplicates on the column PARTY_ID:

```
delete from parties a
where a.rowid <
(select max(b.rowid)
 from parties b
 where a.party_id = b.party_id);
```

Before you issue a delete statement like this, you should run a query similar to the one in recipe 12-1 to determine how much data will be removed.

How It Works

Each row in the database has a unique ROWID. The DELETE statement in the solution section will arbitrarily delete all rows with the same PARTY_ID except the row with the highest ROWID.

If there are multiple columns that comprise your unique identifier, use all of those columns in the correlated subquery WHERE clause. For example, if your primary key logically consists of FIRST_NAME and LAST_NAME, issue the following SQL statement to delete duplicates:

```
delete from parties a
where a.rowid <
(select max(b.rowid)
 from parties b
 where a.first_name = b.first_name
 and    a.last_name  = b.last_name);
```

Listed next is a slight variation of the SQL in the solution section of this recipe:

```
delete from parties
where rowid not in
(select max(rowid)
```

```
from parties
group by party_id);
```

Using this query or the previous one is a matter of SQL coding preference. If you generate execution plans for each query, you'll notice that there isn't much difference in the cost.

12-3. Determining if Data Can Be Loaded as Numeric

Problem

You have a field that has been defined as character string in the old system but will be migrated to a numeric number field in the new database. You have the data loaded into a temporary staging table and you want to determine if any of the character data will not convert cleanly to a numeric data type.

Solution

You need to create a small PL/SQL function:

```
create or replace function isnum(v_in varchar2)
return varchar is
  val_err exception;
  pragma exception_init(val_err, -6502); -- char to num conv. error
  scrub_num number;
begin
  scrub_num := to_number(v_in);
  return 'Y';
exception when val_err then
  return 'N';
end;
/
```

If the value passed into the ISNUM function is a number, then a Y is returned. If the value cannot be converted to a number, then an N is returned.

How It Works

You can use the ISNUM function to detect whether data in a column is numeric. The function defines a PL/SQL pragma exception for the ORA-06502 character-to-number conversion error. When this error is encountered, the exception handler captures it and returns an N.

You can use this function to determine if a character can be converted to a number. For example, say you have a table named STAGE and it contains a column named HOLD_COL with the following values in it:

```
HOLD_COL
-----------------------------
1
c
3
$
1032.22
32423432234234432x
```

The following query uses the ISNUM function to determine if there is any non-numeric data in the table:

```
select hold_col from stage where isnum(hold_col)='N';
```

Here is the expected output:

```
HOLD_COL
-----------------------------
c
$
32423432234234432x
```

12-4. Determining if Data Can Be Loaded as a Date

Problem

You have a field that has been defined as a character string in the old system but will be migrated to a date data type in the new database. You have the data loaded into a temporary holding table and you want to determine if any of the character data will not convert cleanly to a date data type.

Solution

For this solution you'll need to create a small PL/SQL function:

```
create or replace function isdate(p_in varchar2, f_in varchar2)
return varchar is
  scrub_dt date;
```

```
begin
  scrub_dt := to_date(p_in, f_in);
  return 'Y';
exception when others then
  return 'N';
end;
/
```

The ISDATE function accepts two values, the character data and a date format mask. If the value passed into the function is a valid date, a Y is returned. If the value can't be converted to a date, an N is returned.

How It Works

The ISDATE function can be used to detect whether the character data in a column is a valid. For example, say you have a table named STAGE and it contains a column named HOLD_COL with the following values in it:

```
HOLD_COL
-----------------------------
20090130
20090132
20090229
20091430
20090330
```

The following query uses the ISDATE function to determine if there is any character data that does not conform to the YYYYMMDD date format:

```
select hold_col
from stage
where isdate(hold_col,'YYYYMMDD') = 'N';
```

Here are the values that do not map to valid dates:

```
HOLD_COL
-----------------------------
20090132
20090229
20091430
```

12-5. Performing Case-Insensitive Queries

Problem

You have loaded a significant amount of data that is in mixed case. You want to query as if it were all lowercase (or all uppercase).

Solution

If you are using Oracle Database 10*g* or higher, you can use the ALTER SESSION statement to enable case-insensitive searching with the >, <, and = comparison operators. To enable case-insensitive searching, alter the NLS_SORT and NLS_COMP parameters:

```
alter session set nls_sort=binary_ci;
alter session set nls_comp=linguistic;
```

These settings allow case-insensitive searches. You can run the following query to select all values of John, regardless of case:

```
select * from parties where first_name = 'john';
FIRST_NAME
------------------------------
John
JOHN
john
```

How It Works

Prior to Oracle Database 10*g* you would have had to use an UPPER or LOWER SQL function to perform case-insensitive searches, for example:

```
select * from parties where upper(first_name) = 'JOHN';
```

■ **Tip** Oracle will not access an index on a column that has a SQL function applied to it. To get around this, you can create a function-based index.

Other common techniques for making sure case is not an issue in your searches include:

*   Utilizing a trigger to enforce that the string is inserted as all uppercase or all lowercase.

*   Adding a column to the table that contains an all-uppercase or all-lowercase version of the string in question.

In Oracle Database 10g or higher, the combination of setting `NLS_SORT` to `BINARY_CI` and `NLS_COMP` to `LINGUISTIC` instructs SQL to ignore case for comparison operations. The `NLS_SORT` parameter determines the type of sort for character data. The `NLS_SORT` setting of `BINARY_CI` designates that sorting behavior is case-insensitive. The `NLS_COMP` parameter affects the comparison behavior of SQL operations. Setting `NLS_COMP` to `LINGUISTIC` instructs SQL to perform a linguistic comparison of values.

Binary versus Linguistic Sorts

When sorting character data, normally the sort is based on numeric values of the character-encoding scheme. This is known as binary sorting. Binary sorts work well with the English alphabet because the ASCII and EBCDIC character-encoding schemes define the English letters with ascending numeric values. For example the character A has an ASCII decimal value of 65; the B character has a decimal value of 66, and so on.

However, sorting can have undesirable results when characters are present from languages other than English. In such scenarios, a linguistic sorting order based on the language being used is more appropriate. For example, to specify the French linguistic sort:

```
alter session set nls_sort = French;
```

You can override the session setting by directly using the `NLSSORT` function in a SQL statement:

```
select first_name from parties
order by nlssort(first_name,'nls_sort = French');
```

12-6. Obfuscating Values

Problem

Your database is being audited, but it contains information such as names and social security numbers that should remain private. You need to present the data to the auditor in a form in which that data can't be read, but the auditor can still detect patterns in the data. If the audit process detects fraud, then the real names and social security numbers can be provided on a case-by-case basis.

Solution

Use the TRANSLATE built-in SQL function to change each character value to a different value. Here's a simple example:

```
select translate('ORACLE',
  'ABCDEFGHIJKLMNOPQRSTUVWXYZ',
  'ZYXWVUTSRQPONMLKJIHGFEDCBA')
from dual;
```

Here is the output:

```
TRANSL
------
LIZXOV
```

To translate the obfuscated value back to its original value, use the TRANSLATE function again:

```
select translate('LIZXOV',
  'ABCDEFGHIJKLMNOPQRSTUVWXYZ',
  'ZYXWVUTSRQPONMLKJIHGFEDCBA')
from dual;
```

If you're going to obfuscate a large amount of data, it's more efficient to put the TRANSLATE function in a PL/SQL package and use the package to obfuscate data. Here is a simple example:

```
create or replace package obfus is
  function obf(clear_string varchar2) return varchar2;
  function unobf(obs_string varchar2) return varchar2;
end obfus;
/
--
create or replace package body obfus is
  fromstr varchar2(62) := '0123456789ABCDEFGHIJKLMNOPQRSTUVWXYZ' ||
            'abcdefghijklmnopqrstuvwxyz';
  tostr varchar2(62)   := 'defghijklmnopqrstuvwxyzabc3456789012' ||
            'KLMNOPQRSTUVWXYZABCDEFGHIJ';
--
function obf(clear_string varchar2) return varchar2 is
begin
  return translate(clear_string, fromstr, tostr);
end obf;
```

```
--
function unobf(obs_string varchar2) return varchar2 is
begin
  return translate(obs_string, tostr, fromstr);
end unobf;
end obfus;
/
```

Now columns in a table can be obfuscated by calling the OBF function:

```
update emp set emp_name = obfus.obf(emp_name),
               ssn = obfus.obf(ssn);
```

The column values can be set back to their original values using the UNOBF function:

```
update emp set emp_name = obfus.unobf(emp_name),
               ssn = obfus.unobf(ssn);
```

■ **Note** The process of substituting a single alphabet character with another character that is a fixed number of positions further down in the alphabet is known in cryptography as *Caesar's cipher*. For example a single character shift would mean that A is represented by B, and B is represented by C, and so on. This method derives its name from the Roman emperor Julius Caesar who used this encryption technique to communicate with his generals.

In some cases, you may need to obfuscate your data. Obfuscation is changing the data just enough so that real values aren't detected simply by looking at the data. Obfuscation *is not* a secure way of making data unreadable, nor is it a substitute for encryption.

Encryption is a secure method for making data unreadable and not easily decipherable. If you need to encrypt data, use the DBMS_CRYPTO package or encryption features available in the Oracle Advanced Security option.

Obfuscation may be appropriate when you need to make the data unreadable but still preserve the general character patterns. Encryption doesn't work well in these situations because it renders data into values outside of the normal range of ASCII characters.

How It Works

The TRANSLATE function performs a character-for-character substitution, one character at a time. It takes three input arguments: the string to be translated, the source characters, and the target characters. The TRANSLATE function is ideal for data obfuscation.

Sometimes the TRANSLATE function is confused with the REPLACE function, but the REPLACE function substitutes one string for another string while the TRANSLATE function swaps one character for another. Here is a simple example of using REPLACE:

```
select replace('scrappple','ppp','bb')
from dual;
```

The output shows that the ppp string has been replaced with the bb string:

```
REPLACE
--------
scrabble
```

12-7. Dropping All Indexes

Problem

You're inserting a large amount of data into a table and want to load the data as fast as possible. For performance reasons, you want to drop the indexes on the table before you insert the data.

Solution

The easiest way to drop all indexes for a table is to use SQL to generate the SQL required. The following example generates the SQL required to drop all indexes for the F_SALES table:

```
select 'drop index ' || index_name || ';'
from user_indexes where table_name='F_SALES';
```

Here is some sample output:

```
'DROPINDEX'||INDEX_NAME||';'
-----------------------------------------
drop index F_SALES_FK1;
drop index F_SALES_FK2;
drop index F_SALES_FK3;
drop index F_SALES_FK4;
drop index F_SALES_FK5;
```

How It Works

When loading large data warehouse tables, sometimes it's more efficient to drop a table's indexes before a load and then recreate them after the data loading is complete. This is especially true with bitmap indexes associated with a star schema fact table.

Before you drop any indexes, ensure you have the DDL required to recreate the indexes. You don't want to put yourself in the situation of dropping the indexes and then have no idea how to recreate them. Ideally you have the original DDL scripts used to create the indexes. If you don't, use the DBMS_METADATA package to generate the index-creation DDL as shown:

```
select dbms_metadata.get_ddl('INDEX', index_name)
from user_indexes
where table_name = upper('&table_name');
```

If you run the previous SQL from SQL*Plus, be sure to set your LONG variable to a large value so you can view all of the text.

An alternative approach to dropping and recreating indexes is to mark them as unusable and then rebuild them. Here is a script that generates the SQL required to alter all indexes for a table into an unusable state:

```
select 'alter index ' || index_name || ' unusable;'
from user_indexes where table_name=upper('&table_name');
```

And here is a script that generates the SQL required to rebuild all indexes for a table:

```
select 'alter index ' || index_name || ' rebuild;'
from user_indexes where table_name=upper('&table_name');
```

If you want to capture the output of the SQL statement in the solution section in a script, use the SQL*Plus SET command to turn off some of the default feedback settings, as shown in the following code:

```
set verify off feedback off pagesize 0
spool drop_ind.sql
select 'drop index ' || index_name || ';'
from user_indexes where table_name='F_SALES';
spool off;
```

The VERIFY parameter turns off before and after images of lines containing substitution variables. The FEEDBACK parameter controls the display of the number of lines affected by the SQL statement. The PAGESIZE parameter when set to 0 will suppress headings and page breaks.

After the various display settings have been turned off, the script uses the SPOOL command to send the output to a file. You can now run the drop commands contained within the captured output file as follows:

```
SQL> @drop_ind.sql
```

12-8. Disabling Constraints

Problem

You're trying to truncate a table but receive the following error message:

```
ORA-02266: unique/primary keys in table referenced by enabled foreign keys
```

Upon further investigation, you discover that Oracle will not allow a truncate operation on a parent table with a primary key that is referenced by an enabled foreign key in a child table. You need to disable the foreign key constraint before proceeding with the truncate operation.

Solution

If you need to truncate a parent table, you'll first have to disable all of the enabled foreign key constraints that reference the parent table primary key. Run this query to determine the names of the constraints that need to be disabled:

```
select
  b.table_name          primary_key_table
 ,a.table_name          fk_child_table
 ,a.constraint_name     fk_child_table_constraint
from dba_constraints a
    ,dba_constraints b
where a.r_constraint_name = b.constraint_name
and    a.r_owner          = b.owner
and    a.constraint_type  = 'R'
and    b.owner            = upper('&table_owner')
and    b.table_name       = upper('&table_name');
```

For this example, there is only one foreign key dependency:

```
PRIMARY_KEY_TABLE     FK_CHILD_TABLE        FK_CHILD_TABLE_CONST
-------------------   -------------------   --------------------
D_DATES               F_SALES               F_SALES_FK1
```

Use the ALTER TABLE statement to disable constraints on a table. In this case, there is only one foreign key to disable:

```
alter table f_sales disable constraint f_sales_fk1;
```

You can now truncate the parent table:

```
truncate table d_dates;
```

Don't forget to re-enable the foreign key constraints after the truncate operation has completed, like this:

```
alter table f_sales enable constraint f_sales_fk1;
```

In multiuser systems, there is the possibility that another session has inserted data into the child table while the foreign key constraint was disabled. If that happens, you'll see the following error when you attempt to re-enable the foreign key:

```
ORA-02298: cannot validate (<owner>.<constraint>) - parent keys not found
```

In this scenario, you can use the ENABLE NOVALIDATE clause. This instructs Oracle not to validate any existing rows, but to validate rows added after the constraint is re-enabled:

```
alter table f_sales enable novalidate constraint f_sales_fk1;
```

To clean up the rows that violate the constraint, first ensure that you have an EXCEPTIONS table created in your schema. If you don't have an EXCEPTIONS table, use this script to create one:

```
SQL> @?/rdbms/admin/utlexcpt.sql
```

Next populate the EXCEPTIONS table with the rows that violate the constraint with the EXCEPTIONS INTO clause:

```
alter table f_sales modify constraint f_sales_fk1 validate
exceptions into exceptions;
```

This statement will still throw the ORA-02298 error as long as there are rows that violate the constraint. The statement will also insert records into the EXCEPTIONS table for any bad rows. You can now use the ROW_ID column of the EXCEPTIONS table to remove any records that violate the constraint. Here we see that one row needs to be removed from the F_SALES table:

```
select * from exceptions;

ROW_ID              OWNER       TABLE_NAME       CONSTRAINT
------------------  ----------  ---------------  ---------------
AAAFVmAAFAAAAihAAA  INV_MMGT    F_SALES          F_SALES_FK1
```

To remove the offending record, issue a DELETE statement:

```
delete from f_sales where rowid = 'AAAFVmAAFAAAAihAAA';
```

If there are many records in the EXCEPTIONS table, you can run a query such as the following to delete by OWNER and TABLE_NAME:

```
delete from f_sales where rowid in
(select row_id
 from exceptions
 where owner=upper('&owner') and table_name = upper('&table_name'));
```

How It Works

One nice feature of Oracle is that you can disable and enable constraints without dropping and recreating them. This means you avoid having to have on hand the DDL statements that would be required to recreate the dropped constraints.

You can't truncate a table that has a primary key defined that is referenced by an enabled foreign key constraint in a child table—even if the child table has zero rows in it. Oracle prevents you from doing this because in a multiuser system there is a possibility that another session can populate the child table with rows in between the time you truncate the child table and subsequently truncate the parent table. Oracle prudently does not allow you to truncate a parent table in this situation.

Also keep in mind that TRUNCATE is a DDL command, so it automatically commits the current transaction after it executes. Thus, you can't roll back a TRUNCATE operation, and you won't be able to TRUNCATE two separate tables as one transaction. Compare the TRUNCATE behavior to that of DELETE. Oracle does allow you to use the DELETE statement to remove rows from a parent table while the constraints are enabled that reference a child table. This is because DELETE generates undo, is read-consistent, and can be rolled back.

You can disable a primary key and all dependent foreign key constraints with the CASCADE option of the DISABLE clause. For example, this next line of code disables all foreign key constraints related to the D_DATES_PK primary key constraint:

```
alter table d_dates disable constraint d_dates_pk cascade;
```

The prior statement does not cascade through all levels of dependencies. It only disables the foreign key constraints directly dependent on the D_DATES_PK. Also keep in mind that there is no ENABLE...CASCADE statement. To re-enable the constraints, you'll have to query the data dictionary to determine which constraints have been disabled and then re-enable them individually.

Sometimes you'll run into situations when loading data where it's convenient to disable all of the foreign keys before loading data (perhaps from a schema-level import). In these situations, the imp utility simply imports the tables in alphabetical order and doesn't ensure that child tables are imported before parent tables. Also, you might want to run several import jobs in parallel to take advantage of parallel hardware. In such scenarios, you can disable the foreign keys, perform the import, and then re-enable the foreign keys. Here is a script that uses SQL to generate SQL to disable all foreign key constraints for a user:

```
set lines 132 trimsp on head off feed off verify off echo off pagesize 0
spo dis_dyn.sql
select 'alter table ' || a.table_name
   || ' disable constraint ' || a.constraint_name || ';'
from dba_constraints a
   ,dba_constraints b
where a.r_constraint_name = b.constraint_name
and    a.r_owner            = b.owner
and    a.constraint_type   = 'R'
and    b.owner              = upper('&table_owner');
spo off;
```

This script generates a file named dis_dyn.sql that disables all of the foreign key constraints for a user. Listed next is a similar script to generate a file with the commands to re-enable foreign key constraints for a user:

```
set lines 132 trimsp on head off feed off verify off echo off pagesize 0
spo enable_dyn.sql
select 'alter table ' || a.table_name
   || ' enable constraint ' || a.constraint_name || ';'
from dba_constraints a
   ,dba_constraints b
where a.r_constraint_name = b.constraint_name
and    a.r_owner            = b.owner
and    a.constraint_type   = 'R'
and    b.owner              = upper('&table_owner');
spo off;
```

When enabling constraints, by default Oracle will check to ensure that the data doesn't violate the constraint definition. If you are fairly certain that the data integrity is fine and that you don't need to incur the performance hit by revalidating the constraint, you can use the NOVALIDATE clause when re-enabling the constraints. Here's an example:

```
select 'alter table ' || a.table_name
   || ' modify constraint ' || a.constraint_name || ' enable novalidate;'
from dba_constraints a
   ,dba_constraints b
where a.r_constraint_name = b.constraint_name
and    a.r_owner           = b.owner
and    a.constraint_type   = 'R'
and    b.owner             = upper('&table_owner');
```

The NOVALIDATE clause instructs Oracle not to validate the constraints being enabled, but it does enforce that any new DML activities do adhere to the constraint definition.

You may also run into situations where you need to disable primary key or unique constraints. For example, you may want to perform a large data load and for performance reasons you want to disable the primary key and unique key constraints. You don't want to incur the overhead of having every row checked as it is inserted.

The same general techniques used for disabling foreign keys are applicable for disabling primary or unique keys. Run this query to display the primary key and unique key constraints for a user:

```
select
 a.table_name
,a.constraint_name
,a.constraint_type
from dba_constraints a
where a.owner = upper('&table_owner')
and    a.constraint_type in ('P','U')
order by a.table_name;
```

Here is some sample output:

TABLE_NAME	CONSTRAINT_NAME	C
DEPT	SYS_C006507	P
D_DATES	D_DATES_UK1	U
D_DATES	D_DATES_PK	P

Once the table name and constraint name are identified, use the `ALTER TABLE` statement to disable the constraint:

```
alter table d_dates disable constraint d_dates_pk;
```

Oracle will not allow you to disable a primary key or unique key constraint that is referenced in a foreign key. You will first have to disable the foreign key constraints.

Also, consider using the `NOVALIDATE` clause if you're confident that the data does not need to be validated:

```
alter table d_dates modify constraint d_dates_pk enable novalidate;
```

This will instruct Oracle not to verify data when enabling the constraint but will validate any data modified after the constraint is enabled.

12-9. Disabling Triggers

Problem

You're about ready to load a large amount of data. You don't want triggers impacting performance while you're inserting data into a table. Moreover, you want to load the source data as it is; you do not want triggers executing and modifying data as it is loaded. You want to disable the triggers before you perform the data load.

Solution

You can disable single triggers or all triggers on a table. You can view the triggers for a table by querying the `DBA/ALL/USER_TRIGGERS` views. For example:

```
select trigger_name, status
from user_triggers where table_name='CLUSTER_BUCKETS';
```

Here is the output:

```
TRIGGER_NAME                     STATUS
-------------------------------- --------
CLUSTER_BUCKETS_BU_TR1           ENABLED
```

Now use the ALTER TRIGGER statement to disable the trigger:

```
alter trigger CLUSTER_BUCKETS_BU_TR1 disable;
```

If you want to disable all triggers on a table, use the ALTER TABLE...DISABLE ALL TRIGGERS statement:

```
alter table cluster_buckets disable all triggers;
```

After you have loaded the data into the table, you can re-enable all triggers as follows:

```
alter table cluster_buckets enable all triggers;
```

How It Works

If you're performing a large load of data into a table, sometimes for performance reasons it's desirable to disable all of the triggers on a table. If there are many tables involved with the data-loading operation, you can use SQL to generate SQL to disable the triggers for all tables for a user:

```
select 'alter table ' || table_name || ' disable all triggers;'
from user_tables;
```

Once you've completed the data load, you'll need to re-enable the triggers. Here is the SQL to generate SQL to re-enable the triggers for all tables for a user:

```
select 'alter table ' || table_name || ' enable all triggers;'
from user_tables;
```

When you re-enable triggers, the triggers do not run. The status of the trigger is simply changed from DISABLED to ENABLED. Once the trigger is enabled, it will execute for any subsequent SQL statements that cause the trigger to be executed. Therefore, you will have to validate the data with a SQL query to determine if any data has been loaded while the trigger was disabled that violates any critical business rules.

12-10. Removing Data from a Table

Problem

You want to efficiently remove all data from a large table.

Solution

Use the TRUNCATE command to remove data from a table. This example removes all data from the F_SALES table:

```
truncate table f_sales;
Table truncated.
```

By default, Oracle will deallocate all space used for the table except the space defined by the MINEXTENTS table storage parameter. If you don't want the TRUNCATE statement to deallocate the extents, use the REUSE STORAGE parameter:

```
truncate table f_sales reuse storage;
```

How It Works

Oracle defines the high-water mark of a table as the boundary between used and unused space in a segment. When you create a table, Oracle will allocate a number of extents to the table defined by the MINEXTENTS table storage parameter. Each extent contains a number of blocks. Before data is inserted into the table, none of the blocks have been used and the high-water mark is zero.

The TRUNCATE statement sets the high-water mark of a table back to zero. When you use a DELETE statement to remove data from a table, the high-water mark does not change. One advantage to using a TRUNCATE statement and resetting the high-water mark is that full table scans will only search for rows in blocks below the high-water mark. This can have significant performance implications.

■ **Note** You can determine the space usage of blocks beneath the high-water mark via the DBMS_SPACE package.

High-water Mark and Performance

Oracle sometimes needs to scan every block of a table (under the high-water mark) when performing a query. This is known as a full table scan. If there has been a significant amount of data deleted from a table, a full table scan can take a long time to complete, even for an empty table.

You can run this simple test to detect this issue:

1. SQL> set autotrace trace statistics

2. Run the query that performs the full table scan

3. Compare the number of rows processed to the number of logical I/Os

If the number of rows processed is low yet the number of logical I/Os is high, you may have an issue with the number of free blocks below the high- water mark. To readjust the high-water mark you must enable row movement for the table and then use the ALTER TABLE...SHRINK SPACE statement.

The TRUNCATE statement is a DDL statement. This means that Oracle automatically commits the statement (and the current transaction) after it runs, so there is no way to roll back a TRUNCATE statement. If you need to be able to roll back when removing data, you should use the DELETE statement. However, the DELETE statement has the disadvantage that it generates a great deal of undo and redo information. For large tables, therefore, a TRUNCATE statement is usually the most efficient way to remove data.

We should note that another way to remove data from a table is to drop and recreate the table. However, this means you also have to recreate any indexes, constraints, grants, or triggers that belong to the table. Additionally, when you drop a table, it will be temporarily unavailable until you recreate it and reissue any required grants. Usually dropping and recreating a table is acceptable only in a development or test environment.

12-11. Showing Differences in Schemas

Problem

You have test and production databases. You want to determine if there are any object differences between the test database schema and the production database schema. You don't have access to an expensive graphical tool that can show differences between schemas. You wonder what SQL techniques you can use to show the object differences between two schemas.

Solution

A basic technique for showing the differences between two schemas is as follows:

1. If the schemas are in two different databases, create database links to point at the two different environments.

2. Use the MINUS set operator to query the data dictionary views to display differences.

Here is an example that demonstrates how to display schema differences. In this example, we are connected to a central database that has Oracle Net access to two remote databases. We want to view the differences in schemas in the two remote databases. First we create database links that point to the two different environments. This example uses SQL plus variables to define the two different schemas and passwords used to create the database links:

```
define user1=ccim_dev
define user1_pwd=ccim_pwd
define user2=ccim_prod
define user2_pwd=abc123
define conn1=@db1
define conn2=@db2

create database link db1 connect to &&user1 identified by &&user1_pwd
using 'sb-db5:1521/sb6';

create database link db2 connect to &&user2 identified by &&user2_pwd
using 'db-prod1:1521/scaprd';
```

After the database links are created, run SQL statements that display metadata differences from the data dictionary views. The next two statements use the MINUS set operator to determine if there any differences with table names:

```
prompt ...Tables in db1 NOT IN db2
select table_name
from user_tables&&conn1
minus
select table_name
from user_tables&&conn2;

prompt ...Tables in db2 NOT IN db1
select table_name
from user_tables&&conn2
minus
select table_name
from user_tables&&conn1;
```

If you want to compare a local schema with a remote schema, you'll need only one database link. In this situation, you'll also need to define one of the connection variables to be blank, for example:

```
define conn2=''
```

Now you can connect as a local user in your database and compare a remote schema to a local schema.

If you want to compare objects in two schemas in the same database, you'll have to modify the scripts to include an OWNER and use the DBA or ALL data dictionary views (instead of USER).

How It Works

In the solution section of this recipe, we presented a simple example of how to use the data dictionary to determine if there were any differences in table names between two schemas. It compares schemas by using the MINUS set operator to display data dictionary rows that exist for the first schema that don't exist for the second schema. Then another similar query is run, but this time it checks for rows that exist for the second schema which don't exist for the first schema.

Here is a more complete example of comparing two schema's objects. This script compares several different data dictionary views for differences in metadata:

```
spo diff.txt

prompt Default or temp tablespace in db1 NOT IN db2
select default_tablespace, temporary_tablespace
from user_users&&conn1
minus
select default_tablespace, temporary_tablespace
from user_users&&conn2;

prompt Default or temp tablespace in db2 NOT IN db1
select default_tablespace, temporary_tablespace
from user_users&&conn2
minus
select default_tablespace, temporary_tablespace
from user_users&&conn1;

prompt Tablespace quotas in db1 NOT IN db2
select tablespace_name, max_bytes
from user_ts_quotas&&conn1
minus
select tablespace_name, max_bytes
from user_ts_quotas&&conn2;

prompt Tablespace quotas in db2 NOT IN db1
select tablespace_name, max_bytes
from user_ts_quotas&&conn2
minus
select tablespace_name, max_bytes
from user_ts_quotas&&conn1;

prompt Objects in db1 NOT IN db2
select object_name, object_type
```

```
from user_objects&&conn1
minus
select object_name, object_type
from user_objects&&conn2 order by 2;

prompt Objects in db2 NOT IN db1
select object_name, object_type
from user_objects&&conn2
minus
select object_name, object_type
from user_objects&&conn1 order by 2;

prompt Tables in db1 NOT IN db2
select table_name
from user_tables&&conn1
minus
select table_name
from user_tables&&conn2;

prompt Tables in db2 NOT IN db1
select table_name
from user_tables&&conn2
minus
select table_name
from user_tables&&conn1;

prompt Indexes in db2 NOT IN db1
select table_name, index_name, index_type, uniqueness
from user_indexes&&conn2
minus
select table_name, index_name, index_type, uniqueness
from user_indexes&&conn1 order by 1, 2;

prompt Table columns db1 NOT IN db2
select table_name, column_name
from user_tab_columns&&conn1
minus
select table_name, column_name
from user_tab_columns&&conn2 order by 1,2;

prompt Table columns in db2 NOT IN db1
select table_name, column_name
from user_tab_columns&&conn2
```

```
minus
select table_name, column_name
from user_tab_columns&&conn1 order by 1,2;

spo off;
```

The preceding script is just a sample of what you can do with data dictionary views for reporting on metadata differences between schemas. We didn't include every possible type of check into the script. Rather, we included enough here to give you an example of how to find the most common types of differences that developers and DBAs look for. We have included a full version of this script in the source code section of the Apress website (http://www.apress.com).

If you have access to a tool such as Enterprise Manager Change Management Pack, you can also use that to display differences between two schemas. A quick Google search will show dozens of tools available for comparing schemas. The purpose of this recipe is not to compete with these tools, but to show that you can quickly create a set of SQL statements that will display schema differences. These statements can easily be augmented and enhanced as required for your environment.

CHAPTER 13

■ ■ ■

Tree-Structured Data

Tree-structured—hierarchical—data is all around us. In addition to a real tree you might have in your back yard or in the nearby park that has a trunk and branches, you may attend a basketball tournament where the bracket is a time-based version of a tree structure, with only one team ending up at the root at the end of the tournament. At your job, the management structure is, by nature, a tree structure with the boss or owner at the top, and a couple or many levels of management before reaching the hourly workers at the bottom of the tree.

Entire database management systems are built around hierarchical data. One of IBM Corporation's most popular products, Information Management System (IMS), arrived in the late 1960s and is optimized for hierarchical data and transaction speed. Although it is still one of IBM's best-selling products, its implementation makes it difficult to access the data in a variety of ways without additional coding. XML is a relatively new way of representing tree-structured data that offers standardized data interchange, but is challenging if you try to traverse an XML document in an alternative order. In the late 1970s, Oracle and its relational database architecture began to address the inflexibility of the hierarchical model and to provide support for hierarchical traversal of one or more tables using built-in features.

Figure 13-1 shows two hierarchical trees; they could be in different tables or in the same table. Oracle handles more than one tree within the same table without any problem, as you will see in one of the recipes in this chapter. Each node's key within a tree is typically a primary or alternate key. A given node can have zero, one, or many children; a given child node can have only one parent. The concept of a *level* is often used when traversing a tree; it specifies how far a node is from the root node of a tree, with level 1 being the level of the root node(s). A row at each level can be one of two types depending on where in the hierarchy they are. Here are the definitions we'll use throughout the chapter:

Root: the highest row in a hierarchical structure

Child: any non-root row

Parent: any row that has children rows

Leaf: a row without any children rows

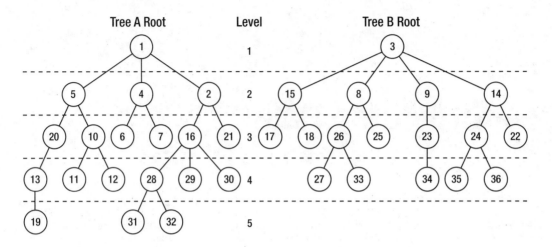

Figure 13-1. *Hierarchical (tree-structured) data in two trees from a single database table*

In Figure 13-1, nodes 1 and 3 are root nodes, 19 and 27 (and many others at the bottom of each tree) are leaf nodes, and all nodes except the leaf nodes are parent nodes. All nodes other than the root nodes are child nodes. A node cannot have three of the four roles, or all four, and a table with one row is the only case where a node can be a root node and a leaf node at the same time.

In this chapter, we'll cover most of the ways to access hierarchical data in a single table or across several tables. The key clauses you'll see in a hierarchical query are CONNECT BY and START WITH. The CONNECT BY clause specifies how you want to link rows to their predecessors and successors; this clause may also contain other filters, as you will see in one of the recipes. Typically, you will also have a START WITH clause in your query, but it is not required. You use START WITH to specify where in the hierarchy you want to begin retrieving rows. This is especially useful if you have more than one hierarchy in your table, as in the example in Figure 13-1. You also might use START WITH to exclude the top node of the hierarchy, for example.

In many situations, your hierarchical data might not be consistent. For example, your database might inadvertently indicate that the employee Smith reports to King, the employee Jones reports to Smith, and the employee King reports to Jones. This is clearly not a valid business condition, and Oracle will automatically detect these conditions and return an error message; alternatively, you can use NOCYCLE with CONNECT_BY_ISCYCLE to easily identify rows that have a successor that is also a predecessor somewhere in the hierarchy.

Other pseudo-columns make your hierarchical queries more useful for reporting. The LEVEL pseudo-column returns the tree depth of the current row. In Figure 13-1, nodes 1 and 3 would return a LEVEL of 1, nodes 5 and 15 will return a LEVEL of 2, and so forth. Qualifying a column with CONNECT_BY_ROOT returns the column's value at the top of the hierarchy, regardless of the level number of the current row in the query results.

Sometimes you want to see the "big picture," and you can use the SYS_CONNECT_BY_PATH function to build a string containing column values from the root of the tree to the current node. The pseudo-column CONNECT_BY_ISLEAF indicates whether the row is a leaf node, at the bottom of a branch in the hierarchy, in other words.

You may find a need to sort the results of your hierarchical query. However, the standard ORDER BY does not produce the desired result, since the ordering is across all rows, and not within each level of the hierarchy. In a hierarchy, you'll use the ORDER SIBLINGS BY clause instead to order a subset of columns within their parent row.

The recipes in this chapter will cover variations of all these clauses to at least give you a template for creating any type of hierarchical query that your application requires. Although you could simulate most, if not all, of these features in a procedural language such as Java or C++, the ease of use, clarity, and efficiency of using Oracle's built-in hierarchical query features make it an easy choice.

13-1. Traversing Hierarchical Data from Top to Bottom

Problem

You need to generate reports from tables with hierarchical data, traversing the hierarchy from top to bottom and clearly denoting the level of each row in the hierarchy.

Solution

Use the CONNECT BY clause to specify a hierarchical query, the PRIOR operator to define the linking condition between the parent nodes, and the combination of the LEVEL pseudo-column and LPAD to provide a visual aid in the report. In the following example, the management team wants a report that displays the management structure of the company, clearly showing subordinates within each higher-level manager:

```
select employee_id, level,
    lpad(' ',(level-1)*3) || last_name || ', ' || first_name full_name
from employees
start with manager_id is null
connect by manager_id = prior employee_id
;
```

EMPLOYEE_ID	LEVEL	FULL_NAME
100	1	King, Steven
101	2	Kochhar, Neena
108	3	Greenberg, Nancy
109	4	Faviet, Daniel
110	4	Chen, John
111	4	Sciarra, Ismael
112	4	Urman, Jose Manuel
113	4	Popp, Luis
200	3	Whalen, Jennifer
203	3	Mavris, Susan
204	3	Baer, Hermann
205	3	Higgins, Shelley
206	4	Gietz, William
102	2	De Haan, Lex
103	3	Hunold, Alexander
104	4	Ernst, Bruce
105	4	Austin, David
106	4	Pataballa, Valli
107	4	Lorentz, Diana
...		
201	2	Hartstein, Michael
202	3	Fay, Pat

```
107 rows selected
```

The query indents the results proportionally to the employee's position in the company management structure.

How It Works

The SQL keywords and clauses you see in the solution are the ones you see in most hierarchical queries: the LEVEL pseudo-column to indicate how far from the root node the current row (node) is, the START WITH clause to indicate where to start the tree navigation, and CONNECT BY to specify how the parent nodes and child nodes are connected. In addition, you almost always use the PRIOR unary operator to specify the column or columns in the parent row that have the same values as the linking columns in the child (current) row.

The START WITH clause indicates that we want to start the navigation on a row where the MANAGER_ID is NULL, in other words, on the owner or president of the company that does not report to anyone else in the company. If there are two owners of the company (both with a MANAGER_ID of NULL), the query still works after the employees for one tree are returned, the query returns all the subordinate (child) rows for the other hierarchy in the table. This scenario is represented by the hierarchical structures in Figure 13-1 where nodes 1 and 3 are the two company owners.

If we know that the employee numbers never change, we could alternatively use this START WITH clause:

```
start with employee_id = 100
```

Furthermore, if there are two hierarchies in the table, and the co-owner of the company has an EMPLOYEE_ID = 250, the START WITH clause would be as follows:

```
start with employee_id in (100,250)
```

This solution adds a visual element along with some additional formatting to make the query result more readable. The LPAD function prefixes blank characters before each full name in proportion to how far down in the hierarchy the current row is, defined by the LEVEL pseudo-column.

Traversing the tree structure from bottom to top instead is as easy and intuitive as switching the linking columns in the CONNECT BY clause. If you want to see the hierarchy in reverse order (from bottom to top) starting with Diana Lorentz (employee number 107), your SELECT statement would look like this:

```
select employee_id, level,
    lpad(' ',(level-1)*3) || last_name || ', ' || first_name full_name
from employees
start with employee_id = 107
connect by employee_id = prior manager_id
;
```

EMPLOYEE_ID	LEVEL	FULL_NAME
107	1	Lorentz, Diana
103	2	Hunold, Alexander
102	3	De Haan, Lex
100	4	King, Steven

```
4 rows selected
```

If you leave off the START WITH clause, you'll get all employees with their managers, and their manager's manager, and so forth, until it gets back to King (at least in this company; King is everyone's manager at the top of the hierarchy). Here are a few rows from the query that leaves out START WITH:

```
select employee_id, level,
    lpad(' ',(level-1)*3) || last_name || ', ' || first_name full_name
from employees
connect by employee_id = prior manager_id
;
```

```
EMPLOYEE_ID            LEVEL                   FULL_NAME
-------------------    -------------------     ---------------------------------------
100                    1                       King, Steven
101                    1                       Kochhar, Neena
100                    2                          King, Steven
102                    1                       De Haan, Lex
100                    2                          King, Steven
103                    1                       Hunold, Alexander
102                    2                          De Haan, Lex
100                    3                             King, Steven
104                    1                       Ernst, Bruce
103                    2                          Hunold, Alexander
102                    3                             De Haan, Lex
100                    4                                King, Steven
...
```

The output from this query includes King as an employee with no supervisor, in addition to showing up at the end of each branch in the hierarchy for every other employee.

13-2. Sorting Nodes Within a Hierarchical Level

Problem

You want to sort the rows at the same level in a hierarchy that are underneath the same parent row.

Solution

Use the SIBLINGS keyword in the ORDER BY clause. If you want to sort the employees by last name within each manager, the standard ORDER BY clause will not work, since it will sort on the last name independent of the level within the tree hierarchy. Instead, you must use the ORDER SIBLINGS BY clause, as in this example:

```
select employee_id, level,
    lpad(' ',(level-1)*3) || last_name || ', ' || first_name full_name
from employees
start with manager_id is null
connect by manager_id = prior employee_id
order siblings by last_name, first_name
;
```

```
EMPLOYEE_ID          LEVEL                  FULL_NAME
-------------------- ---------------------- -----------------------------------
100                  1                      King, Steven
148                  2                          Cambrault, Gerald
172                  3                              Bates, Elizabeth
169                  3                              Bloom, Harrison
170                  3                              Fox, Tayler
173                  3                              Kumar, Sundita
168                  3                              Ozer, Lisa
171                  3                              Smith, William
102                  2                          De Haan, Lex
103                  3                              Hunold, Alexander
105                  4                                  Austin, David
104                  4                                  Ernst, Bruce
107                  4                                  Lorentz, Diana
106                  4                                  Pataballa, Valli
147                  2                          Errazuriz, Alberto
166                  3                              Ande, Sundar
167                  3                              Banda, Amit
163                  3                              Greene, Danielle
165                  3                              Lee, David
164                  3                              Marvins, Mattea
162                  3                              Vishney, Clara
...
149                  2                          Zlotkey, Eleni
174                  3                              Abel, Ellen
178                  3                              Grant, Kimberely
175                  3                              Hutton, Alyssa
179                  3                              Johnson, Charles
177                  3                              Livingston, Jack
176                  3                              Taylor, Jonathon

107 rows selected
```

The sorting occurs at each level. Under King, the direct subordinates are Cambrault, De Haan, and Errazuriz, in alphabetical order within level 2. Under Cambrault at level 3, the direct subordinates are sorted alphabetically as well.

Tree "pruning" is easy. Let's say that the management team does not want to see Gerald Cambrault and his subordinates in this report. This means we're going to prune an entire branch from the tree. To do this, you must filter out the top of the branch to be removed in the CONNECT BY clause as an additional condition, as follows:

```
select employee_id, level,
    lpad(' ',(level-1)*3) || last_name || ', ' || first_name full_name
```

```
from employees
start with manager_id is null
connect by manager_id = prior employee_id
   and not (last_name = 'Cambrault' and first_name = 'Gerald')
order siblings by last_name, first_name
;
```

```
EMPLOYEE_ID          LEVEL                  FULL_NAME
-------------------- ---------------------- ----------------------------------
100                  1                      King, Steven
102                  2                         De Haan, Lex
103                  3                            Hunold, Alexander
105                  4                               Austin, David
104                  4                               Ernst, Bruce
107                  4                               Lorentz, Diana
106                  4                               Pataballa, Valli
147                  2                         Errazuriz, Alberto
166                  3                            Ande, Sundar
167                  3                            Banda, Amit
163                  3                            Greene, Danielle
165                  3                            Lee, David
164                  3                            Marvins, Mattea
162                  3                            Vishney, Clara
...
149                  2                         Zlotkey, Eleni
174                  3                            Abel, Ellen
178                  3                            Grant, Kimberely
175                  3                            Hutton, Alyssa
179                  3                            Johnson, Charles
177                  3                            Livingston, Jack
176                  3                            Taylor, Jonathon
```

```
100 rows selected
```

If someone decides the report should exclude only Gerald Cambrault but still include his subordinate employees, the filter should be in the WHERE clause instead, as follows:

```
select employee_id, level,
   lpad(' ',(level-1)*3) || last_name || ', ' || first_name full_name
from employees
where not (last_name = 'Cambrault' and first_name = 'Gerald')
start with manager_id is null
connect by manager_id = prior employee_id
order siblings by last_name, first_name
;
```

EMPLOYEE_ID	LEVEL	FULL_NAME
100	1	King, Steven
172	3	Bates, Elizabeth
169	3	Bloom, Harrison
170	3	Fox, Tayler
173	3	Kumar, Sundita
168	3	Ozer, Lisa
171	3	Smith, William
102	2	De Haan, Lex
103	3	Hunold, Alexander
105	4	Austin, David
104	4	Ernst, Bruce
107	4	Lorentz, Diana
106	4	Pataballa, Valli
147	2	Errazuriz, Alberto
166	3	Ande, Sundar
167	3	Banda, Amit
163	3	Greene, Danielle
165	3	Lee, David
164	3	Marvins, Mattea
162	3	Vishney, Clara
...		
149	2	Zlotkey, Eleni
174	3	Abel, Ellen
178	3	Grant, Kimberely
175	3	Hutton, Alyssa
179	3	Johnson, Charles
177	3	Livingston, Jack
176	3	Taylor, Jonathon

106 rows selected

There are now several phantom employees at level 3 in the report. It is not clear who the immediate supervisor is, but we do know that they work for a manager whose last name comes before DeHaan in the alphabet! This method of pruning is usually more useful when trimming leaf (bottom) nodes from a tree.

13-3. Generating Pathnames from Hierarchical Tables

Problem

The Linux system administrator is creating directory structures in the file system that match the management structure of the company, and suspects that the DBA can help her out by accessing the hierarchical features of Oracle to save time when creating the directory structure for the first time.

Solution

Use the SYS_CONNECT_BY_PATH operator in a hierarchical query against the EMPLOYEES table. Here's an example of how to do that:

```
select
  '/u01/empl' ||
  sys_connect_by_path(lower(last_name)||'.'||lower(first_name),'/') mgmt_path
from employees
  start with manager_id is null
  connect by prior employee_id = manager_id;
```

```
MGMT_PATH
-----------------------------------------------------------------------
/u01/empl/king.steven
/u01/empl/king.steven/kochhar.neena
/u01/empl/king.steven/kochhar.neena/greenberg.nancy
/u01/empl/king.steven/kochhar.neena/greenberg.nancy/faviet.daniel
/u01/empl/king.steven/kochhar.neena/greenberg.nancy/chen.john
/u01/empl/king.steven/kochhar.neena/greenberg.nancy/sciarra.ismael
/u01/empl/king.steven/kochhar.neena/greenberg.nancy/urman.jose manuel
/u01/empl/king.steven/kochhar.neena/greenberg.nancy/popp.luis
/u01/empl/king.steven/kochhar.neena/whalen.jennifer
/u01/empl/king.steven/kochhar.neena/mavris.susan
/u01/empl/king.steven/kochhar.neena/baer.hermann
/u01/empl/king.steven/kochhar.neena/higgins.shelley
/u01/empl/king.steven/kochhar.neena/higgins.shelley/gietz.william
/u01/empl/king.steven/de haan.lex
/u01/empl/king.steven/de haan.lex/hunold.alexander
...
/u01/empl/king.steven/zlotkey.eleni/grant.kimberely
/u01/empl/king.steven/zlotkey.eleni/johnson.charles
/u01/empl/king.steven/hartstein.michael
/u01/empl/king.steven/hartstein.michael/fay.pat

107 rows selected
```

The Linux system administrator adds the mkdir command at the beginning of each line, and the process is automated, at least for the creation of the initial directory structure.

How It Works

The problem and solution in this recipe seem a bit contrived, but only because we want to use the HR.EMPLOYEES table that is available with any Oracle installation. Furthermore, some of the employee last names and first names have embedded blanks, and this will cause some complaining from Linux when the system administrator tries to create the directories. To fix that, all you need to add is a call to the TRANSLATE function to remove all occurrences of blank characters.

This solution uses a number of hierarchical query features, just as in the previous recipe. In the employees table, the column MANAGER_ID is a foreign key to the row of the employee's manager. Thus the requirement for this part of the SELECT statement:

```
connect by prior employee_id = manager_id
```

The CONNECT BY clause introduces the conditions for linking the root, parent, and child rows. In this example, the CONNECT BY clause connects the MANAGER_ID in the current row to the EMPLOYEE_ID in the parent row. You could rewrite that clause as follows, producing the same results:

```
connect by manager_id = prior employee_id
```

You will typically have only one PRIOR operator, but it is possible to have multiple PRIOR operators in the CONNECT BY clause if the linking conditions span more than one column. You can also use a filtering condition to limit the rows in the result set as we did in the first recipe of this chapter.

You will rarely omit the PRIOR operator, as that is how Oracle links parent and child rows. Under some circumstances, you can leave out the PRIOR operator and only have a filter condition, as you will see in a recipe later in this chapter.

The query uses START WITH to indicate where in the hierarchy to begin. If an employee has no manager (usually the boss or owner), then the MANAGER_ID column is NULL, thus START WITH MANAGER_ID IS NULL gives us the desired result. You could, however, start anywhere in the hierarchical structure based on the value of any other column in the table. In this example, you only want to show the hierarchy for Neena Kochhar and her employees:

```
select
    sys_connect_by_path(lower(last_name)||'.'||lower(first_name),'/') mgmt_path
from employees
    start with last_name = 'Kochhar'
    connect by prior employee_id = manager_id
;

MGMT_PATH
-----------------------------------------------------------------------------
/kochhar.neena
/kochhar.neena/greenberg.nancy
/kochhar.neena/greenberg.nancy/faviet.daniel
/kochhar.neena/greenberg.nancy/chen.john
/kochhar.neena/greenberg.nancy/sciarra.ismael
/kochhar.neena/greenberg.nancy/urman.jose manuel
/kochhar.neena/greenberg.nancy/popp.luis
/kochhar.neena/whalen.jennifer
/kochhar.neena/mavris.susan
/kochhar.neena/baer.hermann
/kochhar.neena/higgins.shelley
/kochhar.neena/higgins.shelley/gietz.william

12 rows selected
```

Finally, the solution uses the SYS_CONNECT_BY_PATH function to give us the full path of nodes from the root node (specified by the START WITH clause) to the child node or leaf node in the current row of the table. It has two arguments: the column you want to appear in the hierarchical result, and the separator to use between nodes in the hierarchy. To rewrite the solution query to work for a Windows operating system, you only have to change the prefix for each row of the result and the separator character:

```
select
  'D:\EMPL' ||
  sys_connect_by_path(lower(last_name)||'_'||lower(first_name),'\') mgmt_path
from employees
    start with manager_id is null
    connect by prior employee_id = manager_id
;
```

```
MGMT_PATH
-------------------------------------------------------------------
D:\EMPL\king_steven
D:\EMPL\king_steven\kochhar_neena
D:\EMPL\king_steven\kochhar_neena\greenberg_nancy
D:\EMPL\king_steven\kochhar_neena\greenberg_nancy\faviet_daniel
D:\EMPL\king_steven\kochhar_neena\greenberg_nancy\chen_john
D:\EMPL\king_steven\kochhar_neena\greenberg_nancy\sciarra_ismael
...
D:\EMPL\king_steven\zlotkey_eleni\johnson_charles
D:\EMPL\king_steven\hartstein_michael
D:\EMPL\king_steven\hartstein_michael\fay_pat

107 rows selected
```

13-4. Identifying Leaf Data in a Hierarchical Table

Problem

The management team wants a report that differentiates managers from non-managers, which means you need to differentiate leaf nodes from root and branch nodes in a hierarchical table.

Solution

Use the CONNECT_BY_ISLEAF pseudo-column to identify rows that are not parents of any other rows—in other words, to identify leaf nodes. Here's an example showing how to do that:

```
select
    lpad(' ',(level-1)*3) || last_name || ', ' || first_name full_name,
```

```
    level, connect_by_isleaf is_leaf
from employees
    start with manager_id is null
    connect by prior employee_id = manager_id
;
```

FULL_NAME	LEVEL	IS_LEAF
King, Steven	1	0
Kochhar, Neena	2	0
Greenberg, Nancy	3	0
Faviet, Daniel	4	1
Chen, John	4	1
Sciarra, Ismael	4	1
Urman, Jose Manuel	4	1
Popp, Luis	4	1
Whalen, Jennifer	3	1
Mavris, Susan	3	1
Baer, Hermann	3	1
Higgins, Shelley	3	0
Gietz, William	4	1
De Haan, Lex	2	0
Hunold, Alexander	3	0
Ernst, Bruce	4	1
Austin, David	4	1
Pataballa, Valli	4	1
Lorentz, Diana	4	1
...		
Hartstein, Michael	2	0
Fay, Pat	3	1

```
107 rows selected
```

For clarity, this solution includes the value of the CONNECT_BY_ISLEAF column. To filter out non-leaf nodes, use a WHERE clause to keep rows where CONNECT_BY_IS_LEAF = 1.

Identifying a root node is easy: a node is a root node if its parent key is NULL. Note that a root node with no siblings is at the same time a leaf node!

How It Works

The CONNECT_BY_ISLEAF pseudo-column is handy when you want to see rows that are at the bottom of each branch of the tree. If you want to see rows at the top of the tree, you can select rows with LEVEL = 1. As you might expect, if you want to see only tree branches (not the root and not the leaves), you can select any rows that are not at level 1 and not a leaf. For example:

```
select
    lpad(' ',(level-1)*3) || last_name || ', ' || first_name full_name,
    level, connect_by_isleaf is_leaf
from employees
where level > 1 and connect_by_isleaf = 0
    start with manager_id is null
    connect by prior employee_id = manager_id
;
```

FULL_NAME	LEVEL	IS_LEAF
Kochhar, Neena	2	0
Greenberg, Nancy	3	0
Higgins, Shelley	3	0
De Haan, Lex	2	0
Hunold, Alexander	3	0
Raphaely, Den	2	0
Weiss, Matthew	2	0
Fripp, Adam	2	0
Kaufling, Payam	2	0
Vollman, Shanta	2	0
Mourgos, Kevin	2	0
Russell, John	2	0
Partners, Karen	2	0
Errazuriz, Alberto	2	0
Cambrault, Gerald	2	0
Zlotkey, Eleni	2	0
Hartstein, Michael	2	0

17 rows selected

In other words, the query returns all middle managers at the company!

Finally, you might want to see only leaf nodes (employees that are not managers), but also include the full tree structure above the leaf node on the same line of the report. To do this, you can use the recipe solution and add the SYS_CONNECT_BY_PATH function presented in recipe 13-3.

```
select
    last_name || ', ' || first_name full_name, level lvl,
    sys_connect_by_path(lower(last_name)||'.'||lower(first_name),'/') mgmt_path
from employees
where connect_by_isleaf = 1
    start with manager_id is null
    connect by prior employee_id = manager_id
;
```

```
FULL_NAME              LVL MGMT_PATH
-------------------    --- --------------------------------------------------------
Faviet, Daniel         4   /king.steven/kochhar.neena/greenberg.nancy/faviet.daniel
Chen, John             4   /king.steven/kochhar.neena/greenberg.nancy/chen.john
Sciarra, Ismael        4   /king.steven/kochhar.neena/greenberg.nancy/sciarra.ismael
Urman, Jose Manuel     4   /king.steven/kochhar.neena/greenberg.nancy/urman.jose manuel
Popp, Luis             4   /king.steven/kochhar.neena/greenberg.nancy/popp.luis
Whalen, Jennifer       3   /king.steven/kochhar.neena/whalen.jennifer
Mavris, Susan          3   /king.steven/kochhar.neena/mavris.susan
Baer, Hermann          3   /king.steven/kochhar.neena/baer.hermann
...
Hutton, Alyssa         3   /king.steven/zlotkey.eleni/hutton.alyssa
Taylor, Jonathon       3   /king.steven/zlotkey.eleni/taylor.jonathon
Livingston, Jack       3   /king.steven/zlotkey.eleni/livingston.jack
Grant, Kimberely       3   /king.steven/zlotkey.eleni/grant.kimberely
Johnson, Charles       3   /king.steven/zlotkey.eleni/johnson.charles
Fay, Pat               3   /king.steven/hartstein.michael/fay.pat

89 rows selected
```

If you only want to see the name of the manager at the top of the hierarchy for each leaf node, and not all the intermediate managers, you can use CONNECT_BY_ROOT to return the row at the top of the hierarchy, as in this example:

```
select
    last_name || ', ' || first_name full_name, level lvl,
    connect_by_root last_name top_last_name,
    connect_by_root first_name top_first_name
from employees
where connect_by_isleaf = 1
    start with manager_id is null
    connect by prior employee_id = manager_id
;
```

```
FULL_NAME               LVL TOP_LAST_NAME   TOP_FIRST_NAME
----------------------  --- --------------- --------------
Ernst, Bruce            4   King            Steven
Austin, David           4   King            Steven
Pataballa, Valli        4   King            Steven
Lorentz, Diana          4   King            Steven
...
Johnson, Charles        3   King            Steven
Fay, Pat                3   King            Steven

80 rows selected
```

To make an even more interesting example, let's take the previous query and start at the second level of the hierarchy, showing employees who do not supervise anyone, along with the intermediate manager right below King. Here is the SELECT statement:

```
select
    last_name || ', ' || first_name full_name, level lvl,
    connect_by_root last_name top_last_name,
    connect_by_root first_name top_first_name
from employees
where connect_by_isleaf = 1
    start with manager_id = 100
    connect by prior employee_id = manager_id
;
```

FULL_NAME	LVL	TOP_LAST_NAME	TOP_FIRST_NAME
Faviet, Daniel	3	Kochhar	Neena
Chen, John	3	Kochhar	Neena
Sciarra, Ismael	3	Kochhar	Neena
Urman, Jose Manuel	3	Kochhar	Neena
Popp, Luis	3	Kochhar	Neena
Whalen, Jennifer	2	Kochhar	Neena
Mavris, Susan	2	Kochhar	Neena
Baer, Hermann	2	Kochhar	Neena
Gietz, William	3	Kochhar	Neena
Ernst, Bruce	3	De Haan	Lex
Austin, David	3	De Haan	Lex
Pataballa, Valli	3	De Haan	Lex
Lorentz, Diana	3	De Haan	Lex
Khoo, Alexander	2	Raphaely	Den
...			
Abel, Ellen	2	Zlotkey	Eleni
Hutton, Alyssa	2	Zlotkey	Eleni
Taylor, Jonathon	2	Zlotkey	Eleni
Livingston, Jack	2	Zlotkey	Eleni
Grant, Kimberely	2	Zlotkey	Eleni
Johnson, Charles	2	Zlotkey	Eleni
Fay, Pat	2	Hartstein	Michael

```
89 rows selected
```

The LVL column now shows the number of management levels plus one between them and the employees that report to King.

13-5. Detecting Cycles in Hierarchical Data

Problem

Updates were made to a hierarchical table and now any hierarchical query run against the table generates this error message:

```
SQL Error: ORA-01436: CONNECT BY loop in user data
```

You need to identify the row that was updated incorrectly, generating this error message.

Solution

Use the `CONNECT_BY_ISCYCLE` pseudo-column and the `NOCYCLE` keyword in the `CONNECT BY` clause to force Oracle to run the query but stop returning rows that cause a cycle in the hierarchy structure. For example:

```
select employee_id, manager_id, level lvl,
    connect_by_iscycle is_cycle,
    lpad(' ',(level-1)*3) || last_name || ', ' || first_name full_name
from employees
start with last_name = 'Kochhar'
connect by nocycle manager_id = prior employee_id
;
```

EMPLOYEE_ID	MANAGER_ID	LVL	IS_CYCLE	FULL_NAME
101	113	1	0	Kochhar, Neena
108	101	2	0	Greenberg, Nancy
109	108	3	0	Faviet, Daniel
110	108	3	0	Chen, John
111	108	3	0	Sciarra, Ismael
112	108	3	0	Urman, Jose Manuel
113	108	3	1	Popp, Luis
200	101	2	0	Whalen, Jennifer
203	101	2	0	Mavris, Susan
204	101	2	0	Baer, Hermann
205	101	2	0	Higgins, Shelley
206	205	3	0	Gietz, William

```
12 rows selected
```

The employee hierarchy in the department headed by Kochhar was incorrectly modified, and the row with IS_CYCLE = 1 identifies the row causing a cycle in the data. The manager for the department, Kochhar, now has a manager with EMPLOYEE_ID = 113 (Popp), whose managerial structure follows up the tree back to Kochhar. The MANAGER_ID for Kochhar has to be changed to another employee who is not one of the subordinates in her management hierarchy.

How It Works

Any application that maintains a table or set of tables in a hierarchical structure should not allow any edits that generate a loop. However, errors occur, such as manual edits to the table that bypass the application logic. Detecting the source of the loop is a two-step process: first, identify the row that is causing the loop. However, as in this scenario, that row may not be the row that was incorrectly updated. The second step is to take the row information (usually a primary key) and find other rows that may incorrectly reference the flagged row. It might be easy to spot the loop with a small result set, as in the example above, but for queries returning hundreds or thousands of rows, you will have to use a query like this:

```
select employee_id, manager_id, last_name, first_name from employees
where manager_id in
(
    select employee_id
    from employees
    where connect_by_iscycle = 1
    start with last_name = 'Kochhar'
    connect by nocycle manager_id = prior employee_id
);
```

Fixing the problem requires identifying the correct parent for the row causing the loop using the previous query, then updating the column in the row that links the rows together:

```
update employees
set manager_id = 100
where employee_id = 101
;
```

Employee Kochhar has now been updated to the original value with the correct manager (King), who is not one of her direct or indirect reports!

13-6. Generating a Fixed Number of Sequential Primary Keys

Problem

You want to generate a virtual table of a sequence of 1000 numbers as the basis of a new table you will populate later. Using a sequence won't work, however, unless you create a table using PL/SQL or some other programming language. You could use an existing table, but it might have too few or too many rows for your needs.

Solution

You can use a little-known (until now) side-effect of Oracle's CONNECT BY hierarchical feature by not specifying the START WITH or CONNECT BY clauses. Here is how to generate 1000 rows in sequence:

```
select level new_pk from dual connect by level <= 1000;
```

```
NEW_PK
----------------------
1
2
3
4
5
6
7
8
9
10
11
...
996
997
998
999
1000
```

```
1000 rows selected
```

You can use this SELECT statement as the basis of a CTAS (Create Table As Select) operation, and add some extra columns, as you will see in the next section.

How It Works

On the surface, it's hard to see how this query works; if you don't use CONNECT BY and START WITH very often, this will probably make even less sense. Let's break it down and remember how CONNECT BY works, starting with the highlighted part of the SELECT statement:

```
select level new_pk from dual connect by level <= 1000;
```

The value returned for LEVEL will be our primary key, and we're assigning a new name to the resulting column. Remember that LEVEL is a pseudo-column, and is only available in hierarchical queries. So far, this is fairly straightforward. But how do we get LEVEL to increment to 1000 or some other user-defined value? Let's look at the next part of the statement:

```
select level new_pk from dual connect by level <= 1000;
```

Again, we're not straying too far from known territory. The table DUAL will always have only one row and one column, DUMMY, whose value is X. If this table were to disappear, or have more than one row, then it is no exaggeration to say that virtually all Oracle database applications would spectacularly fail in short order. But how can we get 1000 rows from only one? Let's look at the next part of the statement:

```
select level new_pk from dual connect by level <= 1000;
```

When you use CONNECT BY, Oracle traverses the tree structure defined in your table, and the column LEVEL indicates how far down the tree you are in the hierarchical structure. But again, DUAL only has one row, so we only have a tree with one level, right? Not exactly. Remember that the CONNECT BY clause usually contains the unary operator PRIOR to tell Oracle how to traverse the tree and connect previous rows to the current row. Since there is no START WITH clause or PRIOR operators, this SELECT statement is evaluated as follows:

1. Oracle finds the root row for the hierarchy. Since there is no START WITH clause, Oracle starts with the only row in the result set, and it is at LEVEL = 1.

2. The next child row is retrieved; since there is no CONNECT BY criterion other than LEVEL <= 1000, Oracle returns the previous row connected to itself as the next child row, incrementing the value of LEVEL.

3. Oracle evaluates the CONNECT BY criteria to see if we're done retrieving rows, and if not, Oracle continues at step 2 to return additional child rows.

4. After the CONNECT BY criteria are satisfied, the query is done returning results.

Finally, we have the last part of the statement, highlighted below:

```
select level new_pk from dual connect by level <= 1000;
```

We have to limit the results somehow, and specifying LEVEL <= 1000 tells Oracle to stop at 1000. If we didn't have this filter, the query would run indefinitely, and would not stop until you cancelled the statement or shut down the database. You cannot specify CONNECT BY without a filter or hierarchical join condition; thus, if you were bound and determined to run a query that would never finish, you would have to write something like to this:

```
select level new_pk from dual connect by 1=1;
```

You can enhance the statement even more by slipping some procedural SQL code into the SELECT statement. In this variation, you want to create a table with a unique primary key, as well as a second column that has a value of ODD when the primary key is an odd number and a value of EVEN when the primary key is an even number:

```
select level new_pk,
    case
        when mod(level,2) = 1 then 'ODD'
        else 'EVEN'
    end odd_or_even
from dual connect by level <= 1000;


NEW_PK                 ODD_OR_EVEN
---------------------- -----------
1                      ODD
2                      EVEN
3                      ODD
4                      EVEN
5                      ODD
6                      EVEN
7                      ODD
8                      EVEN
...
995                    ODD
996                    EVEN
997                    ODD
998                    EVEN
999                    ODD
1000                   EVEN

1000 rows selected
```

■■■

CHAPTER 14

Working with XML Data

Back in the halcyon days of the dot-com boom, it seemed every problem known to humankind could be solved with the application of a single technology—XML was the answer! Fast forward 10 years, and XML has become part of everyday life for information technology. Whether it's as part of the SOAP protocols for web services, the basis for workflow with BPEL (the Business Process Execution Language for Web Services), or as a universal mechanism for data interchange, XML is increasingly entering the database world.

Oracle added support for XML with Oracle 9*i*, and has improved its capabilities so that XML in 11*g* Release 2 is a first-class data citizen, with a wealth of tricks up its metaphorical sleeve. The recipes presented here are a mix of introductory examples, as well as more complex tasks to suit both beginners and experienced hands at XML in Oracle.

14-1. Translating SQL to XML

Problem

You need to convert data stored in traditional form in your database to XML. For instance, you need to dynamically create XML from your employee data for an employee record to send to a third party.

Solution

Oracle possesses many different functions for converting data to XML format. The sheer number of functions stems from the evolution of XML in the database, from its early inclusion in Oracle 9*i* through to its amazing flexibility in Oracle today. Some of the principal functions Oracle provides for converting relational data to XML are the SYS_XMLGEN, DBMS_XMLGEN, and XMLELEMENT functions. Each of these could solve this particular problem, but each has its own idiosyncrasies.

We've chosen to craft our recipe for dynamically converting one row of data with SYS_XMLGEN. We employ a user-defined type to act as a helper type to map our target data from relational to object-relational form, so it can be passed straight to SYS_XMLGEN. The SYS_XMLGEN function returns a block of XML based on a row or row-like expression. It can take a literal value, a single column, or a user-defined type as input parameter. We create the EMPLOYEE_MAP_TYPE shown next to map the relational data in the HR.EMPLOYEES table to a user-defined type that can be used directly by SYS_XMLGEN.

```
create or replace type employee_map_type as object (
  employee_id number(6),
  first_name varchar2(20),
  last_name varchar2(25),
  email varchar2(25),
  phone_number varchar2(20),
  hire_date date,
  job_id varchar2(10),
  salary number(8,2),
  commission_pct number(2,2),
  manager_id number(6),
  department_id number(4)
);
/
```

We now use the EMPLOYEE_MAP_TYPE type as a catalyst to feed data stored relationally for XML processing and output. The next procedure returns a valid, well-formed XML document representing the details of a given employee.

```
create or replace procedure employee_xml (emp_id IN number)
as
  xml_employee xmltype;
begin
  select
  sys_xmlgen
    (employee_map_type
      (e.employee_id,
       e.first_name,
       e.last_name,
       e.email,
       e.phone_number,
       e.hire_date,
       e.job_id,
       e.salary,
       e.commission_pct,
       e.manager_id,
       e.department_id)
    ) into xml_employee
  from hr.employees
  where e.employee_id = emp_id;
  dbms_output.put_line(xml_employee.getclobval());
end;
/
```

We can now call the EMPLOYEE_XML procedure to provide employee data in XML form.

```
call employee_xml(150);

<?xml version="1.0"?>
<ROW>
  <EMPLOYEE_ID>150</EMPLOYEE_ID>
```

```
<FIRST_NAME>Peter</FIRST_NAME>
<LAST_NAME>Tucker</LAST_NAME>
<EMAIL>PTUCKER</EMAIL>
<PHONE_NUMBER>011.44.1344.129268</PHONE_NUMBER>
<HIRE_DATE>30-JAN-97</HIRE_DATE>
<JOB_ID>SA_REP</JOB_ID>
<SALARY>10000</SALARY>
<COMMISSION_PCT>.3</COMMISSION_PCT>
<MANAGER_ID>145</MANAGER_ID>
<DEPARTMENT_ID>80</DEPARTMENT_ID>
</ROW>

Call completed.
```

How It Works

Our recipe works in two parts to build reusable components to convert employee data to XML. One limitation of the SYS_XMLGEN function is that it cannot accept multiple columns or tabular results as an input—such as the result of a SELECT * … statement. While the DBMS_XMLGEN procedure could do this, there's significant extra complexity to using that approach, which we want to avoid. We use SYS_XMLGEN's ability to operate on a user-defined type of arbitrary complexity. Our EMPLOYEE_MAP_TYPE mimics the column names and datatypes of the HR.EMPLOYEES table.

We create the EMPLOYEE_XML procedure by declaring a variable XML_EMPLOYEE to hold the generated XML version of the employee data.

Up to this point, our procedure is very straightforward. The next step calls SYS_XMLGEN:

```
select
sys_xmlgen
  (employee_map_type
    (e.employee_id,
     e.first_name,
     e.last_name,
     e.email,
     e.phone_number,
     e.hire_date,
     e.job_id,
     e.salary,
     e.commission_pct,
     e.manager_id,
     e.department_id)
  ) into xml_employee
from hr.employees
where e.employee_id = emp_id;
```

Here we use our EMPLOYEE_MAP_TYPE to dynamically cast the results from the SELECT statement into our custom user-defined datatype. At this point, we have a parameter that SYS_XMLGEN can accept. The result of the SYS_XMLGEN call is then directed to the XML_EMPLOYEE variable by the INTO clause.

At this point, the XML_EMPLOYEE variable holds our desired data in XML form. For a normal user to see the XML, we need to use a trick that relies on the underlying storage model for XML in Oracle. Under the hood, XML can be stored and managed in several ways. The most common is as a CLOB, and we can use this knowledge to invoke `CLOB` methods to retrieve the XML. The last line of our procedure invokes the `GETCLOBVAL` function on our `XML_EMPOYEE` variable, passing the results to `DBMS_OUTPUT.PUT_LINE` for printing onscreen (If you're running in SQL*Plus, don't forget to issue `SET SERVEROUTPUT ON`).

The Many Forms of XMLTYPE Storage

Oracle provides four different storage mechanisms for `XMLTYPE` data. These different approaches stem from the nature of XML as typically large blocks of text with a readily defined structure. It's this tension between large size and the patterns or structure hidden within that leads to trade-offs in storage efficiency versus indexing, and throughput versus transactional capabilities.

The four storage approaches for the `XMLTYPE` datatype are:

- **Object-Relational:** XML data is shredded into automatically created object-relational rows, ideal for element-based access, updates, and processing. Object-relational storage requires processing overhead to reform the complete XML document each time it is accessed as a single object.

- **CLOB:** Using a character large object approach to storing XML allows for easy processing of the whole XML document, preserving format, whitespace, and more. Extra overhead is introduced when updating individual elements in the XML, or indexing at the element level.

- **Hybrid:** A compromise between object-relational and CLOB storage, hybrid attempts to add element-level performance enhancements to document-centric CLOB storage.

- **Binary XML:** The newest form of XML storage in Oracle, this approach stores XML documents in a "post-parse" format, with checks for XML structure already performed. The underlying storage uses a compressed binary form, adding space efficiency to the processing efficiency gains.

Older applications and designs based on Oracle would normally choose between object-relational and CLOB storage, depending on the element/processing-centric versus document/throughput-centric nature of the system. Any new development with Oracle should favor the new Binary XML storage mechanism—though edge cases that emphasize extreme throughput or heavy element-level manipulation should be benchmarked with the CLOB or object-relational storage options.

In normal operation, you don't necessarily care about displaying the XML, and so can substitute the `DBMS_OUTPUT` call with an assignment to an extra `OUT` parameter value declared with the procedure. The structure of our recipe would change to this general form.

```
create or replace procedure employee_xml
  (emp_id IN number, xml_employee OUT xmltype)
as
  -- no need to specify xml_employee as local variable
```

```
    -- our existing recipe's procedure logic here
    -- no call to dbms_output.put_line
end;
/
```

This variant of the recipe would require the calling application to understand a returned variable of type XMLTYPE.

■ **Tip** Our recipe performs the dynamic conversion to XML using the EMPLOYEE_MAP_TYPE each time the procedure is called. You can increase the speed of this approach, and decrease the complexity of the procedure, by using a materialized column to keep the EMPLOYEE data ready in the form of the user-defined type for when it's needed. This requires more overhead at INSERT and UPDATE time, but speeds up retrieval via this procedure.

14-2. Storing XML in Native Form

Problem

You need to store native XML data into a relational table in your database. The XML needs to be stored as an intact XML document as it received.

Solution

Oracle makes native storage of XML easy by supporting numerous different forms, from native XML-typed tables to a wide range of functions. The trick is finding the approach that takes the least effort. For storing data where your XML doesn't need to be altered, or where a portion of the XML can be extracted with XSLT, using direct XMLTYPE data casting is the easiest approach.

Our recipe uses XMLTYPE to store a new warehouse definition in the OE.WAREHOUSES table. This allows us to store the XML directly in Oracle, effectively making the inner structure of the XML opaque for the purposes of adding it to the database. Oracle's many XML functions enable use and management of the elements, tags, and values within the XML without burdening us with added effort at insert time. The table structure is very simple, as shown here.

```
Name             Null?     Type
---------------  --------  ------------------
WAREHOUSE_ID     NOT NULL  NUMBER(3)
WAREHOUSE_SPEC             SYS.XMLTYPE
WAREHOUSE_NAME            VARCHAR2(35)
LOCATION_ID               NUMBER(4)
WH_GEO_LOCATION           MDSYS.SDO_GEOMETRY
```

We can insert a new warehouse, based in London, with a 15,000-square-foot floor area and other details, using the following INSERT statement with XMLTYPE casting.

```
insert into oe.warehouses
(warehouse_id, warehouse_spec, warehouse_name, location_id)
values
(10,
xmltype('
<?xml version="1.0"?>
  <Warehouse>
    <Building>Owned</Building>
    <Area>15000</Area>
    <Docks>1</Docks>
    <DockType>Side load</DockType>
    <WaterAccess>Y</WaterAccess>
    <RailAccess>Y</RailAccess>
    <Parking>Street</Parking>
    <VClearance>10 ft</VClearance>
  </Warehouse>'),
'London',
2300);
```

Note that the call to XMLTYPE has been formatted for easy reading on the printed page. In use, casting to XMLTYPE will throw an ORA-31011: XML parsing failed error if you include carriage returns, new lines, and spaces between your elements. In the code samples included with *Oracle SQL Recipes*, you'll see the INSERT statement formatted with the XMLTYPE call on one line.

```
insert into oe.warehouses
…
xmltype('<?xml version="1.0"?><Warehouse><Building>Owned</Building>…'),
…
```

How It Works

Our recipe leverages Oracle's ability to work with XML as just another datatype. We use the XMLTYPE call to cast the text provided into the XMLTYPE datatype. Under the hood, XMLTYPE supports CLOB semantics, because it's stored internally as a CLOB. This means we can use the same approach to casting, passing the call to XMLTYPE a string up to 4GB in size. We decided to keep our example short to save trees!

Just as casting to other datatypes enforces rules on precision, length, and so on, casting to XMLTYPE enforces some particular rules for XML data. If your column or table is defined using an XML schema, the schema will be used to validate the data, ensuring that mandatory elements are present and the overall structure conforms to the schema. This is known as testing for validity. Where no schema is used, as in our OE.WAREHOUSES table, the other integrity check of XML data structures is still enforced: the "well-formed" test. Here, Oracle ensures that the XML provided has matching opening and closing tags and that elements are nested correctly.

You can see the well-formed test in action if you attempt to store malformed data as XML. The next code deliberately breaks the XML formatting for our warehouse, omitting the closing </Warehouse> element tag.

```
-- intentionally invalid SQL
insert into oe.warehouses
(warehouse_id, warehouse_spec, warehouse_name, location_id)
values
```

```
(10,
xmltype('<?xml version="1.0"?><Warehouse><Building>Owned</Building>'),
'London',
2300);

xmltype('<?xml version="1.0"?><Warehouse><Building>Owned</Building>'),
*
ERROR at line 5:
ORA-31011: XML parsing failed
ORA-19202: Error occurred in XML processing
LPX-00007: unexpected end-of-file encountered
ORA-06512: at "SYS.XMLTYPE", line 310
ORA-06512: at line 1
```

Note the obscure error message in bold. Unexpected end-of-file is Oracle's way of telling you that it reached the end of the data without finding the expected closing element tag. Not the best error message in the world, but now you know what to look for.

14-3. Shredding XML for Relational Use

Problem

You need to extract individual element values from an XML document for use in other calculations. For instance, you need to extract text and numeric values in an XML document for calculations and details in a report on the space in your warehouses.

Solution

Oracle provides the XMLTABLE function to manipulate XML documents using XQuery and column mapping to traditional Oracle datatypes. Using XMLTABLE, we can identify and use data elements in an XML document in a relational way.

Our next recipe uses XMLTABLE to identify many of the details of warehouses in the OE.WAREHOUSES table, including the building type, the floor space area of the warehouses, dock access, and more.

```
select
  shredded_warehouses."Building",
  shredded_warehouses."FloorArea",
  shredded_warehouses."#Docks",
  shredded_warehouses."DockType",
  shredded_warehouses."WaterAccess",
  shredded_warehouses."RailAccess",
  shredded_warehouses."Parking",
  shredded_warehouses."VertClearance"
from oe.warehouses,
xmltable
  ('/Warehouse'
   passing warehouses.warehouse_spec
```

```
  columns
    "Building" varchar2(8) path '/Warehouse/Building',
    "FloorArea" number path '/Warehouse/Area',
    "#Docks" number path '/Warehouse/Docks',
    "DockType" varchar2(10) path '/Warehouse/DockType',
    "WaterAccess" varchar2(8) path '/Warehouse/WaterAccess',
    "RailAccess" varchar2(7) path '/Warehouse/RailAccess',
    "Parking" varchar2(7) path '/Warehouse/Parking',
    "VertClearance" varchar(9) path '/Warehouse/VClearance'
) shredded_warehouses;
```

Building	FloorArea	#Docks	DockType	WaterAcc	RailAcc	Parking	VertClear
Owned	25000	2	Rear load	Y	N	Street	10 ft
Rented	50000	1	Side load	Y	N	Lot	12 ft
Rented	85700			N	N	Street	11.5 ft
Owned	103000	3	Side load	N	Y	Lot	15 ft

With the data shredded into a table form, we can then use this in normal queries, functions, PL/SQL procedures, and so on.

How It Works

The key to our recipe is using the XMLTABLE function to do the hard work of teasing out the element values from the XML. Looking at the raw XML data, we're looking for the values in bold for a given XML document stored in the WAREHOUSE_SPEC column.

```
<?xml version="1.0"?>
<Warehouse>
  <Building>Owned</Building>
  <Area>25000</Area>
  <Docks>2</Docks>
  <DockType>Rear load</DockType>
  <WaterAccess>Y</WaterAccess>
  <RailAccess>N</RailAccess>
  <Parking>Street</Parking>
  <VClearance>10 ft</VClearance>
</Warehouse>
```

The XMLTABLE function takes one or more XQuery expressions to apply to a reference column or expression of XMLTYPE data. The general form of XMLTABLE is shown next.

```
xmltable(
  <XQuery to apply>,
  <Source XMLTYPE column or expression>,
  <Column definition optionally mapped with XQuery path expression>)
```

We don't have a huge number of spare chapters to devote to working with the DOM and how XQuery differs from SQL, but you can think of the optional PATH expressions for each column as instructing the XMLTABLE function how to walk the XML tree structure on finding the base element specified, which in our case is '/Warehouse'.

Our recipe instructs Oracle to walk through the WAREHOUSE_SPEC column of OE.WAREHOUSES, looking for the <Warehouse> element. Next, we find the sub-element named <Building> nested below the <Warehouse> element, using the XPath expression '/Warehouse/Building' in our columns clause. The value within the tags is cast to the type VARCHAR2(8), and given the name "Building". This process is then repeated for any other columns specified, building up our shredded version of the XML.

The results of the XMLTABLE function are treated just like an inline view in our recipe, as we give the expression an alias SHREDDED_WAREHOUSES. We then use this alias in our SELECT list just as we would use the results of any other inline view. We could equally refer to our SHREDDED_WAREHOUSES result from XMLTABLE in any type of query, function, or PL/SQL block.

14-4. Extracting Key XML Elements from an XML Document

Problem

You need to extract subsections of XML in other processing, including element names, attributes, and values. For instance, you need to extract a portion of XML from your warehouse XML documents for passing to an XSLT process.

Solution

Oracle's EXTRACT function includes support for the XMLTYPE datatype, and provides the ability to preserve XML element name and attribute constructs by returning the results as an XMLTYPE value.

Our recipe uses the EXTRACT function to select the <VClearance> element and its attributes and data from the warehouses in the OE.WAREHOUSES table. The next SQL shows the XPath expression used with the function to find our desired XML subsection.

```
select
  extract(warehouse_spec, 'Warehouse/VClearance') as VClearance_XML
from oe.warehouses;

VCLEARANCE_XML
-------------------------------
<VClearance>10 ft</VClearance>
<VClearance>12 ft</VClearance>
<VClearance>11.5 ft</VClearance>
<VClearance>15 ft</VClearance>
...
```

Each returned value is the XML sub-tree matching the <VClearance> elements found under <Warehouse> elements.

How It Works

The EXTRACT function uses XPath expressions to walk the DOM. It is designed to return well-formed fragments of XML from the source XML document. When the EXTRACT function finds the element matching the lowest level expressed in the XPath query, it returns the portion of the XML document from that element down, while preserving all element names, attributes, and values. In our recipe, that means when EXTRACT encounters the <VClearance> element, it starts returning XML from that element and all sub-elements nested from that point.

The EXTRACT function's operation on XML differs from its behavior when used against other datatypes. For instance, when used on dates or times, EXTRACT will return only the portion of the date or time requested, such as the month. If month is requested, EXTRACT won't return the date or time, or any of the "smaller" measures, such as day, hour, and so on. See Chapter 6 for recipes illustrating this behavior. When operating against XMLTYPE data, EXTRACT returns everything at or below the nesting level of the matching element. The next SQL statement shows the implications of this behavior if we alter our recipe to seek the <Warehouse> element, rather than <VClearance> element within <Warehouse>.

```
select
  extract(warehouse_spec, 'Warehouse') as VClearance_XML
from oe.warehouses
where warehouse_id = 1;

<Warehouse>
  <Building>Owned</Building>
  <Area>25000</Area>
  <Docks>2</Docks>
  <DockType>Rear load</DockType>
  <WaterAccess>Y</WaterAccess>
  <RailAccess>N</RailAccess>
  <Parking>Street</Parking>
  <VClearance>10 ft</VClearance>
</Warehouse>
```

Our modified statement matched the <Warehouse> element, and EXTRACT returned the entire XML sub-tree below the requested element as a result.

14-5. Generating Complex XML Documents

Problem

You need to convert a variety of traditional data in your database to an XML format. You particularly want to create a more complex XML document than a simple table-to-XML conversion, for instance by treating some relational values as attributes, and nesting values at different levels from a sample of employee data.

Solution

Oracle has a bewildering array of functions and procedures for generating XML from regular data. For our stated problem, we'll assume we'd like to use the EMPLOYEE_ID of an employee as an XML attribute to the root element, rather than as an element in its own right. We'd also like to provide added detail on salary, specifying the payment period as an attribute, and adding currency details. Tools like DBMS_XMLGEN or SYS_XMLGEN would require awkward intervention to provide this level of XML-specific massaging of the data.

When dealing with the need to carefully craft an XML result, the lower-level functions XMLROOT, XMLELEMENT, and XMLATTRIBUTE provide fine-grained control over the structure of your desired XML. The next statement uses these functions to produce the XML finesse our recipe demands.

```
select XMLRoot(
  XMLElement("Employee",
    XMLAttributes(employee_id as "Employee_ID"),
    XMLElement("FirstName", first_name),
    XMLElement("LastName", last_name),
    XMLElement("Salary",
      XMLAttributes('Monthly' as "Period"),
      XMLElement("Amount", salary),
      XMLElement("Currency", 'USD'))
    ),
  VERSION '1.0') Employee_XML
from hr.employees
where employee_id = 205;
```

The results yield our required data in a well-formed XML document, including the correct XML header.

```
<?xml version="1.0"?>
<Employee Employee_ID="205">
  <FirstName>Shelley</FirstName>
  <LastName>Higgins</LastName>
  <Salary Period="Monthly">
    <Amount>12000</Amount>
    <Currency>USD</Currency>
  </Salary>
</Employee>
```

How It Works

Our recipe uses the XMLROOT, XMLELEMENT, and XMLATTRIBUTES functions to build the required XML structure to represent our employee data.

Using XMLROOT provides the necessary XML header to turn our results from an XML fragment into a fully formed XML document. XMLROOT produces the header line, shown next.

```
<?xml version="1.0"?>
```

To most people this is just a semantic difference, but when testing XML for validity as a full XML document, the correct header element is required.

You can think of XMLELEMENT as being the XML equivalent of a PUT_LINE and concatenation, ||, command. A call to XMLELEMENT outputs the source column or expression together with the provided element name to form XML building blocks for the result. The trick to using XMLELEMENT is to keep in mind two capabilities. You can string as many calls to XMLELEMENT together as you wish (just as you can concatenate any number of strings), and the expression on which it operates can itself be another call to XMLELEMENT. This nesting of calls produces equivalent nested elements in the output. You can see this in the recipe in this code fragment.

```
...
XMLElement("Salary",
  XMLAttributes('Monthly' as "Period"),
  XMLElement("Amount", salary),
  XMLElement("Currency", 'USD')
...
```

Here we're instructing Oracle that the <Salary> element is composed of a call to XMLATTRIBUTES, and two calls to XMLELEMENT. While this is more laborious than a call to DBMS_XMLGEN or SYS_XMLGEN, the key is the ability to control the structure with simple commands. Neither of those system packages provides the ability to structure your results beyond simple, single-level XML. This is where XMLELEMENT provides the needed capabilities.

Our calls to XMLATTRIBUTES instruct Oracle to place the given columns or expressions as attributes of the element created by the parent call to XMLELEMENT. For instance, in the code fragment just shown, we use XMLATTRIBUTES to create a Period attribute for the <Salary> element, giving the attribute the value Monthly. A very common technique in XML data management is to include the notional primary key value or values as attributes to the root element or parent element of an entity, rather than place them as a sub-elements in their own right. You can see we've taken this approach with the EMPLOYEE_ID value sources from the HR.EMPLOYEES table. We use the call shown next to make this an attribute of the <Employee> element.

```
XMLAttributes(employee_id as "Employee_ID")
```

14-6. Validating XML Schema

Problem

You would like to enforce XML schema validity on XML data stored in your database. Warehouse specifications are currently stored without being checked against a valid schema, and you want to check this data against an appropriate schema to ensure its structure and content adhere to the schema's stipulations.

Solution

Oracle provides the DBMS_XMLSCHEMA.REGISTERSCHEMA function to define XML schemas within the Oracle database. We've created the necessary XML schema and hosted it on a local web server. As shown next, we embed a reference to this schema in a call to REGISTERSCHEMA to enable Oracle to find and register the schema.

```
begin
  dbms_xmlschema.registerschema(
    schemaurl=>'http://localhost/transfer/warehouse_schema.xsd',
    schemadoc=>
      '<?xml version="1.0" encoding="utf-8"?>
       <xs:schema
           targetNamespace="http://tempuri.org/XMLSchema.xsd"
           elementFormDefault="qualified"
           xmlns="http://tempuri.org/XMLSchema.xsd"
           xmlns:mstns="http://tempuri.org/XMLSchema.xsd"
           xmlns:xs="http://www.w3.org/2001/XMLSchema"
           xmlns:xdb="http://xmlns.oracle.com/xdb">
         <xs:element name="warehouse_spec">
           <xs:complexType>
             <xs:sequence>
               <xs:element name="Building" type="xs:string" minOccurs="1"
                 xdb:SQLName="BUILDING" />
               <xs:element name="Area" type="xs:unsignedInt" minOccurs="1"
                 xdb:SQLName="AREA" />
               <xs:element name="Docks" type="xs:unsignedInt" minOccurs="1"
                 xdb:SQLName="DOCKS" />
               <xs:element name="DockType" type="xs:string" minOccurs="1"
                 xdb:SQLName="DOCKTYPE" />
               <xs:element name="WaterAccess" type="xs:boolean" minOccurs="1"
                 xdb:SQLName="WATERACCESS" />
               <xs:element name="RailAccess" type="xs:boolean" minOccurs="0"
                 xdb:SQLName="RAILACCESS" />
               <xs:element name="Parking" type="xs:string" minOccurs="0"
                 xdb:SQLName="PARKING" />
               <xs:element name="VClearance" type="xs:string" minOccurs="0"
                 xdb:SQLName="VCLEARANCE" />
             </xs:sequence>
           </xs:complexType>
         </xs:element>
       </xs:schema>');
end;
/
```

With our schema in place and implicitly parsed for correctness and completeness by DBMS_XMLSCHEMA.REGISTERSCHEMA, we can now use it to examine a corresponding XMLTYPE column in the database to see if the XML present conforms to the schema. In XML parlance, this test determines the validity of the XML.

```
select w.warehouse_id,
  case
    when
      w.warehouse_spec.isSchemaValid
      ('http://localhost/transfer/warehouse_schema.xsd',
```

```
      'warehouse_spec') = 1 then 'Valid'
    when
      w.warehouse_spec.isSchemaValid
      ('http://localhost/transfer/warehouse_schema.xsd',
      'warehouse_spec') is null then 'Undefined'
    else 'Invalid'
  end XML_Validity
from oe.warehouses w;
```

Our results provide a human-readable summary of the validity of each WAREHOUSE_SPEC XML document against the XML schema.

```
WAREHOUSE_ID XML_VALIDITY
------------ ------------
           1 Valid
           2 Valid
           3 Valid
           4 Valid
           5 Undefined
           6 Undefined
           7 Undefined
           8 Undefined
           9 Undefined
```

How It Works

Our recipe starts by using the DBMS_XMLSCHEMA package to process an XML schema using the REGISTERSCHEMA function. This registration provides two features for us. First, it allows Oracle to identify the external location or locations from which it can source the schema. This frees future users of the schema from needing to track the schema's location themselves. Second and most important, REGISTERSCHEMA parses the schema for syntactical correctness and completeness. XML schemas are themselves XML documents, so it's possible to test whether they are well-formed to ensure elements are properly nested, closed, and so forth, and to test them for validity themselves against the W3C standard for XML schemata.

The REGISTERSCHEMA function can take the XML schema from a variety of locations, such as the text presented as a VARCHAR in our recipe, as well as from a BFILE or URI reference. We've included the schema on the website for *Oracle SQL Recipes*, www.oraclesqlrecipes.com, so you don't have to retype the text when exploring this recipe on your own.

Detailing the syntax and design choices of XML schemas could take a whole book. However, there are several noteworthy aspects of our schema that help with Oracle XML management. The first is the inclusion of Oracle's namespace for database-related XML. The "xmlns:xdb="http://xmlns.oracle.com/xdb" entry in our schema header allows us to use Oracle-specific datatypes as type attributes. It also allows us to add a SQLName mapping to assist Oracle to perform sub-element indexing and other administrative tasks.

With our schema validated and registered with Oracle, we know it's safe to use as a validity test (and even as a check constraint) against XML data. Our OE.WAREHOUSES table holds descriptions for warehouses in XML form in the WAREHOUSE_SPEC column, and this schema is designed for that warehouse data. Any XMLTYPE data incorporates member functions to perform a variety of XML processing, and we used the ISSCHEMAVALID function to test the WAREHOUSE_SPEC data against the XML schema. ISSCHEMAVALID returns 1 for valid data, 0 for invalid data, and NULL where no data is found. Instead of presenting this shorthand to the user, we've wrapped the call to ISSCHEMAVALID in a CASE block, to return the human-readable values of Valid, Invalid and Undefined for the three possible results.

14-7. Changing XML in Place

Problem

You need to alter data stored in an XMLTYPE column without affecting other elements in each XML entry. For instance, you need to change XML data describing warehouse floor area from imperial to metric measures.

Solution

Use Oracle's UPDATEXML function to perform updates to any part of an XMLTYPE datatype or XML document. Because our source data for the update is within the WAREHOUSE_SPEC column, of type XMLTYPE, we also use the EXTRACTVALUE function to find the target <Area> element we wish to update, so that we can perform the complete recipe in one statement. The next SQL shows UPDATEXML and EXTRACTVALUE working in unison to change the <Area> element from imperial to metric.

```
update oe.warehouses
set warehouse_spec =
  updatexml(
    warehouse_spec,
    '/Warehouse/Area/text()',
    extractvalue(
      warehouse_spec,
      'Warehouse/Area')*0.09290304
  );
```

We can use the next SQL we developed to view the newly calculated floor area values.

```
select
  extractvalue(warehouse_spec, 'Warehouse/Area')
from oe.warehouses;

EXTRACTVALUE(WAREHOUSE_SPEC,'WAREHOUSE/AREA')
-------------------------------------------
2322.576
4645.152
7961.790528
9569.01312
...
```

> **Note** 1 square foot equals exactly 0.09290304 square meters, thanks to the modern imperial inch being defined as exactly 2.54 centimeters.

How It Works

Our recipe uses two XML functions together to perform the apparent in-place update of the warehouse floor area from square feet to square meters. The overall structure of the update statement is familiar to anyone conversant in SQL.

```
update oe.warehouses
set warehouse_spec = <calculation of new space>;
```

It's the calculation of new space that requires the two XML functions, UPDATEXML and EXTRACTVALUE. A call to UPDATEXML takes this general form.

```
updatexml(<XMLTYPE column>, <XPath Expression>, <New Value>)
```

For our recipe, we target the WAREHOUSE_SPEC column, and use the XPath expression /Warehouse/Area/text() to target the value of the <Area> element. If we omitted the /text() portion of the XPath expression, we'd be telling UPDATEXML to change both the value and the element tags plus any attributes for <Area>.

To calculate the new value for UPDATEXML, we use EXTRACTVALUE to extract the current <Area> element values for each row. EXTRACTVALUE explicitly returns the value from an XPath expression, so we don't need to include the call to /text() in our XPath path. With each value returned, we multiply by 0.09290304 to convert the value in square feet to a value in square meters. This gives us the final value to be used by UPDATEXML to change the <Area> element's value.

When an Update is more than an Update

Our description of UPDATEXML suggests the in-place update of the <Area> element is only apparent. We weren't trying to suggest the update doesn't happen: it certainly does.

However, it's important to note that XMLTYPE data in Oracle can be stored internally as CLOB data as one of the storage options. Just as with CLOB data, you cannot update part of the value. Rather, when updating, you replace the existing data with a newly constructed form of the data. So in our example, the complete WAREHOUSE_SPEC XMLTYPE value is rewritten to Oracle with the new <Area> values. This means that even a small update to a large block of XML can have performance and logging implications.

CHAPTER 15

■■■

Partitioning

If you work with large tables and indexes, at some point you'll experience some performance degradation as the row counts grow into the hundreds of millions. Even efficiently written SQL executing against appropriately indexed tables will eventually slow down as table and index sizes grow into the gigabytes, terabytes, or even higher. For such situations you'll have to devise a strategy that allows your database to scale with increasing data volumes.

Oracle provides two key scalability features: parallelism and partitioning—mechanisms that enable good performance even with massively large databases. Parallelism allows Oracle to start more than one thread of execution to take advantage of multiple hardware resources. Partitioning allows subsets of a table or index to be managed independently. The focus of this chapter is on partitioning strategies.

Partitioning lets you create a logical table or index that consists of separate physical segments. Each partition of a table or index has the same logical structure, such as the column definitions, but can physically reside in separate containers. In other words, you can store each partition in its own tablespace and associated datafiles. This allows you to manage one large logical object as a group of smaller, more maintainable physical pieces.

Throughout this chapter, we will use various terms related to partitioning. Table 15-1 describes the meanings of terms you should be familiar with when using the recipes in this chapter.

Table 15-1. *Oracle Partitioning Terminology*

Term	Meaning
Partitioning	Transparently implementing one logical table or index as many separate, smaller, physical segments.
Partition key	One or more columns that determine which partition a row is stored in.
Partition bound	Boundary between partitions.
Single-level partitioning	Partitioning using a single method.
Composite partitioning	Partitioning using a combination of methods.
Subpartition	Partition within a partition.

Table 15-1. *Oracle Partitioning Terminology (continued)*

Term	Meaning
Partition independence	Ability to access partitions separately to perform maintenance operations without impacting the availability of other partitions.
Partition pruning	Eliminating unnecessary partitions. Oracle detects which partitions need to be accessed by a SQL statement and removes (prunes) any that aren't needed.
Partition-wise join	When two tables are partitioned on the same key and are joined together, Oracle can divide the join into smaller joins that occur between partitions and thereby improve performance.
Local index	Uses the same partition key as its table.
Global index	Does not use the same partition strategy as its table.

If you work with mainly small OLTP databases, you probably don't need to build partitioned tables and indexes. However, if you work with a large OLTP database or in a data warehouse environment, you will most likely benefit from using partitioning. Partitioning is a key to designing and building scalable database systems.

This chapter is for developers and DBAs who work with large databases. Oracle provides a robust set of methods for dividing tables and indexes into smaller subsets. For example, you can divide a table's data by date ranges, such as by month or year. Table 15-2 gives an overview of the many partitioning strategies available.

Table 15-2. *Partitioning Strategies*

Partition type	Description
Range	Allows partitioning based on ranges of dates, numbers, or characters.
List	Useful when the partitions fit nicely into a list of values, like state or region codes.
Hash	Allows even distribution of rows when there is no obvious partitioning key.
Composite	Allows combinations of other partitioning strategies.
Interval	Extends range partitioning by automatically allocating new partitions when new partition key values exceed the existing high range.
Reference	Useful for partitioning a child table based on a parent table column.
Virtual	Allows partitioning on a virtual column.
System	Allows the application inserting the data to determine which partition should be used.

The first few sections of this chapter describe the various partitioning strategies available with Oracle. The later sections delve into a variety of partition maintenance operations.

15-1. Determining if a Table Should be Partitioned

Problem

You have a large table and you wonder whether it should be partitioned.

Solution

Here are some rules of thumb for determining whether to partition a table:

- Tables that are over 2 gigabytes in size

- Tables that have more than 10 million rows and SQL operations are getting slower as more data is added

- Tables you know will grow large; it's better to create a table as partitioned rather than rebuild as partitioned when performance begins to suffer as the table grows

- Rows can be divided in a way that facilitates parallel operations like loading, archiving, retrieval, or backup and recovery

One general rule is that any table over 2 gigabytes in size is a potential candidate for partitioning. Run this query to show the top space-consuming objects in your database:

```
select * from (
select owner, segment_name, segment_type, sum(extents) num_ext, sum(bytes) tot
from dba_segments
group by owner, segment_name, segment_type order by sum(extents) desc)
where rownum < 10;
```

Here is a snippet of the output from the query:

OWNER	SEGMENT_NAME	SEGMENT_TYPE	NUM_EXT	TOT
REP_MV	REG_QUEUE_REP	TABLE	6273	6577717248
CIA_STAR	F_DOWNLOADS_IDX1	INDEX	2927	3069181952
REP_MV	CWP_USER_PROFILE	TABLE	2332	2445279232

The output shows that there are large tables in this database that might benefit from partitioning.

In addition to looking at the size of objects, if you can divide your data so that it facilitates operations such as loading data, querying, backups, archiving, and deleting, you should consider using partitioning. For example, if you work with a large table that contains data that is often accessed by a particular time range, such as by day, week, month, or year, it makes sense to consider partitioning.

How It Works

A large table size combined with a good business reason means you should consider partitioning. Keep in mind that there is more setup work and maintenance when you partition a table. However, it is much easier to partition a table initially during setup, rather than trying to convert it after it's grown to an unwieldy size.

▪ **Note** Currently, partitioning is an extra-cost option that is available only with the Oracle Enterprise Edition. You'll have to decide based on your business requirements whether partitioning is worth the cost.

15-2. Partitioning by Range

Problem

You're working in a data warehouse environment with a star schema. You have a fact table that contains a number column that represents a date. For example, the value 20100101 represents January 1st, 2010. You want to partition the fact table based on this number column.

Solution

Use the PARTITION BY RANGE clause to partition a table by range. The following example creates three partitions based on a range of numbers:

```
create table f_regs
(reg_count number
,d_date_id number
)
partition by range (d_date_id)(
partition p_2009 values less than (20100101),
partition p_2010 values less than (20110101),
partition p_max values less than (maxvalue)
);
```

You can view information about partitioned tables by running the following query:

```
select table_name,partitioning_type,def_tablespace_name
from user_part_tables;
```

Here is a snippet of the output:

```
TABLE_NAME          PARTITION DEF_TABLESPACE_NAME
------------------- --------- -------------------------
F_REGS              RANGE     USERS
```

To view information about the partitions within a table, issue a query like this:

```
select table_name, partition_name, high_value
from user_tab_partitions;
```

Here is some sample output:

```
TABLE_NAME          PARTITION_NAME                  HIGH_VALUE
------------------- ------------------------------- ---------------
F_REGS              P_2009                          20100101
F_REGS              P_2010                          20110101
F_REGS              P_MAX                           MAXVALUE
```

How It Works

The PARTITION BY RANGE clause uses a partitioning column (also called the partition key) to determine which partition a row is inserted into. In the recipe, the D_DATE_ID column is the partitioning column. The VALUES LESS THAN clause creates the partition bound, which defines which partition a row will be inserted into. For example, a row with a partition key value of 20100202 will be inserted into the P_2010 partition (the high value for the P_2010 partition is defined to be 20110101).

The MAXVALUE parameter creates a partition to store rows that don't fit into the other defined partitions. You don't have to specify a MAXVALUE. However, an error will be thrown if you attempt to insert a value that doesn't fit into an existing partition.

You may have noticed that we used a column D_DATE_ID as a number data type instead of a date data type for the F_REGS table. The D_DATE_ID is a foreign key from a D_DATES dimension table into the F_REGS fact table. One technique employed in data warehouse environments is to use a smart surrogate key for the primary key of the D_DATES dimension. The main reason for using smart keys for dates is for the physical database design when you want to use range partitioning on a date field. This allows you to partition on a foreign key number that looks like a date.

15-3. Partitioning by List

Problem

You want to partition a table by values in a list, such as a list of state codes.

Solution

Use the PARTITION BY LIST clause of the CREATE TABLE statement. This example partitions by the column STATE_CODE:

```
create table f_sales
 (reg_sales   number
 ,d_date_id   number
 ,state_code varchar2(20)
)
partition by list (state_code)
 ( partition reg_west values ('AZ','CA','CO','MT','OR','ID','UT','NV')
  ,partition reg_mid  values ('IA','KS','MI','MN','MO','NE','OH','ND')
  ,partition reg_rest values (default)
);
```

How It Works

The partition key for a list-partitioned table can be only one column. Use the DEFAULT list to specify a partition for rows that don't match values in the list. Run this SQL statement to view list values for each partition:

```
select table_name, partition_name, high_value
from user_tab_partitions
order by 1;
```

The HIGH_VALUE column will display the list values defined for each partition. This column is of data type LONG. If you're using SQL*Plus, you may need to set the LONG variable to a value higher than the default (80 bytes) to display the entire contents of the column:

```
SQL> set long 1000
```

15-4. Partitioning by Hash

Problem

You have a table that doesn't contain an obvious column to partition it by range or list. You want to spread out the data evenly among partitions based on an ID column in the table.

Solution

Use the PARTITION BY HASH clause of the CREATE TABLE statement. This example creates a table that is divided into three partitions. Each partition is created in its own tablespace.

```
create table browns(
 brown_id number
,bear_name varchar2(30))
partition by hash(brown_id)
partitions 3
store in(tbsp1, tbsp2, tbsp3);
```

Of course you'll have to modify details like the tablespace names to match those in your environment. Alternatively, you can omit the STORE IN clause and Oracle will place all partitions in your default tablespace. If you want to name both the tablespaces and partitions, you can specify them as follows:

```
create table browns(
 brown_id number
,bear_name varchar2(30))
partition by hash(brown_id)
(partition p1 tablespace tbsp1
,partition p2 tablespace tbsp2
,partition p3 tablespace tbsp3);
```

How It Works

Hash partitioning maps rows to partitions based on an algorithm that will spread data evenly across all partitions. You don't have any control over the hashing algorithm or how Oracle distributes the data. You specify how many partitions you'd like and Oracle divides the data evenly based on the hash key column.

Hash partitioning has some interesting performance implications. All rows that share the same value for the hash key will be inserted into the same partition. This means that inserts are particularly efficient as the hashing algorithm ensures that the data is distributed uniformly across partitions. Also, if you typically select for a specific key value, Oracle only has to access one partition to retrieve those rows. However, if you search by ranges of values, Oracle will most likely have to search every partition to determine which rows to retrieve. Thus range searches can perform poorly in hash-partitioned tables.

15-5. Partitioning a Table in Multiple Ways

Problem

You have a table you want to partition on a number range, but you also want to subdivide each partition by a list of regions.

Solution

Use composite partitioning to instruct Oracle to divide a table in multiple ways. The following example first partitions a table by a number range, then further distributes data via list partitioning:

```
create table f_sales(
  sales_amnt number
 ,reg_code   varchar2(3)
 ,d_date_id  number
)
partition by range(d_date_id)
subpartition by list(reg_code)
(partition p2010 values less than (20100101)
  (subpartition p1_north values ('ID','OR')
  ,subpartition p1_south values ('AZ','NM')
    ),
 partition p2011 values less than (20110101)
  (subpartition p2_north values ('ID','OR')
  ,subpartition p2_south values ('AZ','NM')
  )
);
```

You can view subpartition information by running the following query:

```
select table_name, partitioning_type, subpartitioning_type
from user_part_tables;
```

Here is some sample output:

```
TABLE_NAME          PARTITION SUBPART
------------------- --------- -------
F_SALES             RANGE     LIST
```

Run the next query to view information about the subpartitions:

```
select table_name, partition_name, subpartition_name
from user_tab_subpartitions;
```

Here is a snippet of the output:

```
TABLE_NAME          PARTITION_NAME        SUBPARTITION_NAME
------------------- --------------------- --------------------
F_SALES             P2010                 P1_SOUTH
F_SALES             P2010                 P1_NORTH
F_SALES             P2011                 P2_SOUTH
F_SALES             P2011                 P2_NORTH
```

How It Works

Oracle allows you to combine two partitioning strategies, as follows:

- Range-Range Partitioning
- Range-Hash Partitioning
- Range-List Partitioning
- List-Range Partitioning
- List-Hash Partitioning
- List-List Partitioning

Composite partitioning gives you a great deal of flexibility in the way you divvy up your data. You can use these methods to further refine how data is distributed and maintained.

15-6. Creating Partitions on Demand

Problem

You have a range-partitioned table and want Oracle to automatically add a partition when values are inserted above the highest value defined for the highest range.

Solution

If you are using Oracle Database 11g or higher, you can use the INTERVAL clause of the CREATE TABLE statement to instruct Oracle to automatically add a partition to the high end of a range-partitioned table. This example creates a table that initially has one partition with a high-value range of 01-JAN-2010.

```
create table f_sales(
 sales_amt number
,d_date     date
)
partition by range (d_date)
interval(numtoyminterval(1, 'YEAR'))
(partition p1 values less than (to_date('01-jan-2010','dd-mon-yyyy')));
```

The interval in this example is 1 year, defined by the INTERVAL(NUMTOYMINTERVAL(1, 'YEAR')) clause. If a record is inserted into the table with a D_DATE value greater than or equal to 01-JAN-2010, Oracle will automatically add a new partition to the high end of the table. You can check the details of the partition by running this SQL statement:

```
select table_name, partition_name, partition_position, high_value
from user_tab_partitions order by table_name, partition_name;
```

Here is some sample output (the HIGH_VALUE column has been cut short so the output fits on the page):

```
TABLE_NAME PARTITION_NA PARTITION_POSITION HIGH_VALUE
---------- ------------ ------------------ ----------------------------------------
F_SALES    P1                            1 TO_DATE(' 2010-01-01 00:00:00',...
```

Now we insert some data above the high value for the highest partition:

```
insert into f_sales values(1,sysdate+1000);
```

Here's what the output from selecting from USER_TAB_PARTITIONS now shows:

```
TABLE_NAME PARTITION_NA PARTITION_POSITION HIGH_VALUE
---------- ------------ ------------------ ----------------------------------------
F_SALES    P1                            1 TO_DATE(' 2010-01-01 00:00:00',...
F_SALES    SYS_P93                       2 TO_DATE(' 2013-01-01 00:00:00',...
```

A partition was automatically created named SYS_P93 with a high value of 2013-01-01.

How It Works

As of Oracle Database 11g, you can instruct Oracle to automatically add partitions to range-partitioned tables. Interval partitioning instructs Oracle to dynamically create a new partition when data inserted exceeds the maximum bound of a range-partitioned table. The newly added partition is based on an interval that you specify.

■ **Note** With interval partitioning, you can specify only a single key column from the table and it must be either a DATE or NUMBER data type.

15-7. Partitioning by Referential Constraints

Problem

You have a parent ORDERS table and a child ORDER_ITEMS table that are related by primary key and foreign key constraints on the ORDER_ID column. The parent ORDERS table is partitioned on the ORDER_DATE column. Even though the child ORDER_ITEMS table does not contain the ORDER_DATE column, you wonder if you can partition it so that the records are distributed in the same way as the parent ORDERS table.

Solution

If you are using Oracle Database 11g or higher, you can use the PARTITION BY REFERENCE clause to specify that a child table should be partitioned in the same way as its parent. This example creates a parent table with a primary key constraint on ORDER_ID and range partitions on ORDER_DATE:

```
create table orders(
 order_id    number
,order_date  date
,constraint order_pk primary key(order_id)
)
partition by range(order_date)
(partition p10  values less than (to_date('01-jan-2010','dd-mon-yyyy'))
,partition p11  values less than (to_date('01-jan-2011','dd-mon-yyyy'))
,partition pmax values less than (maxvalue)
);
```

Next the child ORDER_ITEMS table is created. It is partitioned by naming the foreign key constraint as the referenced object:

```
create table order_items(
 line_id  number
,order_id number not null
,sku       number
,quantity number
,constraint order_items_pk  primary key(line_id, order_id)
,constraint order_items_fk1 foreign key (order_id) references orders
)
partition by reference (order_items_fk1);
```

Notice that the foreign key column ORDER_ID must be defined as NOT NULL. The foreign key column must be enabled and enforced.

How It Works

As of Oracle Database 11g, you can partition by reference. This allows a child table to inherit the partitioning strategy of its parent table. Any parent table partitioning maintenance operations are also applied to the child record tables.

Before the advent of the partitioning by reference feature, you would have to physically duplicate and maintain the parent table column in the child table, which not only requires more disk space, it is also prone to errors when maintaining the partitions.

When creating the referenced partition child table, if you don't explicitly name the child table partitions, by default Oracle will create partitions for the child table with the same partition names as its parent table. This example explicitly names the child table referenced partitions:

```
create table order_items(
```

```
 line_id  number
,order_id number not null
,sku      number
,quantity number
,constraint order_items_pk  primary key(line_id, order_id)
,constraint order_items_fk1 foreign key (order_id) references orders
)
partition by reference (order_items_fk1)
(partition c10
,partition c11
,partition cmax
);
```

You can't specify the partition bounds of a referenced table. Partitions of a referenced table will be created in the same tablespace as the parent partition unless you specify tablespaces for the child partitions.

15-8. Partitioning on a Virtual Column

Problem

You've defined a virtual column in a table. You want to partition the table based on the virtual column.

Solution

If you are using Oracle Database 11*g* or higher, you can partition on a virtual column. Here is a sample script that creates a table named EMP with a virtual column of COMMISSION and a corresponding range partition for the virtual column:

```
create table emp (
 emp_id   number
,salary   number
,comm_pct number
,commission generated always as (salary*comm_pct)
)
partition by range(commission)
(partition p1 values less than (1000)
,partition p2 values less than (2000)
,partition p3 values less than (maxvalue));
```

How It Works

A virtual column is a derived calculation from other columns in the table. Starting with Oracle Database 11g, you can create a table with a virtual column, and you can use a virtual column to partition. This strategy allows you to partition on a column that is not stored in the table but is computed dynamically. Virtual-column partitioning is supported with all of the basic indexing strategies.

Virtual-column partitioning is appropriate when there is a business requirement to partition on a column that is not physically stored in a table. This could be a complex calculation, a subset of a column string, a combination of columns, and so on. For example, you may have a ten-character string column where the first two digits represent a region and last eight digits represent a specific location (this is a bad design, but it happens). In this case, it may make sense from the business perspective to partition on the first two digits of this column (by region).

15-9. Application-Controlled Partitioning

Problem

You have a rare situation in which you want the application inserting records into a table to explicitly control which partition it inserts data into.

Solution

If you are using Oracle Database 11g or higher, you can use the PARTITION BY SYSTEM clause to allow an INSERT statement to specify into which partition to insert data. This next example creates a system-partitioned table with three partitions:

```
create table apps
(app_id number
,app_amnt number)
partition by system
(partition p1
,partition p2
,partition p3);
```

When inserting data into this table, you must specify a partition. The next line of code inserts a record into partition P1:

```
insert into apps partition(p1) values(1,100);
```

When updating or deleting, if you don't specify a partition Oracle will scan all partitions of a system-partitioned table to find the relevant rows. Therefore, you should specify a partition when updating and deleting to avoid poor performance.

How It Works

As of Oracle Database 11g, you can create system partitions. A system-partitioned table is for unusual situations in which you need to explicitly control which partition a record is inserted into. This allows your application code to manage the distribution of records among the partitions. We recommend you use this feature in situations where you can't use one of Oracle's other partitioning mechanisms to solve your business requirement.

15-10. Configuring Partitions with Tablespaces

Problem

You want to place each partition of a table in its own tablespace. This will facilitate operations such as backing up and recovering partitions independently of each other.

Solution

If you don't specify a tablespace when creating a partitioned table or index, the partitions will be created in your default tablespace. If you prefer to place each partition in its own tablespace, use the TABLESPACE clause. Of course, you'll have to pre-create the tablespaces you reference before you can use them in your CREATE TABLE statement:

```
create table f_regs
(reg_count number
,d_date_id number
)
partition by range (d_date_id)(
partition p_2009 values less than (20100101)
  tablespace p_2009_tbsp,
partition p_2010 values less than (20110101)
  tablespace p_2010_tbsp,
partition p_max  values less than (maxvalue)
  tablespace p_max_tbsp
);
```

You can also specify any other storage settings. The next example explicitly sets the PCTFREE, PCTUSED, and NOLOGGING clauses:

```
create table f_regs
(reg_count number
,d_date_id number
)
partition by range (d_date_id)(
```

```
partition p_2009 values less than (20100101)
  tablespace p_2009_tbsp pctfree 5 pctused 90 nologging,
partition p_2010 values less than (20110101)
  tablespace p_2010_tbsp pctfree 5 pctused 90 nologging,
partition p_max  values less than (maxvalue)
  tablespace p_max_tbsp pctfree 5 pctused 90 nologging
);
```

How It Works

One advantage to placing partitions in separate tablespaces is that you can back up and recover partitions independently. If you have a partition that is not being modified, you can change its tablespace to read-only and instruct utilities like Oracle Recovery Manager (RMAN) to skip backing up such tablespaces, thus increasing backup performance. And there are other advantages. Creating each partition in its own tablespace facilitates the moving of data from OLTP databases to DSS (decision support system) databases, and it allows specific tablespaces and corresponding datafiles to be placed on separate storage devices to improve scalability and performance

If you have already created a table and want to move its partitions to particular tablespaces, use the `ALTER TABLE...MOVE PARTITION` statement to relocate a table partition to a different tablespace. This example moves the P_2009 partition to the INV_MGMT_DATA tablespace;

```
alter table f_sales move partition p_2009 tablespace inv_mgmt_data;
```

When you move a table partition to a different tablespace, the indexes will be invalidated. Therefore, you must rebuild any local indexes associated with a table partition that has been moved.

When you rebuild an index, you can leave it where it is or move it to a different tablespace. This example rebuilds the P_2009 partition of the D_DATE_ID_FK1 index and moves it to the INV_MGMT_INDEX tablespace:

```
alter index d_date_id_fk1 rebuild partition p_2009 tablespace inv_mgmt_index;
```

When you move a table partition to a different tablespace, this causes the ROWID of each record in the table partition to change. Since a regular index stores the table ROWID as part of its structure, the index partition will be invalidated if the table partition moves. In this scenario you must rebuild the index. When you rebuild the index partition, you have the option of moving to a different tablespace.

15-11. Automatically Moving Updated Rows

Problem

You're attempting to update a partition key to a value that will result in the row belonging in a different partition:

```
update f_regs set d_date_id = 20100901 where d_date_id = 20090201;
```

You receive the following error:

```
ORA-14402: updating partition key column would cause a partition change
```

You wonder if there is some way to modify the table so that Oracle will just move the row when a change to the partition key necessitates that the row be moved to a different partition.

Solution

Use the ENABLE ROW MOVEMENT clause of the ALTER TABLE statement to allow updates to the partition key that would change which partition a value belongs in. For this example the F_REGS table is first modified to enable row movement:

```
alter table f_regs enable row movement;
```

You should now be able to update the partition key to a value that moves the row to a different segment. You can verify that row movement has been enabled by querying the ROW_MOVEMENT column of the USER_TABLES view:

```
select row_movement from user_tables where table_name='F_REGS';
```

You should see the value of ENABLED:

```
ROW_MOVE
--------
ENABLED
```

How It Works

Before you can update a partition key to a value that means the row will need to move to a different partition, you need to enable row movement. This allows Oracle to physically move a row to a different data block.

To disable row movement use the DISABLE ROW MOVEMENT clause:

```
alter table f_regs disable row movement;
```

15-12. Partitioning an Existing Table

Problem

You have a table that has grown quite large and it is currently not partitioned. You wonder if you can partition it.

Solution

There are several methods for converting a non-partitioned table to a partitioned table. In this solution we show one simple approach in which you:

1. Create a new partitioned table from the old with CREATE TABLE <new table>...AS SELECT * FROM <old table>

2. Drop or rename the old table

3. Rename the table created in Step 1 to the name of the dropped table

In this example, we first create a new partitioned table named F_REGS_NEW with the CREATE TABLE statement selecting from the old, non-partitioned table named F_REGS:

```
create table f_regs_new
partition by range (d_date_id)
(partition p2008 values less than(20090101),
 partition p2009 values less than(20100101),
 partition pmax values less than(maxvalue)
)
nologging
as select * from f_regs;
```

Now you can drop (or rename) the old non-partitioned table and rename the new partitioned table to the old table name:

```
drop table f_regs purge;
rename f_regs_new to f_regs;
```

Lastly, build any constraints, grants, indexes, and statistics for the new table. You should now have a partitioned table that replaces the old, non-partitioned table.

For the last step, if the original table contains many constraints, grants, and indexes, you may want to use Data Pump EXPDP or EXP to export the original table without data, and then after the new table is created, use then use Data Pump IMPDP or IMP to create the constraints, grants, indexes, and statistics on the new table.

How It Works

Converting tables from non-partitioned to partitioned can be a time-consuming process. In the solution section we showed a simple way to convert a table. Table 15-3 lists the pros and cons of techniques used to create partitioned tables from non-partitioned tables. Needless to say, you'll need to plan carefully and test your conversion process.

Table 15-3. Methods of Converting a Non-Partitioned Table

Conversion method	Advantages	Disadvantages
CREATE <new_part_tab> AS SELECT * FROM <old_tab>	Simple, can use NOLOGGING and PARALLEL options. Direct path load.	Requires space for both old and new table.
INSERT /*+ APPEND */ INTO <new_part_tab> SELECT * FROM <old_tab>	Fast, simple. Direct path load.	Requires space for both old and new table.
Data Pump EXPDP old table, IMPDP new table (or EXP IMP if using older version of Oracle)	Fast, less space required. Takes care of grants, privileges, and so on. Loading can be done per partition with filtering conditions.	More complicated because you need to use a utility.
Create partitioned <new_part_tab>, exchange partitions with <old_tab>	Potentially less down time.	Many steps, complicated.
Use DBMS_REDEFINITION package (newer versions of Oracle)	Converts existing table inline.	Many steps, complicated.
Create CSV file or external table, load <new_part_tab> with SQL*Loader	Loading can be done partition by partition.	Many steps, complicated.

15-13. Adding a Partition to a Partitioned Table

Problem

You have a table that is already partitioned but you want to add another partition to the table.

Solution

The solution will depend on the type of partitioning you've implemented. For a range-partitioned table, if the table's highest bound is not defined with a MAXVALUE, you can use the ALTER TABLE...ADD PARTITION statement to add a partition to the high end of the table. This example adds a partition to the high end of a range-partitioned table:

```
alter table f_regs add partition p2011 values less than (20120101)
pctfree 5 pctused 95 tablespace p_tbsp;
```

If you have a range-partitioned table with the high range bounded by MAXVALUE, you can't add a partition. In this situation you'll have to split an existing partition (see recipe 15-16 for details).

If you have a hash-partitioned table, use the ADD PARTITION clause as follows to add a partition:

```
alter table browns add partition new_part tablespace p_tbsp update indexes;
```

If you don't specify the UPDATE INDEXES clause, any global indexes and local indexes for the new partition on a hash-partitioned table will have to be rebuilt.

For a list-partitioned table, you can only add a new partition if there is not a DEFAULT partition defined. The next example adds a partition to a list-partitioned table:

```
alter table f_sales add partition reg_east values('GA');
```

How It Works

After adding a partition to a table, always check the indexes to ensure that they all still have a usable STATUS:

```
select index_name, partition_name, status from user_ind_partitions;
```

Consider using the UPDATE INDEXES clause of the ALTER TABLE statement to automatically rebuild indexes when performing maintenance operations. In some cases, you may not be able to use the UPDATE INDEXES clause and will have to rebuild any unusable indexes. We highly recommend that you always test a maintenance operation in a non-production database to determine any unforeseen side effects.

15-14. Exchanging a Partition with an Existing Table

Problem

You have loaded a staging table with data. You now want to make the table a partition in a partitioned table.

Solution

Use the partition exchange feature to swap a stand-alone table with a table partition. A simple example will illustrate the process. Say you have a range-partitioned table created as follows:

```
create table f_sales
(sales_amt number, d_date_id number)
partition by range (d_date_id)
(partition p_2007 values less than (20080101),
 partition p_2008 values less than (20090101),
 partition p_2009 values less than (20100101)
);
```

Also, a bitmap index has been created on the D_DATE_ID column:

```
create bitmap index d_date_id_fk1 on
f_sales(d_date_id) local;
```

Now add a new partition to the table that will store new data:

```
alter table f_sales add partition p_2010
values less than(20110101);
```

Next, create a staging table and insert data that falls within the range of values for the newly added partition:

```
create table workpart(sales_amt number, d_date_id number);
insert into workpart values(100,20100101);
insert into workpart values(120,20100102);
```

Create a bitmap index on the WORKPART table that matches the structure of the bitmap index on F_SALES:

```
create bitmap index d_date_id_fk2 on workpart(d_date_id);
```

Now exchange the WORKPART table with the P_2010 partition:

```
alter table f_sales exchange partition p_2010
with table workpart including indexes without validation;
```

A quick query of the F_SALES table verifies the partition was exchanged successfully:

```
select * from f_sales partition(p_2010);
```

Here is the output:

```
SALES_AMT   D_DATE_ID
---------- ----------
      100   20100101
      120   20100102
```

This query will display that the indexes are all still usable:

```
select index_name, partition_name, status from user_ind_partitions;
```

You can also verify that a local index segment was created for the new partition:

```
select segment_name,segment_type,partition_name
from user_segments
where segment_name IN('F_SALES','D_DATE_ID_FK1');
```
Here is the output:

```
SEGMENT_NAME          SEGMENT_TYPE          PARTITION_NAME
--------------------  --------------------  --------------------
D_DATE_ID_FK1         INDEX PARTITION       P_2007
D_DATE_ID_FK1         INDEX PARTITION       P_2008
D_DATE_ID_FK1         INDEX PARTITION       P_2009
D_DATE_ID_FK1         INDEX PARTITION       P_2010
F_SALES               TABLE PARTITION       P_2007
F_SALES               TABLE PARTITION       P_2008
F_SALES               TABLE PARTITION       P_2009
F_SALES               TABLE PARTITION       P_2010
```

How It Works

The ability to exchange partitions is a powerful feature. It allows you to take a partition of an existing table and make it a stand-alone table, and at the same time, make a stand-alone table part of a partitioned table. When you exchange a partition, Oracle simply updates the entries in the data dictionary to perform the exchange.

When you exchange a partition with the WITHOUT VALIDATION clause, you instruct Oracle not to validate that the rows in the incoming partition (or subpartition) are valid entries for the defined range. This has the advantage of making the exchange a very quick operation because Oracle is only updating pointers in the data dictionary to perform the exchange operation. You will need to make sure that your data is accurate if you use WITHOUT VALIDATION.

If you have a primary key defined for the partitioned table, the table being exchanged must also have the same primary key structure defined. If there is a primary key, the WITHOUT VALIDATION clause does not stop Oracle from enforcing unique constraints.

15-15. Renaming a Partition

Problem

You want to rename a partition so that it conforms to your naming standards.

Solution

You can rename both table partitions and index partitions. This example uses the ALTER TABLE statement to rename a table partition:

```
alter table f_regs rename partition reg_p_1 to reg_part_1;
```

This next line of code uses the ALTER INDEX statement to rename an index partition:

```
alter index f_reg_dates_fk1 rename partition reg_p_1 to reg_part_1;
```

How It Works

Sometimes it's necessary to rename a table partition or index partition. For example, you might want to rename a partition before you drop it. Also, you may want to rename objects so that they conform to standards. In these scenarios, use the appropriate ALTER TABLE or ALTER INDEX statement to do so. You can query the data dictionary to verify the information regarding renamed objects. This query shows partitioned table names:

```
select table_name,partition_name,tablespace_name from user_tab_partitions;
```

Similarly, this query displays partitioned index information:

```
select index_name,partition_name,status,high_value,tablespace_name
from user_ind_partitions;
```

15-16. Splitting a Partition

Problem

You have identified a partition that has too many rows. You want to split the partition into two partitions.

Solution

Use the ALTER TABLE...SPLIT PARTITION statement to split an existing partition. The following example splits a partition in a range-partitioned table:

```
alter table f_regs split partition p2010 at (20100601)
into (partition p2010_a, partition p2010) update indexes;
```

If you don't specify UPDATE INDEXES, you will need to rebuild any local indexes associated with the split partition as well as any global indexes. You can verify the status of indexes with the following SQL:

```
select index_name, partition_name, status from user_ind_partitions;
```

The next example splits a list partition. First the CREATE TABLE statement is shown so that you can see how the list partitions were originally defined:

```
create table f_sales
 (reg_sales  number
 ,d_date_id  number
 ,state_code varchar2(20)
)
partition by list (state_code)
```

```
( partition reg_west values ('AZ','CA','CO','MT','OR','ID','UT','NV')
 ,partition reg_mid  values ('IA','KS','MI','MN','MO','NE','OH','ND')
 ,partition reg_rest values (default)
);
```

Next, the REG_MID partition is split:

```
alter table f_sales split partition reg_mid values ('IA','KS','MI','MN') into
(partition reg_mid_a,
 partition reg_mid_b);
```

The REG_MID_A partition now contains the values of IA, KS, MI, and MN, while the REG_MID_B is assigned the remaining values of MO, NE, OH, and ND.

How It Works

The split-partition operation allows you to create two new partitions from a single partition. Each new partition has its own segment, physical attributes, and extents. The segment associated with the original partition is deleted.

15-17. Merging Partitions

Problem

You have two partitions that don't contain enough data to warrant separate partitions. You want to combine the two partitions into one.

Solution

Use the ALTER TABLE...MERGE PARTITIONS statement to combine partitions. This example merges the REG_P_1 partition into the REG_P_2 partition:

```
alter table f_regs merge partitions reg_p_1, reg_p_2 into partition reg_p_2;
```

In this example, the partitions were organized by a range of dates. The merged partition will be defined to accept rows with the highest range of the two merged partitions. Any local indexes are also merged into the new single partition.

Be aware that merging partitions will invalidate any local indexes associated with the merged partitions. Additionally, all partitions of any global indexes that exist on the table will be marked as unusable. You can verify the status of the partitioned indexes by querying the data dictionary:

```
select index_name, partition_name, tablespace_name, high_value,status
from user_ind_partitions
order by 1,2;
```

Here is some sample output showing what a global index and a local index look like after a partition merge:

```
INDEX_NAME            PARTITION_NAME   TABLESPACE_NAME  HIGH_VALUE       STATUS
-------------------   ---------------  ---------------  ---------------  ----------
F_GLO_IDX1            SYS_P680         IDX1                              UNUSABLE
F_GLO_IDX1            SYS_P681         IDX1                              UNUSABLE
F_GLO_IDX1            SYS_P682         IDX1                              UNUSABLE
F_LOC_FK1             REG_P_2          USERS            20110101         UNUSABLE
F_LOC_FK1             REG_P_3          TBSP3            20120101         USABLE
```

When merging partitions, you can use the UPDATE INDEXES clause of the ALTER TABLE statement to instruct Oracle to automatically rebuild any associated indexes:

```
alter table f_regs merge partitions reg_p_1, reg_p_2 into partition reg_p_2
tablespace tbsp2
update indexes;
```

Keep in mind that the merge operation will take longer when you use the UPDATE INDEXES clause. If you want to minimize the merge operation time, don't use this clause. Instead, manually rebuild local indexes associated with a merged partition:

```
alter table f_regs modify partition reg_p_2 rebuild unusable local indexes;
```

You can rebuild each partition of a global index with the ALTER INDEX...REBUILD PARTITION statement:

```
alter index f_glo_idx1 rebuild partition sys_p680;
alter index f_glo_idx1 rebuild partition sys_p681;
alter index f_glo_idx1 rebuild partition sys_p682;
```

How It Works

You can merge two or more partitions with the ALTER TABLE...MERGE PARTITIONS statement. The partition name you are merging into can be the name of one of the partitions you are merging or it can be a completely new name.

When merging partitions, make sure you rebuild any indexes associated with the merged partitions. You can either rebuild or re-create any invalidated indexes. Rebuilding the indexes is probably the easiest method because you don't need the DDL required to re-create the index.

Before you merge two (or more partitions), make certain that the merged partition has enough space in its tablespace to accommodate all of the merged rows. If there isn't enough space, you'll receive an error that the tablespace was unable to extend to the necessary size.

15-18. Dropping a Partition

Problem

You have some data that is obsolete. It is contained within a partition and you want to drop the partition.

Solution

First identify the name of the partition you want to drop. Run the following query to list partitions for a particular table for the currently connected user:

```
select segment_name, segment_type, partition_name
from user_segments
where segment_name = upper('&table_name');
```

Next use the ALTER TABLE...DROP PARTITION statement to remove a partition from a table. This example drops the P_2008 partition from the F_SALES table:

```
alter table f_sales drop partition p_2008;
```

You should see the following message:

```
Table altered.
```

If you want to drop a subpartition, use the DROP SUBPARTITION clause:

```
alter table f_sales drop subpartition p2_south;
```

You can query USER_TAB_SUBPARTITIONS to verify that the subpartition has been dropped.

■ **Note** Oracle will not allow you to drop all subpartitions of a composite-partitioned table. There must be at least one subpartition per partition.

How It Works

When you drop a partition there is no undrop operation. Therefore, before you drop a partition, ensure that you're in the correct environment and really do need to drop it. If you need to preserve the data in a partition to be dropped, merge the partition to another partition instead of dropping it.

You can't drop a partition from a hash-partitioned table. For hash-partitioned tables, you must coalesce partitions to remove one. And you can't explicitly drop a partition from a reference-partitioned table. When a parent table partition is dropped, it will also be dropped from corresponding child reference-partitioned tables.

15-19. Removing Rows from a Partition

Problem

You want to efficiently remove all records from a partition.

Solution

First identify the name of the partition you want to remove records from.

```
select segment_name, segment_type, partition_name
from user_segments
where partition_name is not null;
```

Use the ALTER TABLE...TRUNCATE PARTITION statement to remove all records from a partition. This example truncates the P_2008 partition of the F_SALES table:

```
alter table f_sales truncate partition p_2008;
```

You should see the following message:

```
Table truncated.
```

In this scenario, that message does not mean the entire table was truncated. It's only confirming that the specified partition was truncated.

How It Works

Truncating a partition is an efficient way to quickly remove large amounts of data. When you truncate a partition, however, there is no rollback mechanism. The truncate operation permanently deletes the data from the partition.

If you need the option of rolling back a transaction, use the DELETE statement:

```
delete from f_sales partition(p_2008);
```

The downside to this approach is that if you have millions of records, the DELETE operation could take a long time to run. Also, for a large number of records, DELETE generates a great deal of rollback information. This could cause performance issues for other SQL statements contending for resources.

15-20. Generating Statistics for a Partition

Problem

You have just loaded data into a single partition and need to generate statistics to reflect the newly inserted data.

Solution

Use the EXECUTE statement to run the DBMS_STATS package to generate statistics for a particular partition. In this example, the owner is STAR, the table is F_SALES, and the partition being analyzed is P_2009:

```
exec dbms_stats.gather_table_stats(ownname=>'STAR',-
tabname=>'F_SALES',-
partname=>'P_2009');
```

If you're working with a large partition, you'll probably want to specify the percentage sampling size, degree of parallelism, and also generate statistics for any indexes:

```
exec dbms_stats.gather_table_stats(ownname=>'STAR',-
tabname=>'F_SALES',-
partname=>'P_2009',-
estimate_percent=>dbms_stats.auto_sample_size,-
degree=>dbms_stats.auto_degree,-
cascade=>true);
```

How It Works

For a partitioned table, you can generate statistics either on a single partition or the entire table. We recommend that you generate statistics whenever a significant amount of data changes within the partition. You need to understand your tables and data well enough to determine whether generating new statistics will be required.

15-21. Creating an Index that Maps to a Partition (Local Index)

Problem

You find that you often use the partition key in the WHERE clause when querying a partitioned table. You want to improve the performance of your queries.

Solution

Here is the SQL to create a simple partitioned table:

```
create table f_regs(
 reg_count number
,d_date_id number
)
partition by range(d_date_id)
(partition p2009 values less than (20100101) tablespace tbsp1
,partition p2010 values less than (20110101) tablespace tbsp2
);
```

Next, use the LOCAL clause of the CREATE INDEX statement to create a local index on the partitioned table: This example creates a local index on the D_DATE_ID column of the F_REGS table:

```
create index f_regs_dates_fk1 on f_regs(d_date_id) local;
```

Run the following query to view information about partitioned indexes:

```
select index_name, table_name, partitioning_type from user_part_indexes;
```

Here's some sample output:

```
INDEX_NAME                      TABLE_NAME           PARTITI
------------------------------  -------------------- -------
F_REGS_DATES_FK1                F_REGS               RANGE
```

Now query the USER_IND_PARTITIONS table to view information about the locally partitioned index:

```
select index_name, partition_name, tablespace_name
from user_ind_partitions;
```

Notice that an index partition has been created for each partition of the table, and that the index is created in the same tablespace as the table partition:

```
INDEX_NAME           PARTITION_NAME       TABLESPACE_NAME
-------------------- -------------------- --------------------
F_REGS_DATES_FK1     P2009                TBSP1
F_REGS_DATES_FK1     P2010                TBSP2
```

If you want the local index partitions be created in a tablespace (or tablespaces) separate from the table partitions, specify those when creating the index:

```
create index f_regs_dates_fk1 on f_regs(d_date_id) local
```

```
(partition p2009 tablespace idx1
,partition p2010 tablespace idx2);
```

If you specify the partition information when building a local partitioned index, the number of partitions must match the number of partitions in the table on which the partitioned index is built.

How It Works

A local partitioned index is partitioned in exactly the same manner as the partitioned table that the local index is built on. Each table partition will have a corresponding index that contains ROWID values and index key values for just that table partition. In other words, a ROWID in a local partitioned index will only point to rows in its corresponding table partition.

Oracle keeps local index partitions in sync with the table partitions. You cannot explicitly add or drop a partition from a local index. When you add or drop a table partition, Oracle automatically performs the corresponding work for the local index. Oracle manages the local index partitions regardless of how the local indexes have been assigned to tablespaces.

Local indexes are common in data-warehouse and decision-support systems. If you query frequently by using the partitioned column(s), a local index is appropriate. This lets Oracle use the appropriate index and table partition to quickly retrieve the data.

There are two types of local indexes, local *prefixed* and local *nonprefixed*. A local prefixed index is one in which the leftmost column of the index matches the table partition key. The example in the solution section is a local prefixed index because its leftmost column (D_DATE_ID) is also the partition key for the table.

A nonprefixed local index is one in which its leftmost column does not match the partition key used to partition the corresponding table. For example, this is a local nonprefixed index:

```
create index f_regs_idx1 on f_regs(reg_count) local;
```

The index is partitioned with the REG_COUNT column, which is not the partition key of the table, and is therefore a nonprefixed index. You can verify whether an index is considered prefixed by querying the ALIGNMENT column from USER_PART_INDEXES:

```
select index_name,table_name,alignment,locality
from user_part_indexes;
```

Here is some sample output:

```
INDEX_NAME            TABLE_NAME            ALIGNMENT     LOCALITY
--------------------  --------------------  ------------  ----------
F_REGS_DATES_FK1      F_REGS                PREFIXED      LOCAL
F_REGS_IDX1           F_REGS                NON_PREFIXED  LOCAL
```

You may be asking why even make the distinction between prefixed and nonprefixed? A local nonprefixed index means the index doesn't include the partition key as a leading edge of its index definition. This could have performance implications in that a range scan accessing a nonprefixed index may need to search every index partition. If there are a large number of partitions, this could result in poor performance.

You can create all local indexes as prefixed by including the partition key column in the leading edge of the index. For example, we could create the F_REGS_IDX1 index as prefixed as follows:

```
create index f_regs_idx2 on f_regs(d_date_id,reg_count) local;
```

Is a prefixed index better than a nonprefixed index? It depends on how you query your tables. You'll have to generate explain plans for the queries you use and examine whether a prefixed index is able to better take advantage of partition pruning (eliminating partitions to search in) than a nonprefixed index. Also keep in mind that a multi-column prefixed local index will consume more space and resources than a nonprefixed local index.

15-22. Creating an Index with Its Own Partitioning Scheme (Global Index)

Problem

You query your partitioned table by a column that is not a partition key. You want to improve performance by creating an index on this column.

Solution

You can create either a range-partitioned global index or hash-based global index. Use the keyword GLOBAL to specify that the index will be built with a partitioning strategy separate from its corresponding table. You must always specify a MAXVALUE when creating a range-partitioned global index. The following example creates a range-based global index:

```
create index f_sales_gidx1 on f_sales(sales_id)
global partition by range(sales_id)
(partition pg1 values less than (100)
,partition pg2 values less than (200)
,partition pg3 values less than (maxvalue));
```

The other type of global partitioned index is hash based. This example creates a hash-partitioned global index:

```
create index f_count_idx1 on f_regs(reg_count)
global partition by hash(reg_count) partitions 3;
```

How It Works

An index that is partitioned differently from its base table is known as a *global index*. An entry in a global index can point to any of the partitions of its base table. A global index can be created on any type of partitioned table. A global index itself can be either partitioned by range or hash.

In general, global indexes are more difficult to maintain than local indexes. We recommend that you try to avoid using global indexes and use local indexes whenever possible. There is no automatic maintenance of a global index (as there is with local indexes). With global indexes, you are responsible for adding and dropping index partitions. Also, many maintenance operations on the underlying partitioned table often require that the global index partitions be rebuilt. The following operations on a heap-organized table will render a global index unusable:

- ADD (HASH)
- COALESCE (HASH)
- DROP
- EXCHANGE
- MERGE
- MOVE
- SPLIT
- TRUNCATE

Consider using the UPDATE INDEXES clause when performing maintenance operations. This will keep the global index available during the operation and eliminates the need for rebuilding. The downside to using UPDATE INDEXES is that the maintenance operation will take longer due to the indexes being maintained during the action.

Global indexes are useful for queries that retrieve a small set of rows via an index. In these situations, Oracle can eliminate (prune) any unnecessary index partitions and efficiently retrieve the data. For example, global range-partitioned indexes are useful in OLTP environments where you need efficient access to individual records.

CHAPTER 16

■ ■ ■

LOBs

Large objects, generically known as LOBs, seem to keep the hard-drive manufacturers in business. Whether it's images, word-processing documents, video clips, full-length movies, or XML documents, large objects are frequently found on web sites for download by customers who *want them now*.

Storing these types of objects on disk is only half the picture—they need to be easily managed, organized, and retrieved. Not only do LOBs need to be easily and quickly accessible, they need to be backed up and kept consistent with their associated metadata. In other words, an Oracle database with its high level of redundancy, availability, and recoverability becomes an ideal platform in which to store LOBs.

LOBs come in a number of different flavors. Character large objects, or CLOBs, include all kinds of text-based objects that will likely exceed 4000 characters (the maximum size for a VARCHAR2 column). CLOBs include word-processing documents, XML documents, log files, and so forth, that are typically and more conveniently accessed as a single column in a database row.

Binary large objects (BLOBs), in contrast, are not tied to a specific locale or character set and represent binary information that is not usually human-readable without a viewer of some type. Images and video clips are the most common forms of BLOBs. The task of decoding the contents of a BLOB is typically performed by a middleware or client application. The type of a BLOB (such as JPEG or MPEG) can be stored within the BLOB itself or as another column in the same row in which the BLOB is stored.

For those applications where it is not feasible to store LOBs in the database, you can use BFILES. A BFILE is a data type whose metadata is stored in the database, but whose actual content is stored in operating system files outside of the database. In essence, a BFILE object is a pointer to an operating system file.

In this chapter we'll cover a few tasks involving CLOBs, BLOBs, and BFILE objects. We'll show you how to get LOBs into the database. We'll show how to perform bulk loads using SQL*Loader. And, of course, we'll show you how to query LOB data, as well as how to retrieve LOBs using the HTTP protocol. Retrieval by HTTP is handy when there is no other convenient way to load a LOB, such as from a disk file system or via some other file transfer protocol such as FTP.

16-1. Loading Large Documents into CLOB Columns

Problem

You want to manage your large text files in the database. Your files are in a directory on the file system (a local file system, a Windows network share, or an NFS-mounted directory), and you need to load them into a database table that has other attributes about each file.

Solution

Create a directory object, a sequence, and a table to hold your CLOB documents as follows:

```
create directory lob_src as '/Download/Docs2Load';

create sequence doc_seq;

create table txt_docs
(
    doc_num         number,
    doc_nm          varchar2(100),
    doc_clb         clob,
    ins_ts          timestamp
);
```

Next, create an anonymous PL/SQL block (or a stored procedure) to create a reference to the file in the file system (a LOB pointer), insert a row into the database with an empty CLOB column, then use a built-in PL/SQL procedure to populate the CLOB column in the row you just inserted. It should look like the following:

```
declare
    src_clb         bfile;         /* point to source CLOB on file system */
    dst_clb         clob;          /* destination CLOB in table            */
    src_doc_nm      varchar2(100) := 'Baseball Roster.doc';
    src_offset      integer := 1; /* where to start in the source CLOB    */
    dst_offset      integer := 1; /* where to start in the target CLOB    */
    lang_ctx        integer := dbms_lob.default_lang_ctx;
    warning_msg     number;        /* returns warning value if we find     */
                                   /* unconvertible characters             */
begin
    src_clb := bfilename('LOB_SRC',src_doc_nm);  -- assign pointer to file
                                                 -- within the Oracle directory
    insert into txt_docs (doc_num, doc_nm, doc_clb, ins_ts)
        values(doc_seq.nextval, src_doc_nm, empty_clob(), systimestamp)
```

```
    returning doc_clb into dst_clb;  -- create LOB placeholder  column first
  dbms_lob.open(src_clb, dbms_lob.lob_readonly);
  dbms_lob.loadclobfromfile
    (
     dest_lob =>      dst_clb,
     src_bfile =>     src_clb,
     amount =>        dbms_lob.lobmaxsize,
     dest_offset =>   dst_offset,
     src_offset =>    src_offset,
     bfile_csid =>    dbms_lob.default_csid,
     lang_context =>  lang_ctx,
     warning =>       warning_msg
    );
  dbms_lob.close(src_clb);
  commit;
  dbms_output.put_line('Wrote CLOB to table: ' || src_doc_nm);
end;
```

The procedure creates a pointer, SRC_CLB, to the CLOB on the file system, initializes the database row containing the CLOB, and returns a pointer in the PL/SQL variable DST_CLB to the empty CLOB column in the newly inserted row. DBMS_LOB.LOADCLOBFROMFILE uses the variable SRC_CLB to access the LOB in the file system and the variable DST_CLB to access the CLOB column in the table, and copies the document from the file system to the CLOB column. Finally, the change is committed.

How It Works

The various documents and images are in a file system directory containing the following files:

```
[oracle@dw ~]$ ls -l /Download/Docs2Load
total 718
-rwxr-xr-x  1 root root   80896 Mar 15 22:59 Baseball Roster.txt
-rwxr-xr-x  1 root root   47104 Jan 25 17:40 Display Table.php
-rwxr-xr-x  1 root root   78336 Apr 11 23:20 My Antiques.docx
-rwxr-xr-x  1 root root  451638 May 30 22:08 Screen Capture.bmp
-rwxr-xr-x  1 root root   76800 Feb 16 23:02 Water Table Analysis.doc
[oracle@dw ~]$
```

In the recipe solution, we create an Oracle directory object LOB_SRC to reference an operating system file directory. An Oracle *directory object* is a logical abstraction of a physical file directory. It has a number of benefits and uses; in this example, we use it to access the LOBs from the PL/SQL block. From the DBA's perspective, it has the advantages of transparency and security. The DBA can change the file system referenced by the directory object without requiring a change to any SQL or PL/SQL code, since the directory object name stays the same. In addition, the DBA can grant privileges on the directory object to one or more users, and thus control who can read from or write to objects within the file system directory.

After specifying the file name in the SRC_DOC_NM variable and running the anonymous block, the output is as follows:

```
Wrote CLOB to table: Baseball Roster.txt
```

Now you can run the following SELECT statement against the table and see that a CLOB has been loaded:

```
SQL> select doc_num, doc_nm, ins_ts, length(doc_clb) from txt_docs;
```

DOC_NUM	DOC_NM	INS_TS	LENGTH(DOC_CLB)
1	Baseball Roster.txt	07-JUN-09 07.52.41.229794 PM	80896

The steps in the PL/SQL block are straightforward when you take them one at a time:

1. Create a pointer to the CLOB on disk using the BFILENAME function.

2. Create a new row in the database table and initialize the CLOB column using EMPTY_CLOB.

3. Open the CLOB on disk with DBMS_LOB.OPEN.

4. Copy the CLOB from disk to table using DBMS_LOB.LOADCLOBFROMFILE.

5. Close the source CLOB with DBMS_LOB.CLOSE.

6. Commit the transaction.

Most of the defaults for DBMS_LOB.LOADCLOBFROMFILE are demonstrated in the solution. For example, you typically want to copy from source to destination starting at the beginning (SRC_OFFSET and DST_OFFSET), using the default language context (DBMS_LOB.DEFAULT_LANG_CTX), and copying the entire CLOB into the database column (DBMS_LOB.LOBMAXSIZE).

■ **Note** An alternative to DBMS_LOB.LOADCLOBFROMFILE is DBMS_LOB.LOADFROMFILE. It has fewer parameters and is a bit easier to use; however, it does not support multi-byte character sets.

If you have a long list of CLOBs to load into your database, running this procedure repeatedly will be resource-intensive for the database and error-prone for you. It's more efficient to use SQL*Loader to load a long list of CLOBs, and you will find an example of this later in the chapter.

16-2. Loading Image Data into BLOB Columns

Problem

You have various JPG, PNG, GIF, and BMP image files that need to be managed and backed up in the database, and you need a way to do an initial load into the database.

Solution

Loading binary LOBs is a bit simpler than loading text-based LOBs. You don't have to worry about character-set conversions—or character sets at all; a picture is worth a thousand words, and an image file in the database means that you don't need to store an equivalent text document with those one thousand words!

Create a sequence for your image table's unique identifier, plus the table itself:

```
create sequence img_seq;
```

```
create table image
(
    img_num         number,
    img_nm          varchar2(100),
    img_blb         blob,
    ins_ts          timestamp
);
```

Next, run an anonymous block to load the image SCREEN CAPTURE.BMP into your database table:

```
declare
    src_blb         bfile;          /* point to source BLOB on file system  */
    dst_blb         blob;           /* destination BLOB in table            */
    src_img_nm      varchar2(100) := 'Screen Capture.bmp';
    src_offset      integer := 1; /* where to start in the source BLOB      */
    dst_offset      integer := 1; /* where to start in the target BLOB      */
begin
    src_blb := bfilename('LOB_SRC',src_img_nm);
    insert into image (img_num, img_nm, img_blb, ins_ts)
        values(img_seq.nextval, src_img_nm, empty_blob(), systimestamp)
        returning img_blb into dst_blb;
    dbms_lob.open(src_blb, dbms_lob.lob_readonly);
    dbms_lob.loadblobfromfile
        (
        dest_lob =>     dst_blb,
        src_bfile =>    src_blb,
```

```
            amount =>         dbms_lob.lobmaxsize,
          dest_offset =>  dst_offset,
          src_offset =>   src_offset
        );
    dbms_lob.close(src_blb);
    commit;
    dbms_output.put_line('Wrote BLOB to table: ' || src_img_nm);
end;
```

How It Works

Loading binary objects into a BLOB column is very similar to loading text files into CLOB columns. Unlike with text documents, however, you will rarely find a situation where you copy only part of an image file into a BLOB column. This is due to the nature of the structure of most image files. You either load all of an image, or none at all.

Querying the table IMAGE, you see the metadata for the image file you just loaded:

```
select img_num, img_nm, ins_ts, length(img_blb) from image;
```

IMG_NUM	IMG_NM	INS_TS	LENGTH(IMG_BLB)⏎
-------	------------------	----------------------------	----------------⏎
1	Screen Capture.bmp	07-JUN-09 10.25.02.984755 PM	451638

To further automate this process (assuming you are still dealing only with a relatively small number of objects), you could create a stored procedure instead of using an anonymous procedure. Your parameters would consist of, at a minimum, the name of the file to be loaded. Here is an example of such a procedure:

```
create or replace procedure load_blob ( src_img_nm in varchar2 )
is
    src_blb        bfile;       /* point to source BLOB on file system  */
    dst_blb        blob;        /* destination BLOB in table            */
    src_offset     integer := 1; /* where to start in the source BLOB   */
    dst_offset     integer := 1; /* where to start in the target BLOB   */
begin
...   /* same code as in the anonymous block version */
end;
```

Calling the procedure is easy from a loop in another stored procedure or from an anonymous block. For example:

```
begin
    load_blob('Screen Capture.bmp');
end;
```

You may also consider parameterizing the directory object, and creating a new column for the description of the image file and parameterizing that as well. Typically the file name itself is not a very good description of the contents of the image!

Note This recipe uses the same directory object as the CLOB example at the beginning of the chapter. As you might surmise, you could treat all objects, whether CLOB or BLOB, as binary objects if you did not have to worry about character conversions.

16-3. Using SQL*Loader to Bulk-Load Large Objects

Problem

You want to load thousands of binary objects from a local file system, and you want to minimize manual intervention as well as the time it takes to load the objects.

Solution

Previous solutions used an Oracle directory object and PL/SQL procedures. If the binary files are accessible from an Oracle client, you can use SQL*Loader to easily load the BLOBs. Here is a SQL*Loader control file named load_lobs.ctl:

```
load data
infile load_lobs.list
append into table image
fields terminated by ','
trailing nullcols
(
 img_num        char,
 img_nm         char(100),
 img_file_nm    filler char(100),
 img_blb        lobfile(img_file_nm) terminated by EOF,
 ins_ts         "systimestamp"
)
```

Here is the referenced data file load_lobs.list, containing the location of the BLOBs:

```
101,Water Table Analysis,E:\Download\Docs2Load\Water Table Analysis.doc
102,My Antiques,My Antiques.docx
103,Screen Capture for Book,Screen Capture.bmp
```

Your SQL*Loader command line will look something like this:

```
sqlldr userid=rjb/rjb@recipes control=load_lobs.ctl
```

How It Works

Using SQL*Loader for LOBs is much the same as using SQL*Loader for traditional data types, except that the SQL*Loader INFILE contains a pointer to the location of the LOB in the file system.

You specify the other table columns as you would in a typical SQL*Loader job. For BLOB data, however, you need to specify two columns: the location of the BLOB and the column in the table that will hold the BLOB. In the solution, the column IMG_FILE_NM is marked as FILLER, which means that IMG_FILE_NM is not a real column, but will be referenced later when loading the BLOB data. The SQL*Loader line containing the BLOB column is as follows:

```
img_blb        lobfile(img_file_nm) terminated by EOF,
```

The LOBFILE clause references the SQL*Loader column containing the BLOB's location in the file system. Note in the example that you can provide an absolute file location (E:\Download\Docs2Load\Water Table Analysis.doc) or a file name relative to the directory where you run SQL*Loader.

Finally, the clause TERMINATED BY EOF tells SQL*Loader to stop reading the BLOB at the end. In other scenarios, you may only want to read part of the CLOB or BLOB, up to a specific delimiter, which you specify with a constant in the TERMINATED BY clause along with an optional maximum size, as in this example:

```
paragraph_clb  lobfile(chapter_file_nm) char(2000) terminated by '[PARA]'
```

After loading the BLOBs into the IMAGE table from the solution, the contents of the table look like this:

```
select img_num, img_nm, ins_ts, length(img_blb) from image;
```

IMG_NUM	IMG_NM	INS_TS	LENGTH(IMG_BLB)
101	Water Table Analysis	11-JUN-09 10.49.44.154432000 PM	76800
102	My Antiques	11-JUN-09 10.49.44.154432000 PM	78336
103	Screen Capture for Book	11-JUN-09 10.49.44.154432000 PM	451638

```
3 rows selected
```

As you might expect, you can load multiple BLOB and CLOB columns in the same SQL*Loader job, just make sure that your LOBFILE locators are defined as FILLER columns if they are not the values for actual columns in the table.

This method works very well even when the client is on a different platform from the database instance. In the solution provided, the client and the BLOB objects are on a Microsoft Windows platform (MS-Word DOC and DOCX files are essentially binary files), whereas the database containing the tables with the BLOB columns are on a Linux platform. Remember that we don't worry about platform character set conversion issues when we are using BLOB large object types.

Whether you use SQL*Loader or PL/SQL with directory objects to load your BLOBs and CLOBs depends on a number of factors. If you do not need any procedural logic to load your data and your developers are more familiar with SQL*Loader, that may be the best option. SQL*Loader is also a good choice if the data to be loaded is not accessible via Oracle directory objects or if the data is not always available in the same file system location. On the other hand, if the LOBs are on the same server as the Oracle database and all of the directory objects are in place, loading the LOBs using PL/SQL calls is more efficient than using SQL*Loader on a client workstation, which must then copy the data from the source location to the client location and then back to the database server.

16-4. Accessing Large Objects Using HTTP

Problem

You need to load LOBs from a remote server to your database, but the only protocol available to transfer data is via HTTP (port 80).

Figure 16-1 shows the desired data, its destination, and the roadblocks to moving the data from the source to the target.

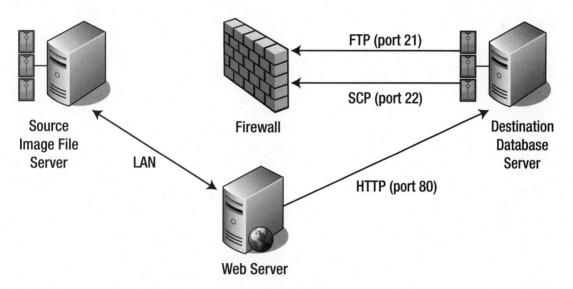

Figure 16-1. *Transferring LOBs between servers with firewall restrictions*

Firewall restrictions on the network containing the image file server prevent any direct access to the image server from the database server, other than web page access on port 80 to a web server front end used to serve images on the source system. In other words, the only way to get images from the image server is via HTTP.

Solution

The images for Apress.com must be migrated to another database server; the servers are separated by thousands of miles and there is no network access between the servers other than the HTTP (port 80) protocol. You don't have time to do an export/import to a DVD or to a tape and ship the DVD or tape to the physical location of the local database server. However, you do have a local database table containing the list of URLs to be transferred.

To facilitate this transfer, use the Oracle PL/SQL packages UTL_HTTP and DBMS_LOB to transfer the files over the network using the HTTP protocol. For this solution, the table IMG_LIST contains the list of URLs holding the images, and the table WEB_IMG contains the metadata for each image along with the image itself.

Here is the code to access the remote objects using HTTP and copy the remote objects to LOB columns in your local database tables:

```
-- create image table with list of URLs
-- and retrieve those images via HTTP

declare

    cursor img_list is -- image URLs to retrieve
        select img_url from img_list;

    r_img_list              img_list%rowtype;

    lBlob           blob;             -- locator for current image
    l_http_request  utl_http.req;
    l_http_response utl_http.resp;
    l_raw           raw(32767);    -- blob buffer

begin
    dbms_output.put_line('*** Begin image load.');
    open img_list;

    loop
        fetch img_list into r_img_list;
        exit when img_list%notfound;
        -- initialize image table row with empty blob
        insert into web_img(img_num, img_url, img_blb, ins_ts)
            values(web_img_seq.nextval, r_img_list.img_url, empty_blob(), systimestamp)
            returning img_blb into lBlob;  -- save pointer for local use
        dbms_output.put_line('Attempt retrieval of: ' || r_img_list.img_url);
        -- attempt to retrieve image via HTTP
        l_http_request  := utl_http.begin_request(r_img_list.img_url); -- request
        l_http_response := utl_http.get_response(l_http_request); -- response back
        dbms_output.put_line('  HTTP stat code: ' || l_http_response.status_code);
```

```
        dbms_output.put_line('   HTTP resp reason phrase: ' ||
                              l_http_response.reason_phrase);

    if l_http_response.status_code = 200 then /* image file found */
        dbms_lob.open(lBlob, dbms_lob.lob_readwrite);
        begin
           loop
             utl_http.read_raw(l_http_response, l_raw, 32767);
             dbms_lob.writeappend (lBlob, utl_raw.length(l_raw), l_raw);
           end loop;
           exception
             when utl_http.end_of_body then
                 utl_http.end_response(l_http_response);
        end; /* retrieving BLOB parts */
        dbms_lob.close(lBlob);
        dbms_output.put_line('   Image URL loaded: '
                             || web_img_seq.currval || ' '
                             || r_img_list.img_url);
      else /* image not found */
        dbms_output.put_line('   No Image at this URL');
        utl_http.end_response(l_http_response);
      end if;
  end /* img_list */ loop;

  close img_list;
  commit;

  dbms_output.put_line('*** Done importing images.');

  exception /* unexpected error, close everything and get out */
     when others then
        dbms_output.put_line('Unexpected error');
        utl_http.end_response(l_http_response);
        close img_list;
        raise;
end;
```

This anonymous procedure reads each row in the URL table, attempts to retrieve the contents of each URL, and writes a row to the new table. A status is recorded for the success or failure of each URL.

How It Works

The solution uses this list of URLs, and they are stored in the IMG_LIST table:

```
select img_url from img_list;

IMG_URL
-----------------------------------------------------------
http://apress.com/img/masthead_logo.gif
http://apress.com/img/dealofdaysanstimer_v2.gif
http://apress.com/img/AlphaProgram_140.gif
http://apress.com/img/mini_toe_logo.gif
http://apress.com/img/banner/1515banner.gif

5 rows selected
```

Here is the SQL you use to create the image list, the destination image table, and the image table's sequence generator:

```
create table img_list
(
    img_url        varchar2(255)
);

create table web_img
(
    img_num        number,
    img_url        varchar2(255),
    img_blb        blob,
    ins_ts         timestamp
);

create sequence web_img_seq;
```

The cursor IMG_LIST retrieves each URL. For each URL, the procedure uses two built-in PL/SQL packages: DBMS_LOB and UTL_HTTP. Previous solutions in this chapter use DBMS_LOB.LOADBLOBFROMFILE to copy a binary object from a file system to a BLOB column in a database table. In contrast, we're using DBMS_LOB.WRITEAPPEND to write the contents of the image in 32KB chunks after receiving each 32KB chunk from the call to UTL_HTTP.READ_RAW.

The PL/SQL package UTL_HTTP is what you'd expect: sending HTTP requests to a web site and receiving HTTP replies. For each URL, here are the steps that the procedure performs:

1. Request the URL using UTL_HTTP.BEGIN_REQUEST.

2. Receive response from web site using UTL_HTTP.GET_RESPONSE.

3. If the response code is 200 (URL found), open the BLOB in the table, otherwise go back to step 1 with the next URL.

4. Read the contents of the URL in 32K chunks using UTL_HTTP.READ_RAW in a local PL/SQL block until you've reached the end of the URL and append each 32K chunk to the end of the destination BLOB using DBMS_LOB.WRITE_APPEND.

5. Close the destination BLOB.

6. Get the next URL in step 1; if there are no more, proceed to step 7

7. Close the cursor, commit all transactions.

The logging from running this procedure indicates that one of the URLs did not exist:

```
*** Begin image load.
Attempt retrieval of: http://apress.com/img/masthead_logo.gif
    HTTP stat code: 200
    HTTP resp reason phrase: OK
    Image URL loaded: 16 http://apress.com/img/masthead_logo.gif
Attempt retrieval of: http://apress.com/img/dealofdaysanstimer_v2.gif
    HTTP stat code: 200
    HTTP resp reason phrase: OK
    Image URL loaded: 17 http://apress.com/img/dealofdaysanstimer_v2.gif
Attempt retrieval of: http://apress.com/img/AlphaProgram_140.gif
    HTTP stat code: 200
    HTTP resp reason phrase: OK
    Image URL loaded: 18 http://apress.com/img/AlphaProgram_140.gif
Attempt retrieval of: http://apress.com/img/mini_toe_logo.gif
    HTTP stat code: 404
    HTTP resp reason phrase: Not Found
    No Image at this URL
Attempt retrieval of: http://apress.com/img/banner/1515banner.gif
    HTTP stat code: 200
    HTTP resp reason phrase: OK
    Image URL loaded: 20 http://apress.com/img/banner/1515banner.gif
*** Done importing images.
```

No doubt you have received a 404 error on many occasions while using your favorite web browser. After running the procedure, here are the contents of the WEB_IMG table:

```
select img_num, img_url, length(img_blb)
from web_img
order by img_num;
```

IMG_NUM	IMG_URL	LENGTH(IMG_BLB)
16	http://apress.com/img/masthead_logo.gif	2959
17	http://apress.com/img/dealofdaysanstimer_v2.gif	4349
18	http://apress.com/img/AlphaProgram_140.gif	2932
19	http://apress.com/img/mini_toe_logo.gif	0
20	http://apress.com/img/banner/1515banner.gif	14029

```
5 rows selected
```

Note that the procedure in its current form will write a row into the WEB_IMG table whether or not it is found. For missing URLs, the BLOB is empty, thus its length is zero.

After reviewing this solution, you may notice some of the similarities between this anonymous procedure and your favorite web browser: it sends a URL request; if the page or item exists, it returns the page or item to the browser and displays it. In other words, with a GUI front end, you could use PL/SQL with the UTL_HTTP package to create an Oracle-flavored server-based web browser, impractical as that might be.

16-5. Making External Large Objects (BFILEs) Available to the Database

Problem

You want to manage your images and other binary files in an Oracle table, but the end-user application needs to access the files from the file system, and there is not enough disk space in the database's tablespaces to hold the images as BLOBs.

Solution

You can use BFILE pointers in Oracle tables to reference binary objects on the file system. In addition, you can read and manage the objects using the DBMS_LOB and UTL_FILE packages.

Create a table to hold the image metadata, along with a sequence to supply the table's primary key:

```
create table web_img2
(
    img_num         number primary key,
    img_url         varchar2(255),
    img_blb         bfile,
    ins_ts          timestamp,
constraint ak1_web_img2 unique(img_url)
);

create sequence web_img2_seq;
```

Here is a procedure that accepts an Oracle directory name and a file within that directory and loads the file's metadata into the table WEB_IMG2 if the file exists:

```
create or replace procedure load_bfile ( dir_name varchar2, src_img_nm in varchar2 )
is
    src_blb        bfile;         /* point to source BLOB on file system */
    file_exists    boolean;       /* return value from UTL_FILE.FGETATTR */
    file_len       number;
    blksize        binary_integer;
begin
    src_blb := bfilename(dir_name, src_img_nm);
    insert into web_img2 (img_num, img_nm, img_blb, ins_ts)
        values(web_img2_seq.nextval, src_img_nm, src_blb, systimestamp);
    -- check to see if file is there at this moment
    utl_file.fgetattr(dir_name, src_img_nm, file_exists, file_len, blksize);
    if file_exists then
        commit;
        dbms_output.put_line('Wrote BFILE pointer to table: ' || src_img_nm);
    else
        rollback;
        dbms_output.put_line('BLOB ' || src_img_nm
                    || ' in directory '
                    || dir_name
                    || ' does not exist.');
    end if;
end;
```

How It Works

The solution is very similar to a recipe earlier in this chapter where we store the object in the database; in this solution, we still store the metadata in the table WEB_IMG2, but not the BLOB itself. Instead, we store a pointer to the file in the operating system file system. This does facilitate sharing the file with other applications that need to access the file outside of Oracle, but it can cause problems with referential integrity (RI). Usually with referential integrity, a database table references rows in another database table, and DBMS constraints prevent the deletion of a row that is referenced. Here, however, the table references files in a file system. If another application or an administrator deletes or moves the file, the BFILE pointer in the database table is still there, but it's invalid. Thus, you can use UTL_FILE.FGETATTR to check for existence of a BFILE in the operating system directory.

Running this procedure with a file that exists looks like this:

```
begin
    load_bfile('LOB_SRC','Screen Capture.bmp');
end;
```

```
Wrote BFILE pointer to table: Screen Capture.bmp
```

In contrast, trying to store a file that does not exist produces the following output:

```
begin
   load_bfile('LOB_SRC','Cake Boss.bmp');
end;


BLOB Cake Boss.bmp in directory LOB_SRC does not exist.
```

When you query the table, it returns these results:

```
select * from web_img2;


IMG_NUM    IMG_NM               IMG_BLB   INS_TS
-------    --------------------   -------   --------------------------------
1          Screen Capture.bmp   (BFILE)   13-JUN-09 10.43.16.737554000 PM
```

You may be wondering how to decode the BFILE contents referenced in the IMG_BLB column. The procedure DBMS_LOB.FILEGETNAME can help you with that, too. Here is a function that returns the Oracle directory name and file name within the directory:

```
create or replace function get_bfile_attrs (bfile_obj in bfile)
return varchar2 is
   dir_alias        varchar2(30);
   file_name        varchar2(100);
begin
   dbms_lob.filegetname(bfile_obj, dir_alias, file_name);
   return('BFILE: Directory=' || dir_alias || ' File=' || file_name);
end;


select img_num, img_nm, get_bfile_attrs(img_blb) from web_img2;


IMG_NUM    IMG_NM               GET_BFILE_ATTRS(IMG_BLB)
-------    --------------------   --------------------------------------------------
1          Screen Capture.bmp   BFILE: Directory=LOB_SRC File=Screen Capture.bmp
```

You can use the DBMS_LOB package to copy an image or a Word document on a file system to a BLOB or CLOB column in a table; see the recipes earlier in this chapter.

16-6. Deleting or Updating LOBs in a Database Table

Problem

Several LOBs in your database tables are either obsolete or need to be replaced.

Solution

To delete a LOB, you can set the contents of a LOB column to either EMPTY_CLOB() or EMPTY_BLOB(), as in this example:

```
update web_img
set img_blb = empty_blob()
where img_num = 19
;
```

Although you can alternatively set the column IMG_BLB to NULL, you will have to set it to EMPTY_CLOB() or EMPTY_BLOB() before reinserting a LOB into that column. Allowing a LOB column to have NULLs keeps it consistent with use of other columns that can have NULLs: you can differentiate a LOB column that has an unknown value from a LOB column that has an empty LOB of zero length.

Updating the value of a LOB column is identical to updating an empty LOB column—retrieve the pointer to the LOB column and use DBMS_LOB to populate the column. If you know which part of the LOB needs to be replaced, you can use other parameters of DBMS_LOB.COPY. Here are the parameters for DBMS_LOB.COPY:

```
DBMS_LOB.COPY
(
  dest_lob    IN OUT NOCOPY BLOB,    -- BLOB to be updated
  src_lob     IN            BLOB,    -- BLOB containing new content
  amount      IN            INTEGER, -- number of bytes to copy
  dest_offset IN            INTEGER := 1,  -- where to start in the destination
  src_offset  IN            INTEGER := 1   -- where to start in the source
);
```

As you might expect, Oracle provides reasonable defaults for where to start in the source and target LOBs. Here is how you would copy 5000 bytes from the 10th byte of a new LOB to the 125th byte of the existing LOB:

```
dbms_lob.copy (existing_blb, new_blb, 5000, 125, 10);
```

Updating a CLOB uses the same procedure (it is overloaded, as are many other Oracle PL/SQL procedures), except that DEST_LOB and SRC_LOB are of type CLOB and will be converted from the source character set to the destination character set.

How It Works

Because of their potential size, large object columns (BLOBs and CLOBs) have several restrictions in SELECT and DDL statements, including the following:

- LOBs cannot be used in a SELECT DISTINCT, ORDER BY, or GROUP BY clauses

- You cannot use LOB columns as a JOIN column

- LOB columns are not allowed in UNION, INTERSECTION, and MINUS

- A LOB column cannot have a bitmap index, unique index, or a B-tree index—only function-based or domain indexes

- A LOB column cannot be a primary key

Most of these restrictions seem reasonable considering the amount of overhead that would be required, for example, to make a LOB column a primary key. However, you can treat them as any other database column in other operations, such as updating a LOB column to another LOB column in the same table or another table, or setting the LOB column to a NULL or an empty value using EMPTY_CLOB(). LOBs can also be rolled back in a transaction, although the old version of the LOB is stored in the LOB segment instead of the undo tablespace.

PART 5

Administration

■ ■ ■

CHAPTER 17

Database Administration

The term *database administration* refers to a wide variety of tasks that DBAs perform to ensure the availability, scalability, usability, and maintainability of a database management system. Entire books have been written on this topic. This chapter does not cover every aspect of SQL a DBA might use. Rather, its goal is to show you how to use SQL to perform the common database administrator tasks.

Many of the tasks covered in this chapter can also be performed using graphical tools like Enterprise Manager. Graphical tools are excellent for quickly carrying out basic database administration tasks, especially if you're not comfortable with running SQL commands directly. They are fine for most scenarios.

However, you will eventually find yourself in a situation where you'll need to implement a SQL feature that just doesn't work with a graphical tool. For example, you may need to use some new aspect or special command syntax that isn't available in the graphical tool. Or you may want to write a somewhat complicated script that has to run in batch mode. In such circumstances, you'll need the SQL scripting skills required to perform the operation.

The Five-command Rule

One of us worked at a company where a junior DBA had recently been hired. When it came time for the junior DBA to be on call, the youngster fretted over whether the knowledge was there to perform database administration tasks in the production environment. One of the senior DBAs took the junior DBA aside and explained that there really are only five SQL commands you need to know to be a DBA:

- STARTUP
- SHUTDOWN
- RECOVER
- ALTER DATABASE
- ALTER SYSTEM

The senior DBA was being a bit facetious in stating that DBAs needed only a handful of SQL commands. Of course, DBAs also need to know how to backup and restore a database—among other tasks.

Still, there is some truth to the five-command rule. The key is acquiring a solid foundation in Oracle database architecture, as well as the know-how to use SQL to interact with the database. When serious problems arise, SQL is the tool that a DBA uses to troubleshoot and fix problems. You must be knowledgeable about the basic commands a DBA uses, as well as how to look up commands for scenarios that fall outside of the basic SQL commands.

17-1. Creating a Database

Problem

You've just installed the Oracle binaries. You want to create a database.

Solution

Before you run a CREATE DATABASE command, you must connect to SQL*Plus and start your database in NOMOUNT mode:

```
$ sqlplus / as sysdba
SQL> startup nomount;
```

Listed next is a typical Oracle CREATE DATABASE statement:

```
create database invrep controlfile reuse
    maxlogfiles 16
    maxlogmembers 4
    maxdatafiles 1024
    maxinstances 1
    maxloghistory 680
    character set "UTF8"
logfile group 1
        ('/ora01/oradata/INVREP/redo01a.log',
         '/ora01/oradata/INVREP/redo01b.log')  size 200m reuse,
      group 2
        ('/ora01/oradata/INVREP/redo02a.log',
         '/ora01/oradata/INVREP/redo02b.log' ) size 200m reuse,
      group 3
        ('/ora01/oradata/INVREP/redo03a.log',
         '/ora01/oradata/INVREP/redo03b.log' ) size 200m reuse
datafile
'/ora01/oradata/INVREP/system01.dbf'
    size 500m
    reuse
undo tablespace undotbs1 datafile
'/ora01/oradata/INVREP/undotbs01.dbf'
```

```
    size 800m
    reuse
sysaux datafile
'/ora01/oradata/INVREP/sysaux01.dbf'
    size 200m
    reuse
default temporary tablespace temp tempfile
'/ora01/oradata/INVREP/temp01.dbf'
    size 800m
    reuse;
```

After your database is successfully created, you can then instantiate the data dictionary with the next two scripts from Oracle. You must run these scripts as the SYS schema:

```
SQL> show user
USER is "SYS"
SQL> @?/rdbms/admin/catalog
SQL> @?/rdbms/admin/catproc
```

Now, as the SYSTEM schema, create the product user profile tables:

```
SQL> connect system/manager
SQL> @?/sqlplus/admin/pupbld
```

These tables allow SQL*Plus to disable commands on a user-by-user basis. If the pupbld.sql script is not run, then all non-sys users will see the following warning when logging into SQL*Plus:

```
Error accessing PRODUCT_USER_PROFILE
Warning: Product user profile information not loaded!
You may need to run PUPBLD.SQL as SYSTEM
```

How It Works

Before you can run the CREATE DATABASE statement, you must start the background processes and allocate memory via the STARTUP NOMOUNT statement. The CREATE DATABASE statement is dependent on an initialization file that defines the location(s) for the control file and memory configuration.

On Linux/Unix systems, the initialization file (either a text init.ora or binary spfile) is by default located in the ORACLE_HOME/dbs directory. On Windows, the default directory is ORACLE_HOME\database. When starting your instance, Oracle will look in the default location for a binary initialization file named spfile<ORACLE_SID>.ora. If there is no binary spfile, Oracle will look for a text file with the name of init<ORACLE_SID>.ora. Oracle will throw an error if it can't find an initialization file in the default location. You can explicitly tell Oracle which directory and file to use by specifying the PFILE clause of the STARTUP command, which allows you to specify a non-default directory and name of a text initialization file.

Here is a typical Oracle Database 11*g* init.ora text file:

```
db_name=INVREP
```

```
db_block_size=8192
compatible=11.1.0
memory_target=800M
memory_max_target=800M
processes=200
control_files=(/ora01/oradata/INVREP/control01.ctl,
/ora02/oradata/INVREP/control02.ctl)
diagnostic_dest=/orahome/oracle
job_queue_processes=10
open_cursors=300
fast_start_mttr_target=500
undo_management=AUTO
undo_tablespace=UNDOTBS1
remote_login_passwordfile=EXCLUSIVE
```

And this is a typical Oracle Database 10g init.ora text file:

```
db_name=INVREP
db_block_size=8192
pga_aggregate_target=400M
workarea_size_policy=AUTO
sga_max_size=500M
sga_target=500M
processes=400
control_files=(/ora01/oradata/INVREP/control01.ctl,
/ora01/oradata/INVREP/control02.ctl)
job_queue_processes=10
open_cursors=300
fast_start_mttr_target=500
background_dump_dest=/orahome/oracle/admin/INVREP/bdump
user_dump_dest=/orahome/oracle/admin/INVREP/udump
core_dump_dest=/orahome/oracle/admin/INVREP/cdump
undo_management=AUTO
undo_tablespace=UNDOTBS1
remote_login_passwordfile=EXCLUSIVE
```

17-2. Dropping a Database

Problem

You want to drop a database and remove all datafiles, control files, and online redo logs associated with the database.

Solution

Ensure that you're on the correct server and are connected to the correct database. On a Linux/Unix system, issue the following OS command from the operating system prompt:

```
$ uname -a
```

Next connect to SQL*Plus and ensure that you're connected to the database you really want to drop:

```
select name from v$database;
```

Once you've verified that you're in the correct database environment, issue the following SQL commands from a SYSDBA privileged account:

```
shutdown immediate;
startup mount exclusive restrict;
drop database;
```

■ **Caution** Obviously, you should be careful when dropping a database. You are *not* prompted when dropping the database and, as of this writing, there is no UNDROP ACCIDENTALLY DROPPED DATABASE command.

How It Works

Use *extreme* caution when dropping a database as this operation will remove datafiles, control files, and online redo log files.

The DROP DATABASE command is useful when you have a database that needs to be removed. This could be a test database or an old database that is no longer used.

The DROP DATABASE command will not remove old archive redo log files. You will need to manually remove those files with an operating system command (such as the rm in Linux/Unix or DEL at the Windows command prompt). You can also instruct RMAN to remove archive redo log files.

17-3. Verifying Connection Information

Problem

You're running several DDL scripts as part of an application upgrade. You want to ensure you're connected to the correct database environment before you issue commands.

Solution

The easiest way to verify your environment is to connect to the database and query the V$DATABASE view:

```
select name from v$database;
```

You can also run the SHOW USER command to quickly verify the schema you're connected to the database as:

```
SQL> show user;
```

If you want your SQL prompt to display user and instance information, you can set it via the following command:

```
SQL> set sqlprompt '&_user.@&_connect_identifier.> '
```

Here's an example of what your SQL command prompt might look like:

```
SYS@RMDB11>
```

If you want the prompt to change when you connect to the database as a different user, then add the previous line of code to either your glogin.sql file or your login.sql file. The glogin.sql file is usually located in the ORACLE_HOME/sqlplus/admin directory and will be run each time any user connects to SQL*Plus.

If you only want the change to show when you connect to the database, create a login.sql in the directory you initiate SQL*Plus from, or ensure that the login.sql file is in a directory contained in your SQLPATH operating system environment variable.

How It Works

There are at least two aspects of ensuring that you are connected properly. First, you must make certain you've connected to the correct database. Next, you must ensure that you are connected to the proper user within that database. The solution shows how to verify both database and user. Having verified those, you can run your DDL script with confidence.

Sometimes when deploying code through various development, test, and production environments, it's handy to be prompted as to whether you're in the right environment. The technique for accomplishing that requires two files: answer_yes.sql and answer_no.sql. Here are the contents of answer_yes.sql:

```
-- answer_yes.sql
PROMPT
PROMPT Continuing...
```

And here's answer_no.sql:

```
-- answer_no.sql
PROMPT
PROMPT Quitting and Discarding changes...
ROLLBACK;
EXIT;
```

Now you can place the following code into the first part of a deployment script that will prompt you as to whether you're in the right environment and if you want to continue:

```
WHENEVER SQLERROR EXIT FAILURE ROLLBACK;
WHENEVER OSERROR EXIT FAILURE ROLLBACK;
SELECT name FROM v$database;
SHOW user;
SET ECHO OFF;
PROMPT
ACCEPT answer PROMPT 'Correct environment?  Enter yes to continue: '
@@answer_&answer..sql
```

If you type in *yes*, then the answer_yes.sql script will run and you will continue to run any other scripts you call. If you type in *no*, then the answer_no.sql script will run and you will exit from SQL*Plus and end up at the OS prompt. If you press *Enter* without typing either, you will also exit and wind up back at the OS prompt.

17-4. Creating Tablespaces

Problem

You want to create a tablespace.

Solution

Use the CREATE TABLESPACE statement to create a tablespace. This example shows common options used when creating a tablespace:

```
create tablespace inv_data
  datafile '/ora02/RMDB11/invdata01.dbf'
  size 100m
  extent management local
  uniform size 256k
  segment space management auto;
```

This statement creates a file named invdata01.dbf in the /ora02/RMDB11 directory that is 100 megabytes in size. You'll see this message if the CREATE TABLESPACE statement runs correctly:

```
Tablespace created.
```

How It Works

We recommend you create all tablespaces with EXTENT MANAGEMENT LOCAL to specify that each tablespace manage its extents locally. A locally managed tablespace uses a bitmap image within the datafile to efficiently determine if an extent is in use or not. The storage parameters NEXT, PCTINCREASE, MINEXTENTS, MAXEXTENTS, and DEFAULT STORAGE are not valid for extent options in locally managed tablespaces.

You should also use a UNIFORM SIZE when creating a tablespace, which tells Oracle to make each extent the same size (as space is needed by objects such as tables and indexes).

The SEGMENT SPACE MANAGEMENT AUTO clause instructs Oracle to manage the space within the block. When you use this clause there is no need to specify parameters such as PCTUSED, FREELISTS, and FREELIST GROUPS.

If you create a tablespace with the AUTOEXTEND feature, we recommend that you also specify a MAXSIZE so that a runaway SQL process doesn't inadvertently fill up a tablespace that in turn fills up a mount point. Here's an example of creating an autoextending tablespace with a cap on its maximum size:

```
create tablespace users
  datafile '/ora01/oradata/INVREP/users_01.dbf'
  size 100m
  autoextend on maxsize 1000m
  extent management local
  uniform size 128k
  segment space management auto;
```

When using CREATE TABLESPACE scripts in different environments, it's useful to be able to parameterize portions of the script. For example, in development, you may size the datafiles at 100MB, whereas in production the datafiles may be 5,000MB. Use ampersand variables to make CREATE scripts more portable. The next listing defines ampersand variables at the top of the script, and those variables determine the sizes of datafiles created for the tablespaces:

```
define tbsp_large=1000M
define tbsp_med=500M
--
create tablespace exp_data
  datafile '/ora01/oradata/INVREP/exp_data01.dbf'
  size &&tbsp_large
  autoextend on maxsize 1000m
  extent management local
  uniform size 128k
  segment space management auto;
--
create tablespace reg_data
  datafile '/ora01/oradata/INVREP/reg_data01.dbf'
  size &&tbsp_med
  autoextend on maxsize 1000m
  extent management local
```

```
uniform size 128k
segment space management auto;
```

Using ampersand variables allows you to modify the script once and have the variables reused throughout the script.

You can also pass the values to the ampersand variables into the CREATE TABLESPACE script from the SQL*Plus command line. To accomplish this, first define at the top of the script the ampersand variables to accept the values being passed in:

```
define tbsp_large=&1
define tbsp_med=&2
-- the rest of the script goes here...
```

Now you can pass in variables to the script from the SQL*Plus command line. The following example executes a script named cretbsp.sql and passes in two values that will set the ampersand variables to 1000m and 500m respectively:

```
SQL> @cretbsp 1000m 500m
```

17-5. Dropping a Tablespace

Problem

You want to drop a tablespace.

Solution

If you need to drop a tablespace, use the DROP TABLESPACE statement. We recommend that you first take the tablespace offline before you drop it. Taking a tablespace offline ensures that no SQL statements are operating against objects in that tablespace.

This example first takes the INV_DATA tablespace offline and then drops it using the INCLUDING CONTENTS AND DATAFILES clause:

```
alter tablespace inv_data offline;
drop tablespace inv_data including contents and datafiles;
```

■ **Note** You can drop a tablespace whether it is online or offline. The exception to this is the SYSTEM tablespace, which cannot be dropped.

How It Works

Dropping a tablespace using INCLUDING CONTENTS AND DATAFILES will permanently remove a tablespace and any of its datafiles. Make certain the tablespace doesn't contain any data you want to keep before you drop it.

If the tablespace to be dropped contains a table with a primary key that is referenced by a foreign key constraint from a table in a different tablespace, you will not be able to drop the tablespace. You can either drop the constraint or use the CASCADE CONSTRAINTS clause of the DROP TABLESPACE statement:

```
drop tablespace inv_data including contents and datafiles cascade constraints;
```

This statement will drop any referential integrity constraints from tables outside of the tablespace being dropped that reference tables within the dropped tablespace.

17-6. Adjusting Tablespace Size

Problem

You're getting this error when attempting to insert data into a table:

```
ORA-01653: unable to extend table INVENTORY by 128 in tablespace INV_IDX
```

You determine that you need to add more space to the tablespace associated with the table.

Solution

There are two common techniques for resizing a tablespace:

- Increasing (or decreasing) the size of an existing datafile

- Adding an additional datafile

Before you resize a datafile, you should first verify its current size and location using a query similar to this:

```
select name, bytes from v$datafile;
```

Once you determine which datafile you want to resize, use the ALTER DATABASE DATAFILE ... RESIZE command to increase its size. This example resizes the datafile to one gigabyte:

```
alter database datafile '/ora01/oradata/INVREP/reg_data01.dbf' resize 1g;
```

To add a datafile to an existing tablespace, use the ALTER TABLESPACE ... ADD DATAFILE statement:

```
alter tablespace reg_data add datafile
'/ora01/oradata/INVREP/reg_data02.dbf' size 100m;
```

How It Works

Resizing datafiles can be a daily task when managing databases with heavy transaction loads. Increasing the size of an existing datafile allows you to add space to a tablespace without adding more datafiles. If there isn't enough disk space left on the storage device that contains an existing datafile, you can add a datafile in a different location to an existing tablespace.

You can also modify an existing datafile to turn AUTOEXTEND on and off. This next example modifies a datafile to AUTOEXTEND with a maximum size of 1000MB:

```
alter database datafile '/ora01/oradata/INVREP/reg_data02.dbf'
autoextend on maxsize 1000m;
```

Many DBAs are uncomfortable enabling AUTOEXTEND because they worry that a storage device could fill up if an erroneous SQL INSERT statement executes a large number of times. Instead of enabling AUTOEXTEND, DBAs will implement monitoring scripts that alert them when a tablespace is becoming full.

If you want to add space to a temporary tablespace, first query the V$TEMPFILE view to verify the current size and location of temporary datafiles:

```
select name, bytes from v$tempfile;
```

Next use the TEMPFILE option of the ALTER DATABASE statement:

```
alter database tempfile '/ora01/oradata/INVREP/temp01.dbf' resize 500m;
```

You can also add a file to a temporary tablespace via the ALTER TABLESPACE statement:

```
alter tablespace temp add tempfile '/ora01/oradata/INVREP/temp02.dbf' size 5000m;
```

17-7. Limiting Database Resources per Session

Problem

You want to limit the amount of resources a user can consume in your database.

Solution

First you need to ensure that the RESOURCE_LIMIT initialization parameter is set to TRUE for your database. You can do this either in the initialization file (init.ora or spfile) or use the ALTER SYSTEM command. Issue the following SQL statement to view the current setting of RESOURCE_LIMIT in your database:

```
select name, value from v$parameter where name='resource_limit';
```

Use the CREATE PROFILE command to create a resource-limiting profile. You can then assign that profile to any existing database users. The following SQL statement creates a profile that limits resources, such as the amount of CPU an individual session can consume:

```
create profile user_profile_limit
limit
sessions_per_user 20
cpu_per_session 240000
logical_reads_per_session 1000000
connect_time 480
idle_time 120;
```

After a profile has been created, you can assign it to a user. In the next example, user HEERA is assigned the USER_PROFILE_LIMIT:

```
alter user heera profile user_profile_limit;
```

■ **Note** Oracle recommends you use Database Resource Manager to manage database resource limits. However, we find database profiles (implemented via SQL) to be an effective and easy mechanism for limiting resources.

How It Works

Oracle database profiles are used for two main reasons:

- Setting resource limits
- Enforcing password security settings

When creating a user, if no profile is specified, the DEFAULT profile is assigned to the newly created user. You can modify a profile with the ALTER PROFILE statement. The next example modifies the DEFAULT profile to limit the CPU_PER_SESSION to 240000 (in hundredths of seconds):

```
alter profile default limit cpu_per_session 240000;
```

This limits any user with the DEFAULT profile to 2400 seconds of CPU use. There are various limits you can set in a profile. Table 17-1 describes the database resource settings that can be limited via a profile.

Table 17-1. *Database Resource Profile Settings*

Profile resource	Meaning
COMPOSITE_LIMIT	Limit based on weighted sum algorithm for these resources CPU_PER_SESSION, CONNECT_TIME, LOGICAL_READS_PER_SESSION, and PRIVATE_SGA.
CONNECT_TIME	Connect time in minutes.
CPU_PER_CALL	CPU time limit per call in hundredths of seconds.
CPU_PER_SESSION	CPU time limit per session in hundredths of seconds.
IDLE_TIME	Idle time in minutes.
LOGICAL_READS_PER_CALL	Blocks read per call.
LOGICAL_READS_PER_SESSION	Blocks read per session.
PRIVATE_SGA	Amount of space consumed in shared pool.
SESSIONS_PER_USER	Number of concurrent sessions.

As part of the CREATE USER statement, you can specify a profile other than DEFAULT:

```
create user heera identified by foo profile user_profile_limit;
```

A profile is also used to enforce password security settings (see Table 17-2 for descriptions of password profile settings). For example, say you wanted to alter the DEFAULT profile so that there was a cap on the maximum number of days a password can be used. This next line of code sets the PASSWORD_LIFE_TIME of the DEFAULT profile to 300 days:

```
alter profile default limit password_life_time 300;
```

Table 17-2. *Password Security Settings*

Password Setting	Description	11g default	10g default
FAILED_LOGIN_ATTEMPTS	Number of failed login attempts before schema is locked.	10 attempts	10 attempts
PASSWORD_GRACE_TIME	Number of days after a password expires that owner can login with old password.	7 days	Unlimited

Table 17-2. *Password Security Settings (continued)*

Password Setting	Description	11g default	10g default
PASSWORD_LIFE_TIME	Number of days password is valid.	180 days	Unlimited
PASSWORD_LOCK_TIME	Number of days account is locked after FAILED_LOGIN_ATTEMPTS has been reached.	1 day	Unlimited
PASSWORD_REUSE_MAX	Number of days before a password can be reused.	Unlimited	Unlimited
PASSWORD_REUSE_TIME	Number of times a password must change before a password can be reused.	Unlimited	Unlimited
PASSWORD_VERIFY_FUNCTION	Database function used to verify the password.	Null	Null

The PASSWORD_REUSE_TIME and PASSWORD_REUSE_MAX settings must be used in conjunction. If you specify an integer for one parameter (doesn't matter which one) and then UNLIMITED for the other parameter, the current password can never be reused.

If you want to specify that the DEFAULT profile password has to be changed 10 times within 100 days before it can be reused, use a line of code similar to this:

```
alter profile default limit password_reuse_time 100 password_reuse_max 10;
```

17-8. Associating a Group of Privileges

Problem

You want to group privileges together so you can assign those privileges in one operation to a schema.

Solution

First connect to the database as a user who has the CREATE ROLE system privilege. Next create a role and assign to it the system or object privileges you want to group together. This example uses the CREATE ROLE command to create the JR_DBA role:

```
create role jr_dba;
```

The next several lines of SQL grant system privileges to the newly created role:

```
grant select any table to jr_dba;
grant create any table to jr_dba;
grant create any view to jr_dba;
grant create synonym to jr_dba;
grant create database link to jr_dba;
```

Next, grant the role to any schema you want to possess those privileges:

```
grant jr_dba to lellison;
grant jr_dba to cphillips;
```

Now the schemas LELLISON and CPHILLIPS can perform tasks such as creating synonyms, views, and so on. As a DBA schema, to view schemas assigned to roles, query the DBA_ROLES_PRIVS view:

```
select grantee, granted_role from dba_role_privs order by 1;
```

To view roles granted to your currently connected user, query from the USER_ROLE_PRIVS view:

```
select * from user_role_privs;
```

To revoke a privilege from a role, use the REVOKE command:

```
revoke create database link from jr_dba;
```

Similarly, use the REVOKE command to remove a role from a schema:

```
revoke jr_dba from lellison;
```

■ **Note** Unlike other database objects, roles do not have owners. A role is defined by the privileges assigned to it.

How It Works

A database *role* is a logical grouping of system or object privileges that can be assigned to schemas or other roles. Roles help you manage aspects of database security. They also provide a central object that has privileges assigned to it; the role can subsequently be assigned to multiple users.

A typical use of a role is when you need to grant several users read-only access to another user's tables. To implement this, first create a role named SELECT_APP:

```
create role select_app;
```

Next grant SELECT TABLE access for every table that read-only access is required for. The following code dynamically creates a script that grants SELECT access for every table in the schema to the specified role:

```
CONN &user_name/&password
DEFINE sel_user=SELECT_APP
SET LINES 132 PAGES 0 ECHO OFF FEEDBACK OFF VERIFY OFF HEAD OFF TERM OFF TRIMS ON
SPO gen_grants_dyn.sql
--
SELECT 'grant select on ' || table_name || ' to &&sel_user ;'
FROM user_tables;
--
SPO OFF;
SET ECHO ON FEEDBACK ON VERIFY ON HEAD ON TERM ON;
--
@@gen_grants_dyn
```

Now you can assign the SELECT_APP role to any user who requires read-only access to the tables within the schema that owns the tables.

PL/SQL and Roles

If you work with PL/SQL, sometimes you'll get this error when attempting to compile a procedure or a function:

`PL/SQL: ORA-00942: table or view does not exist`

What confuses you is that you can describe the table:

`SQL> desc app_table;`

So why doesn't PL/SQL seem to be able to recognize the table? It's because PL/SQL requires that the owner of the package, procedure, or function must be explicitly granted privileges to any objects referenced in the code. The owner of the PL/SQL code cannot have obtained the grants through a role.

Try this as the owner of the PL/SQL code:

`SQL> set role none;`

Now try to run a SQL statement that accesses the table in question:

`SQL> select count(*) from app_table;`

If you can no longer access the table, then you have been granted access through a role. To resolve the issue, explicitly grant access to any tables to the owner of the PL/SQL code (as the owner of the table):

`SQL> connect owner/pass`

`SQL> grant select on app_table to proc_owner;`

Now you should be able to connect as the owner of the PL/SQL code and successfully compile your code.

17-9. Creating Users

Problem

You need to create a new user.

Solution

Use the CREATE USER statement to create a user. This example creates a user named HEERA with a password of CHAYA and assigns the default temporary tablespace of TEMP and default tablespace of USERS:

```
create user heera identified by chaya
  default tablespace users
  temporary tablespace temp;
```

This creates a bare-bones schema that has no privileges to do anything in the database. To make the schema useful, it must be minimally granted the CREATE SESSION system privilege:

```
grant create session to heera;
```

If the new schema needs to be able to create tables, it will need to be granted additional privileges like CREATE TABLE.

```
grant create table to heera;
```

The new schema will also need to have quota privileges granted for any tablespace it needs to create objects in:

```
alter user heera quota unlimited on users;
```

■ **Note** A common technique that DBAs use is to grant the predefined roles of CONNECT and RESOURCE to newly created schemas. These roles contain system privileges such as CREATE SESSION and CREATE TABLE (and several others, it varies by release). We recommend against doing this as Oracle has stated those roles may not be available in future releases.

How It Works

A user is a database account, which is the mechanism that allows you to log on to a database. You must have the CREATE USER system privilege to create a user. When you create a user, you establish the initial security and storage attributes. These user attributes can be modified with the ALTER USER statement.

You can view user information by selecting from the DBA_USERS view:

```
select username, default_tablespace, temporary_tablespace from dba_users;
```

Here is some sample output:

```
USERNAME              DEFAULT_TABLESPACE    TEMPORARY_TABLESPACE
--------------------  --------------------  ------------------------------
C2R                   USERS                 TEMP
REP_MV_SEL            USERS                 TEMP
STAR_SEL              USERS                 TEMP
SYS                   SYSTEM                TEMP
```

All of your users should be assigned a temporary tablespace that has been created as type *temporary*. If a user has a temporary tablespace of SYSTEM, then any sort area that they require temporary disk storage for will acquire extents in the SYSTEM tablespace. This can lead to the SYSTEM tablespace temporarily filling up. None of your users, other than the SYS user, should have a default tablespace of SYSTEM. You don't want any users other than SYS creating objects in the SYSTEM tablespace. The SYSTEM tablespace should be reserved for the SYS user's objects.

17-10. Dropping Users

Problem

You want to drop a user.

Solution

Use the DROP USER statement to remove a database account. This next example drops the user HEERA:

```
drop user heera;
```

This command won't work if the user owns any database objects. Use the CASCADE clause to remove a user and have its objects dropped:

```
drop user heera cascade;
```

■ **Note** The DROP USER statement may take an inordinate amount of time to execute if the user being dropped owns a vast number of database objects. In these situations, you may want to consider dropping the user's objects before dropping the user.

How It Works

When you drop a user, any tables that it owns will also be dropped. Additionally, all indexes, triggers, and referential integrity constraints will be removed. If referential integrity constraints exist in other schemas that depend on any dropped primary key and unique key constraints, the referential constraints in other schemas will also be dropped. Oracle will invalidate but not drop any views, synonyms, procedures, functions, or packages that are dependent on the dropped user's objects.

Sometimes you'll run into a situation where you want to drop a user, but are not sure if anybody is using it. In these scenarios it's safer to first lock the user and see who screams:

```
alter user heera account lock;
```

Any user or application attempting to connect to this user will now receive this error:

```
ORA-28000: the account is locked
```

To view the users and lock dates in your database, issue this query:

```
select username, lock_date from dba_users;
```

To unlock an account issue this command:

```
alter user heera account unlock;
```

The locking of users is a very handy technique for securing your database and discovering which users are used.

17-11. Modifying Passwords

Problem

You want to modify a user's password.

Solution

Use the ALTER USER command to modify an existing user's password. This example changes the HEERA user's password to foobar:

```
alter user heera identified by foobar;
```

You can only change the password of another account if you have the ALTER USER privilege granted to your user. This privilege is granted to the DBA role.

How It Works

After you change a password for a user, any subsequent connection to the database by that user must use the password changed by the ALTER USER statement.

In Oracle Database 11g or higher, when you modify a password it is by default case sensitive. See recipe 17-12 for details on how to disable password case-sensitivity. If you are using Oracle Database 10g or lower, the password is not case-sensitive.

SQL*Plus Password Command

You can change the password for a user with the SQL*Plus PASSWORD command. (Like all SQL*Plus commands, it can be abbreviated.) You will be prompted for a new password:

```
SQL> passw heera
Changing password for heera
New password:
Retype new password:
Password changed
```

This method has the advantage of changing a password for a user without displaying the new password on the screen.

17-12. Enforcing Password Complexity

Problem

You want to ensure that your database users are creating passwords that cannot be easily guessed by a hacker.

Solution

Run the following script as the SYS schema:

```
SQL> @?/rdbms/admin/utlpwdmg
Function created.
Profile altered.
Function created.
```

For Oracle Database 11g, set the PASSWORD_VERIFY_FUNCTION of the DEFAULT profile to be verify_function_11G:

```
alter profile default limit PASSWORD_VERIFY_FUNCTION verify_function_11G;
```

For Oracle Database 10g, set the PASSWORD_VERIFY_FUNCTION of the DEFAULT profile to VERIFY_FUNCTION:

```
alter profile default limit PASSWORD_VERIFY_FUNCTION verify_function;
```

If you need to back out of the new security for any reason, run this statement to disable the password function:

```
alter profile default limit PASSWORD_VERIFY_FUNCTION null;
```

How It Works

When enabled, the password verification function ensures that users are correctly creating or modifying their passwords. The utlpwdmg.sql script creates a function that checks a password to ensure that it meets basic security standards such as minimum password length, password not the same as username, and so on. In Oracle Database 11g, the password security PL/SQL function name is VERIFY_FUNCTION_11G. Once this PL/SQL function is created in the SYS schema, it can be assigned to the PASSWORD_VERIFY_FUNCTION parameter of a profile.

By default, the DEFAULT profile is assigned to all new users created in the database. In the solution section of this recipe, the PASSWORD_VERIFY_FUNCTION parameter of the DEFAULT profile is assigned the VERIFY_FUNCTION_11G function. From that point on, any user assigned the DEFAULT profile will have the VERIFY_FUNCTION_11G function execute when his password is created or modified.

You can verify that the new security function is in effect by attempting to change the password of a user who has been assigned the DEFAULT profile. In this example an attempt is made to change the password to less than the minimum length:

```
SQL> password
Changing password for HEERA
Old password:
New password:
Retype new password:
ERROR:
ORA-28003: password verification for the specified password failed
ORA-20001: Password length less than 8
Password unchanged
```

■ **Note** For Oracle Database 11g, the minimum length is eight characters. For Oracle Database 10g, the minimum length is four characters.

Starting with Oracle Database 11g, password case-sensitivity is enforced. You can disable this feature by setting the SEC_CASE_SENSITIVE_LOGON initialization parameter to FALSE:

```
alter system set sec_case_sensitive_logon = FALSE;
```

However, this is not recommended.

CHAPTER 18

■ ■ ■

Object Management

This chapter focuses on SQL techniques used to manage database objects, including object types such as tables, indexes, views, and synonyms. The SQL statements you use to create and modify objects are often referred to as data definition language (DDL) statements. Managing DDL is part of a database administrator's daily job. DBAs frequently generate and modify DDL scripts to build development, test, staging, and production databases. For these reasons a DBA needs to be particularly deft at writing DDL.

Some will argue that only a database administrator should maintain and manage DDL and that developers should keep their hands out of schema management. However, the reality is that developers often find themselves in environments where they need to write and maintain DDL. For example, you might be in a shop that doesn't have a DBA or perhaps you've created your own personal database to use for development and testing. In these situations the developer is required to perform database administration tasks and therefore must be familiar with writing DDL statements.

This chapter doesn't cover every object manipulation statement available. Instead, it focuses on the most commonly encountered user objects and how to manage them. We'll look first at basic table creation and modification statements, then progress to other typical object maintenance tasks.

18-1. Creating a Table

Problem

You want to perform the basic task of creating a table.

Solution

Not surprisingly, you use the CREATE TABLE command to accomplish this task. Here's a simple example:

```
create table d_sources(
    d_source_id number not null,
    source_type    varchar2(32),
    create_dtt     date default sysdate not null,
    update_dtt     timestamp(5)
);
```

This code creates a table with just basic column definitions, which is usually sufficient if you're in a hurry. If you don't specify any tablespace information, the table will be created in the default tablespace assigned to your user account.

Query the USER_TABLES to view metadata regarding tables within your currently connected account Select from the ALL_TABLES to display information about tables that your account has been granted privileges on. Use the DBA_TABLES view to display information regarding all tables in the database.

■ **Note** Why use the VARCHAR2 datatype instead of the VARCHAR datatype? Oracle says so. Although VARCHAR is currently synonymous with VARCHAR2, the documentation states that in the future VARCHAR will be redefined as a separate datatype.

How It Works

The Oracle table is a flexible and feature-rich container for storing data. If you look in Oracle's documentation for the CREATE TABLE command, you'll find about seventy pages of details. It can be daunting to wade through lengthy documentation when what you really need are a few good examples.

The following code shows the most common features you'll use when creating a table. For example, this DDL defines primary keys, foreign keys, and tablespace information:

```
create table computer_systems(
    computer_system_id      number(38, 0)  not null,
    agent_uuid              varchar2(256),
    operating_system_id     number(19, 0)  not null,
    hardware_model          varchar2(50),
    create_dtt              date           default sysdate not null,
    update_dtt              date,
    constraint computer_systems_pk primary key (computer_system_id)
    using index tablespace inv_mgmt_index
) tablespace inv_mgmt_data;
--
comment on column computer_systems.computer_system_id is
'Surrogate key generated via an Oracle sequence.';
--
create unique index computer_system_uk1 on computer_systems(agent_uuid)
tablespace inv_mgmt_index;
--
alter table computer_systems add constraint computer_systems_fk1
    foreign key (operating_system_id)
    references operating_systems(operating_system_id);
```

In the table and index creation statements, notice that we did not specify any table physical space properties. We only specified the tablespace for the table and the index. If no table-level space properties are specified, the table inherits its space properties from the tablespace. This simplifies table administration and maintenance.

It's a good idea to let a table inherit its physical space properties from the tablespace. If you have tables that require different physical space properties, you can create separate tablespaces to hold tables with differing needs. For example, you might create a DATA_LARGE tablespace with extent sizes of 16M, and a DATA_SMALL tablespace with extents sizes of 128K. (See Chapter 10 for a discussion of extents and other logical structures, and recipe 17-4 for an example of creating a tablespace.)

18-2. Storing Data Temporarily

Problem

You want to store the results of a query temporarily for later use by a session.

Solution

Use the CREATE GLOBAL TEMPORARY TABLE statement to create a table that stores data only provisionally. You can specify that the temporary table retain the data for a session or until a transaction commits. Use ON COMMIT PRESERVE ROWS to specify the data should be deleted at the end of the user's session. In this example, the rows will be retained until the user either explicitly deletes data or until the user terminates the session:

```
create global temporary table today_regs
on commit preserve rows
as select * from f_registrations
where create_dtt > sysdate - 1;
```

Specify ON COMMIT DELETE ROWS to indicate the data should be deleted at the end of the transaction. The following example creates a temporary table named TEMP_OUTPUT and specifies that records should be deleted at the end of each committed transaction:

```
create global temporary table temp_output(temp_row varchar2(30))
on commit delete rows;
```

■ **Note** If you don't specify a commit method for a global temporary table, then the default is ON COMMIT DELETE ROWS.

You can create a temporary table and grant other users access to it. However, a session can only view the data that it inserts into a table. In other words, if two sessions are using the same temporary table, a session cannot select any data inserted into the temporary table by a different session.

How It Works

A global temporary table is useful for applications that need to briefly store data in a table structure. Global temporary tables store session private data that exists only for the duration of the session or transaction. Once you create a temporary table, it exists until you drop it. In other words, the definition of the temporary table is permanent; it's the data that is short-lived.

You can view whether a table is temporary by querying the TEMPORARY column of DBA/ALL/USER_TABLES:

```
select table_name, temporary from user_tables;
```

Temporary tables are designated with a Y in the TEMPORARY column. Regular tables contain an N in the TEMPORARY column.

When you create records within a temporary table, space is allocated in your default temporary tablespace. You can verify this by running the following SQL:

```
select username, contents, segtype from v$sort_usage;
```

If you are working with a large number of rows and need better performance when selectively retrieving rows, you may want to consider creating an index on the appropriate columns in your temporary table:

```
create index temp_index on temp_output(temp_row);
```

Use the DROP TABLE command to drop a temporary table:

```
drop table temp_output;
```

Temporary Table Redo

No redo data is generated for changes to blocks of a global temporary table. However, rollback data is generated for a transaction against a temporary table. Since the rollback data generates redo, there is some redo data associated with a transaction for a temporary table. You can verify this by turning on statistics tracing (see recipe 19-7 for more details) and viewing the redo size as you insert records into a temporary table:

```
SQL> set autotrace on
```

Next insert a few records into the temporary table:

```
insert into temp_output values(1);
```

```
insert into temp_output values(1);
```

Here is a partial snippet of the output (only showing the redo size):

```
140  redo size
```

The redo load is less for temporary tables than normal tables because the redo generated is only associated with the rollback data for a temporary table transaction.

18-3. Moving a Table

Problem

You want to move a table to a different tablespace.

Solution

Use the ALTER TABLE MOVE statement to move a table from one tablespace to another. This example moves the PARTIES table to the MTS tablespace.

```
alter table parties move tablespace mts;
```

You can verify that the table has been moved by querying USER_TABLES:

```
select table_name, tablespace_name from user_tables where table_name='PARTIES';
TABLE_NAME           TABLESPACE_NAME
-------------------- --------------------
PARTIES              MTS
```

How It Works

Occasionally you will need to move a table from one tablespace to another. There may be manageability issues or perhaps the table is being used in a different way than originally intended and for organizational purposes it makes more sense for the table to be in a different tablespace.

When you move a table, all of its indexes are rendered unusable. This is because a table's index includes the ROWID as part of the structure. The table ROWID contains information about the physical location. Since the ROWID of a table changes when the table moves from one tablespace to another (because the table rows are now physically located in different datafiles), any indexes on the table contain incorrect information. To rebuild the index, use the ALTER INDEX ... REBUILD command.

Oracle Rowid

Every row in every table has an address. The address of a row is determined from a combination of the following:

- datafile number
- block number
- location of row within the block
- object number

The address of a row in a table can be displayed by querying the ROWID pseudo-column. For example:

```
select rowid, emp_id from emp;
```

Here is some sample output:

```
ROWID                    EMP_ID

------------------ ----------

AAAFWXAAFAAAAlWAAA           1
```

The ROWID pseudo-column value is not physically stored in the database. Oracle calculates its value when you query it. The ROWID contents are displayed as base 64 values that can contain the characters A-Z, a-z, 0-9, +, and /. You can translate the ROWID value into meaningful information via the DMBS_ROWID package. For example to display the relative file number that a row is stored in, issue this statement:

```
select dbms_rowid.rowid_relative_fno(rowid), emp_id from emp;
```

Here is some sample output:

```
DBMS_ROWID.ROWID_RELATIVE_FNO(ROWID)     EMP_ID

------------------------------------ ----------

                                   5          1
```

The ROWID value can be used in the SELECT and WHERE clauses of a SQL statement. In most cases the ROWID uniquely identifies a row. However, it is possible to have rows in different tables that are stored in the same cluster and so contain rows with the same ROWID.

18-4. Renaming Objects

Problem

You have an obsolete table in a schema. Before you drop the table, you want to rename it and see if anybody complains that they no longer have access.

Solution

Use the ALTER TABLE ... RENAME statement to rename a table. This example renames a table from PRODUCTS to PRODUCTS_OLD:

```
alter table products rename to products_old;
```

After you're sure the table is not being used, you can drop it:

```
drop table products_old;
```

■ **Note** See recipe 18-5 for full details on dropping a table.

How It Works

In Oracle, you can rename many different objects such as:

- Tables
- Columns
- Indexes
- Constraints
- Triggers

Renaming a table before you drop it is a common practice because it gives you a quick way to recover in the event the table is still being used. Another good reason to rename an object is to make sure it conforms to your database naming standards.

Here are some brief examples showing how to rename other object types. The following code renames one of the PRODUCTS table's columns from PRODUCT_ID to PRODUCT_NO:

```
alter table products rename column product_id to product_no;
```

The next line renames an index from PRODID to PROD_IDX1:

```
alter index prodid rename to prod_idx1;
```

Similarly, you can rename a constraint. The next line of code renames a constraint from MAST_CON to MAST_FK1:

```
alter table details rename constraint mast_con to mast_fk1;
```

The next example renames a trigger from F_SHIPMENTS_BU_TR1 to F_AU_TR2:

```
alter trigger f_shipments_bu_tr1 rename to f_au_tr2;
```

Note that it is possible to create two objects within the same schema with the same name. For example, you can create a table and an index in the same schema with the same name. However, you can't create a table and a view with the same name within the same schema.

To understand which objects can (or cannot) be created with the same name within a schema, you must understand the concept of a namespace. A *namespace* is a grouping of objects within a schema in which no two objects can have the same name. Objects in different groupings (that is, different namespaces) within a schema can have the same name.

The following objects share the same namespace within a schema:

- tables
- views
- materialized views
- private synonyms
- sequences
- procedures
- functions
- packages
- user defined types

Each of the follow objects has its own namespace within a schema:

- indexes
- constraints
- triggers
- clusters
- private database links
- dimensions

Thus it is possible to create a trigger with the same name as a function or procedure. However, a table and a view are in the same namespace and therefore can't have the same name. Each schema has its own namespace for the objects that it owns. Two different schemas can therefore create a table with the same name.

These objects each have their own namespaces within a database:

- roles
- public synonyms
- public database links
- tablespaces
- profiles
- initialization files (spfile and init.ora)

Because the previous objects' namespaces aren't contained within a schema, these objects must have unique names across the entire database.

18-5. Dropping a Table

Problem

You want to remove an object such as a table from a user.

Solution

Use the DROP TABLE statement to remove a table. This example drops a table named INVENTORY:

```
drop table inventory;
```

You should see the following confirmation:

```
Table dropped.
```

If you attempt to drop a table that has a primary key or unique keys referenced as a foreign key in a child table, you'll see an error such as:

```
ORA-02449: unique/primary keys in table referenced by foreign keys
```

You'll either need to drop the referenced foreign key constraint(s), or use the CASCADE CONSTRAINTS option when dropping the parent table:

```
drop table inventory cascade constraints;
```

How It Works

You must be the owner of the table or have the DROP ANY TABLE system privilege to drop a table. If you have the DROP ANY TABLE privilege, you can drop a table in a different schema by prepending the schema name to the table name:

```
drop table inv_mgmt.inventory;
```

If you don't prepend the table name with a user name, Oracle assumes you are dropping a table in your current user.

If you're using the RECYCLEBIN feature, DROP TABLE logically marks a table as dropped and renames it. The renamed table is placed in a logical container called the RECYCLEBIN. The table remains in your RECYCLEBIN until you manually remove it or until Oracle needs the space for other objects.

This means that the space associated with the dropped table is not released until you purge your RECYCLEBIN. If you want to purge the entire contents of the RECYCLEBIN, use the PURGE RECYCLEBIN statement:

```
SQL> purge recyclebin;
```

If you want to bypass the RECYCLEBIN feature and permanently drop a table a table, use the PURGE option of the DROP TABLE statement:

```
drop table inventory purge;
```

If you use the PURGE option, the table is permanently dropped. You can't use the FLASHBACK TABLE statement (see recipe 18-6 for details) to retrieve the table. All space used by the table is released and any associated indexes and triggers are also dropped.

18-6. Undropping a Table

Problem

You accidentally dropped a table and you want to restore it.

Solution

First verify that the table you want to restore is in the recycle bin:

```
SQL> show recyclebin;
ORIGINAL NAME    RECYCLEBIN NAME                  OBJECT TYPE  DROP TIME
---------------  -------------------------------  -----------  -------------------
PURCHASES        BIN$YzqKOhN3Fh/gQHdAPLFgMA==$0 TABLE          2009-02-18:17:23:15
```

Next, use the FLASHBACK TABLE...TO BEFORE DROP statement to recover a dropped table:

```
flashback table purchases to before drop;
```

■ **Note** You cannot FLASHBACK TABLE...TO BEFORE DROP for a table created in the SYSTEM tablespace.

How It Works

In Oracle Database 10g and higher, when a DROP TABLE statement is issued, the table is actually renamed (to a name that starts with BIN$) and placed in the recycle bin. The recycle bin is a mechanism that allows you to view some of the metadata associated with a dropped object. You can view complete metadata regarding renamed objects by querying DBA_SEGMENTS:

```
select segment_name, segment_type, tablespace_name
from dba_segments
where segment_name like 'BIN%';
```

```
SEGMENT_NAME                    SEGMENT_TYPE        TABLESPACE_NAME
------------------------------  ------------------  ---------------
BIN$YzqKOhN4Fh/gQHdAPLFgMA==$0 TABLE               MTS
```

The FLASHBACK TABLE statement simply renames the table back to its original name. By default, the RECYCLEBIN feature is enabled in Oracle Database 10g and higher. You can change the default by setting the RECYCLEBIN initialization parameter to OFF.

We recommend that you don't disable the RECYCLEBIN feature. It's safer to leave this feature enabled and purge the RECYCLEBIN to remove objects that you want permanently deleted. If you want to permanently drop a table, use the PURGE option of the DROP TABLE statement.

18-7. Creating an Index

Problem

You are experiencing performance issues. You've identified a selective column that is used as a search criterion. You want to add an index to the table.

Solution

The default index type in Oracle is a B-tree (balanced tree) index. To create a B-tree index on an existing table, use the CREATE INDEX statement. This example creates an index on the D_SOURCES table, specifying D_SOURCE_ID as the column:

```
create index d_sources_idx1 on d_sources(d_source_id);
```

By default, Oracle will try to create an index in your default tablespace. Use the following syntax to instruct Oracle to build an index in a specific tablespace:

```
create index d_sources_idx1 on d_sources(d_source_id) tablespace dim_index;
```

If you don't specify any physical storage properties for an index, the index will inherit its properties from the tablespace. This is usually an acceptable method for managing index storage.

To view index metadata information, query the DBA/USER/ALL_INDEXES data dictionary views. For example, this query displays all index information for the currently connected user:

```
select
  table_name
 ,index_name
 ,index_type
 ,tablespace_name
 ,status
from user_indexes
order by table_name;
```

To Rebuild or not

In the olden days (version 7 or so), in the name of performance, DBAs would religiously rebuild indexes on a regular basis. Just about every DBA had a script similar to the one listed next that would use SQL to generate the SQL required to rebuild indexes for a schema:

```
SPO ind_build_dyn.sql

SET HEAD OFF PAGESIZE 0 FEEDBACK OFF;

SELECT 'ALTER INDEX ' || index_name || ' REBUILD;'

FROM user_indexes;

SPO OFF;

SET FEEDBACK ON;
```

However, it's debatable as to whether rebuilding an index with the newer versions of Oracle will achieve any kind of performance gain. Refer to Oracle's My Oracle Support (formerly known as MetaLink) web site for more details. In particular, document ID 555284.1 contains a script that detects whether an index might need to be rebuilt.

How It Works

An index is an optional database object that is used primarily to increase performance. An index in Oracle works much like an index in the back of a book that associates a page number with information of interest. When looking for information in a book, it's usually much faster to look in the index first, then go to the page of interest. If there were no index, you would have to scan every page of the book to find the information.

An index is a separate object from the table and can be created and dropped independently of the table. Just like a table, indexes require storage. Additionally, there is some overhead with an index as Oracle has to maintain the indexes as data is inserted, updated, or deleted in the associated table. Therefore, you should only add an index when you are certain it will improve performance. See Chapter 19 for details on improving SQL query performance.

The index definition is associated with a table and column(s). The index structure stores a mapping of a row's ROWID and the column data on which the index is built. A ROWID usually uniquely identifies a row within a database. The ROWID contains information to physically locate a row (datafile, block, and row position within block).

By default, when you create an index in Oracle, its type will be a balanced B-tree structure. Figure 18-1 shows the balanced, tree-like structure of a B-tree index created on a first-name column. When Oracle accesses the index, it starts with the top node called the root block. It uses this block to determine which second-level block to read next. The second-level block points to several leaf nodes that contain a ROWID and the name value. In this structure, it will take three I/O operations to find the ROWID. Once the ROWID is determined, Oracle will use it to read the table block that contains the ROWID.

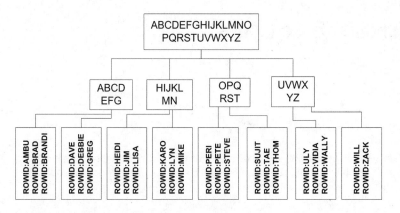

Figure 18-1. *Balanced B-tree index structure*

Separate Tablespaces for Tables and Indexes

DBAs debate the merits of separating tables and indexes into different tablespaces. If you have the luxury of setting up a storage system from scratch and can set up mount points that have their own sets of disks and controllers, you may see some I/O benefits by specifying tables to be built in tablespaces based on datafiles on one mount point, and indexes to be built in tablespaces based on datafiles on a separate mount point.

However, nowadays it's often the case where your storage administrator will just give you a large slice of storage in a SAN and there's no way to guarantee that data and indexes will be stored physically on separate disks (and controllers). Nevertheless, there are still valid reasons to separate index tablespaces from the table tablespaces:

- You may want to implement different physical storage characteristics (such as extent size) for tables and indexes, and you prefer to allow the table and index to inherit their storage attributes from the tablespace.

- You prefer to have the option of being able to back up, restore, and recover table and index tablespaces separately.

- When running maintenance reports, you find it easier to manage tables and indexes when the reports have sections separated by tablespace.

If any of these reasons are valid for your environment, it's probably worth the extra effort to employ different tablespaces for tables and indexes.

18-8. Creating a Function-Based Index

Problem

You're running this SQL query:

```
select emp_name from emp where UPPER(emp_name) = 'DAVE';
```

You've created a normal B-tree index on the EMP_NAME column, but you notice that Oracle is not using the index whenever you apply the UPPER function to the EMP_NAME column. You wonder if you can create an index that Oracle will use.

Solution

Create a function-based index to improve performance of queries that use a SQL function in the WHERE clause. This example creates a function-based index on UPPER(EMP_NAME):

```
create index user_upper_idx on emp(upper(emp_name));
```

Why use a function-based index? Because that's the only kind Oracle will use in this scenario. Oracle will disregard a regular index on a column if you apply a SQL function to it in the WHERE clause.

How It Works

Function-based indexes allow index lookups on columns referenced by functions in the WHERE clause of a SQL query. The function-based index can be as simple as the preceding example, or it can be based on complex logic stored in a PL/SQL function.

Any user-created SQL functions must be declared deterministic before they can be used in a function-based index. Deterministic means that for a given set of inputs, the function will always return the same results. You must use the key word DETERMINISTIC when creating a user-defined function you want to use in a function-based index.

Select from the DBA/ALL/USER_IND_EXPRESSIONS view to display the SQL associated with a function-based index:

```
select index_name, column_expression from user_ind_expressions;
```

If you're running this SQL from SQL*Plus, don't forget to use the SET LONG command in order to display the entire contents of the COLUMN_EXPRESSION column. For example:

```
SQL> set long 500
```

18-9. Creating a Bitmap Index

Problem

You've built a star schema in a data warehouse. You want to ensure that SQL queries that join fact and dimension tables return data efficiently.

Solution

Create bitmap indexes on columns used to join the fact and dimension tables. Bitmap indexes are created by using the keyword BITMAP of the CREATE INDEX statement. This example creates a bitmap index on the column D_DATE_ID of the F_DOWNLOADS table:

```
create bitmap index f_down_date_fk1 on f_downloads(d_date_id);
```

If your fact table is partitioned, you must create the bitmap index as locally partitioned. Do this by specifying the LOCAL keyword:

```
create bitmap index f_down_date_fk1 on f_downloads(d_date_id) local;
```

How It Works

Bitmapped indexes are used extensively in data warehouse environments, typically on fact table foreign key columns. Bitmap indexes are less appropriate for OLTP environments where you have multiple-session DML activity on a table. This is because with a bitmap-indexed column, the internal structure of the bitmap index often requires that many rows be locked during the update. Therefore, if you have more than one session performing UPDATES, INSERTS, and DELETES, you will encounter locking and deadlock problems.

Bitmap indexes in data warehouse environments are usually dropped and re-created as needed. Typically, before a large amount of data is loaded, the bitmap indexes are dropped, and then re-created after the table is populated. To improve the performance of creating a bitmap index, you can turn off the generation of redo via the NOLOGGING option:

```
create bitmap index f_down_date_fk1 on f_downloads(d_date_id) local nologging;
```

Because the index can easily be re-created, there's usually no reason to generate redo for the CREATE INDEX operation.

18-10. Creating an Index-Organized Table

Problem

You have an application that mainly accesses the table data through queries that select on the primary key or a range of primary key values. You want to efficiently query this table.

Solution

Index-organized tables (IOTs) are efficient objects when the table data is typically accessed through querying on the primary key. Use the ORGANIZATION INDEX clause to create an index-organized table:

```
create table prod_sku
(prod_sku_id number,
 sku          varchar2(256),
 create_dtt   timestamp(5),
 constraint prod_sku_pk primary key(prod_sku_id)
)
organization index
including sku
pctthreshold 30
tablespace inv_mgmt_data
overflow
tablespace mts;
```

How It Works

An index-organized table stores the entire contents of the table's row in a B-tree index structure. Index-organized tables provide fast access for queries that have exact matches and/or range searches on the primary key.

The INCLUDING clause specifies the start of which columns to store in the overflow data segment. In the previous example, the SKU and CREATE_DTT columns are stored in the overflow segment.

The PCTTHRESHOLD specifies the percentage of space reserved in the index block for the index-organized table row. This value can be from 1 to 50, and defaults to 50 if no value is specified. There must be enough space in the index block to store the primary key.

The OVERFLOW clause details which tablespace should be used to store overflow data segments.

You'll notice that there will be an entry in DBA/ALL/USER_TABLES for the table name used when creating an IOT. Additionally, there will be a record in DBA/ALL/USER_INDEXES with the name of the primary key constraint specified. The INDEX_TYPE column will contain a value of IOT - TOP for index organized tables:

```
select index_name,table_name,index_type from user_indexes;
```

Here's a sample of the output:

```
INDEX_NAME           TABLE_NAME           INDEX_TYPE
-------------------- -------------------- ---------------------------
PROD_SKU_PK          PROD_SKU             IOT - TOP
```

18-11. Creating a View

Problem

You want to store a SQL query that is run frequently.

Solution

Use the CREATE VIEW command to create a view. The following code creates a view (or replaces it if the view already exists) that selects a subset of columns and rows from the SALES table:

```
create or replace view sales_rockies as
select sales_id, amnt, state
from sales
where state in ('CO','UT','WY','ID','AZ');
```

Now you can treat the SALES_ROCKIES view as if it were a table. Views that only select from one table are called simple views. The schema that has access to the view can perform any SELECT, INSERT, UPDATE, or DELETE operation that it has object grants for and the DML operation will result in the underlying table data being changed.

If you want to allow only the underlying table data within the scope of the view to be changed, then specify the WITH CHECK OPTION:

```
create or replace view sales_rockies as
select sales_id, amnt, state
from sales
where state in ('CO','UT','WY','ID','AZ')
with check option;
```

Using the WITH CHECK OPTION means that you can only insert or update rows that would be returned by the view query. For example, this update statement will work because we are not changing the underlying data in a way that would cause it not to be returned by the view:

```
update sales_rockies set state='CO' where sales_id=160;
```

However this next update statement will fail because it attempts to update the STATE column to a state that is not selectable by the view:

```
update sales_rockies set state='CA' where sales_id=160;
```

If you don't want a user to be able to perform INSERT, UPDATE, or DELETE operations on a view, then don't grant those object privileges on the underlying table(s) to that user. If you don't want an account that owns the underlying tables (or has privileges to modify the table data) to be able to change underlying table data through a view, create the view with the WITH READ ONLY clause:

```
create or replace view sales_rockies as
select sales_id, amnt, state
from sales
where state in ('CO','UT','WY','ID','AZ')
with read only;
```

If you need to modify the SQL query that a view is based on, then either drop and re-create it or use the CREATE OR REPLACE syntax as in the previous examples. The advantage to the CREATE OR REPLACE method is that you don't have to reestablish access to the view for users with previously granted permissions. If you drop and re-create the view, you'll need to regrant privileges to any users or roles that previously had been granted access to the dropped and re-created object.

■ **Note** There is an ALTER VIEW command that is used for modifying constraint attributes of the view. You can also use the ALTER VIEW command to recompile a view.

How It Works

You can think of a view as a SQL statement stored in the database. When you select from a view, Oracle looks up the view definition in the data dictionary, executes the query that the view is based on, and returns the results. Or put another way, views are logical tables built on other tables and/or views. Views are used to:

- create an efficient method of storing a SQL query for reuse.
- provide an interface layer between application and physical tables.
- hide the complexity of a SQL query from the application.
- report on only a subset of columns and/or rows to a user.

As long as a user has select access on a view, they can issue the following SQL statements to display the SQL the view is based on:

```
select text from all_views where view_name like upper('&view_name');
```

If you're running this SQL from SQL*Plus, use the SET LONG command in order to display the entire view. For example:

```
SQL> set long 5000
```

18-12. Creating an Alternate Name for an Object

Problem

You have been granted access to another user's tables. You wonder if there's a way to create a pointer to those tables so you don't have to place the schema name in front of the table name every time you access a table.

Solution

Use the CREATE SYNONYM command to create an alias for another database object. The following example creates a synonym for a table named INV that's owned by the INV_MGMT user:

```
create or replace synonym inv for inv_mgmt.inv;
```

Once you've created the INV synonym, you can operate on the INV_MGMT.INV table directly. If select access has been granted to the INV_MGMT.INV table, you can now select by referencing the synonym INV. For example:

```
select * from inv;
```

The creation of the synonym does not create the privilege to access an object. Such privileges must be granted separately, usually before creating the synonym.

How It Works

Creating a synonym that points to another object eliminates the need to specify the schema owner or name of the object. This lets you create a layer of abstraction between an object and the user, often referred to as object transparency. Synonyms allow you to transparently manage objects separately from the users who access the objects.

For example, you can use synonyms to set up multiple application environments within one database. Each environment would have its own synonyms that point to a different user's objects, allowing you to run the exact same code against several different schemas within one database. You might do this because you can't afford to build a separate box or database for development, testing, quality assurance, production, and so on.

You can create synonyms for the following types of database objects:

- Tables
- Views or object views
- Other synonyms
- Remote objects via a database link
- PL/SQL packages, procedures and functions
- Materialized views

- Sequences

- Java class schema object

- User defined object types

You can also define a synonym to be public, which means that any user in the database has access to the synonym. Sometimes, what lazy (or inexperienced) DBAs do is the following:

```
grant all on books to public;
create public synonym books for inv_mgmt.books;
```

Now any user that can connect to the database can perform any INSERT, UPDATE, DELETE, or SELECT operation on the BOOKS table that exists in the INV_MGMT schema. DBAs might be tempted to do this so they don't have to bother setting up individual grants and synonyms for each schema that needs access. This is almost always a bad idea. There are a few issues with using public synonyms:

- Troubleshooting can be problematic if you're not aware of globally defined (public) synonyms.

- Applications that share one database can have collisions on object names if multiple applications use public synonyms that are not unique within the database

- Security should be administered as needed, not on a wholesale basis.

Sometimes it's useful to dynamically generate synonyms for all tables or views for a schema that needs private synonyms. The following script uses SQL*Plus commands to format and capture the output of a SQL script that generates synonyms for all tables within a schema:

```
CONNECT &&master_user/&&master_pwd.@&&tns_alias
--
SET LINESIZE 132 PAGESIZE 0 ECHO OFF FEEDBACK OFF VERIFY OFF HEAD OFF TERM OFF TRIMSPOOL ON
--
SPO gen_syns_dyn.sql
--
select 'create synonym ' || table_name || ' for ' || '&&master_user..' ||
  table_name || ';'
from user_tables;
--
SPO OFF;
--
SET ECHO ON FEEDBACK ON VERIFY ON HEAD ON TERM ON;
```

Notice the &&MASTER_USER variable with the two dots appended to it in the SELECT statement. A single dot at the end of an ampersand variable instructs SQL*Plus to concatenate anything after the single dot to the ampersand variable. So when you place two dots together, that tells SQL*Plus to concatenate a single dot to the string contained in the ampersand variable.

18-13. Enforcing Unique Rows in a Table

Problem

You want to ensure that the data entered into the database conforms to certain business rules. For example, you need to ensure that a new department will not be mistakenly added under the same department number as an existing one. You want to enforce uniqueness with a primary key constraint.

Solution

When implementing a database, most tables you create will require a primary key constraint that guarantees every record in the table can be uniquely identified. There are multiple techniques for adding a primary key constraint to a table. The first example creates the primary key inline with the column definition:

```
create table dept(dept_id number primary key,
                  dept_desc varchar2(30));
```

If you select the CONSTRAINT_NAME from USER_CONSTRAINTS, you'll notice that Oracle generates a cryptic name for the constraint (something like SYS_C003682). Use the following syntax to explicitly give a name to a primary key constraint:

```
create table dept(
    dept_id number constraint dept_pk primary key using index tablespace users,
    dept_desc varchar2(30));
```

■ **Note** When you create a primary key constraint, Oracle will also create a unique index with the same name as the constraint.

You can also specify the primary key constraint definition after the columns have been defined. The advantage of doing this is that you can define the constraint on multiple columns. The next example creates the primary key when the table is created, but not inline with the column definition:

```
create table dept(
  dept_id number,
  dept_desc varchar2(30),
  constraint dept_pk primary key (dept_id)
  using index tablespace prod_index);
```

If the table has already been created and you want to add a primary key constraint, use the ALTER TABLE statement. This example places a primary key constraint on the DEPT_ID column of the DEPT table:

```
alter table dept add constraint dept_pk primary key (dept_id)
using index tablespace users;
```

When a primary key constraint is enabled, Oracle will automatically create a unique index associated with the primary key constraint. Some DBAs prefer to first create a non-unique index on the primary key column and then define the primary key constraint:

```
create index dept_pk on dept(dept_id);
alter table dept add constraint dept_pk primary key (dept_id);
```

The advantage to this approach is that you can drop or disable the primary key constraint independently of the index. When working with large data sets, you may want that sort of flexibility. If you don't create the index before creating the primary key constraint, then whenever you drop or disable the primary key constraint, the index is automatically dropped.

Confused as to which method to use to create a primary key? All of the methods are valid and have their merits. Table 18-1 summarizes the primary key and unique key constraint creation methods. We've used all of the methods to create primary key constraints. Usually, we use the ALTER TABLE command that just adds the constraint.

Table 18-1. *Primary Key and Unique Key Constraint Creation Methods*

Constraint Creation Method	Advantages	Disadvantages
Inline, no name	Very simple	Oracle-generated name makes troubleshooting harder; less control over storage attributes; only applied to single column
Inline, with name	Simple; user-defined name makes troubleshooting easier	Requires more thought than inline without name
Inline, with name and tablespace definition	User-defined name and tablespace; makes troubleshooting easier	Less simple
After column definition (out of line)	User-defined name and tablespace, can operate on multiple columns	Less simple
ALTER TABLE add just constraint	Manage constraints in separate statements (and files) from table creation scripts; can operate on multiple columns	More complicated
CREATE INDEX, ALTER TABLE add constraint	Separation of index and constraint so you can drop/disable constraints without affecting index; can operate on multiple columns	Most complicated, more to maintain, more moving parts

How It Works

Primary key constraints are used to guarantee that each record in a table can be uniquely identified. A common table design technique is to create a non-meaningful numeric column to contain a unique system-generated sequence number (also called a surrogate key). A primary key constraint is placed on the surrogate key column to ensure its uniqueness.

In addition to a primary key constraint, we also recommend that you place a unique key constraint on the column(s) a business user would use to uniquely identify a record (also called a logical key). Using both a surrogate key and logical key

- lets you efficiently join parent and child tables on a single numeric column;

- allows updates to logical key columns without changing the surrogate key.

A unique key guarantees uniqueness on the defined columns within a table. There are some subtle differences between primary key and unique constraints. You can define only one primary key per table but there can be several unique keys. A primary key does not allow a null value in any of its columns whereas a unique key allows null values.

As with the primary key constraint, there are several methods for creating a unique column constraint. This method uses the UNIQUE keyword inline with the column:

```
create table dept(dept_id number, dept_desc varchar2(30) unique);
```

If you want to explicitly name the constraint, use the CONSTRAINT keyword:

```
create table dept(dept_id number,
    dept_desc varchar2(30) constraint dept_desc_uk1 unique);
```

You can also add the tablespace information inline to be used for the associated unique index that is automatically created for unique constraints:

```
create table dept(dept_id number,
    dept_desc varchar2(30) constraint dept_desc_uk1
    unique using index tablespace prod_index);
```

■ **Note** When you create a unique key constraint, Oracle will also create a unique index with the same name as the constraint.

As with the primary key, the unique constraint can be specified out of line from the column definitions:

```
create table dept(dept_id number,
    dept_desc varchar2(30),
    constraint dept_desc_uk1 unique (dept_desc) using index tablespace prod_index);
```

You can also alter a table to include a unique constraint:

```
alter table dept add constraint dept_desc_uk1 unique (dept_desc);
```

And you can create an index on the columns of interest before you define a unique key constraint:

```
create index dept_desc_uk1 on dept(dept_desc);
alter table dept add constraint dept_desc_uk1 unique(dept_desc);
```

This can be helpful when working with large data sets and you want to be able to disable or drop the unique constraint without dropping the associated index.

18-14. Ensuring Lookup Values Exist

Problem

You have a business rule that states that a column must always be a value in a valid list of values. For example, any DEPT_ID entered in the EMP table must always exist in the master DEPT table.

Solution

Create a foreign key constraint to ensure that a value entered into a foreign key column exists as a unique or primary key value in the parent table. There are several methods for creating a foreign key constraint. The following creates a foreign key constraint on the DEPT_ID column in the EMP table:

```
create table emp(
 emp_id number,
 name varchar2(30),
 dept_id constraint emp_dept_fk references dept(dept_id));
```

Notice that the DEPT_ID data type is not explicitly defined. It derives the data type from the referenced DEPT_ID column of the DEPT table. You can also explicitly specify the data type when defining a column (regardless of the foreign key definition):

```
create table emp(
 emp_id number,
 name varchar2(30),
 dept_id number constraint emp_dept_fk references dept(dept_id));
```

The foreign key definition can also be specified out of line from the column definition in the CREATE TABLE statement:

```
create table emp(
 emp_id number,
```

```
name varchar2(30),
dept_id number,
constraint emp_dept_fk foreign key (dept_id) references dept(dept_id)
);
```

You can also alter an existing table to add a foreign key constraint:

```
alter table emp add constraint emp_dept_fk foreign key (dept_id)
references dept(dept_id);
```

■ **Note** Unlike with primary key and unique key constraints, Oracle does not automatically add an index to the foreign key column(s). You must explicitly create indexes on foreign key columns.

How It Works

Foreign key constraints are used to ensure that a column value is contained within a defined list of values. Using database constraints is an efficient way of enforcing that data must be a predefined value before an insert or update is allowed. Constraints are advantageous because once enabled, there's no way to enter data that violates a given constraint.

The foreign key constraint is a technique that stores in a table the list of valid values. This technique works well for the following scenarios:

- Many entries in the list of values

- Other information about the lookup value needs to be stored

- Easy to select, insert, update, or delete values lookup via SQL

For example, you may have a STATES lookup table that has columns such as STATE_CODE, STATE_NAME, STATE_DESC, and REGION. Your business rule may be that you have an ADDRESSES table that contains a STATE_CODE column and any values entered in this column must exist in the STATES table. A separate table with a foreign key constraint works well for this scenario.

If the condition you want to check for is a small list that doesn't change very often, consider using a check constraint instead of a foreign key constraint (see recipe 18-15 for details). For example, if you have a column that will always be defined to contain either a 0 or a 1, a check constraint is an efficient solution.

18-15. Checking Data for a Condition

Problem

You have a business rule that a column must contain the values of 0 or 1. You want to ensure that the business rule will not be violated.

Solution

Use a check integrity constraint to define a SQL check for a column. There are several methods for creating a check constraint. For example, you can define a check constraint when you create a table. The following defines that the ST_FLG column must be either a 0 or a 1:

```
create table emp(
    emp_id   number,
    emp_name varchar2(30),
    st_flg   number(1) CHECK (st_flg in (0,1))
);
```

A slightly better method is to give the check constraint a name:

```
create table emp(
    emp_id   number,
    emp_name varchar2(30),
    st_flg   number(1) constraint st_flg_chk CHECK (st_flg in (0,1))
);
```

A more descriptive way to name the constraint would be to embed information in the constraint name that actually describes the condition that was violated. For example:

```
CREATE table emp(
    emp_id   number,
    emp_name varchar2(30),
    st_flg   number(1) constraint "st_flg must be 0 or 1" check (st_flg in (0,1))
);
```

You can also alter an existing column to include a constraint. The column must not contain any values that violate the constraint being enabled:

```
alter table emp add constraint "st_flg must be 0 or 1" check (st_flg in (0,1));
```

How It Works

A check constraint works well for lookups when you have a short list of fairly static values, such as a column that can be either a Y or N. In this situation, the list of values will most likely not change and there is no other information that needs to be stored other than the Y or N, so a check constraint is the appropriate solution.

If you have a long list of values that needs to be periodically updated, then a table and foreign key constraint would be a better solution (see recipe 18-14 for details). If you have sophisticated business logic that must be validated, then the application code would be more appropriate. A check constraint works well for a business rule that must always be enforced and can be written with a simple SQL expression.

For example, if you could have a business rule where you want to ensure that an amount is always greater than zero, you could use a check constraint:

```
alter table sales add constraint "sales_amt must be > 0" check(sales_amt > 0);
```

The check constraint must evaluate to a true or unknown (null) value in the row being inserted or updated. You cannot use subqueries or sequences in a check constraint. Also you cannot reference the SQL functions of UID, USER, SYSDATE or USERENV, or the pseudo-columns of LEVEL or ROWNUM.

Another common condition to check for is whether a column is null, and the NOT NULL constraint should be used for this. The NOT NULL constraint can be defined in several ways. The simplest technique is shown here:

```
create table emp(
 emp_id number,
 emp_name varchar2(30) not null);
```

A slightly better approach is to give the NOT NULL constraint a name that makes sense to you:

```
create table emp(
 emp_id number,
 emp_name varchar2(30) constraint emp_name_nn not null);
```

Use the ALTER TABLE command if you need to modify a column for an existing table. For the following command to work, there must not be any NULL values in the column being defined as NOT NULL.

```
alter table emp modify(emp_name not null);
```

If there are currently NULL values in a column that is being defined as NOT NULL, then either first update the column to a NOT NULL value or specify a default value for the column:

```
alter table emp modify(emp_name default 'not available');
```

18-16. Creating a Connection Between Databases

Problem

You want to run SQL statements against a table in a remote database while connected to a local database.

Solution

Use a database link to create a connection between two databases. You must use a naming method for the database link to resolve the location of the remote database. Two common methods used to resolve the location of the remote database are:

- Easy connect naming

- Local naming

The *easy connect naming* method directly embeds the location of the remote database into the database link. In this example, the remote host is OSS.EAST, the port number of the remote listener is 1521, and the remote instance name is BRDSTN:

```
create database link mss connect to e123 identified by e123
using 'oss.east:1521/BRDSTN';
```

The CONNECT TO and IDENTIFIED BY clauses identify the remote user and password respectively. The remote user account doesn't have to be the owner of the remote objects. It can be a regular account with the privileges to access the remote objects.

The *local naming* method resolves the remote service through entries in a tnsnames.ora file. This file needs to be located in a directory that the Oracle client library will look in when attempting to connect to a remote database, such as the directory specified by the TNS_ADMIN operating system variable. In this example, the TNS (Transparent Network Substrate, Oracle's network architecture) information is first placed in the tnsnames.ora file:

```
mss =
(DESCRIPTION =
  (ADDRESS = (PROTOCOL=TCP) (HOST=oss.east)(PORT=1521))
  (CONNECT_DATA=(SERVICE_NAME=BRDSTN)(SERVER=DEDICATED)))
```

Now the database link can be created by referencing the TNS information in the tnsnames.ora file:

```
create database link mss connect to E123 identified by E123 using 'MSS';
```

To drop a database link, use the DROP DATABASE LINK command:

```
drop database link mss;
```

■ **Note** There are two other remote database name resolution methods—*directory naming* (LDAP) and *external naming*. See the *Oracle Database Net Services Administrator's Guide* for details on how to implement these. This documentation is available at http://www.oracle.com/technology.

How It Works

A database link is nothing more than a named connection to another database. It enables you to access objects that exist in a different database. In other words, a database link allows you to perform insert, update, delete, and select statements on tables and views that exist in a remote database. The other database doesn't need to be an Oracle database. However, you must use Oracle Heterogeneous Services to access non-Oracle databases.

After you have created a database link, you can reference remote tables and views using the syntax <REMOTE_OBJECT>@<DATABASE_link>. This example selects a count from the remote view INVENTORY_V:

```
select count(*) from inventory_v@mss;
```

You can also reference a database link in a local view, synonym, or a materialized view to provide a transparency layer between the remote objects and the local objects. This example creates a local synonym that points at the remote INVENTORY_V view:

```
create synonym inventory_v for inventory_v@mss;
```

The following query will display information about database links for a user:

```
select db_link,username,password,host from user_db_links;
```

To view information on all database links in the database, query the DBA_DB_LINKS view. Use the ALL_DB_LINKS to view all database links your account has access to. Query the USER_DB_LINKS to show database links owned by your account.

You can also create a public database link that is accessible to all users in the database. To create a public link, use the PUBLIC clause:

```
create public database link mss connect to e123 identified by e123
using 'oss.east:1521/BRDSTN';
```

18-17. Creating an Auto-incrementing Value

Problem

You want to be able to automatically increment a value used to populate a primary key in a table.

Solution

Create a sequence and then reference it in INSERT statements. The following example uses a sequence to populate the primary key value of a parent table, and then uses the same sequence to populate corresponding foreign key values in a child table:

```
create sequence inv_seq;
```

Now use the sequence in INSERT statements. The first time you access the sequence, use the NEXTVAL pseudo-column:

```
insert into inv(inv_id, inv_desc) values (inv_seq.nextval, 'Book');
```

If you want to re-use that same sequence value, you can reference it via the CURRVAL pseudo-column. Next, a record is inserted into a child table that uses the same value for the foreign key column as its parent primary key value:

```
insert into inv_lines(inv_line_id,inv_id,inv_item_desc)
    values (1, inv_seq.currval, 'Tome1');
insert into inv_lines(inv_line_id,inv_id,inv_item_desc)
    values (2, inv_seq.currval, 'Tome2');
```

How It Works

A *sequence* is a database object that users can access to select unique integers. Sequences are typically used to generate integers for populating primary key and foreign key columns. A sequence is incremented by accessing it via a SELECT, INSERT, or UPDATE statements. Oracle guarantees that a sequence number will be unique when selected. No two sessions can select the same sequence number.

If you don't specify a starting number and a maximum number for a sequence, by default the starting number will be 1, the increment will be 1, and the maximum value will be 10^27. This example specifies a starting value of 1000 and a maximum value of 1000000:

```
create sequence inv2 start with 10000 maxvalue 1000000;
```

To drop a sequence, use the DROP SEQUENCE statement:

```
drop sequence inv;
```

If you have DBA privileges, you can query the DBA_SEQUENCES view to display information on all sequences in the database. To view sequences that your schema owns, query the USER_SEQUENCES view:

```
select
  sequence_name
 ,min_value
 ,max_value
 ,increment_by
from user_sequences;
```

To reset a sequence number, you can drop and re-create the sequence with the desired starting point. The following code drops and then re-creates a sequence to start at the number 1:

```
drop sequence cia_seq;
create sequence cia_seq start with 1;
```

One issue with the previous method of resetting a sequence number is that if there are other schemas that access the sequence, they will have to be re-granted select access to the sequence. This is because when you drop an object, any grants that were associated with that object are also dropped.

An alternative approach to dropping and re-creating the sequence is to alter the sequence's INCREMENT BY to one integer below where you want to reset it to and then alter the sequence's INCREMENT

BY to 1. This effectively resets the sequence without having to drop and re-create it and removes the need to re-grant select access to the sequence. This technique is shown in the next several lines of SQL code:

```
UNDEFINE seq_name
UNDEFINE reset_to
PROMPT "sequence name" ACCEPT '&&seq_name'
PROMPT "reset to value" ACCEPT &&reset_to
COL seq_id NEW_VALUE hold_seq_id
COL min_id NEW_VALUE hold_min_id
--
SELECT &&reset_to - &&seq_name..nextval - 1 seq_id
FROM dual;
--
SELECT &&hold_seq_id - 1 min_id FROM dual;
--
ALTER SEQUENCE &&seq_name INCREMENT BY &hold_seq_id MINVALUE &hold_min_id;
--
SELECT &&seq_name..nextval FROM dual;
--
ALTER SEQUENCE &&seq_name INCREMENT BY 1;
```

To ensure that the sequence has been set to what you want, select the NEXTVAL from it:

```
select &&seq_name..nextval from dual;
```

■ ■ ■

CHAPTER 19

SQL Monitoring and Tuning

SQL is the language used to create, retrieve, update, and delete (CRUD) data from databases. If your SQL statements are slow, the whole system suffers. Whether you're a developer or a DBA, effectively tuning SQL is a critical job requirement. When troubleshooting performance issues, you must know how to identify and tune resource-intensive queries.

A good developer must be familiar with query-tuning techniques. Ideally, developers will proactively evaluate queries for potential performance issues before they are deployed to production. In reality, bad SQL often makes it into production because it wasn't adequately tested, or the test environment does not accurately reflect the production environment (in terms of hardware, data volumes, load on box, and so on). In scenarios where inefficient SQL is deployed, developers must be familiar with reactive techniques for identifying and fixing poorly performing queries.

DBAs (who want to keep their jobs) must also be adept at identifying SQL queries that hog resources. The DBA is often the first person looked to when the database code is performing poorly. DBAs should also be able to help developers generate query execution plans and implement solutions to poorly performing SQL queries.

Most application performance issues can be attributed to code ineffectively accessing the database. This could be in the form of SQL, PL/SQL, JDBC, and so on. This chapter focuses on techniques used to identify and tune resource-intensive SQL statements. If you are new to SQL, this chapter will lay the foundation for critical tuning skills. If you are already familiar with SQL, this chapter covers new features in Oracle related to SQL tuning. We start with basic tasks such as monitoring and identifying resource-intensive SQL statements and then progress to topics such as generating and interpreting a SQL execution plan.

19-1. Monitoring Real-Time SQL Execution Statistics

Problem

You want to identify in real time SQL statements consuming the most resources.

Solution

If your database is Oracle Database 11g, you can use the following query to select from the V$SQL_MONITOR to monitor the near real-time resource consumption of SQL queries:

```
select * from (
select
 a.sid session_id
,a.sql_id
,a.status
,a.cpu_time/1000000 cpu_sec
,a.buffer_gets
,a.disk_reads
,b.sql_text sql_text
from v$sql_monitor a
    ,v$sql b
where a.sql_id = b.sql_id
order by a.cpu_time desc)
where rownum <=20;
```

The output of this query doesn't fit easily onto a page. Here is a subset of the output:

```
SESSION_ID SQL_ID        STATUS     CPU_SEC    BUFFER_GETS    DISK_READS SQL_TEXT
---------- ------------- ---------- ---------- -----------    ---------- ------------
       194 4k8runghhh31d DONE         7 8.66             0             0 select count(*)
       191 9tjq6dfrwgzfr EXECUTING     45.57          1944             7 select output f
```

In the query, an inline view is utilized to first retrieve all records and organize them by CPU_TIME in descending order. The outer query then limits the result set to the top twenty rows using the ROWNUM pseudocolumn. You can modify the previous query to order by the statistic of your choice. You can also modify it to display only the queries that are currently executing. For example, the next SQL statement monitors executing queries ordered by the number of disk reads:

```
select * from (
select
 a.sid session_id
,a.sql_id
,a.status
,a.cpu_time/1000000 cpu_sec
,a.buffer_gets
,a.disk_reads
,substr(b.sql_text,1,15) sql_text
from v$sql_monitor a
    ,v$sql b
where a.sql_id = b.sql_id
and   a.status='EXECUTING'
order by a.disk_reads desc)
where rownum <=20;
```

■ **Note** If you're using Oracle Database 10*g* or lower, see recipe 19-4 for displaying resource-consuming queries.

How It Works

The statistics in V$SQL_MONITOR are updated every second so you can view resource consumption as it changes. These statistics are gathered by default if a SQL statement runs in parallel or consumes more than 5 seconds of CPU or I/O time.

The V$SQL_MONITOR view includes a subset of statistics contained in the VSQL, VSQLAREA, and V$SQLSTATS views. The V$SQL_MONITOR view displays real-time statistics for each execution of a resource-intensive SQL statement, whereas VSQL, VSQLAREA, and V$SQLSTATS contain cumulative sets of statistics over several executions of a SQL statement.

Once the SQL statement execution ends, the run time statistics are not immediately flushed from V$SQL_MONITOR. Depending on activity in your database, the statistics can be available for some period of time. If you have a very active database, the statistics could potentially be flushed soon after the query finishes.

■ **Tip** You can uniquely identify an execution of a SQL statement in V$SQL_MONITOR from a combination of the following columns: SQL_ID, SQL_EXEC_START, SQL_EXEC_ID.

19-2. Displaying a Query's Progress in the Execution Plan

Problem

You want to view exactly where Oracle is taking time within a SQL execution plan. You are using Oracle Database 11g.

Solution

If you're working with Oracle Database 11g, you can watch a SQL query's execution plan progress while the SQL is running. The V$SQL_PLAN_MONITOR view contains a row for each step of a SQL statement's execution plan.

This query will show the number of rows and memory used for each step of the execution plan while the query is running. You'll have to use some SQL*Plus formatting commands to make the output readable:

```
COL SID FORMAT 99999
COL status FORMAT A15
COL start_time FORMAT A12
COL plan_line_id FORMAT 99999 HEAD "Plan ID"
COL plan_options FORMAT A16
COL mem_bytes FORMAT 99999999
COL temp_bytes FORMAT 99999999
SET LINESIZE 132 PAGESI 100 TRIMSP ON
BREAK ON sid on status on start_time NODUP SKIP 1
--
```

```
select
  a.sid
 ,a.status
 ,to_char(a.sql_exec_start,'yymmdd hh24:mi') start_time
 ,a.plan_line_id
 ,a.plan_operation
 ,a.plan_options
 ,a.output_rows
 ,a.workarea_mem     mem_bytes
 ,a.workarea_tempseg temp_bytes
from v$sql_plan_monitor a
    ,v$sql_monitor      b
where a.status NOT LIKE '%DONE%'
and    a.key = b.key
order by a.sid, a.sql_exec_start, a.plan_line_id;
```

Here is a partial listing of the output (the memory columns have been removed to fit the output on the page):

SID	STATUS	START_TIME	Plan ID	PLAN_OPERATION	PLAN_OPTIONS	OUTPUT_ROWS
184	EXECUTING	090326 17:31	0	SELECT STATEMENT		0
			1	SORT	ORDER BY	0
			2	HASH	GROUP BY	0
			3	HASH JOIN		693940
			4	TABLE ACCESS	FULL	7
			5	TABLE ACCESS	FULL	693940

You can now watch Oracle step through each line in the explain plan and update the relevant number of rows, bytes used in memory, and bytes used in temporary space.

How It Works

When tuning a SQL query, you may wonder which steps within the execution plan are consuming the most resources. The V$SQL_PLAN_MONITOR provides you with information on the steps that are using the most resources. The statistics in V$SQL_PLAN_MONITOR are updated every second.

You can also generate a real-time text, HTML, or XML report of query progress within an execution plan by using the REPORT_SQL_MONITOR function of the DBMS_SQLTUNE package.

■ **Note** As of the writing of this book, an extra license is required for the DBMS_SQLTUNE package, which is part of the Oracle Tuning Pack.

The next example demonstrates how to generate such a report. If you are running this from SQL*Plus, be sure you use the SET command to set variables to appropriate values so you can view the results:

```
SQL> SET LINES 3000 PAGES 0 LONG 1000000 TRIMSPOOL ON
```

If you don't pass any parameters to REPORT_SQL_MONITOR, then by default Oracle will report on the last query monitored:

```
select dbms_sqltune.report_sql_monitor from dual;
```

Here is small snippet of the output:

```
Global Information
  Status             :  DONE (ALL ROWS)
  Instance ID        :  1
  Session ID         :  185
  SQL ID             :  1nzw6bfkm0pry
  SQL Execution ID   :  16777218
  Plan Hash Value    :  2855621993
  Execution Started  :  07/17/2009 15:35:31
  First Refresh Time :  07/17/2009 15:35:37
  Last Refresh Time  :  07/17/2009 15:37:21
```

| Elapsed | Cpu | IO | Fetch | Buffer | Reads | Writes |
Time(s)	Time(s)	Waits(s)	Calls	Gets		
100	13	86	275	22827	24866	6231

You can also instruct REPORT_SQL_MONITOR to report on a specific session ID or SQL ID. This example reports on the SQL being monitored for the session ID of 185:

```
select dbms_sqltune.report_sql_monitor(session_id=>185) from dual;
```

By default, REPORT_SQL_MONITOR generates a text report. If you prefer, you can create a report in HTML or XML. This example generates an HTML report, using the SQL*Plus SPOOL command to capture the output to a file:

```
SET LINES 3000 PAGES 0 LONG 1000000 TRIMSPOOL ON
SPOOL out.html
select dbms_sqltune.report_sql_monitor(session_id=>185,
  event_detail => 'YES' ,report_level => 'ALL' ,type => 'HTML'
  )
from dual;
SPOOL OFF;
```

Now you can open the HTML file from a browser and view a nicely formatted graphical report like the one shown in Figure 19-1.

SQL Text

select mytab from mytab union select a.table_name from dba_tables a ,dba_indexes c ,dba_constraints d ,dba_objects e union select c.index_name fro
c ,dba_constraints d ,dba_objects e ,dba_synonyms f

Global Information: EXECUTING

Instance ID	: 1				
Session ID	: 185		**Buffer Gets**	**IO Count**	**Database Time**
SQL ID	: 4tb8s6tyxm9nu				
SQL Execution ID	: 16777220		49456	29767 IO	462s
Plan Hash Value	: 3109003328				
Execution Started	: 08/30/2009 16:31:21				
First Refresh Time	: 08/30/2009 16:31:25				
Last Refresh Time	: 08/30/2009 16:39:03				
Fetch Calls	:				

SQL Plan Monitoring Details:

Id	Operation	Name	Estimated Rows	Cost	Active Period (463s)	Starts	Actual Rows	Memory	Temp	CPU Activity
0	SELECT STATEMENT			1111T		1				
1	SORT UNIQUE		1010 P	1111T		1	0			7.9%
> 2	UNION-ALL					1	11651K			2.2%
3	TABLE ACCESS FULL	MYTAB	1829K	4537		1	3670K			.66%
> 4	FILTER					1	7980K			9.5%
> 5	HASH JOIN		318T	256G		1	7980K	1573K		6.2%
6	INDEX FULL SCAN	I_USER2	42	1		1	42			

Figure 19-1. An HTML Report Generated Using DBMS_SQLTUNE.REPORT_SQL_MONITOR

19-3. Determining How Much SQL Work Is Left

Problem

A SQL query has been running for quite some time and you wonder if there's a way to tell how much longer it will take to finish.

Solution

Use the V$SESSION_LONGOPS view to approximate how much time a query has left to run. To view the output from SQL*Plus, you'll need to use the SET and COLUMN commands to format the output. Run the following query to get an estimate of the progress of currently running SQL statements:

```
SET LINESIZE 141 TRIMSPOOL ON PAGES 66
COL username    FORMAT A8       HEAD "User|Name"
COL opname      FORMAT A16      HEAD "Operation|Type"
COL sql_text    FORMAT A33      HEAD "SQL|Text" TRUNC
COL start_time  FORMAT A15      HEAD "Start|Time"
```

```
COL how_long    FORMAT 99,990    HEAD "Time|Run"
COL secs_left   FORMAT 99,990    HEAD "Appr.|Secs Left"
COL sofar       FORMAT 9,999,990 HEAD "Work|Done"
COL totalwork   FORMAT 9,999,990 HEAD "Total|Work"
COL percent     FORMAT 999.90    HEAD "%|Done"
--
select
  a.username
 ,a.opname
 ,b.sql_text
 ,to_char(a.start_time,'DD-MON-YY HH24:MI') start_time
 ,a.elapsed_seconds how_long
 ,a.time_remaining secs_left
 ,a.sofar
 ,a.totalwork
 ,round(a.sofar/a.totalwork*100,2) percent
from v$session_longops a
     ,v$sql            b
where a.sql_address     = b.address
and   a.sql_hash_value = b.hash_value
and   a.sofar <> a.totalwork
and   a.totalwork != 0;
```

How It Works

The V$SESSION_LONGOPS view displays the status of various database operations that have been running for longer than six seconds. To use V$SESSION_LONGOPS, you must use the cost-based optimizer and have the following in place:

- TIMED_STATISTICS initialization parameter set to TRUE

- Statistics generated for the objects in the query

The V$SESSION_LONGOPS view gives you a rough idea of how long a currently running query has left to finish. In our experience, the results are not 100% accurate, so allow some fudge-factor time into what it reports.

19-4. Identifying Resource-Intensive SQL Statements

Problem

You want to identify which SQL statements are consuming the most resources.

Solution

Use the following query to identify the ten most resource-intensive queries based on CPU time:

```
select * from(
select
  sql_text
 ,buffer_gets
 ,disk_reads
 ,sorts
 ,cpu_time/1000000 cpu_sec
 ,executions
 ,rows_processed
from v$sqlstats
order by cpu_time DESC)
where rownum < 11;
```

An inline view is utilized to first retrieve all records and sorts the output by CPU_TIME in descending order. The outer query then limits the result set to the top ten rows using the ROWNUM pseudocolumn.

The query can be easily modified to sort by a column other than CPU_TIME. For example, if you want to report resource usage by BUFFER_GETS, simply change the ORDER BY clause to use BUFFER_GETS instead of CPU_TIME. The CPU_TIME column is calculated in microseconds; to convert it to seconds it is divided by 1000000.

How It Works

The V$SQLSTATS view displays performance statistics for SQL statements that have recently executed. You can also use V$SQL and V$SQLAREA to report on SQL resource usage. V$SQLSTATS is faster and retains information for a longer period of time, but contains only a subset of the columns in V$SQL and V$SQLAREA. Thus there are scenarios where you may want to query from V$SQL or V$SQLAREA. For example, if you want to display information like the user who first parsed the query, you use the PARSING_USER_ID column of V$SQLAREA:

```
select * from(
select
  b.sql_text
 ,a.username
 ,b.buffer_gets
 ,b.disk_reads
 ,b.sorts
 ,b.cpu_time/1000000 cpu_sec
from v$sqlarea b
    ,dba_users a
where b.parsing_user_id = a.user_id
order by b.cpu_time DESC)
where rownum < 11;
```

19-5. Using Oracle Performance Reports to Identify Resource-Intensive SQL

Problem

You want to use one of Oracle's performance-tuning reports to identify resource-intensive queries.

Solution

If you notice that your database performance slowed down for a day or was sluggish for a few hours, you should run one of the following reports for the timeframe in which performance issues were noticed:

- Automatic Workload Repository (AWR)

- Automatic Database Diagnostic Monitor (ADDM)

- Active Session History (ASH)

- Statspack

Each of these reports is described in the next several subsections.

■ **Note** As of the writing of this book, you need to purchase an additional license from Oracle Corporation to use the AWR, ADDM, and ASH utilities. If you don't have a license, you can use the free Statspack utility.

Using AWR

An AWR report is good for viewing the entire system performance and identifying the top resource-consuming SQL queries. Run the following script to generate an AWR report:

```
SQL> @?/rdbms/admin/awrrpt
```

From the AWR output, identify top resource-consuming statements in the "SQL ordered by Elapsed Time" or the "SQL ordered by CPU Time" sections of the report. Here is some sample output:

```
SQL ordered by CPU Time           DB/Inst: DWREP/DWREP  Snaps: 11384-11407
-> Resources reported for PL/SQL code includes the resources used by all SQL
   statements called by the code.
-> % Total DB Time is the Elapsed Time of the SQL statement divided
   into the Total Database Time multiplied by 100

   CPU      Elapsed                    CPU per  % Total
  Time (s)  Time (s)  Executions     Exec (s) DB Time   SQL Id
---------- ---------- ------------ ----------- ------- -------------
   4,809     13,731           10      480.86     6.2   8wx77jyhdr31c
```

```
Module: JDBC Thin Client
SELECT D.DERIVED_COMPANY ,CB.CLUSTER_BUCKET_ID ,CB.CB_NAME ,CB.SOA_ID ,COUNT(*)
TOTAL ,NVL(SUM(CASE WHEN F.D_DATE_ID > TO_NUMBER(TO_CHAR(SYSDATE-30,'YYYYMMDD'))
THEN 1 END), 0) RECENT ,NVL(D.BLACKLIST_FLG,0) BLACKLIST_FLG FROM F_DOWNLOADS F
,D_DOMAINS D ,D_PRODUCTS P ,PID_DF_ASSOC PDA ,( SELECT * FROM ( SELECT CLUSTER_
```

As of Oracle Database 10g, Oracle will automatically take a snapshot of your database once an hour and populate the underlying AWR tables that store the statistics. By default, seven days of statistics are retained.

You can also generate an AWR report for a specific SQL statement by running the awrsqrpt.sql report. When you run the following script, you will be prompted for the SQL_ID of the query of interest:

```
SQL> @?/rdbms/admin/awrsqrpt.sql
```

Using ADDM

The ADDM report provides useful suggestions on which SQL statements are candidates for tuning. Use the following SQL script to generate an ADDM report:

```
SQL> @?/rdbms/admin/addmrpt
```

Look for the section of the report labeled "SQL statements consuming significant database time." Here is some sample output:

```
FINDING 2: 29% impact (65043 seconds)
-------------------------------------
SQL statements consuming significant database time were found.

   RECOMMENDATION 1: SQL Tuning, 6.7% benefit (14843 seconds)
      ACTION: Investigate the SQL statement with SQL_ID "46cc3t7ym5sx0" for
         possible performance improvements.
         RELEVANT OBJECT: SQL statement with SQL_ID 46cc3t7ym5sx0 and
         PLAN_HASH 1234997150
   MERGE INTO d_files a
         USING
         ( SELECT
```

The ADDM report analyzes data in the AWR tables to identify potential bottlenecks and high resource-consuming SQL queries.

Using ASH

The ASH report allows you to focus on short-lived SQL statements that have been recently run and may have only executed for a brief amount of time. Use the following script to generate an ASH report:

```
SQL> @?/rdbms/admin/ashrpt
```

Search the output for the section labeled "Top SQL". Here is some sample output:

	SQL ID	Planhash	Sampled # of Executions	% Activity
Event		% Event Top Row Source		% RwSrc
	4k8runghhh31d	3219321046	12	51.61
CPU + Wait for CPU		51.61 HASH JOIN		12.26
select countryimp0_.COUNTRY_ID as COUNTRY_ID, countryimp0_.COUNTRY_NAME				

The previous output indicates that the query is waiting for CPU resources. In this scenario, it may actually be another query that is consuming the CPU resources that is the problem.

When is the ASH report more useful than the AWR or ADDM reports? The AWR and ADDM output shows top-consuming SQL in terms of total database time. If the SQL performance problem is transient and short-lived, it may not appear on the AWR and ADDM reports. In these situations an ASH report is more useful.

■ **Note** You can also run the AWR, ADDM, and ASH reports from Enterprise Manager, which you may find more intuitive than manually running the scripts from SQL*Plus.

Using Statspack

If you don't have a license to use the AWR, ADDM, and ASH reports, the free Statspack utility can help you identify poorly performing SQL statements. Run the following script as SYS to install Statspack:

```
SQL> @?/rdbms/admin/spcreate.sql
```

This script creates a PERFSTAT user that owns the Statspack repository. To enable the automatic gathering of Statspack statistics, run this script:

```
SQL> @?/rdbms/admin/spauto.sql
```

After some snapshots have been gathered, you can run the following script as the PERFSTAT user to create a Statspack report:

```
SQL> @?/rdbms/admin/spreport.sql
```

Once the report is created, search for the section labeled "SQL ordered by CPU." Here is some sample output:

```
SQL ordered by CPU  DB/Inst: DW11/DW11  Snaps: 11-14
-> Total DB CPU (s):        107
-> Captured SQL accounts for  246.0% of Total DB CPU
-> SQL reported below exceeded  1.0% of Total DB CPU
```

```
       CPU              CPU per          Elapsd                       Old
     Time (s)  Executions Exec (s) %Total Time (s)  Buffer Gets Hash Value
    ---------- ---------- ---------- ------ ---------- ---------------- ----------
       254.95          4     63.74 238.1    249.74           12,811 2873951798
    Module: SQL*Plus
    select count(*) from dba_indexes, dba_tables
```

■ **Tip** View the `ORACLE_HOME/rdbms/admin/spdoc.txt` file for Statspack documentation.

How It Works

Oracle maintains a massive collection of dynamic performance views that track and accumulate metrics of database performance. For example, if you run the following query, you'll notice that for Oracle Database 11g, there are over 400 dynamic performance views:

```
select count(*) from dictionary where table_name like 'V$%';

   COUNT(*)
----------
       481
```

The Oracle performance utilities rely on periodic snapshots gathered from these internal performance views. Two of the most useful views with regard to performance statistics are the V$SYSSTAT and V$SESSTAT views. The V$SYSSTAT view contains over 400 types of database statistics. This V$SYSSTAT view contains information about the entire database, whereas the V$SESSTAT view contains statistics for individual sessions.

A few of the values in the V$SYSSTAT and V$SESSTAT views contain the current usage of the resource. These values are:

- opened cursors current

- logons current

- session cursor cache current

- workarea memory allocated

The rest of the values are cumulative. The values in V$SYSSTAT are cumulative for the entire database from the time the instance was started. The values in V$SESSTAT are cumulative per session from the time the session was started. Some of the more important performance-related cumulative values are:

- CPU used

- consistent gets

- physical reads

- physical writes

For the cumulative statistics, the way to measure periodic usage is to note the value of a statistic at a starting point, and then note the value at a later point in time and capture the delta. This is the approach used by the Oracle performance utilities such as AWR and Statspack. Periodically Oracle will take a snapshot of the dynamic wait interface views and store them in a repository.

You can access statistics regarding top-resource consuming SQL statements in the DBA_HIST_SQLSTAT AWR view. There is another related view, DBA_HIST_SNAPSHOT, which shows a record for each AWR snapshot. Similarly, the Statspack historical performance statistical data is stored in the STATS$SQL_SUMMARY table and the STATS$SNAPSHOT table contains a record for each Statspack snapshot.

19-6. Using the Operating System to Identify Resource-Intensive Queries

Problem

You have multiple Oracle, MySQL, and PostgreSQL databases running on a single server. The performance of the box seems sluggish. You want to pinpoint which operating system session is consuming the most resources and determine if that session is associated with a database and ultimately a specific SQL query.

Solution

First, use an operating system utility to identify the process consuming the most resources. This example uses the Linux/Unix ps utility to identify the operating system sessions consuming the most CPU:

```
$ ps -e -o pcpu,pid,user,tty,args | sort -n -k 1 -r | head
```

Here is some sample output:

```
7.8 14028 oracle ? oracleDW11 (DESCRIPTION=(LOCAL=YES)(ADDRESS=(PROTOCOL=beq)))
0.1 17012 oracle ? ora_j003_SCDEV
0.1 17010 oracle ? ora_j002_SCDEV
```

From the output, the operating system session of 14028 is consuming the most CPU resources at 7.8 percent. In this example, the 14028 process is associated with the DW11 database. Next, log onto the appropriate database and use the following SQL statement to determine what type of program is associated with the operating system process of 14028:

```
select
  'USERNAME : ' || s.username|| chr(10) ||
  'OSUSER   : ' || s.osuser  || chr(10) ||
  'PROGRAM  : ' || s.program || chr(10) ||
  'SPID     : ' || p.spid    || chr(10) ||
  'SID      : ' || s.sid     || chr(10) ||
  'SERIAL#  : ' || s.serial# || chr(10) ||
  'MACHINE  : ' || s.machine || chr(10) ||
  'TERMINAL : ' || s.terminal
from v$session s,
```

```
     v$process p
where s.paddr = p.addr
and   p.spid  = '&PID_FROM_OS';
```

Here is the output for this example:

```
'USERNAME:'||S.USERNAME||CHR(10)||'OSUSER:'||S.OSUSER||CHR(10)||'PROGRAM:'
--------------------------------------------------------------------------
USERNAME : INV_MGMT
OSUSER   : oracle
PROGRAM  : sqlplus@rmougprd.rmoug.org (TNS V1-V3)
SPID     : 14028
SID      : 198
SERIAL#  : 57
MACHINE  : rmougprd.rmoug.org
TERMINAL :
```

In this output, the PROGRAM value is sqlplus@rmougprd.rmoug.org. This indicates that a SQL*Plus session is the program consuming the inordinate amount of resources on the rmougprd.rmoug.org server. Next run the following query to display the SQL statement associated with the operating system process ID (in this example, the SPID is 14028):

```
select
  'USERNAME : '  ||  s.username  ||  chr(10)  ||
  'OSUSER   : '  ||  s.osuser    ||  chr(10)  ||
  'PROGRAM  : '  ||  s.program   ||  chr(10)  ||
  'SPID     : '  ||  p.spid      ||  chr(10)  ||
  'SID      : '  ||  s.sid       ||  chr(10)  ||
  'SERIAL#  : '  ||  s.serial#   ||  chr(10)  ||
  'MACHINE  : '  ||  s.machine   ||  chr(10)  ||
  'TERMINAL : '  ||  s.terminal  ||  chr(10)  ||
  'SQL TEXT : '  ||  q.sql_text
from v$session s
    ,v$process p
    ,v$sql     q
where s.paddr  = p.addr
and   p.spid   = '&PID_FROM_OS'
and   s.sql_id = q.sql_id;
```

The result shows the resource-consuming SQL as part of the output in the SQL TEXT column:

```
'USERNAME:'||S.USERNAME||CHR(10)||'OSUSER:'||S.OSUSER||CHR(10)||'PROGRAM:'
--------------------------------------------------------------------------
USERNAME : INV_MGMT
OSUSER   : oracle
PROGRAM  : sqlplus@rmougprd.rmoug.org (TNS V1-V3)
SPID     : 14028
SID      : 198
SERIAL#  : 57
MACHINE  : rmougprd.rmoug.org
TERMINAL :
SQL TEXT : select  count(*) ,object_name from dba_objects,dba_segments
```

How It Works

When you run multiple databases on one server and are experiencing server performance issues, it can sometimes be difficult to pinpoint which database and associated process are causing the problems. In these situations you have to use an operating system tool to identify the top-consuming sessions on the system.

In a Linux or Unix environment, you can use utilities such as ps, top, or vmstat to identify top-consuming operating system processes. The ps utility is handy because it lets you identify processes consuming the most CPU or memory. In the solution section, we used the ps command to identify the most CPU-intensive queries. Here we use it to identify the top Oracle memory-using processes:

```
$ ps -e -o pmem,pid,user,tty,args | grep -i oracle | sort -n -k 1 -r | head
```

Once you have identified a top-consuming process associated with a database, you can query the data dictionary views based on the server process ID to identify what the database process is executing.

OS Watcher

Oracle provides a collection of Linux/Unix scripts that gather and store metrics for CPU, memory, disk, and network usage. The OS Watcher tool suite automates the gathering of statistics using tools such as top, vmstat, iostat, mpstat, netstat, and traceroute.

You can obtain OS Watcher from Oracle's My Oracle Support (MetaLink) website. Search for document ID 301137.1 or for the document titled "OS Watcher User Guide". Navigate to the Contents page and search for the Download link.

This utility also has an optional graphical component for visually displaying performance metrics. The OS Watcher utility is currently supported on the following platforms: Linux, Solaris, AIX, Tru64, and HP-UX.

19-7. Displaying an Execution Plan Using AUTOTRACE

Problem

You're experiencing performance problems when executing a SQL statement and you want to see how the optimizer is planning to retrieve data to build the query result set.

Solution

One easy way to generate an execution plan is to use the AUTOTRACE utility. Before you generate an explain plan, you must first make AUTOTRACE available in your database.

Setting up AUTOTRACE

Follow these steps to set up the AUTOTRACE facility to display an explain plan.

1. Ensure that the PLAN_TABLE table exists. To see if your schema has a PLAN_TABLE, try to describe it:

```
SQL> desc plan_table;
```

If the PLAN_TABLE doesn't exist, you need to create one. Run this script to create the PLAN_TABLE in your schema:

```
SQL> @?/rdbms/admin/utlxplan
```

2. Your schema also needs access to the PLUSTRACE role. You can verify access to the PLUSTRACE role using the following:

```
select username,granted_role from user_role_privs
where granted_role='PLUSTRACE';
```

If you don't have access to the PLUSTRACE role, run steps 3 and 4 as the SYS schema:

3. Connect as SYS and run the plustrce.sql script:

```
SQL> conn / as sysdba
SQL> @?/sqlplus/admin/plustrce
```

4. Grant the PLUSTRACE role to developers (or to a specific role) who want to use the AUTOTRACE facility:

```
SQL> grant plustrace to star1;
```

Generating an Execution Plan

Here's the simplest way to use the AUTOTRACE facility:

```
SQL> set autotrace on;
```

Now any SQL you run will generate an explain plan.

```
select emp_name from emp;
```

Here is a partial listing of the output:

```
---------------------------------------------------------------------
| Id | Operation         | Name | Rows | Bytes | Cost (%CPU)| Time     |
---------------------------------------------------------------------
|  0 | SELECT STATEMENT  |      |    1 |    17 |     5   (0)| 00:00:01 |
|  1 |  TABLE ACCESS FULL| EMP  |    1 |    17 |     5   (0)| 00:00:01 |
---------------------------------------------------------------------

Note
-----
   - dynamic sampling used for this statement
```

```
Statistics
-----------------------------------------------------------
        28  recursive calls
         0  db block gets
        33  consistent gets
```

To turn off AUTOTRACE use the OFF option:

```
SQL> set autotrace off;
```

■ **Note** An execution pan is also commonly referred to as an explain plan. This is because you can use the SQL EXPLAIN PLAN statement to generate an execution plan.

How It Works

The AUTOTRACE facility can be invoked in several modes. For example, if you only want to generate statistics (and not generate a result set), use AUTOTRACE in this mode:

```
SQL> set autotrace trace explain
```

To view all AUTOTRACE options, type in this statement:

```
SQL> set autotrace help
Usage: SET AUTOT[RACE] {OFF | ON | TRACE[ONLY]} [EXP[LAIN]] [STAT[ISTICS]]
```

Actually, the previous statement displays help because the HELP option doesn't exist, and AUTOTRACE will automatically display the usage when an incorrect option has been entered. Table 19-1 explains the different modes in which AUTOTRACE can be invoked.

Table 19-1. AUTOTRACE Options

Option(s)	Result
SET AUTOTRACE ON	Query output, explain plan, statistics
SET AUTOTRACE OFF	Turns AUTOTRACE off
SET AUTOTRACE ON EXPLAIN	Query output, explain plan, no statistics
SET AUTOTRACE ON EXPLAIN STAT	Query output, explain plan, statistics
SET AUTOTRACE ON STAT	Query output, statistics, no explain plan
SET AUTOTRACE TRACE	Explain plan, statistics, result generated but not displayed

Table 19-1. *AUTOTRACE Options (continued)*

Option(s)	Result
SET AUTOTRACE TRACE EXPLAIN	Explain plan only, no result set generated
SET AUTOTRACE TRACE STAT	Statistics only, result set generated but not displayed.

19-8. Generating an Execution Plan Using DBMS_XPLAN

Problem

You want a handy way to view an execution plan.

Solution

A useful way for viewing statistics is to use the DBMS_XPLAN package. Before you use this technique, ensure that a PLAN_TABLE is available:

```
SQL> desc plan_table
```

If the PLAN_TABLE doesn't exist, you'll need to create one. Run this query to create the PLAN_TABLE in your schema:

```
SQL> @?/rdbms/admin/utlxplan
```

Now create an entry in the PLAN_TABLE for the SQL statement you want explained. Use the EXPLAIN PLAN FOR statement to do this:

```
explain plan for select emp_id from emp;
```

Next, display the explain plan by calling the DBMS_XPLAN package via a SELECT statement:

```
select * from table(dbms_xplan.display);
```

Here is partial listing of the output:

```
Plan hash value: 610802841

--------------------------------------------------------------------------
| Id  | Operation            | Name | Rows  | Bytes | Cost (%CPU)| Time     |
--------------------------------------------------------------------------
|   0 | SELECT STATEMENT     |      |     3 |    27 |     3   (0)| 00:00:01|
|   1 |  PARTITION RANGE ALL |      |     3 |    27 |     3   (0)| 00:00:01|
|   2 |   TABLE ACCESS FULL  | EMP  |     3 |    27 |     3   (0)| 00:00:01|
--------------------------------------------------------------------------
```

For ease of use, you can create a view that selects from the DBMS_XPLAN.DISPLAY function:

```
create view pt as select * from table(dbms_xplan.display);
```

You can now select from the PT view:

```
select * from pt;
```

How It Works

DBMS_XPLAN is a useful tool for displaying the explain plan in several different formats. There are a number of helpful functions included with DBMS_XPLAN package (see Table 19-2 for details). For example, if a particular query shows up in the top CPU-consuming SQL statements section of your AWR report, you can run an explain plan for that query via the DISPLAY_AWR function:

```
select * from table(dbms_xplan.display_awr('413xuwws268a3'));
```

Table 19-2. Functions Available in DBMS_XPLAN

Procedure	Purpose
DISPLAY	Displays execution plan for PLAN_TABLE contents.
DISPLAY_AWR	Displays execution plan for a SQL statement stored in AWR repository.
DISPLAY_CURSOR	Displays execution for a cursor.
DISPLAY_SQL_PLAN_BASELINE	Displays execution plan for SQL identified by SQL handle.
DISPLAY_SQLSET	Displays execution plan for SQL contained in SQL tuning set.

DBMS_XPLAN is also handy for displaying the contents of V$SQL_PLAN for a query using DISPLAY_CURSOR. For example, to display the explain plan for the current query, first run the query:

```
select * from parties where party_id = 1;
```

Now generate the explain plan for the most recently executed query in the session:

```
select * from table(dbms_xplan.display_cursor(null, null));
```

Here is a partial listing of the output (truncated in order to fit on the page):

```
--------------------------------------------------------------------------
| Id  | Operation        | Name         | Rows  | Bytes | Cost (%CPU)| Time     |
--------------------------------------------------------------------------
|   0 | SELECT STATEMENT |              |       |       |    1 (100)|          |
|   1 |  TABLE ACCESS BY | PARTIES      |     1 |    47 |    1   (0)| 00:00:01 |
|*  2 |   INDEX UNIQUE SC| SYS_C0047742 |     1 |       |    1   (0)| 00:00:01 |
--------------------------------------------------------------------------
```

19-9. Tracing All SQL Statements for a Session

Problem

A user running an application that calls hundreds of SQL statements is having performance issues. You want to determine specifically which statements are consuming the most resources.

Solution

You can instruct Oracle to capture resources consumed and execution plans for all SQL statements run by a session. One technique for enabling SQL tracing is to use the DBMS_SESSION package. You'll need the ALTER SESSION privilege granted to your schema before you can execute this:

```
SQL> exec dbms_session.set_sql_trace(sql_trace=>true);
```

■ **Note** The TIMED_STATISTICS initialization parameter must be set to TRUE (the default setting) before you can generate SQL trace statistics.

Now any SQL you run will be traced. For demonstration purposes, we'll trace the following SQL statement:

```
select 'my_trace' from dual;
```

To turn off SQL tracing for a session, you can either log out of SQL*Plus or use DBMS_SESSION to disable tracing:

```
SQL> exec dbms_session.set_sql_trace(sql_trace=>false);
```

Now inspect the value of your USER_DUMP_DEST initialization parameter:

```
SQL> show parameter user_dump_dest

NAME                         TYPE        VALUE
---------------------------- ----------- ---------------------------------------
user_dump_dest               string      /oracle/diag/rdbms/rmdb11/RMDB11/trace
```

From the operating system, navigate to the user dump destination directory:

```
$ cd /oracle/diag/rdbms/rmdb11/RMDB11/trace
```

■ **Tip** You can assign your trace file an easily identifiable name by setting the `TRACEFILE_IDENTIFIER` initialization parameter before you enable tracing. For example, `ALTER SESSION SET TRACEFILE_IDENTIFIER=FOO` will produce a trace file with the name of `<SID>_ora_<PID>_FOO.trc`.

There may be hundreds of trace files in your user dump destination directory. Look for the most recent files. In this example, we know that our trace file will contain the string of `my_trace` within it (from running the SQL above). In a Unix environment, you can search for that string with the grep command:

```
$ grep -i my_trace *.trc
RMDB11_ora_21846.trc: select 'my_trace' from dual
```

Oracle provides the `tkprof` command line utlity to translate the contents of a trace file into human-readable format. This utility is located in the `ORACLE_HOME/bin` directory (along with all other standard Oracle utilities like `sqlplus`, `expdp`, and so on). Provide `tkprof` with the username and password of the schema you used to generate the trace file (in this example it's `heera`/`foo`):

```
$ tkprof RMDB11_ora_21846.trc readable.txt explain=heera/foo sys=no
```

■ **Tip** Run `tkprof` from the command line without any parameters to view all options for this utility. By default, SQL statements are reported in the order in which they were run. You can alter the sort order using the SORT parameter to order the output by CPU, disk reads, elapsed time, and so on.

Now inspect the `readable.txt` file with a text editor. Here is some sample output from the text file:

call	count	cpu	elapsed	disk	query	current	rows
Parse	1	0.01	0.01	0	0	0	0
Execute	1	0.00	0.00	0	0	0	0
Fetch	2	0.00	0.00	2	3	0	1
total	4	0.01	0.01	2	3	0	1

```
Misses in library cache during parse: 1
Optimizer mode: ALL_ROWS
Parsing user id: 28  (HEERA)
Rows     Row Source Operation
-------  ---------------------------------------------------
      1   SORT AGGREGATE (cr=3 pr=2 pw=2 time=0 us)
    103    TABLE ACCESS FULL EMP (cr=3 pr=2 pw=2 time=4 us cost=2 size=0 card=103)
```

```
Rows     Execution Plan
-------  ------------------------------------------------------
      0  SELECT STATEMENT    MODE: ALL_ROWS
      1    SORT (AGGREGATE)
    103    TABLE ACCESS   MODE: ANALYZED (FULL) OF 'EMP' (TABLE)
```

The tkprof output gives detailed information on the resources consumed by each SQL statement issued while tracing was enabled. Use this utility to identify which SQL statements are potential bottlenecks and tune them accordingly.

■ **Tip** By default, the permissions on trace files only permit the Oracle software operating system owner to view the files. To enable public read permissions on the trace files, set the initialization parameter _TRACE_FILES_PUBLIC to TRUE. However, you should do this only on test or development systems where developers need access to trace files for tuning purposes.

How It Works

Sometimes a user may be running an application in which hundreds of queries are executed. In such scenarios, it may be hard to pinpoint exactly which SQL statement is causing performance issues (especially when it's the cumulative cost rather than the unitary cost that is high). In these situations you can turn on SQL tracing to capture statistics regarding all SQL statements run by a user.

Moreover, when SQL is dynamically generated via the application, there's no way for you to tell from the source code what SQL may be causing performance issues. You may have a situation in which the SQL generated by the application changes from one run to the next. In such situations you'll have to turn on SQL tracing for a session to record resources consumed by all SQL statements issued for that session. Also, the tracing output allows you to view the actual execution plan.

Here are the general steps to take to trace a session:

1. Enable tracing.

2. Run the SQL statements you want traced.

3. Disable tracing.

4. Use a utility such as tkprof, trcsess, or the Oracle Trace Analyzer to translate the trace file into a human-readable format

Oracle provides a wide variety of methods to generate a SQL resource usage trace file (quite frankly, to the point of being confusing), including:

DBMS_SESSION

DBMS_MONITOR

DBMS_SYSTEM

DBMS_SUPPORT

ALTER SESSION

ALTER SYSTEM

oradebug

The method you use depends on your personal preferences and various aspects of your environment, such as the version of the database and PL/SQL packages installed. Each of these tracing methods is described briefly in the following subsections.

Using DBMS_SESSION

Using the DBMS_SESSION package was covered in the solution section of this recipe. Here's a brief summary of how to enable and disable tracing using DBMS_SESSION:

```
SQL> exec dbms_session.set_sql_trace(sql_trace=>true);
SQL> -- run sql statements that you want to trace...
SQL> exec dbms_session.set_sql_trace(sql_trace=>false);
```

Using DBMS_MONITOR

If you are using Oracle Database 10*g* or higher, we recommend using the DBMS_MONITOR package, which offers a high degree of flexibility, for facilitating tracing. To enable and disable tracing within the current session use the following statements:

```
SQL> exec dbms_monitor.session_trace_enable;
SQL> -- run sql statements that you want to trace...
SQL> exec dbms_monitor.session_trace_disable;
```

Use the WAIT and BINDS parameters to enable tracing with wait and bind variable information:

```
SQL> exec dbms_monitor.session_trace_enable(waits=>TRUE, binds=>TRUE);
```

■ **Note** Wait events track the amount of time spent waiting for a resource. Bind variables are substitution variables used in place of literal variables.

Use the SESSION_ID and SERIAL_NUM parameters to enable and disable tracing for an already connected session. First run this SQL query to determine the SESSION_ID and SERIAL_NUM for target session:

```
select username,sid,serial# from v$session;
```

Now use the appropriate values when calling DBMS_SESSION:

```
SQL> exec dbms_monitor.session_trace_enable(session_id=>1234, serial_num=>12345);
SQL> -- run sql statements that you want to trace...
SQL> exec dbms_monitor.session_trace_disable(session_id=>1234, serial_num=>12345);
```

You can also enable the tracing of wait and bind variable information as follows:

```
SQL> exec dbms_monitor.session_trace_enable(session_id=>1234, -
> serial_num=>12345, waits=>TRUE, binds=>TRUE);
```

Using DBMS_SYSTEM

To enable SQL tracing in another session, you can use the DBMS_SYSTEM package. You first must identify the session you want to trace:

```
select username,sid,serial# from v$session;
```

Pass the appropriate values to the following lines of code:

```
SQL> exec dbms_system.set_sql_trace_in_session(sid=>200,serial#=>5,-
> sql_trace=>true);
```

Run the following to disable tracing for the session:

```
SQL> exec dbms_system.set_sql_trace_in_session(sid=>200,serial#=>5,-
> sql_trace=>false);
```

You can also use DBMS_SYSTEM to capture wait events:

```
SQL> exec dbms_system.set_ev(si=>123, se=>1234, ev=>10046, le=>8, nm=>' ');
SQL> exec dbms_system.set_ev(si=>123, se=>1234, ev=>10046, le=>0, nm=>' ');
```

Using DBMS_SUPPORT

This technique requires that you first load the DBMS_SUPPORT package (it's not created by default):
```
SQL> @?/rdbms/admin/dbmssupp.sql
```

Use the following syntax to enable and disable tracing in your current session:

```
SQL> exec dbms_support.start_trace(waits=>TRUE, binds=>TRUE);
SQL> exec dbms_support.stop_trace;
```

Use this syntax to enable and disable tracing in session other than your own:

```
SQL> exec dbms_support.start_trace_in_session(sid=>123, serial=>1234,-
> waits=>TRUE, binds=>TRUE);
SQL> exec dbms_support.stop_trace_in_session(sid=>123, serial=>1234);
```

Altering Your Session

You can use ALTER SESSION to turn tracing on and off:

```
SQL> alter session set sql_trace=true;
SQL> -- run sql commands...
SQL> alter session set sql_trace=false;
```

■ **Note** The `SQL_TRACE` parameter is deprecated. Oracle recommends that you use the `DBMS_MONITOR` or `DBMS_SESSION` packages to enable tracing.

Sometimes it's useful to see where the SQL statement is waiting for resources within the database. To instruct Oracle to write wait information to the trace file, use the following syntax:

```
SQL> alter session set events '10046 trace name context forever, level 8';
SQL> -- run sql commands...
SQL> alter session set events '10046 trace name context off';
```

The `LEVEL 8` instructs Oracle to write wait events to the trace file. If you want to view wait events and bind variables, specify `LEVEL 12`.

■ **Tip** On Unix systems inspect the `ORACLE_HOME/rdbms/mesg/oraus.msg` file for a description of Oracle events.

Oracle provides a tool called the Trace Analyzer that will parse SQL trace files and produce comprehensive tuning reports. See My Oracle Support (formerly known as MetaLink) note 224270.1 for details.

Sometimes when tracing an application, the trace files can span multiple files. In such cases, use the `trcsess` utility to translate multiple trace files into one readable output file.

Altering the System

You can turn on tracing for all sessions in the database by using this `ALTER SYSTEM` statement:

```
SQL> alter system set sql_trace=true;
```

Use the following SQL to disable system-wide tracing:

```
SQL> alter system set sql_trace=false;
```

■ **Caution** We recommend that you don't set SQL tracing at the system level as it can severely degrade system performance.

Using oradebug

The oradebug utility can be used to enable and disable tracing for a session. You need SYSDBA privileges to run this utility.

You can identify a process to trace either by its operating system process ID or its Oracle process ID. To determine these IDs, run the following SQL query for the username you want to trace (in this example the user is HEERA):

```
select spid os_pid, pid ora_pid from v$process
where addr=(select paddr from v$session where username='HEERA');
```

Here is the output for this example:

```
OS_PID                          ORA_PID
------------------------ ----------
31064                                23
```

Next, use oradebug with either the SETOSPID or SETORAPID option to attach oradebug to a session. This example uses the SETOSPID option:

```
SQL> oradebug setospid 31064;
```

Now you can set tracing on for the session:

```
SQL> oradebug EVENT 10046 TRACE NAME CONTEXT FOREVER, LEVEL 8;
```

You can verify that tracing is enabled by viewing the trace file name:

```
SQL> oradebug TRACEFILE_NAME;
```

Use the following syntax to disable tracing:

```
SQL> oradebug EVENT 10046 TRACE NAME CONTEXT OFF;
```
Use the HELP option to view all features available in the oradebug utility:

```
SQL> oradebug help
```

DBMS_TRACE

The DBMS_TRACE package isn't a SQL tracing utility, it's a PL/SQL debugging tool. To prepare an environment to use DBMS_TRACE, first run the following SQL scripts as SYS:

```
SQL> @?/rdbms/admin/tracetab.sql
SQL> @?/rdbms/admin/dbmspbt.sql
```

You can now enable PL/SQL tracing in either of two ways. The first method is with the ALTER SESSION command:

```
SQL> alter session set plsql_debug=true;
```

The second method is to use the `ALTER` command to compile with the `DEBUG` option:

```
SQL> alter <procedure | function | package body> compile debug;
```

Now you can trace the PL/SQL code by calling the `DBMS_TRACE` package as follows:

```
SQL> exec dbms_trace.set_plsql_trace(dbms_trace.trace_all_lines);
```

Any PL/SQL you run will now be traced. Issue the following to turn tracing off:

```
SQL> exec dbms_trace.clear_plsql_trace();
```

To view PL/SQL tracing information, query the `SYS`-owned `PLSQL_TRACE_EVENTS` table:

```
select
  event_seq, stack_depth, event_kind,
  event_unit, event_line, event_comment
from sys.plsql_trace_events;
```

The `DBMS_TRACE` package gives you a useful technique for debugging PL/SQL code.

19-10. Interpreting an Execution Plan

Problem

You're looking at the formatted output of an execution plan from a utility such as AUTOTRACE (see recipe 19-7 for details on AUTOTRACE). You wonder how to interpret the output.

Solution

An *execution plan* is a line-by-line description of how Oracle will retrieve and process a result set for a SQL statement. Each line in the execution plan describes how Oracle will physically retrieve rows from the database or process rows that have been retrieved in previous steps. Here are some guidelines for determining the order in which the steps are run in a formatted execution plan (such as the output of AUTOTRACE):

- If there are two steps at the same level of indentation then the topmost step is executed first.

- For a given step, the most heavily indented substep is executed first.

- When the operation completes, it passes its results up to the next level.

A simple example will help illustrate these concepts. An explain plan is generated for this query with the SET AUTOTRACE statement:

```
SET AUTOTRACE TRACE EXPLAIN
select
  p.first_name
 ,a.address1
```

```
   ,i.invoice_id
from parties   p
    ,addresses a
    ,invoice_transactions i
where a.party_id   = p.party_id
and    p.first_name = 'HEERA'
and    p.party_id   = i.party_id;
```

Here is a partial listing of the corresponding plan:

```
--------------------------------------------------------------------------------
| Id  | Operation              | Name                | Rows  | Bytes | Cost (%CPU)|
--------------------------------------------------------------------------------
|   0 | SELECT STATEMENT       |                     |    39 |  1716 |  375   (1)|
|*  1 |  HASH JOIN             |                     |    39 |  1716 |  375   (1)|
|*  2 |   HASH JOIN            |                     |     2 |    70 |   32   (4)|
|*  3 |    TABLE ACCESS FULL   | PARTIES             |     2 |    22 |   22   (0)|
|   4 |    TABLE ACCESS FULL   | ADDRESSES           |  1664 | 39936 |    9   (0)|
|   5 |    TABLE ACCESS FULL   | INVOICE_TRANSACTIONS| 34072 |  299K |  342   (1)|
--------------------------------------------------------------------------------
```

From this output, the rightmost indented operations are full table scans of the PARTIES and ADDRESSES tables. Since they are at the same level of indentation, the topmost full table scan on PARTIES is performed first (ID 3). Next the ADDRESSES table is scanned (ID 4). The output of these two operations is combined through a hash join (ID 2). Another hash join (ID 1) combines the output of the previous hash join (ID 2) with the full table access of the INVOICE_TRANSACTIONS table (ID 5). The result is returned to the calling SQL SELECT statement.

The explain plan output indicates that the full table scan operation in step ID 5 has a cost of 342 and does a full table scan of the INVOICE_TRANSACTIONS table. The INVOICE_TRANSACTIONS table is joined to the PARTIES table on the PARTY_ID column. In an attempt to lower the cost, an index is added to the PARTY_ID column of INVOICE_TRANSACTIONS:

```
SQL> create index inv_trans_idx1 on invoice_transactions(party_id);
```

An explain plan is regenerated by running the original query again:

```
select
  p.first_name
 ,a.address1
 ,i.invoice_id
from parties   p
    ,addresses a
    ,invoice_transactions i
where a.party_id   = p.party_id
and    p.first_name = 'HEERA'
and    p.party_id   = i.party_id;
```

Here's the partial output showing that the cost has been significantly reduced:

```
----------------------------------------------------------------------------
| Id | Operation                    | Name                 | Rows |Bytes|Cost(%CPU)|
----------------------------------------------------------------------------
|   0 |SELECT STATEMENT             |                      |   39 | 1716|  55 (0) |
|   1 | NESTED LOOPS                |                      |      |     |         |
|   2 |  NESTED LOOPS               |                      |   39 | 1716|  55 (0) |
|*  3 |   HASH JOIN                 |                      |    2 |   70|  32 (4) |
|*  4 |    TABLE ACCESS FULL        | PARTIES              |    2 |   22|  22 (0) |
|   5 |    TABLE ACCESS FULL        | ADDRESSES            | 1664 |39936|   9 (0) |
|*  6 |   INDEX RANGE SCAN          | INV_TRANS_IDX1       |   20 |     |   1 (0) |
|   7 |  TABLE ACCESS BY INDEX ROWID| INVOICE_TRANSACTIONS |   20 |  180|  22 (0) |
----------------------------------------------------------------------------
```

The preceding exercise was a simple example of how adding an index improved the performance of one query. Be aware that adding an index that speeds up one query can potentially have adverse effects on other aspects of the application. An index will minimally add the overhead of additional disk space and processing to maintain the index when the table is inserted, updated, or deleted from. You should add the index in a test environment and verify that it improves performance without unintended side effects. Additional considerations would be the type of index (B-tree, bitmap, and so on), storage characteristics, and the index's tablespace.

■ **Note** The *cost* of each row is the optimizer's weighted estimate of how expensive each step is in terms of system resources such as CPU, I/O, and memory. The cost doesn't have a unit of measurement per se; rather it's a number that the optimizer uses to compare execution plans and steps. In general, the lower the cost the better the expected performance of the operation and query.

How It Works

When interpreting each step of the execution plan, each ID in the plan is associated with an operation. The two types of operations that have the biggest impact on performance are:

- Access Path
- Join Method

The *access path* describes how data is retrieved from the database. Table 19-3 describes the most common execution plan access paths. In general, when a small subset of a table's data is to be retrieved, an index access path should be used. When a large portion of a table's data is returned, a full table scan may be more appropriate.

Table 19-3. *Most Common Access Paths*

Access Path	Description
Full table scan	All rows from a table are read, which is efficient when large portions of a table's rows need to be read. When only small portions of the table need to be read, an index may be created to eliminate full table scans.
Rowid scan	Locates a row by ROWID. The ROWID contains the physical location of the row within a datafile and a block, efficient when a relatively small number of rows are retrieved, less efficient when large portion of a table is read.
Index scan	An index contains key values and a ROWID. If the query only needs information contained in the index key values, Oracle returns those values, otherwise it uses the ROWID to retrieve additional data from the table row.

Join methods are techniques the optimizer uses to retrieve data from multiple tables. Join statements result from tables joined in the WHERE clause. Table 19-4 provides an overview of the various join methods. The optimizer must compute the following for each join statement:

- Access path for returning rows for each table in the join

- Join method

- Join order when more than two tables are involved in the join

Table 19-4. *Join Methods*

Join Method	Description
Nested loop	Useful when joining small subsets of data and there is a unique index or highly selective indexed access to the second table (inner) in the join.
Hash join	Efficient for joining large sets of data. A hash table is built in memory on the join key of the smaller table or result set. The larger table is scanned and uses the hash table to retrieve rows.
Sort merge join	Joins rows from two independent tables or result sets. Sort merge joins are efficient when rows are already sorted. Hash joins are usually more efficient than sort merge joins.
Cartesian join	Used when no join condition is present.
Outer join	Returns from one table rows that don't satisfy the join condition.

The execution plan (sometimes referred to as the explain plan) is a handy tool used by DBAs and developers for improving the performance of SQL queries. If you're new to using execution plans, follow these heuristics to get started:

- Establish how fast the query needs to run.

- Ensure that accurate statistics have been generated (see recipe 19-13 for details).

- Determine if indexes exist for columns used in the WHERE clause (see recipe 10-5 for viewing indexes created on a table).

- Focus on the most costly steps in the execution plan and determine if an index on a column involved in the operation might reduce the cost (see recipe 18-7 for details on creating indexes).

- When querying large tables, determine if a parallel hint might help.

- Determine if the query (or parts of it) can be rewritten for better performance.

The results of an execution plan can sometimes be non-intuitive because the optimizer will determine that using an index is too costly. Or the optimizer might determine that a full table scan is more efficient than using an index.

When developing queries, it's sometimes useful to write in stages and analyze the execution plan after each stage. For example, you may have a query that joins five tables and has several conditions in the WHERE clause. Don't wait until you have the fully developed query to generate an explain plan. Instead, generate an execution plan as you iteratively add tables and conditions to the WHERE clause.

If you generate an explain plan with statistics turned on (via SET AUTOTRACE ON STATISTICS) you will also see output such as this:

```
Statistics
----------------------------------------------------------
        276  recursive calls
          0  db block gets
         51  consistent gets
          7  physical reads
          0  redo size
        583  bytes sent via SQL*Net to client
        524  bytes received via SQL*Net from client
          2  SQL*Net roundtrips to/from client
          4  sorts (memory)
          0  sorts (disk)
          3  rows processed
```

These statistics are described in Table 19-5. In general, one of the goals of query tuning is to try to reduce the number of consistent gets required by a query.

Table 19-5. *Execution Plan Statistics*

Statistic	Description
recursive calls	Preliminary work performed by Oracle such as checking syntax, semantics, permissions, looking up data dictionary information, and so on.
db block gets	Number of times Oracle needs the current version of a block.

Table 19-5. *Execution Plan Statistics (continued)*

Statistic	Description
consistent gets	Number of times consistent versions of blocks were read. The consistent versions of the blocks are the blocks as they were when the SQL statement started. Logical reads are db block gets plus consistent gets.
physical reads	Number of blocks read from disk because the block was not found in memory.
redo size	Amount of information Oracle writes to the redo stream for a SQL operation.
bytes sent via SQL*Net to client	Number of bytes sent to the client tool.
bytes received via SQL*Net from client	Number of bytes received from the client tool.
SQL*Net roundtrips to/from client	Number of times data was sent to and from client.
sorts (memory)	Number of sorting operations performed in memory.
sorts (disk)	Number of sorting operations performed on disk.
rows processed	Total number of rows returned by query.

19-11. Obtaining SQL Tuning Advice

Problem

You want advice on how to improve performance of a problem query.

Solution

Use the SQL Tuning Advisor to display suggestions on how to improve the performance of a query.

■ **Note** As of the writing of this book, the SQL Tuning Advisor is part of the Oracle Database Tuning Pack and requires an extra-cost license.

Follow these steps to get tuning suggestions from the Advisor:

1. Connect as a privileged user and issue the following grants to the schema that will be performing the tuning analysis:

```
GRANT ADMINISTER SQL TUNING SET TO &&tune_user;
GRANT ADVISOR TO &&tune_user;
GRANT CREATE ANY SQL PROFILE TO &&tune_user;
GRANT ALTER ANY SQL PROFILE TO &&tune_user;
GRANT DROP ANY SQL PROFILE TO &&tune_user;
```

If you're using Oracle Database 11g, the previous GRANT ... ANY SQL PROFILE statements can be replaced with:

```
GRANT ADMINISTER SQL MANAGEMENT OBJECT TO &&tune_user;
```

2. Create a tuning task using the DBMS_SQLTUNE package. Change the following code to match the query you're attempting to tune and also your user name:

```
DECLARE
 tune_task_name VARCHAR2(30);
 tune_sql CLOB;
BEGIN
 tune_sql := 'select a.emp_name, b.dept_name from emp a, dept b';
 tune_task_name := DBMS_SQLTUNE.CREATE_TUNING_TASK(
   sql_text     => tune_sql,
   user_name    => 'STAR_APR',
   scope        => 'COMPREHENSIVE',
   time_limit   => 1800,
   task_name    => 'tune1',
   description  => 'Basic tuning example'
);
END;
/
```

3. Verify that your tuning task exists by querying the USER_ADVISOR_LOG view:

```
SQL> SELECT task_name FROM user_advisor_log WHERE task_name LIKE 'tune1';
```

4. Run the tuning task:

```
SQL> EXEC DBMS_SQLTUNE.EXECUTE_TUNING_TASK(task_name=>'tune1');
```

5. Display the SQL Tuning Advisor report. Run the following SQL statements to display the output:

```
SET LONG 10000
SET LONGCHUNKSIZE 10000
SET LINESIZE 132
SET PAGESIZE 200
--
SELECT DBMS_SQLTUNE.REPORT_TUNING_TASK('tune1') FROM dual;
```

Here is a partial snippet of the output:

```
3- Restructure SQL finding (see plan 1 in explain plans section)
-----------------------------------------------------------------
 An expensive cartesian product operation was found at line ID 1 of the
 execution plan.
```

```
Recommendation
--------------
- Consider removing the disconnected table or view from this statement or
  add a join condition which refers to it.

Rationale
---------
  A cartesian product should be avoided whenever possible because it is an
  expensive operation and might produce a large amount of data.
```

As you can see from the previous output, the SQL Tuning Advisor report correctly recommends rewriting the query so that it doesn't use a cartesian join.

How It Works

The SQL Tuning Advisor helps automate the task of tuning poorly performing queries. The tool is fairly easy to use and the tuning output report provides detailed suggestions on how to tune a query.

If you need to drop a tuning task, use the DBMS_SQLTUNE package as follows:

```
SQL> EXEC DBMS_SQLTUNE.DROP_TUNING_TASK(task_name=>'tune1');
```

■ **Note** The SQL Tuning Advisor is also available in Oracle Enterprise Manager. If you have access to Enterprise Manager, you may find it easier to use the graphical interface.

19-12. Forcing Your Own Execution Plan on a Query

Problem

You suspect that the optimizer isn't using an index that is available. You want to force the optimizer to use the index and see if the cost of the query is reduced.

Solution

The syntax for a hint is to place the following comment /*+ <hint> */ immediately after the SELECT keyword. The following code uses the INDEX hint to instruct the optimizer to use the EMP_IDX1 index on the EMP table:

```
SELECT /*+ INDEX (emp emp_idx1) */
  ename
FROM emp
WHERE ename='Chaya';
```

If you use table aliases, ensure that the alias is referenced in the hint, not the table name. When using aliases, the hint will be ignored if you use the table name within the hint. The following example references the table alias within the full table scan hint:

```
SELECT /*+ FULL(a) */ ename
FROM emp a
WHERE ename='Heera';
```

If you misspell the name of a hint or make a typo in a table alias or index name, Oracle will ignore the hint. You can verify that a hint is being used by setting AUTOTRACE ON and viewing the execution plan. Keep in mind that in some situations Oracle will ignore a hint. Oracle may determine that the hint directive is not feasible for a given scenario and thus reject your suggestion.

How It Works

SQL hints allow you to override the optimizer's choices in an execution plan. Sometimes query performance issues can be improved because you know something about your environment that the optimizer isn't aware of (much like the sport or landscape settings on your camera).

For example, suppose you have a data warehouse database that is using the system-wide setting of ALL_ROWS, but you also want to run an OLTP reporting query against the database that will execute more efficiently with the FIRST_ROWS setting. In this situation, you can hint the optimizer to use FIRST_ROWS instead of ALL_ROWS.

We recommend that you use hints sparingly. Before using a hint, first try to figure out why the optimizer isn't choosing an efficient execution plan. Investigate if the query can be rewritten or if adding an index or generating fresh statistics will help. Relying on hints for good performance is time-consuming and could cause you issues when upgrading to newer versions of the database.

In the most recent versions of Oracle, there are well over 200 different hints. It's beyond the scope of this recipe to describe every hint. Table 19-6 describes the major categories of hints.

■ **Tip** Starting with Oracle Database 11*g*, you can query V$SQL_HINT for information about hints.

Table 19-6 .*SQL Hint Categories*

Category of Hint	Description	Hint Examples
Optimizer goal	Optimizes throughput or responsiveness.	ALL_ROWS, FIRST_ROWS
Access paths	Path to retrieve data.	INDEX, NO_INDEX, FULL
Query transformations	Execute query in a different manner.	STAR_TRANSFORMATION, MERGE, FACT, REWRITE
Join Orders	Alter the order of the tables to be joined.	ORDERED, LEADING

Table 19-6. *SQL Hint Categories (continued)*

Category of Hint	Description	Hint Examples
Parallel operations	Execute in parallel.	PARALLEL, PARALLEL_INDEX, NOPARALLEL
Join operations	How to join tables.	USE_NL, USE_MERGE, USE_HASH
Miscellaneous	Sometimes useful hints that don't fit in a specific category.	APPEND, CACHE, DRIVING_SITE

19-13. Viewing Optimizer Statistics

Problem

You're experiencing performance issues. You want to determine if statistics exist for the tables being queried.

Solution

A quick and easy way to check if statistics are accurate is to compare the NUM_ROWS column in USER_TABLES with the actual row count of a table. The following script will prompt you for a table name:

```
select a.num_rows/b.actual_rows
from user_tables a
   ,(select count(*) actual_rows from &&table_name) b
where a.table_name=upper('&&table_name');
```

The next script uses SQL to generate the prior SQL for all tables for a user. The script uses SQL*Plus formatting commands to turn off headings and page breaks:

```
set head off pages 0 lines 132 trimspool on
spo show_stale.sql
select
  'select ' || '''' || table_name || ': ' || '''' || '||' || chr(10) ||
  ' round(decode(b.actual_rows,0,0,a.num_rows/b.actual_rows),2) ' || chr(10) ||
  'from user_tables a ' ||
  ',(select count(*) actual_rows from ' || table_name || ') b' || chr(10) ||
  'where a.table_name=(' || '''' || table_name || '''' || ');'
from user_tables;
spo off;
```

This script produces a file named show_stale.sql that you can execute to display the staleness of table statistics.

How It Works

The scripts in the solution section use the NUM_ROWS column that is populated when statistics are gathered. If the percentage of NUM_ROWS to actual rows is more than 10% different from the actual rows, the statistics are probably stale.

There are a few other techniques for determining if statistics have been recently generated. For example, you can check the LAST_ANALYZED column of the USER_TABLES and USER_INDEXES views to determine the last time your tables and indexes were analyzed. This following query displays the last time tables were analyzed for the current schema:

```
select
  table_name
 ,last_analyzed
 ,monitoring
from user_tables
order by last_analyzed;
```

This next query reports the last time indexes were analyzed for the current schema:

```
select
  index_name
 ,last_analyzed
from user_indexes
order by last_analyzed;
```

Viewing the last time statistics were generated for tables and indexes in a vacuum can be somewhat misleading. The LAST_ANALYZED column does tell you if statistics have ever been generated, but that's about it. The LAST_ANALYZED time doesn't provide enough information to determine whether the statistics might need to be re-generated.

For more detailed information about table statistics use the USER_TAB_STATISTICS view. This view contains information about the many optimizer statistics that are generated for tables. For example, this view has a STALE_STATS column that is an indicator of whether or not Oracle thinks the statistics are stale. The following query displays statistics such as SAMPLE_SIZE and STALE_STATS:

```
select
  table_name
 ,partition_name
 ,last_analyzed
 ,num_rows
 ,sample_size
 ,stale_stats
from user_tab_statistics
order by last_analyzed;
```

Similar to the table statistics, you can also view index statistics by querying the USER_IND_STATISTICS view:

```
select
  index_name
 ,partition_name
```

```
  ,last_analyzed
  ,num_rows
  ,sample_size
  ,stale_stats
from user_ind_statistics
order by last_analyzed;
```

If you want to determine how much INSERT, UPDATE, DELETE, and TRUNCATE activity has occurred since the last time statistics were generated, query the USER_TAB_MODIFICATIONS view. For example, you may have a situation in which a table is truncated before a large load of new records are inserted. You can run a query like the following to verify that that type of activity has occurred since the last time statistics were generated:

```
select
  table_name
 ,partition_name
 ,inserts
 ,updates
 ,deletes
 ,truncated
 ,timestamp
from user_tab_modifications
order by table_name;
```

If you detect that there have been significant changes to the data in a table, you should consider generating the statistics manually (see recipe 19-14 for details).

■ **Note** The USER_TAB_MODIFICATIONS view isn't updated instantaneously. Oracle will periodically flush results to this table from memory. To force Oracle to flush these statistics from memory, run the DBMS_STATS.FLUSH_DATABASE_MONITORING_INFO procedure.

19-14. Generating Statistics

Problem

You just finished loading a large amount of new data into a table. You're now experiencing performance problems and you want to generate statistics for the table that was just loaded.

Solution

Use the DBMS_STATS package to generate fresh statistics. In this next bit of code, statistics are generated for the STAR1 schema.

```
SQL> exec dbms_stats.gather_schema_stats(ownname => 'STAR1',-
  estimate_percent => DBMS_STATS.AUTO_SAMPLE_SIZE,-
  degree => DBMS_STATS.AUTO_DEGREE,-
  cascade => true);
```

The ESTIMATE_PERCENT parameter is set to AUTO_SAMPLE_SIZE. This instructs Oracle to determine the optimal sample size.

The DEGREE parameter is set to AUTO_DEGREE. This allows Oracle to choose the optimal parallel degree depending on the hardware and initialization parameters.

The CASCADE value of TRUE instructs Oracle to additionally gather index statistics (for any table being analyzed).

■ **Note** You can also generate statistics with the ANALYZE statement using the COMPUTE or ESTIMATE clauses. However, Oracle highly recommends *not* using the ANALYZE statement for generating object statistics. Instead you should use the DBMS_STATS package.

How It Works

There are numerous methods for invoking DBMS_STATS. For example, if you want to generate statistics for just one table, use the GATHER_TABLE_STATS procedure. This example gathers statistics for the D_DOMAINS table:

```
SQL> exec dbms_stats.gather_table_stats(ownname=>'STAR2',tabname=>'D_DOMAINS',-
> cascade=>true, estimate_percent=>20, degree=4);
```

Starting with Oracle Database 10g, there is a default DBMS_SCHEDULER job that runs once a day that automatically analyzes your database objects. To view the last time this job ran, execute the following query:

```
select
  owner
 ,job_name
 ,last_start_date
from dba_scheduler_jobs
where job_name IN
('GATHER_STATS_JOB', -- 10g
 'BSLN_MAINTAIN_STATS_JOB' -- 11g
);
```

For many databases, this automatic statistics-gathering job is adequate. However, you may experience poor performance after a large proportion of data has been modified in the tables the SQL queries are based on. In situations where the table data changes significantly, you may want to manually generate statistics as shown in the solution section of this recipe.

When you run a query, if there are no statistics generated for a table, Oracle will by default dynamically attempt to estimate optimizer statistics. For dynamic sampling to take place, the

OPTIMIZER_DYNAMIC_SAMPLING initialization parameter must be set. In Oracle Database 10*g* and higher, the default value of this parameter is 2. If you have AUTOTRACE enabled, Oracle will denote the usage of dynamic sampling for a SQL statement as follows:

```
Note
-----
   - dynamic sampling used for this statement
```

■ ■ ■

CHAPTER 20

Database Troubleshooting

Database troubleshooting is a general term that can apply to vast a range of topics, such as resolving storage issues, investigating sluggish performance, or monitoring database objects. SQL is often the first tool you'll use to get an idea of what might be amiss in the database. Therefore, you must be familiar with SQL techniques for extracting and analyzing database information.

The recipes in this chapter are mainly for DBAs. However, if you're a developer, many of these topics will indirectly impact your ability to work efficiently with the database. Knowing the solutions to the problems described in this chapter will give you a better understanding of the Oracle architecture and will also arm you with information for troubleshooting application issues with the crusty old territorial database administrator.

DBAs, of course, need to be experts at identifying problem areas within their databases. The DBA is the go-to team member for any connectivity, performance, or availability issues. A good DBA must be proficient with SQL, especially with regard to troubleshooting.

It would be impossible to cover every type of SQL statement you can use to troubleshoot issues with your database. Rather, we present SQL insights for dealing with common database pain points. We'll begin by showing you how to identify potential problems, then explore how to deal with storage issues and database auditing.

20-1. Determining Causes of Database Problems

Problem

Users are reporting that the application using the database is acting odd. Your manager wants you to check to see if anything is wrong with the database.

Solution

When diagnosing database problems, you have to have a strategy for determining where to look for issues. For example, if a user is reporting a specific database error or if there is a detailed message in the alert log, then it's obvious to begin by investigating those reported problems.

If there's not a clear starting point, you can run an Automatic Workload Repository (AWR) report (requires a license) or a Statspack report; see Chapter 19 for more details on how to run these reports. If you don't have either of these tools at your disposal, you can query the data dictionary directly to determine if the database is stressed and what might be the root cause of the issue.

The next query uses the V$SYSSTAT view to determine the database time spent processing user requests and CPU time to infer the database wait time (by subtraction). This relates to the available time, which is the wall-clock time multiplied by the number of CPUs. The purpose of this query is to determine whether your database is spending an inordinate amount of time waiting for resources (indicative of an overloaded system):

```
select
 round(100*CPU_sec/available_time,2) "ORACLE CPU TIME AS % AVAIL."
,round(100*(DB_sec - CPU_sec)/available_time,2) "NON-IDLE WAITS AS % AVAIL."
,case
  sign(available_time - DB_sec)
  when 1 then round(100*(available_time - DB_sec) / available_time, 2)
  else 0
  end "ORACLE IDLE AS % AVAIL."
from
(
  select
    (sysdate - i.startup_time) * 86400 * c.cpus available_time
   ,t.DB_sec
   ,t.CPU_sec
  from v$instance i
 ,(select value cpus
   from v$parameter
   where name = 'cpu_count') c
 ,(select
    sum(case name
        when 'DB time' then round(value/100)
        else 0
        end) DB_sec
   ,sum(case name
        when 'DB time' then 0
        else round(value/100)
        end) CPU_sec
   from v$sysstat
   where name in ('DB time', 'CPU used by this session')) t
where i.instance_number = userenv('INSTANCE')
);
```

Here is some output:

```
ORACLE CPU TIME AS % AVAIL. NON-IDLE WAITS AS % AVAIL. ORACLE IDLE AS % AVAIL.
-------------------------- -------------------------- -----------------------
                     31.97                     129.59                       0
```

As indicated by the non-idle waits, this database is clearly under a heavy load. Now that we know we have a problem relating to waiting for resources, the next question is to determine specifically where the waits occur. The following query details where Oracle is spending its wait time. The query uses some standard SQL*Plus formatting commands to make the output more readable:

```
col wait_class format A15
col event format A35 trunc
col "CLASS AS % OF WHOLE" format 990.00 HEAD "CLASS AS|% OF WHOLE"
col "EVENT AS % OF CLASS" like "CLASS AS % OF WHOLE" HEAD "EVENT AS|% OF CLASS"
col "EVENT AS % OF WHOLE" like "CLASS AS % OF WHOLE" HEAD "EVENT AS|% OF WHOLE"
set pagesize 30
break on wait_class on "CLASS AS % OF WHOLE"
--
select
  wait_class,
  round(100 * time_class / total_waits, 2) "CLASS AS % OF WHOLE",
  event,
  round(100 * time_waited / time_class, 2) "EVENT AS % OF CLASS",
  round(100 * time_waited / total_waits, 2) "EVENT AS % OF WHOLE"
from
(select
  wait_class
 ,event
 ,time_waited
 ,sum(time_waited) over (partition by wait_class) time_class
 ,rank() over (partition by wait_class order by time_waited desc) rank_within_class
 ,sum(time_waited) over () total_waits
from v$system_event
where wait_class <> 'Idle')
where rank_within_class <= 3
order by time_class desc, rank_within_class;
```

Here is a snippet of the output:

WAIT_CLASS	CLASS AS % OF WHOLE	EVENT	EVENT AS % OF CLASS	EVENT AS % OF WHOLE
System I/O	15.50	log file parallel write	60.14	9.32
		db file parallel write	18.59	2.88
		control file parallel write	17.80	2.76
Commit	14.34	log file sync	100.00	14.34
User I/O	12.40	db file scattered read	59.47	7.37
		db file sequential read	26.11	3.24
		direct path read	5.99	0.74

From the System I/O section of the report, the log file parallel write event could indicate contention in the online redo log files. Similarly, from the User I/O section, the db file scattered read wait event could indicate that excessive full table scans are being performed by SQL queries. If you think your problem is with SQL performance, see Chapter 19 for details on how to isolate poorly performing SQL.

Table 20-1 lists some common wait events that affect performance. This is by no stretch of the imagination an exhaustive list. It is just a sample of the many types of wait events, with descriptions and possible courses of action. There are currently over 900 different types of wait events (this varies by the version of Oracle you're using). For a complete list and description of all wait events, refer to Oracle's Database Reference Guide at otn.oracle.com.

Table 20-1. *Common Database Wait Events*

Wait Event	Description	Further Examination
db file scattered read	Actual time to do I/O for multiple blocks (often caused by full table scans).	Excessive I/O, poorly performing SQL; see Chapter 19 for tuning SQL.
db file sequential read	Actual time to do I/O for single blocks (often associated with index scans).	Excessive I/O, poorly performing SQL; see Chapter 19 for tuning SQL.
free buffer waits	Wait time when no free buffers are found after inspecting cache for free buffers or waiting for dirty buffers to be written to disk.	Indicates lack of free buffers in cache; check buffer cache statistics for an undersized or oversized cache.
buffer busy waits	Wait time until buffer becomes available.	Inspect V$SESSION to determine type of block contention.
db file parallel write	Database writer wait time until I/O is complete.	Disk I/O contention.
log file parallel write	Time for I/O to complete writing redo from log buffer to disk.	Reduce I/O contention in online redo logs; move logs to dedicated disks or faster disks.
log file sync	Time flushing redo when user commits.	Reduce I/O contention in online redo logs; move logs to dedicated disks or faster disks.
log file switch (archiving needed)	Waiting for log switch because log writer will be switching to an unarchived redo log.	Archive destination possibly running out of space or archive can't read redo logs fast enough.
log file switch (checkpoint incomplete)	Waiting for log switch because checkpoint for log has not completed.	Possibly too few or undersized redo logs (see recipe 20-3).
control file parallel write	Time to finish writes to all control files.	I/O contention in control files.
SQL*Net more data to client	Time to send data from server to client to complete.	Possible network or middle-tier bottleneck.
SQL*Net more data from client	Server waiting for client to send more data.	Possible network or middle-tier bottleneck.
SQL*Net message to/from client	Communication time between user client and server.	Possibe network or middle-tier bottleneck.
enq: TX - row lock contention	Internal transaction lock.	Potential locking issue, query V$LOCK.
enq: TM - contention	Internal DML lock.	Potential locking issue, query V$LOCK.

How It Works

Sometimes developers and DBAs take the old "Battleship" approach to database troubleshooting. They randomly lob queries at the database that might help reveal an issue in a hit or miss fashion. That's an inefficient way to troubleshoot, though. Instead, we recommend you take the more focused approach to troubleshooting. First run a utility (such as AWR) or the queries provided in the solution section of this recipe to point you toward the real issue.

The queries in the solution section use Oracle's dynamic performance views V$SYSSTAT and V$SYSTEM_EVENT to help pinpoint the possible source of a database issue. Table 20-2 lists descriptions of views commonly used in troubleshooting database problems.

We realize that selecting from views such as V$SYSSTAT and V$SYSTEM_EVENT has inherent limitations because these views report on averages collected since instance startup. It would be better to query the AWR or Statspack historical views (if available). However, despite these known limitations, the solution section queries will give you a place to begin your database troubleshooting. The point is that you should start your analysis with a set of tools that will direct your efforts.

Table 20-2. *CommonlyUsed Oracle Dynamic Performance Views*

View	Description
V$SYSSTAT	System-level cumulative workload statistics.
V$SESSTAT	Session-level cumulative workload statistics.
V$SEGSTAT	Segment-level cumulative workload statistics.
V$EVENT_NAME	All wait events and associated classes.
V$SYSTEM_EVENT	Total number of times all sessions have waited for an event.
V$SESSION_EVENT	Total number of times individual sessions have waited for an event.
V$SESSION_WAIT	Events for sessions that are currently waiting or have recently completed.

20-2. Displaying Open Cursors

Problem

An application accessing the database is throwing the following error:

```
ORA-01000: maximum open cursors exceeded
```

You want to query the data dictionary to determine the number of cursors that are open per session.

Solution

The following query will show the currently open cursors per session:

```
select
  a.value
 ,c.username
 ,c.machine
 ,c.sid
 ,c.serial#
from v$sesstat  a
    ,v$statname b
    ,v$session  c
where a.statistic# = b.statistic#
and   c.sid       = a.sid
and   b.name      = 'opened cursors current'
and   a.value     != 0
and   c.username IS NOT NULL
order by 1,2;
```

We recommend that you query V$SESSION instead of V$OPEN_CURSOR to determine the number of open cursors. V$SESSION provides a more accurate number of the cursors currently open.

How It Works

The OPEN_CURSORS initialization parameter determines the maximum number of cursors a session can have open. This setting is per session. The default value of 50 is usually too low for any application. It's common to set OPEN_CURSORS to a value such as 1000.

However, if a single session has over 1000 open cursors, there is probably something in the code that is not closing a cursor. When this limit is reached, somebody should inspect the application code to determine if a cursor is not being closed.

If you work in an environment that has thousands of connections to the database, you may want to view only the top cursor-consuming sessions. The following query uses an inline view and the pseudo-column ROWNUM to display the top twenty values:

```
select * from (
select
  a.value
 ,c.username
 ,c.machine
 ,c.sid
 ,c.serial#
from v$sesstat  a
    ,v$statname b
    ,v$session  c
where a.statistic# = b.statistic#
and   c.sid       = a.sid
and   b.name      = 'opened cursors current'
and   a.value     != 0
and   c.username IS NOT NULL
```

```
order by 1 desc,2)
where rownum < 21;
```

20-3. Determining If Online Redo Logs Are Sized Properly

Problem

You notice that there are an inordinate number of log file switch (checkpoint incomplete) wait events (see Table 20-1 for a description). You want to verify the frequency with which the redo logs are switching in a production database.

Solution

The V$LOG_HISTORY contains history information about the online redo logs. Execute this query to view the number of log switches per hour:

```
select count(*)
 ,to_char(first_time,'YYYY:MM:DD:HH24')
from  v$log_history
group by to_char(first_time,'YYYY:MM:DD:HH24')
order by 2;
```

Here's a snippet of the output:

```
  COUNT(*) TO_CHAR(FIRST
---------- -------------
        15 2009:07:20:00
        31 2009:07:20:01
        47 2009:07:20:02
        14 2009:07:20:03
         3 2009:07:20:04
         1 2009:07:20:05
```

From the previous output, you can see that a lot of redo generation occurred on July 20th, from about midnight to 3:00 a.m. This could be due to a nightly batch job or users running the database application on the opposite side of the world (where your nighttime is their daytime).

How It Works

The V$LOG_HISTORY derives its data from the control file. Each time there is a log switch, an entry is recorded in this view that details information, such as the time of the switch and system change number (SCN).

A general rule of thumb is that you should size your online redo log files so that they switch about two or three times per hour. You don't want them switching too often because there is overhead with the log switch. Oracle initiates a checkpoint as part of a log switch. During a checkpoint, the database writer background process writes all modified (dirty) blocks to disk, which is resource-intensive.

On the other hand, you don't want online redo log files to never switch because there are transactions in the current online redo log that you may need in the event of a recovery. If you were to have a disaster that caused a media failure in your current online redo log, you could lose those transactions that haven't been archived yet.

■ **Tip** Use the `ARCHIVE_LAG_TARGET` initialization parameter to set a maximum amount of time (in seconds) between log switches. A typical setting for this parameter is 1800 seconds (30 minutes). A value of 0 (default) disables this feature. This parameter is commonly used in Oracle Data Guard environments to force log switches after the specified amount of time lapses.

You can also query the `OPTIMAL_LOGFILE_SIZE` column from the `V$INSTANCE_RECOVERY` view to determine if your online redo log files have been sized correctly:

```
select optimal_logfile_size from v$instance_recovery;
```

Here is some sample output:

```
OPTIMAL_LOGFILE_SIZE
--------------------
                 349
```

This reports the redo log file size (in megabytes) that is considered optimal based on the initialization parameter setting of `FAST_START_MTTR_TARGET`. Oracle recommends you configure all online redo logs to be at least the value of `OPTIMAL_LOGFILE_SIZE`. However, when sizing your online redo logs, you must take into consideration information about your environment (such as the frequency of the switches).

You can view the current size of your online redo log files by issuing the following query:

```
select a.group#
 ,a.member
 ,b.status
 ,b.bytes/1024/1024 meg_bytes
from v$logfile a,
     v$log     b
where a.group# = b.group#
order by a.group#;
```

Here is some sample output:

```
GROUP# MEMBER                        STATUS               MEG_BYTES
------ ----------------------------- -------------------- ---------
     1 /oralogs01/DWREP/redo01a.log  INACTIVE                   256
     1 /oralogs02/DWREP/redo01b.log  INACTIVE                   256
     2 /oralogs01/DWREP/redo02a.log  CURRENT                    256
     2 /oralogs02/DWREP/redo02b.log  CURRENT                    256
     3 /oralogs01/DWREP/redo03a.log  INACTIVE                   256
     3 /oralogs02/DWREP/redo03b.log  INACTIVE                   256
```

20-4. Determining If Undo Is Sized Properly

Problem

You have a long-running SQL statement that is throwing an ORA-01555 "snapshot too old" error. You want to determine if you have properly sized your undo tablespace.

Solution

Run this next query to identify potential issues with your undo tablespace. The query checks for issues with the undo tablespace that have occurred within the last day:

```
select
 to_char(begin_time,'MM-DD-YYYY HH24:MI') begin_time
,ssolderrcnt    ORA_01555_cnt
,nospaceerrcnt  no_space_cnt
,txncount       max_num_txns
,maxquerylen    max_query_len
,expiredblks    blck_in_expired
from v$undostat
where begin_time > sysdate - 1
order by begin_time;
```

Here is some sample output. Part of the output has been omitted to fit this on the page:

BEGIN_TIME	ORA_01555_CNT	NO_SPACE_CNT	MAX_NUM_TXNS	MAX_QUERY_LEN
07-20-2009 18:10	0	0	249	0
07-20-2009 18:20	0	0	290	0
07-20-2009 18:30	0	0	244	0
07-20-2009 18:40	0	0	179	0

The ORA_01555_CNT column indicates the number of times your database has encountered the ORA-01555 "snapshot too old" error. If this column reports a non-zero value, you need to do one or more of the following:

- Ensure that code does not contain COMMIT statements within cursor loops.

- Tune the SQL statement throwing the error so that it runs faster.

- Ensure that you have good statistics (so your SQL runs efficiently).

- Increase the UNDO_RETENTION initialization parameter.

The NO_SPACE_CNT column displays the number of times space was requested in the undo tablespace but none was to be found. If the NO_SPACE_CNT is reporting a non-zero value, you may need to add more space to your undo tablespace.

How It Works

There is a maximum of four days' worth of information stored in the V$UNDOSTAT view. The statistics are gathered every ten minutes for a maximum of 576 rows in the table. If you've stopped and started your database within the last four days, this view will only have information in it from the time you last started your database.

Another way to get advice on the undo tablespace sizing is to use the Oracle Undo Advisor, which you can invoke by querying the PL/SQL DBMS_UNDO_ADV package from a SELECT statement. The following query displays the current undo size and the recommended size for an undo retention setting of 900 seconds:

```
select
  sum(bytes)/1024/1024                      cur_mb_size
  ,dbms_undo_adv.required_undo_size(900)  req_mb_size
from dba_data_files
where tablespace_name LIKE 'UNDO%';
```

Here is some sample output:

```
CUR_MB_SIZE REQ_MB_SIZE
----------- -----------
      36864       20897
```

The output shows that the undo tablespace currently has 36.8 gigabytes allocated to it. In the prior query we used 900 seconds for the amount of time to retain information in the undo tablespace. To retain undo information for 900 seconds, the Oracle Undo Advisor estimates that the undo tablespace should be 20.8 gigabytes. For this example, the undo tablespace is sized adequately. If it were not sized adequately, you would either have to add space to an existing datafile or add a datafile to the undo tablespace.

Here's a slightly more complex example of using the Oracle Undo Advisor to find the required size of the undo tablespace. This example uses PL/SQL to display information about potential issues and recommendations to fix the problem.

```
SET SERVEROUT ON SIZE 1000000
DECLARE
  pro    VARCHAR2(200);
  rec    VARCHAR2(200);
  rtn    VARCHAR2(200);
  ret    NUMBER;
  utb    NUMBER;
  retval NUMBER;
BEGIN
  DBMS_OUTPUT.PUT_LINE(DBMS_UNDO_ADV.UNDO_ADVISOR(1));
  DBMS_OUTPUT.PUT_LINE('Required Undo Size (megabytes): ' ||
DBMS_UNDO_ADV.REQUIRED_UNDO_SIZE (900));
  retval := DBMS_UNDO_ADV.UNDO_HEALTH(pro, rec, rtn, ret, utb);
  DBMS_OUTPUT.PUT_LINE('Problem:   ' || pro);
  DBMS_OUTPUT.PUT_LINE('Advice:    ' || rec);
  DBMS_OUTPUT.PUT_LINE('Rational:  ' || rtn);
  DBMS_OUTPUT.PUT_LINE('Retention: ' || TO_CHAR(ret));
```

```
  DBMS_OUTPUT.PUT_LINE('UTBSize:    ' || TO_CHAR(utb));
END;
/
```

If no issues are found, a 0 will be returned for the retention size. Here is some sample output:

```
Finding 1:The undo tablespace is OK.
Required Undo Size (megabytes): 20897
Problem:   No problem found
Advice:
Rational:
Retention: 0
UTBSize:   0
```

20-5. Determining If Temporary Tablespace Is Sized Correctly

Problem

You're trying to build an index and Oracle is throwing this error:

```
ORA-01652: unable to extend temp segment by 128 in tablespace TEMP
```

You want to determine if your temporary tablespace is sized correctly.

Solution

If you are using Oracle Database 11g or higher, run the following query to show both the allocated and free space within the temporary tablespace:

```
select
 tablespace_name
,tablespace_size/1024/1024 mb_size
,allocated_space/1024/1024 mb_alloc
,free_space/1024/1024      mb_free
from dba_temp_free_space;
```

Here is some sample output:

```
TABLESPACE_NAME   MB_SIZE   MB_ALLOC   MB_FREE
---------------   -------   --------   -------
TEMP                  200        200       170
```

If the FREE_SPACE (MB_FREE) value drops to near zero, there are SQL operations in your database consuming most of the available space. The FREE_SPACE (MB_FREE) column is the total free space available, including space currently allocated and available for reuse.

If you are using an Oracle Database 10g database, run this query to view space being used in your temporary tablespace:

```
select tablespace_name, sum(bytes_used)/1024/1024 mb_used
from v$temp_extent_pool
group by tablespace_name;
```

Here is some sample output:

```
TABLESPACE_NAME     MB_USED
--------------- ----------
TEMP                    120
```

If the used amount is getting near your current allocated amount, you may need to allocate more space to the temporary tablespace datafiles. Run the following query to view the temporary datafile names and allocated sizes:

```
select name, bytes/1024/1024 mb_alloc from v$tempfile;
```

Here is some typical output:

```
NAME                              MB_ALLOC
------------------------------- ----------
/ora02/DWREP/temp01.dbf             12000
/ora03/DWREP/temp03.dbf             10240
/ora01/DWREP/temp02.dbf              2048
```

How It Works

The temporary tablespace is used as a sorting area on disk when a process has consumed the available memory and needs more space. Operations that require a sorting area include:

- Index creation

- SQL sorting operations

- Temporary tables and temporary indexes

- Temporary LOBs

- Temporary B-trees

There is no exact formula for determining if your temporary tablespace is sized correctly. It depends on the number and types of queries, index build operations, parallel operations, and size of your memory sort space (program global area). You'll have to use one of the queries in the solution section to monitor your temporary tablespace while there is a load on your database to determine its usage patterns.

If Oracle throws the ORA-01652 error, that is one indicator that your temporary tablespace is too small. However, Oracle may throw that error if it runs out of space because of a one-time event, like a large index build. You'll have to decide whether a one-time index build or a query that consumes large amounts of sort space in the temporary tablespace warrants adding space.

If you determine that you need to add space, you can either resize an existing datafile or add a new datafile. To resize a temporary tablespace datafile, use the ALTER DATABASE TEMPFILE...RESIZE statement. The following resizes a temporary datafile to 12 gigabytes:

```
alter database tempfile '/ora03/DWREP/temp03.dbf' resize 12g;
```

You can add a datafile to a temporary tablespace as follows:

```
alter tablespace temp add tempfile '/ora04/DWREP/temp04.dbf' size 2g;
```

20-6. Displaying Tablespace Fullness

Problem

You're getting an ORA-01653 "unable to extend table" error. You want to find out how much free space remains in each tablespace.

Solution

Run the following script to view the amount of free and allocated bytes in your database:

```
select
  a.tablespace_name
 ,(f.bytes/a.bytes)*100 pct_free
 ,f.bytes/1024/1024 mb_free
 ,a.bytes/1024/1024 mb_allocated
from
(select nvl(sum(bytes),0) bytes, x.tablespace_name
from dba_free_space y, dba_tablespaces x
where x.tablespace_name = y.tablespace_name(+)
and x.contents != 'TEMPORARY' and x.status != 'READ ONLY'
and x.tablespace_name not like 'UNDO%'
group by x.tablespace_name) f,
(select sum(bytes) bytes, tablespace_name
from dba_data_files
group by tablespace_name) a
where a.tablespace_name = f.tablespace_name
order by 1;
```

Here's some sample output:

TABLESPACE_NAME	PCT_FREE	MB_FREE	MB_ALLOCATED
DOWN_TBSP_9	79.1992188	8110	10240
DTS_STAGE_DATA	84.3	843	1000
DTS_STAGE_INDEX	96.7	967	1000
INST_TBSP_1	96.8	484	500

How It Works

Monitoring a tablespace for freespace is a basic activity of a database administrator. You can use the AUTOEXTEND feature for tablespace datafiles, which allows a datafile to grow as it needs space. Some DBAs are reluctant to use the AUTOEXTEND feature for fear of a runaway process with many transactions that causes a datafile to fill up the existing disk space. If you're not using AUTOEXTEND for your datafiles, you'll need to monitor the tablespaces with a script such as the one in the solution section of this recipe.

Sometimes when you're performing physical file maintenance on a database, it's useful to list all of the files associated with your database. In these situations you'll need a script that displays datafiles, control files and online redo log files. This is particularly true in production support situations where you may have a tablespace that is getting full and you want to add space to one of the many datafiles associated with a tablespace.

This next script allows you to quickly identify tablespaces that are getting full and which datafiles are candidates for more space. We use many SQL*Plus formatting commands here to make the output readable:

```
REM ****************************************************
REM * File : freesp.sql
REM ****************************************************
SET PAGESIZE 100 LINES 132 ECHO OFF VERIFY OFF FEEDB OFF SPACE 1 TRIMSP ON
COMPUTE SUM OF a_byt t_byt f_byt ON REPORT
BREAK ON REPORT ON tablespace_name ON pf
COL tablespace_name FOR A17    TRU HEAD 'Tablespace|Name'
COL file_name        FOR A40   TRU HEAD 'Filename'
COL a_byt            FOR 9,990.999 HEAD 'Allocated|GB'
COL t_byt            FOR 9,990.999 HEAD 'Current|Used GB'
COL f_byt            FOR 9,990.999 HEAD 'Current|Free GB'
COL pct_free         FOR 990.0     HEAD 'File %|Free'
COL pf               FOR 990.0     HEAD 'Tbsp %|Free'
COL seq NOPRINT
DEFINE b_div=1073741824
--
COL db_name NEW_VALUE h_db_name NOPRINT
COL db_date NEW_VALUE h_db_date NOPRINT
SELECT name db_name, TO_CHAR(sysdate,'YYYY_MM_DD') db_date FROM v$database;
--
SPO &&h_db_name._&&h_db_date..lis
PROMPT Database: &&h_db_name, Date: &&h_db_date
--
SELECT 1 seq, b.tablespace_name, nvl(x.fs,0)/y.ap*100 pf, b.file_name file_name,
  b.bytes/&&b_div a_byt, NVL((b.bytes-SUM(f.bytes))/&&b_div,b.bytes/&&b_div) t_byt,
  NVL(SUM(f.bytes)/&&b_div,0) f_byt, NVL(SUM(f.bytes)/b.bytes*100,0) pct_free
FROM dba_free_space f, dba_data_files b
 ,(SELECT y.tablespace_name, SUM(y.bytes) fs
   FROM dba_free_space y GROUP BY y.tablespace_name) x
 ,(SELECT x.tablespace_name, SUM(x.bytes) ap
   FROM dba_data_files x GROUP BY x.tablespace_name) y
WHERE f.file_id(+) = b.file_id
AND    x.tablespace_name(+) = y.tablespace_name
and    y.tablespace_name = b.tablespace_name
AND    f.tablespace_name(+) = b.tablespace_name
```

```
GROUP BY b.tablespace_name, nvl(x.fs,0)/y.ap*100, b.file_name, b.bytes
UNION
SELECT 2 seq, tablespace_name, j.bf/k.bb*100 pf, b.name file_name, b.bytes/&&b_div a_byt,
  a.bytes_used/&&b_div t_byt, a.bytes_free/&&b_div f_byt,
  a.bytes_free/b.bytes*100 pct_free
FROM v$temp_space_header a, v$tempfile b
 ,(SELECT SUM(bytes_free) bf FROM v$temp_space_header) j
 ,(SELECT SUM(bytes) bb FROM v$tempfile) k
WHERE a.file_id = b.file#
ORDER BY 1,2,4,3;
--
COLUMN name FORMAT A60 HEAD 'Control Files'
SELECT name FROM v$controlfile;
--
COL member    FORMAT A50 HEAD 'Redo log files'
COL status    FORMAT A9  HEAD 'Status'
COL archived  FORMAT A10 HEAD 'Archived'
--
SELECT
  a.group#, a.member, b.status,
  b.archived, SUM(b.bytes)/1024/1024 mb
FROM v$logfile a, v$log b
WHERE a.group# = b.group#
GROUP BY a.group#, a.member, b.status, b.archived
ORDER BY 1, 2;
--
SPO OFF;
```

This script spools the output to a file with the database name and date embedded into the filename. For example, if you run the script on the 22nd of July in 2009 for the database named DW11, the output file will be named DW11_2009_07_22.lis. The script also uses a B_DIV parameter to divide all of the byte columns by a value of 1073741824, which results in the output being displayed in gigabytes.

20-7. Showing Object Sizes

Problem

You want to proactively run a report that shows which tables and indexes are consuming the most space in your database.

Solution

Here is a typical script that shows the top space-consuming objects (tables and indexes) in the database:

```
select * from
(
select
```

```
  segment_name
 ,partition_name
 ,segment_type
 ,owner
 ,bytes/1024/1024 mb
 from dba_segments
 order by bytes desc)
 where rownum <=20;
```

Here is some sample output:

```
SEGMENT_NAME             PARTITION_NAME   SEGMENT_TYPE        OWNER            MB
------------------------ ---------------- ------------------- --------- ----------
 _SYSSMU1$                                TYPE2 UNDO          SYS       18481.4375
CIA_DOWNLOADS                             TABLE               CIA             7868
REG_QUEUE_REP                             TABLE               REP_MV          6874
F_DOWNLOADS              DOWN_P_7         TABLE PARTITION     STAR2           3180
F_DOWNLOADS_IDX1                          INDEX               CIA_STAR        2927
```

How It Works

Sometimes when you're troubleshooting disk space issues, it's useful to view which objects (tables and indexes) are consuming the most storage. The script in the solution section uses an inline view to first select all segments in the database and order them by the BYTES column in descending order. The outer query then limits the output to the top twenty space-consuming objects in the database.

If you're interested in seeing information such as which objects are consuming space in which datafiles, you'll need to query the DBA_DATA_FILES view. Listed next is a script that prompts you for an owner and then displays tables and the space consumed in the associated datafiles:

```
select
  a.table_name
 ,b.tablespace_name
 ,b.partition_name
 ,c.file_name
 ,sum(b.bytes)/1024/1024 mb
from dba_tables      a
    ,dba_extents     b
    ,dba_data_files c
where a.owner        = upper('&owner')
and   a.owner        = b.owner
and   a.table_name   = b.segment_name
and   b.file_id      = c.file_id
group by
  a.table_name
 ,b.tablespace_name
 ,b.partition_name
 ,c.file_name
order by a.table_name, b.tablespace_name;
```

20-8. Monitoring Index Usage

Problem

You want to remove any indexes that aren't being used in your database. You need a simple yes or no answer as to whether an index is being used.

Solution

Use the `ALTER INDEX...MONITORING USAGE` statement to enable basic index monitoring. The following example enables index monitoring on an index named `F_DOWN_DOM_FK9`:

```
alter index F_DOWN_DOM_FK9 monitoring usage;
```

From this point on, the first time the index is accessed, Oracle will record this and it can be viewed via the `V$OBJECT_USAGE` view. To report which indexes are being monitored and have ever been used, run this query:

```
select * from v$object_usage;
```

Most likely you're not going to monitor only only one index. Rather, you're going to want to monitor all indexes for a user. In this situation, use SQL to generate SQL to create a script you can run to turn on monitoring for all indexes. Here is such a script:

```
select 'alter index ' || index_name || ' monitoring usage;'
from user_indexes;
```

How It Works

The `V$OBJECT_USAGE` view will only show information for the currently connected user. If you inspect the `TEXT` column of `DBA_VIEWS`, you'll notice the following line:

```
where io.owner# = userenv('SCHEMAID')
```

If you're logged in as a DBA account and want to view the status of all indexes that have monitoring enabled (regardless of the user), execute this query:

```
select io.name, t.name,
       decode(bitand(i.flags, 65536), 0, 'NO', 'YES'),
       decode(bitand(ou.flags, 1), 0, 'NO', 'YES'),
       ou.start_monitoring,
       ou.end_monitoring
from sys.obj$ io, sys.obj$ t, sys.ind$ i, sys.object_usage ou
where i.obj# = ou.obj#
and io.obj# = ou.obj#
and t.obj# = i.bo#;
```

20-9. Auditing Object Usage

Problem

You wonder which tables in your database are actually being used.

Solution

Use database auditing to determine if an object is being accessed by SELECT, INSERT, UPDATE, and DELETE statements. Follow these steps to enable and use database auditing:

1. Enable auditing on the database by setting the AUDIT_TRAIL initialization parameter to a valid value such as DB. If you are using an SPFILE, then set the AUDIT_TRAIL parameter with the ALTER SYSTEM statement:

```
SQL> alter system set audit_trail=db scope=spfile;
```

If you are using an init.ora file, open it with a text editor and set the value to DB (see Table 20-3 for a description of valid values for the AUDIT_TRAIL parameter):

```
AUDIT_TRAIL=DB
```

Table 20-3. *Valid AUDIT_TRAILSettings*

Setting	Meaning
DB	Enables auditing and sets the SYS.AUD$ table as the audit repository.
DB, EXTENDED	Enables auditing and sets the SYS.AUD$ table as the audit repository and includes the SQLTEXT and SQLBIND columns.
OS	Enables auditing and specifies that an operating system file will store auditing information.
XML	Enables auditing and writes audit records in XML format to an OS file.
XML, EXTENDED	Enables auditing and writes audit records in XML format to an OS file including values for SqlText and SqlBind.
NONE	Disables database auditing.

2. Next, stop and start your database.

```
SQL> shutdown immediate;
SQL> startup;
SQL> show parameter audit_trail;
```

NAME	TYPE	VALUE
audit_trail	string	DB

3. Now you can enable auditing by object, privilege, or statement. For example, the following statement enables auditing on all DML access to the EMP table owned by INV_MGMT:

```
SQL> audit select, insert, update, delete on inv_mgmt.emp;
```

4. From this point on, any DML access to the INV_MGMT.EMP table will be recorded in the SYS.AUD$ table. You can use a query such as this to report on DML access to a table:

```
select
  username
 ,obj_name
 ,timestamp
 ,substr(ses_actions,4,1)  del
 ,substr(ses_actions,7,1)  ins
 ,substr(ses_actions,10,1) sel
 ,substr(ses_actions,11,1) upd
from dba_audit_object;
```

To turn off auditing on an object, use the NOAUDIT statement:

```
SQL> noaudit select, insert, update, delete on inv_mgmt.inv;
```

You should periodically purge the AUD$ table so that it doesn't consume inordinate amounts of space in your SYSTEM tablespace. If you need to save the AUD$ data, you can first export the table and then use the TRUNCATE command to remove records.

▪ **Tip** If you want to move the AUD$ table to a non-SYSTEM tablespace, refer to My Oracle Support (MetaLink) note 72460.1 for instructions.

How It Works

Oracle auditing is a powerful feature that allows you to determine what types of SQL activities are occurring against a table. For example, you may want to determine which tables are being used or not. If a table is not being used, you may want to rename and then drop the table. Auditing allows you to capture the types of SQL statements being used to access a table.

In step 4 of the solution we use the SUBSTR function to reference the SES_ACTIONS column of the DBA_AUDIT_OBJECT view. That column contains a 16-character string in which each character means that a certain operation has occurred. The 16 characters represent the following operations in this order: ALTER, AUDIT, COMMENT, DELETE, GRANT, INDEX, INSERT, LOCK, RENAME, SELECT, UPDATE, REFERENCES, and EXECUTE. Positions 14, 15, and 16 are reserved by Oracle for future use. The character of S represents success, F represents failure, and B represents both success and failure.

Once you have identified tables that are not being used, you can simply rename the tables and see if this breaks the application or if any users complain. If there are no complaints, then after some time you can consider dropping the tables. Make sure you take a good backup of your database with both RMAN and Data Pump before you drop any tables you might have to later recover.

■ **Tip** If you simply need to know whether a table is being inserted, updated, or deleted from, you can use the USER_TAB_MODIFICATIONS view to report on that type of activity. This view has columns such as INSERTS, UPDATES, DELETES, and TRUNCATED that will provide information as to how data in the table is being modified.

20-10. Auditing at a Granular Level

Problem

You have some sensitive data regarding employee salaries. You want to audit any type of access to a particular column in a table. You need to audit at a more granular level than is available with standard auditing.

Solution

Use Oracle fine-grained auditing (FGA) to monitor any user selecting from a particular column. Follow the next several steps to implement FGA:

■ **Note** The fine-grained auditing feature requires the Enterprise Edition of Oracle.

---

1. Create a policy using the DBMS_FGA package. This example creates a policy for the INV table and specifies that any INSERT, UPDATE, DELETE, or SELECT statement against the SALARY column of the EMP table will be recorded in the audit trail:

```
begin
dbms_fga.add_policy (
object_schema => 'INV',
object_name => 'EMP',
audit_column=> 'SALARY',
policy_name => 'S1_AUDIT',
statement_types => 'INSERT, UPDATE, DELETE, SELECT',
audit_trail => DBMS_FGA.DB_EXTENDED
);
end;
/
```

   2. Verify that the policy exists by querying the DBA_AUDIT_POLICIES view:

```
select object_schema
 ,object_name
 ,policy_name
 ,sel, ins, upd, del, policy_column
from dba_audit_policies;
```

Here's the output for this example:

```
OBJECT_SCHEMA   OBJECT_NAME   POLICY_NAME    SEL    INS    UPD    DEL    POLICY_COL
-------------   -----------   -----------    -----  -----  -----  -----  ----------
INV             EMP           S1_AUDIT       YES    YES    YES    YES    SALARY
```

   3. To view the recorded SQL statements in the FGA audit trail, select from the DBA_FGA_AUDIT_TRAIL view:

```
select
  db_user
 ,to_char(timestamp,'dd-mon-yy hh24:mi:ss') ts
 ,sql_text
from dba_fga_audit_trail
order by timestamp;
```

■ **Note** The DBA_FGA_AUDIT_TRAIL view is based on the FGA_LOG$ table.

Here's some sample output:

```
DB_USER         TS                        SQL_TEXT
-------------   -----------------------   ------------------------
INV             21-jul-09 21:47:07        select * from emp
SYSTEM          21-jul-09 21:58:36        select salary from inv.emp
```

   If you need to disable a policy, use the DISABLE_POLICY procedure:

```
SQL> exec dbms_fga.disable_policy('INV','EMP','S1_AUDIT');
```

   To drop a policy, use the DROP_POLICY procedure:

```
SQL> exec dbms_fga.drop_policy('INV','EMP','S1_AUDIT');
```

   As the SYS schema you can purge records from the fine-grained auditing audit table as follows:

```
truncate table fga_log$;
```

How It Works

Fine-grained auditing allows you to audit SQL at a more granular level than simple INSERT, UPDATE, DELETE, and SELECT operations. FGA auditing allows you to audit for SQL activities that occur at the column level. FGA auditing also allows you to perform a Boolean check on an operation, such as "if the value selected is in a range then audit the activity".

You manage fine-grained auditing through the use of FGA policies. The DBMS_FGA package allows you to add, disable, enable, and drop FGA policies. You need execute privilege on the DBMS_FGA package to administer audit policies.

■ **Tip** For more details on fine-grained auditing, see Oracle's Security Guide available from the otn.oracle.com web site.

Index

USER_TAB_STATISTICS view, 493
USING clause, and ANSI SQL 99 join syntax, 60
UTLDTREE script, 250
UTL_FILE package, 396–397
UTL_HTTP package, 392–394

■V

validating
  numbers in strings, 194–196
  XML schema, 346–349
values
  See also datetime values; nulls/null values
  accessing from subsequent or preceding rows, 42–45
  assigning ranking to rows in query results, 45–47
  auto-incrementing, creating, 453–455
  changing nulls into real, 109–111
  in columns, summarizing, 23–25
  finding first and last, within groups, 47–48
  obfuscating sensitive, 294–297
  predicting beyond series end, 130–133
  in rows, changing, 10–11
  unique, finding in tables, 35–37
VARCHAR2 datatype, VARCHAR datatype compared to, 426
variables
  bind, 268
  substitution, 268
verifying connection information, 407–409
VERIFY parameter, 298
vertical bars (||) operator, 97
viewing
  metadata about databases, 229–230
  optimizer statistics, 492–494
views
  See also displaying; specific views
  ALL_TAB_COLS, 130
  ALL_TAB_COLUMNS, 129–130
  creating, 441–442
  data dictionary

    dynamic performance, 231–232
    overview of, 213
    static, 230–231
  dynamic performance, 213, 501
  dynamically generating synonyms for, 444
  internal, definitions of, 252
  privilege-related data dictionary, 259
  space-management, 239–240
view text, displaying, 251–252
V$INSTANCE_RECOVERY view, OPTIMAL_LOGFILE_SIZE column, 504
virtual columns
  definition for, 86
  determining, 86
  partitioning on, 362–363
  restrictions on, 87
V$LOCKED_OBJECT view, 214
V$LOCK view, 213–214
V$LOG_HISTORY view, 503
V$OBJECT_USAGE view, 513
V$SESSION_LONGOPS view, 462–463
V$SESSION view, 214, 502
V$SESSTAT view, 468
V$SQLAREA view, 459, 464
V$SQL_MONITOR view, 457–459
V$SQL_PLAN_MONITOR view, 459–460
V$SQLSTATS view, 459, 464
V$SQL view, 459, 464
V$SYSSTAT view, 468, 498, 501
V$SYSTEM_EVENT view, 501
V$UNDOSTAT view, 506
V$ view, 231–232

■W

wait events, common, affecting performance, 499–501
web-page reports, producing directly from databases, 280–285
web pages, displaying query results on, 113–117
web sites, tracking unique users for number of days, 164–165

You Need the Companion eBook

Your purchase of this book entitles you to buy the companion PDF-version eBook for only $10. Take the weightless companion with you anywhere.

We believe this Apress title will prove so indispensable that you'll want to carry it with you everywhere, which is why we are offering the companion eBook (in PDF format) for $10 to customers who purchase this book now. Convenient and fully searchable, the PDF version of any content-rich, page-heavy Apress book makes a valuable addition to your programming library. You can easily find and copy code—or perform examples by quickly toggling between instructions and the application. Even simultaneously tackling a donut, diet soda, and complex code becomes simplified with hands-free eBooks!

Once you purchase your book, getting the $10 companion eBook is simple:

❶ Visit **www.apress.com/promo/tendollars/**.

❷ Complete a basic registration form to receive a randomly generated question about this title.

❸ Answer the question correctly in 60 seconds, and you will receive a promotional code to redeem for the $10.00 eBook.

233 Spring Street, New York, NY 10013

Offer valid through 4/10.